Basic statistics for social research

Both students and professionals are increasingly reliant on computers for the analysis of data. This accessible introduction to statistics using the program Minitab assumes no prior knowledge of statistics or computing, and has details of the different versions and options available. It also explains when to apply and how to calculate and interpret a wide range of statistical procedures commonly used in the social sciences. Ranging from chi-square and the *t* test to analysis of covariance and multiple regression, Duncan Cramer covers a wide choice of statistics, including tests not found in other introductory texts, such as tests for determining whether correlations differ and the extent of agreement between observers. Important statistical points are illustrated with worked numerical examples, and exercises are provided at the end of chapters.

Basic Statistics for Social Research will prove an invaluable introductory statistics text for students, and a useful resource for graduates and professionals engaged in research in the social sciences.

Duncan Cramer is Senior Lecturer in Social Psychology at Loughborough University. He is the author of *Quantitative Data Analysis with Minitab: A guide for social scientists* (1996), with Alan Bryman; *Introducing Statistics for Social Research: Step-by-step calculations and computer techniques using SPSS* (1994); and *Quantitative Data Analysis for Social Scientists* (SPSS version) (1990, revised 1994), with Alan Bryman.

Basic statistics for social research

Step-by-step calculations and computer techniques using Minitab

Duncan Cramer

London and New York

MINITAB is a registered trademark of Minitab Inc., 3081 Enterprise Drive, State College, PA 16801–3008, USA, telephone 814–238–3280, fax 814–238–4383.

First published 1997
by Routledge
11 New Fetter Lane, London EC4P 4EE

Simultaneously published in the USA and Canada
by Routledge
29 West 35th Street, New York, NY 10001

© 1997 Duncan Cramer

Typeset in Times by J&L Composition Ltd, Filey, North Yorkshire
Printed and bound in Great Britain by TJ Press (Padstow) Ltd, Padstow, Cornwall

British Library Cataloguing in Publication Data
A catalogue record for this book is available from the British Library

Library of Congress Cataloguing in Publication Data
Cramer, Duncan, 1948–
    Basic statistics for social research: step-by-step calculations
    and computer techniques using Minitab / Duncan Cramer.
    p.   cm.
    Includes bibliographical references and index.
    1. Social sciences–Statistical methods.   2. Social sciences–Data
    processing.   3. Minitab for Windows.   I. Title.
    HA29.C7747   1996
    519.5–dc20   96–11415

ISBN 0–415–12004–7
ISBN 0–415–12005–5 (pbk)

To Stella

Contents

Figures

Tables

Preface

Statistics play a vital role in the description of the results of empirical research in the social sciences. Consequently, an understanding of the way in which such data have been analysed is essential to be able to evaluate those results fully and critically. A knowledge of statistics is also necessary for running our own statistical analyses. This book describes when to apply, how to calculate and how to interpret a comprehensive selection of statistical tests used in the social sciences, ranging from chi-square and the t test to analysis of covariance and multiple regression. It shows how to calculate these tests by hand as well as with the aid of a computer program called Minitab. The widespread availability of computers and programs for carrying out statistics means that statistics can now be more efficiently and accurately computed with these means. Minitab was chosen because it has an extensive variety of statistical procedures, is considered easy to learn and, as a consequence, is widely taught and used in the social sciences.

However, in order to understand what these tests involve it is still necessary to work out the computations by hand. To make the calculations easier the examples employ small sets of data consisting of small numbers. The same set of data is often used to illustrate more than one test so that the results of different tests can be compared and less time is spent on introducing new examples. Where possible, important statistical points have been illustrated with worked numerical examples. Statistical symbols have been kept to a minimum so that there is less need to remember what these symbols represent. Exercises at the end of chapters (together with the answers at the back of the book) enable readers to test their understanding of the computational steps involved in the tests described, as well as providing additional examples of data and their statistical analysis. Once readers have learned how to operate Minitab, they can generate their own exercises and assess their knowledge by comparing their answers with those produced by Minitab. This book contains information which is not present in many other introductory statistical textbooks. Where this occurs, a reference is given for further information or for an additional explanation chosen to be as nontechnical as possible. If the examples use variables which seem less relevant to the reader's own interests, then replace them with variables of more immediate concern.

The version of Minitab covered in the relevant chapters of the book is the latest version which, at the time of writing, is *Release 10Xtra for Windows and Macintosh* (Minitab 1995). The Windows version requires a 386 or higher processor. *Release 9* is available for some mainframe computers. Any differences between these versions and *Release 8* and *Release 7* are described. Minitab commands and output have been printed in **bold** to distinguish them from the rest of the text.

I would like to thank Longman Group UK Ltd, on behalf of the Literary Executor of the late Sir Ronald A. Fisher, F.R.S., and Dr Frank Yates, F.R.S., for permission to reproduce Tables II, IV and VII from *Statistical Tables for Biological, Agricultural and Medical Research*, 6th ed. (1974).

Duncan Cramer
Loughborough University

Chapter 1

Role of statistics in social research

A major aim of the social and behavioural sciences is to develop principles which explain and provide new insights into human behaviour. One way of evaluating what appear to be sound and promising principles is to examine the extent to which they are consistent with carefully controlled observations of human behaviour. In other words, the validity of principles needs to be tested by conducting empirical research wherever possible. If the data do not agree with the principle under scrutiny, the principle may have to be modified and then re-examined. Alternatively, the way in which the controlled observations were made may have been mistaken and a new set of data may have to be collected. Suppose, for example, we tested the idea that people are likely to repeat the aggressive behaviour they see in others but we found no evidence to support such a relationship. In this case, it might be necessary to make the principle more specific by proposing that individuals are likely to imitate aggression which is rewarded rather than punished, and then to test this revised proposition. On the other hand, the test of aggression we used may have been unsuitable for the purpose and may have to be replaced with a more appropriate test.

Statistics play a vital role in collecting, summarising and interpreting data designed to empirically evaluate a principle. Consequently, an understanding of this important subject is necessary both to carry out research and to be able to critically evaluate research that has been, or is going to be, conducted. The function that statistics serves in social research can best be briefly illustrated by looking at the ways in which it is involved in testing a principle. Take, for example, the simple idea that we have already introduced that people tend to imitate what they have observed. If this is the case, then individuals who, say, have watched a violent incident shown on television should be more likely to behave in this way than those who have not seen this incident. One approach to testing this idea would be to select two groups of people and to show one group (known as the *experimental* group, condition or treatment) a film or video with a violent incident and the other group (the *control* group) a similar film not containing the violent sequence. After viewing the film, the aggression displayed by both groups of people would be observed to see if the groups differed as expected.

Suppose that the people who had watched the violent incident showed more aggression subsequently than those who had not been exposed to this violence. Before it could be concluded that these results confirm the principle that individuals tend to imitate what they have observed, at least three essential and related statistical considerations need to have been met. The first is that participants should have been *randomly sampled* from the population. A random sample is one in which each member of the population has an equal chance of being selected for the sample. The second is that the sampled participants should have been *randomly assigned* to the two groups. Random assignment means that individuals have an equal probability of being assigned to each group. The third is that the difference in observed aggression between the two groups should be *statistically significant*, which means that the difference has a one in twenty probability or less of occurring simply by chance.

RANDOM SAMPLING

When testing a principle, we usually want to know how valid it is of people in general. Since it is not possible to test everyone when examining a particular generalisation, we carry out our study on a *sample* or subset of people. The idea of a sample implies that there is a larger *population* from which it is drawn. This population is often not specified because we assume the principle to be generally true. For example, when we postulate that watching violence on television causes aggression, we presumably believe that this holds true for all people where watching television is part of their cultural experience and that this principle does not simply apply to the people we have tested. In other words, we want to be able to generalise the findings from our sample to the population.

There are two main ways in which we can select a sample of objects or cases, which need not be people, of course. The first method is to draw a *simple random* sample where every object in a given population has an equal probability of being chosen. To do this, the population of objects needs to be specified and known and some random procedure employed for selecting objects. To give a simple example, suppose we wanted to draw a small sample of five people from a class of twenty which was the population of interest. We could assign a number from 1 to 20 to each of the individuals in the class. We could then go to a table of random numbers and select the first five numbers which fell between 1 and 20, which may be 13, 9, 17, 18 and 5. The five people who had those numbers would constitute our sample. In this method, everybody would have a one in five probability of being selected.

The second method of sampling is to generate a *non-random* sample where the probability of choosing an object from a specified population is not known. An example of this approach would be if we selected the first five people according to whether their surname started with letters closest to the beginning of the alphabet. This method would be non-random because people whose surname began with these letters would have the highest probability of being chosen.

Because of the difficulty of obtaining a random sample, many studies in the social sciences use non-random samples and assume that the sample can be thought of as random. If, however, we believed that the principle we were investigating only applied to people with certain characteristics, then we could see if this assumption was true by testing this principle on people with and without those characteristics. For example, if we thought that watching violence only made males more aggressive and did not affect females, then we could test this idea on a sample of males and females. If, on the other hand, we wanted to know how common a particular behaviour was in a specified population, we would require a random sample to answer this question. For example, we would need a random sample to find out how many adults living in Britain viewed violent programmes on television. How accurate our estimate was would partly depend on the size of that sample. If we had used a non-random sample, we would not be able to estimate this figure because we would not know how representative that non-random sample was of the population.

RANDOM ASSIGNMENT

Having obtained our sample, we then need to randomly assign them to the two conditions. One way of trying to do this is to flip an unbiased coin. The two faces of the coin are used to represent the two groups. For example, it can be agreed beforehand that if the coin lands with the side showing the head ('heads up'), then the first of two people will be assigned to the group that will see the violent episode. The second person will be allocated to the group that will not be shown the violent incident. If, on the other hand, the coin lands with the side which does not display the head ('tails up'), then the first person will be assigned to the group which will not see the violent sequence, while the second participant will be allocated to the group which will be shown the violent episode. This procedure of assigning two people at a time with one coin throw will ensure that the number of people in both groups will be similar, although a similar number of people in each group is not itself a statistical requirement.

The reason for random assignment of participants to conditions is to try and ensure that there is no bias in the way that people are allocated to the two groups and that every person has an equal chance of being in either group. If random assignment is not used, then there is the possibility that one group will contain individuals who may be more prone to show aggression. If this happened, the results obtained could not be explained in terms of which films the participants had seen. Because this is a very important point to grasp, it will be further elaborated.

There are potentially a very large number of factors which may predispose individuals to be aggressive, some of which we may not readily recall or even be aware. For example, participants who had had a poor night's sleep or gone without breakfast may be more irritable than those who had slept well or had had a hearty breakfast. Men may be more inclined to show their aggression than women, and so on. Now, it is possible to control for some of these factors by holding them constant such as restricting participation to men or to women. Alternatively, the roles of these factors may themselves be investigated by including both women and men in the study. However, because we are not necessarily aware of all the factors that might influence aggressiveness and because it would be difficult to study or to hold constant all those variables that we were conscious of, it would be better to try to control for these extraneous factors through random assignment. By randomly assigning participants to treatments, it is more likely that the people in both groups will be similar in terms of a whole host of other characteristics. For example, random assignment will make it more probable that the two groups will contain the same number of people who had a disturbed night's sleep, missed breakfast or were male.

However, when only a small number of participants are involved in a study and are randomly assigned to conditions, there is a greater probability that the number or proportion of people who have the same characteristic will differ in the two conditions. This point can be illustrated by looking at the possible results of tossing a varying number of coins. The two sides of the coin can be thought of as denoting any variable which can take on two equiprobable values such as being a woman or man. If we tossed the coin once, then the probability of it turning up heads would be one of two possibilities (a head or a tail), which can be represented as the proportion 0.5 (i.e. $1/2 = 0.5$).

If we tossed two coins once, there are four possible or theoretical outcomes as shown in Table 1.1: (1) a head on the first coin and a tail on the second; (2) a tail on the first coin and a head on the second; (3) two

Table 1.1 Four possible outcomes of tossing two coins once and their probability

	Coin 1	Coin 2	Probability (p)
1	Head	Tail	0.25 } = 0.5
2	Tail	Head	0.25
3	Head	Head	0.25
4	Tail	Tail	0.25

heads on both coins; and (4) two tails on both coins. The probability of obtaining both a head and a tail (regardless of the coin) would be two out of four possibilities or 0.5 (2/4 = 0.5). The probability (or p value) of obtaining two heads would be one out of four possibilities or 0.25 (1/4 = 0.25). Similarly, the probability of having two tails would also be one out of four possibilities or 0.25.

If we assume that we are randomly assigning only two participants to one of the two conditions, then we can see that the probability of having all women or all men in this condition is 0.5. We can calculate the probability of this particular outcome from any number of coins by simply multiplying the probability of the two outcomes of each of the coins being used. So this probability would be 0.25 for two coins as we have already noted (0.5 $\times$ 0.5 = 0.25), 0.125 for three coins (0.5 $\times$ 0.5 $\times$ 0.5 = 0.125) and 0.0625 for four coins (0.5 $\times$ 0.5 $\times$ 0.5 $\times$ 0.5 = 0.0625). For any number of coins, there can only be one outcome which contains all heads and only one which consists of all tails. To work out the probability of obtaining both these outcomes, we simply add up their separate probabilities, which is 0.5 for two coins (0.25 + 0.25 = 0.5) as we have already calculated, 0.25 for three coins (0.125 + 0.125 = 0.25) and 0.125 for four coins (0.0625 + 0.0625 = 0.125). It should be clear then that as the number of participants increases, the probability that random assignment will lead to participants in any one group having all of one characteristic should decrease.

Of course, it is possible to check whether random assignment has resulted in the participants in the two conditions being similar in various ways before being shown the two films. However, in order not to overtax the participants' good will, it is preferable to limit this *pre-testing* to those variables of most direct interest, which in this case would be their aggressiveness before seeing the film. A pre-test is a measure taken before the experimental manipulation is carried out as opposed to a *post-test* which is taken after the manipulation has been carried out. This pre-test information can be used in three ways. First, participants with similar pre-test aggressiveness can be *matched*, *blocked* or *paired* in terms of their scores and then randomly assigned to one of the two conditions. This matching procedure will ensure that the participants in the two conditions will be similar in terms of their initial aggressiveness.

Second, without resorting to matching, the pre-test aggressiveness scores of the participants in the two conditions can be compared after all the data have been collected. If the scores in the two conditions differ, then random assignment has not been effective so far as the key variable of aggressiveness is concerned. The way of determining whether two groups of scores differ is itself a statistical issue which will be introduced below. If the pre-test scores differ, then there are statistical procedures, such as *analysis of covariance*, which take these differences into consideration. This particular procedure will be described in Chapter 8.

Third, if the pre-test scores do not differ, then they may be compared with the post-test aggressiveness scores of the participants after they have seen the film to determine the nature and statistical significance of any change that has occurred.

STATISTICAL SIGNIFICANCE

Having tested our participants, we then need to determine how likely it is that the results of our study are due to chance. Findings which have a one in twenty probability or less of occurring by chance are considered to be statistically significant in the sense that they are not thought to be due to chance. This level of significance is usually expressed as the proportion 0.05 (1/20 = 0.05). There are numerous tests for assessing the statistical significance of a finding. Indeed, most of this book is devoted to describing the more commonly used tests. However, the general principle which underlies significance testing can be simply illustrated as follows.

Assume that people's behaviour in this study is rated as being either aggressive or non-aggressive. If watching the violent film had no effect and if the probability of being aggressive was the same as being non-aggressive (that is 0.5), then the proportion of people who were rated as being aggressive after viewing the film should differ by chance between the two conditions. This situation is like tossing two sets of coins once, where heads depict being aggressive and tails being non-aggressive. The two sets of coins represent the people who have been randomly assigned to watching either the violent or non-violent film. If we toss two coins once (representing one person from each of the two conditions), then there are four possible outcomes as shown in Table 1.1: (1) a head and a tail; (2) a tail and a head; (3) two heads; and (4) two tails. If the first coin represents people viewing the violent film and the second coin those watching the non-violent film, then the probability is 0.25 of finding the person watching the violent film being aggressive (heads on coin 1) and the person viewing the non-violent film being non-aggressive (tails on coin 2). If we obtained this result and if we use the conventional criterion that for a difference to be statistically significant it has to have a probability of 0.05 or less, then we would have to conclude that there was no statistically significant difference in aggressiveness between the two conditions.

We can now extend this idea to the theoretical outcomes of tossing two sets of two coins once, which are shown in Table 1.2. There is one outcome (outcome 2 in Table 1.2) in which two heads were obtained with the two coins in the first set and two tails were found with the two coins in the second set. This outcome represents the situation in which the two people watching the violent film were both rated as being aggressive subsequently while the two people watching the non-violent film were both described as being non-aggressive. The probability of this outcome is 0.0625. If we

Table 1.2 Probability of the same outcome from tossing two sets of two coins once

Outcome	Set 1 (Violent film)	Set 2 (Non-violent film)	Probability (p)
1	HH	HH	0.0625
2	HH	TT	0.0625
3	HH	HT	0.0625
4	HH	TH	0.0625
5	TT	HH	0.0625
6	TT	TT	0.0625
7	TT	HT	0.0625
8	TT	TH	0.0625
9	HT	HH	0.0625
10	HT	TT	0.0625
11	HT	HT	0.0625
12	HT	TH	0.0625
13	TH	HH	0.0625
14	TH	TT	0.0625
15	TH	HT	0.0625
16	TH	TH	0.0625

obtained this result from our study, then we could conclude that this difference just failed to reach statistical significance at the 0.05 level.

Suppose, however, we had found that only one of the two people watching the violent film had been rated as being aggressive subsequently and that, as before, neither of the two people viewing the non-violent film had been described as being aggressive. From Table 1.2, we can see that there are two outcomes (outcomes 10 and 14) which reflect this situation. Consequently, the probability of finding that only one of the two people watching the violent film was rated as being aggressive (and neither of the other two in the non-violent condition) is the combined probability of these two outcomes which is 0.125 (0.0625 + 0.0625 = 0.125). If we obtained this result, then this difference is clearly not significant at the 0.05 level.

The basic aim of many statistical tests is to determine the probability of obtaining a particular finding by chance. Which test to use depends on a number of considerations which are outlined in Chapter 4.

TRUE EXPERIMENTAL DESIGNS

The design of the study which has so far been used to illustrate the role of statistics in social research has been referred to as a *true experimental* design (Campbell and Stanley 1966). There are two essential features to such a design. First, only the presence of the factor (or factors) whose effects are of interest should be varied or manipulated. Everything else should be kept as similar and as constant as possible. Second, participants should be randomly assigned to the conditions which represent these variations, or to the order in which these conditions are run if participants take part in more than one condition. An example of the latter procedure would be where participants saw both the film with the violence and the one without it.

A design in which different participants (or *subjects* as they were traditionally called in psychology) are randomly assigned to different conditions has been referred to as a *between-subjects* design or one involving *independent, unrelated* or *uncorrelated* groups or samples. Whereas a design in which the same participants are randomly allocated to more than one condition has been described as a *within-subjects* design or one involving *repeated measures* or *dependent, related* or *correlated* groups or samples.

The advantage of a within-subjects design, apart from requiring fewer participants, is that it holds constant all those factors which are unique to any one person (such as their genetic makeup and previous personal experiences) and which may affect the way they respond to the manipulation. However, since the order in which conditions are run may alter the responses to them, it is essential to control for any potential *order effect* by making sure that the different orders are conducted the same number of times. Suppose, for instance, that watching violent films does not increase aggression but that the more often people see a film (no matter what its content), the less aggressive they feel. If the violent film is shown first more often, then it will appear that seeing violence produces aggression. Random assignment of participants to different orders, on the other hand, is necessary to determine if the order of the conditions has an effect. With non-random assignment, it is more likely that people who are prone to aggression will be allocated to one or other of the two orders. If aggressive people are more frequently assigned to seeing the violent film first, then there may appear to be an order effect (such that seeing violence first makes people more aggressive) when there is none.

Within-subjects designs (where it is possible in principle to use them) have two potential drawbacks which may outweigh their advantages. The first disadvantage is that there may be a *carryover* or *asymmetrical transfer effect* where a change induced by the first condition will carry over to the second. For instance, watching the violent film first may increase a person's tendency to be aggressive so that they are more likely to act aggressively after seeing the non-violent film. If this happens, then the difference in aggressiveness between the two conditions will be less in a within- than a between-subjects design and consequently may not be statistically significant. The second potential disadvantage of the within-subjects design is that participants will have more information about the experiment as a result of being exposed to more than one condition. This knowledge may affect what they think the experiment is about which in turn may influence their subsequent behaviour.

The great strength of a true experimental design is that by virtue of trying to hold all other extraneous variables constant and to only vary those factors of interest, it enables us to determine with more certainty whether the effects we observe are due to the factors that have been manipulated. For example, suppose we find that, with everything else held constant, participants who watched the violent film behaved more aggressively than those who saw the non-violent film. Then, provided that this effect occurred more frequently than is likely to have happened just by chance, it seems reasonable to conclude that the greater aggression shown resulted from watching the violent film.

NON-EXPERIMENTAL DESIGNS

Experimental designs which do not entail the random assignment of participants to the systematic manipulation of one or more variables have been called *non-*, *pre-* or *quasi-experimental* designs (Campbell and Stanley 1966). Perhaps the most common of these designs is one in which two or more variables are measured at one moment in time. This kind of design is very similar to what Campbell and Stanley (1966) term the *static-group comparison* and often takes the form of a survey. Suppose, for example, we wanted to find out whether people who watched more violence on television also behaved more aggressively. In other words, we wished to determine if the amount of violence seen on television was related to the level of aggression displayed. The simplest way of examining whether there was such a relationship between these two characteristics would be to ask a number of individuals how much violence they watched on television and how aggressively they behaved and to work out what the association was between these two variables.

There are two main statistical approaches for determining whether there is a statistically significant association between these two factors. The first approach is essentially a test of difference. It examines whether there is a statistical difference in aggression between the two groups of people and is the same as that previously used in the true experiment described above to find out if there was a significant difference between those participants who saw the violent film and those who did not. In the static-group comparison we could divide the participants into two groups according to how much violence they watched on television. Individuals in one group will have watched little or no violence on television, while those in the other group will have seen more violence on television. The exact criterion we use to form the two groups need not concern us here. We can then compare the amount of aggression reported by the people in the two groups.

As before, any difference we find between the two groups may be due to chance and so we would have to work out what the statistical probability was of coming up with any such difference by chance. Suppose we noted that those who watched more violence on television also reported being more aggressive than those who saw less violence. If the probability of finding this difference was calculated to be 0.05 or less, we could conclude that those who watched more violence on television behaved significantly more aggressively than those who saw less violence. If the probability of obtaining this difference was greater than 0.05, we would have to conclude that there was no significant difference between these two groups of individuals.

The second statistical approach for calculating whether there is a significant association between two factors (such as watching violence on television and aggression) is essentially a test of the strength of that association. We are interested in estimating how strong the relationship is between two factors. To illustrate the principle behind this test, suppose that of four people questioned about their television viewing habits and aggressive behaviour, two could be classified as watching little or no violence on television while the other two could be categorised as viewing violence on television. Furthermore, the two who did not watch violence on television did not behave aggressively, while the two who viewed violence on television did act aggressively. We could summarise these results in the form of a simple table as shown in Table 1.3.

To work out the strength of the relationship between watching violence on television and being aggressive, we can count the number of people who watch violence and are aggressive (which is 2) and the number of people who do not watch violence and are not aggressive (which is also 2). We can then calculate the proportion of people who fall into either of these two categories by adding these two figures together and dividing by the total number of people in the sample. This proportion is 1.00 [(2 + 2)/4 = 1.00]. In other words, since both the persons who watch violence on televison are aggressive while both those who do not watch violence on television are not aggressive, we have a perfect relationship between watching violence on television and being aggressive.

It should be noted that an index of association can also be worked out for

Table 1.3 Results showing a perfect relationship between watching violence on television and aggression

		Aggression	
		No	Yes
Violence watched	No	2	0
	Yes	0	2

the results of a true experiment between the manipulated variable (e.g. watching the violent or non-violent film) and the measured variable (e.g. aggression). However, this is done less often with data from true experimental designs. The important point to remember is that statistical tests of difference and association can be used with either true or non-experimental designs and that the choice of which test to use depends primarily on the purpose of the analysis.

The static-group comparison design includes the following three advantages. First, it is relatively simple and inexpensive to carry out. Second, information on a large number of potentially relevant factors can be assessed which is useful in exploring which factors are likely to be the most influential. And third, these factors can be studied in the natural, everyday context in which they occur.

The main drawback of this design, however, is that it does not enable us to determine the causal nature of the relationship between any two variables. Suppose, for instance, we found that people who watched violence on television also behaved more aggressively in general. The causal connection between these two variables can be explained in four possible ways. First, as originally suggested, watching violence on television may produce aggression.

1 Watching violence ⎯⎯⎯⎯→ Aggression

But, this is by no means the only possible explanation. Indeed, the causal direction of this association may be reversed, with aggression resulting in watching violence on television. In other words, aggressive people may like to view violence on television.

2 Watching violence ←⎯⎯⎯⎯ Aggression

In both these explanations, only one variable affects the other. Consequently, these causal directions are sometimes referred to as *one-way*, *unidirectional*, *unilateral*, *non-reciprocal* or *recursive*.

However, it is also possible that both variables affect each other. Watching violence on television may encourage aggression while aggression itself may lead to viewing violence on television.

3 Watching violence ←⎯⎯⎯⎯→ Aggression

Relationships in which both variables influence each other are sometimes described as *two-way*, *bidirectional*, *bilateral*, *reciprocal* or *non-recursive*.

Finally, two variables may appear to be related when in reality they are not because they are both associated with a third variable. For example, adolescents may both watch more violence on television and be more aggressive than adults. In other words, if age is strongly related to both these variables, then the two variables will themselves appear to be directly associated when they are not.

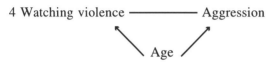

This kind of relationship is described as *spurious* because it is due to other factors. Note, however, that although age may be a *confounding* variable in this case, an alternative possibility is that aggression is an *intervening* or *mediating* variable through which age acts to affect watching violence. Whether age is better seen as a confounding variable or aggression as an intervening variable depends partly on the size of the associations between the variables and partly on theoretical argument.

On the other hand, if we find no relationship between watching violence on television and aggression, then it is still possible that there is an association between these two variables but that it has been suppressed by some other factor(s). For instance, if the more physically active watched less violence on television and behaved more aggressively, then the relationship between these two variables may be hidden by the fact that the less physically active watched more violence on television but behaved less aggressively. Where we believe that the relationship between two variables may be either spurious or suppressed, we should try to measure the factor(s) that are bringing this about and to remove or control the influence of these factor(s) statistically. Statistical tests for doing this are described in Chapters 9 and 10.

It is important to realise that making claims about the causal relationship between two (or more) variables depends primarily on the experimental design used to examine the relationship and not on the statistical analysis of the results. True experimental designs enable causality to be ascertained with more confidence because an attempt is made to hold constant all other variables except the ones of interest which are systematically varied. Non-experimental designs, such as the static-group comparison, do not allow causality to be inferred because they do not systematically manipulate the variables of concern. The same statistical tests can be used to analyse the appropriate results of both non- and true experimental designs. What these tests generally do is to provide us with an estimate of the size of any relationship and the probability of finding that relationship by chance.

Factors whose effects we are interested in are often called *independent variables* while the effects themselves are usually referred to as the *dependent variables* because it is assumed that these effects *depend* on the independent variables. Consequently, if we believed that watching violence on television increased aggressiveness, we would call the degree to which violence was watched on television the independent variable and the level of aggressiveness displayed the dependent variable. If we thought that the direction of causality was the other way round, we would call the level of aggressiveness the independent variable and the degree to which violence was watched on television the dependent variable. Strictly speaking, however, the terms independent variable and dependent variable should be respectively reserved for the manipulated variable and the measured effect in a true experimental design. In such a design the independent variable should be manipulated independently of other features of the design so that any observed effect is more likely to be due to this manipulated variable than to the other features of the study. Factors in a true experimental design which cannot be independently manipulated, such as the age and gender of the participants, are sometimes more appropriately referred to as *subject variables* since they cannot be separated from the individual. Often, however, these factors are also described as independent variables.

MEASURING CONCEPTS

Finally, an understanding of statistics is required for making decisions about how a concept or variable should be measured and for assessing how reliable and valid that measure is. For example, we have to decide how we should quantify or score how aggressive someone is. Do we simply categorise people as being aggressive or non-aggressive? Do we order them in terms of how aggressive they are from the most to the least aggressive? Or do we rate them in some way in terms of how aggressive they are? Various ways of quantifying concepts are outlined in Chapter 2. When comparing levels of aggressiveness in two or more groups, we have to summarise or aggregate the scores of the individuals in the groups being compared. Different procedures for doing this are also covered in the next chapter. Statistics for describing sets of scores or the relationship between them are called *descriptive statistics* while statistics which make inferences from these sets of scores to the population from which they are drawn are known as *inferential statistics*.

Whatever method we use for assessing aggressiveness, we also need to know how reliable and valid our measures are. By reliable, we mean how similar the scores of aggressiveness are for a particular individual when measured on more than one occasion not too far apart, or by more than one person or item. A valid measure of aggressiveness, on the other hand, is one that behaves in a way which indicates that it seems to be assessing aggressiveness. For example, we would expect a measure of aggressiveness to be more highly related to other measures of aggressiveness than to measures of dissimilar constructs such as self-esteem. The reliability and validity of a measure are usually assessed statistically. Statistical procedures for assessing validity are the same as those used for determining relationships between variables or differences between groups. Some specific statistical tests, however, have been devised for measuring reliability and agreement between observers. These tests are covered in Chapter 12.

SUMMARY

Statistics play a vital role in collecting, summarising and interpreting data in quantitative social science research. Random assignment of participants to experimental conditions is essential in increasing the likelihood that participants assigned to different treatments will be similar and that as a consequence any observed difference between conditions will be more likely due to the experimental manipulation. Random selection of participants from a population, on the other hand, is necessary when a sample is used to gather information about that population. The reliability and validity of the measures employed have to be ascertained. The data collected need to be summarised in order to determine the nature of the results. The size of the association between variables and of the difference between groups indicates how important a variable might be in relationship to one or more other variables. The statistical significance of a finding estimates the likelihood of that result occurring simply by chance in the population.

## Chapter 2

Measurement and univariate analysis

MEASUREMENT

Statistical analysis depends on being able to measure or to quantify those aspects of objects which interest us. Measurement involves assigning numbers to observations according to certain rules. Since the type of statistical procedure used to describe and to draw inferences from empirical observations partly rests on the way in which an attribute or variable is measured, it is important to be familiar with the kinds of measurement that have been distinguished. Stevens (1946) suggested four levels or scales of measurement which are frequently referred to in discussions on the types of statistical procedures to be followed with different kinds of measurement. Although each level has its own characteristics, the levels are hierarchical. The higher levels have more sophisticated properties than the lower levels but they also include the more basic features of the lower levels.

Nominal level

The nominal level is the lowest and crudest form of measurement. Numbers are simply used to identify or to 'name' the attribute or category being described, hence the term 'nominal'. For example, the gender of participants may be coded as numbers, with 1 for females and 2 for males. Similarly, the treatments in a true experiment may be given a number. Participants who watched the violent film may be ascribed as 1 and those who saw the non-violent film as 2. The assignment of numbers is arbitrary. So, males may be coded 5 and females 9. Since the numbers have no quantitative meaning, it makes no sense to carry out mathematical operations on them such as addition, subtraction, multiplication and division. The only mathematical operation that can be performed on them is to count the frequency of each number. For instance, there may be four 1's and six 2's, denoting four females and six males respectively. Data which correspond to this level of measurement are sometimes referred to as *categorical* or *frequency* data. Numbers are often used to consecutively label and identify people or objects, such as the participants in a study. Some writers include this use of numbers as being nominal.

Ordinal level

The next higher level of measurement is the ordinal one in which the numbers indicate increasing amounts of a particular attribute. As the term 'ordinal' implies, individuals (objects or events) can be rank 'ordered' from the smallest to the largest in terms of the characteristic being evaluated. For example, ten participants can be rank ordered in terms of how aggressive they seem with 1 indicating the least aggressive person and 10 the most. The intervals between the numbers do not represent equal amounts of the quality being measured. For instance, the difference in aggressiveness between someone ranked 2 and someone ranked 4 need not be the same as the difference between someone ranked 6 and someone ranked 8. Furthermore, the numbers do not indicate absolute quantities, so that someone ranked 8 is not necessarily twice as aggressive as someone ranked 4. In some instances, it is not possible to distinguish between cases and no attempt is made to order these cases. In this situation a *tie* is said to exist and the tied cases receive the same number.

Interval level

With interval level measurement, the intervals between numbers denote equal amounts of the attribute being assessed, hence the term 'interval'. A clear example of a measure having an interval scale is a Celsius thermometer. The difference in temperature between the two readings of 5°C and 10°C is said to be the same as that between the two readings of 15°C and 20°C. However, because interval scales have no absolute zero point, we cannot say that a value which is twice as big as another value denotes twice the amount of the quality being assessed. Although a Celsius thermometer has a zero point, this point does not represent absolute zero since the scale registers temperatures below zero. Consequently, while we can say that 20°C is hotter than 10°C, we cannot claim that it is twice as hot as 10°C. This point will be easier to demonstrate when we consider the highest level of measurement.

Ratio level

The ratio scale represents the highest level of measurement and so has all the properties of the lower measurement levels in that it has equal intervals and it also categorises and rank orders scores. Unlike the other levels, however, it also includes an absolute zero point which means that a value which is twice as large as another reflects twice the amount of the attribute being measured. In other words, we can express two values on such a scale as a ratio. Age is an example of a ratio measure. Someone who is 20 is twice as old as someone of 10. In other words, these two ages can be expressed as a ratio of 2(0):1(0). If age was made to be an interval scale in which zero was arbitrarily set at 5 years, 10 would become 15 (5 + 10 = 15) and 20 would become 25 (5 + 20 = 25) in which case the interval scale value of 25 is not twice that of 15.

As we shall see, many social scientists treat what appear to be ordinal scales as if they were interval or ratio ones. Suppose we developed a simple rating scale for participants to report how aggressive they generally saw themselves as being. The rating scale has four points which represent the following degrees of aggression: 0 = not aggressive; 1 = slightly aggressive; 2 = moderately aggressive; and 3 = very aggressive. Participants have to select the number which best describes them. Although this scale has a zero point, it is neither an interval nor a ratio scale since it cannot be argued that the interval or difference in aggression between, say, points of 0 and 1 is the same as that between 2 and 3. In effect, this scale is a simple ordinal one in which the numbers indicate increasing degrees of aggression and nothing more.

None the less, many social scientists will interpret ordinal scales as interval or ratio ones. Perhaps, the main reason for this is that in many cases the main interest is not with the level of measurement as such but with whether two (or more) conditions differ or whether two (or more) variables are related. Since the statistical tests themselves only apply to numbers and not to what they mean (Lord 1953), no attention has to be paid to the measurement scales when undertaking the statistical analysis. Furthermore, there is no need to be primarily concerned with measurement levels should we, for example, find that those who watch more violence on television also rate themselves as being more aggressive. However, the failure to find a difference between the two conditions may result from using a relatively crude (i.e. ordinal level) measure of aggression. Consequently, the absence of a difference or association may be due to the low level of the measure employed.

UNIVARIATE ANALYSIS

Once we have collected the data of our study, we usually need to carry out one or more *univariate* analyses in which the data for a single variable are looked at on their own. For example, we may begin by wanting to know how many participants are married or what the average number of hours of television watched per week by each participant is. In describing such data, we are primarily concerned with differentiating between nominal variables (such as marital status) and non-nominal variables (such as hours of television watched). Since at this stage we are simply describing the numerical characteristics of the distribution of scores in our study and are not concerned with making any inferences from them about their distribution in the population, these kinds of statistics are known as descriptive statistics.

Proportions, percentages and ratios

With nominal variables, all we can do is to count the number or frequency of participants within each category and to report either the total number for each category or that total number as a *proportion* (or *percentage*) of the total sample. Suppose, for example, we had three categories of marital status (married, divorced and single) and that 40 people were married, 20 divorced and 10 single.

Rather than simply presenting the total numbers in each group, the numbers in any one category can be expressed as a proportion or percentage of the whole sample. A proportion is the frequency of cases within a category divided by the total number of cases. Since it is often easier to grasp a statistical concept in terms of a formula, we will provide formulae for such concepts wherever possible. So the formula for a proportion can be expressed as follows.

$$\text{proportion} = \frac{\text{frequency of cases in one category}}{\text{total number of cases}}$$

In our example, the proportion of single people is 0.14, rounded to two decimal places (10/70 = 0.143). The sum of proportions always equals one (10/70 + 20/70 + 40/70 = 70/70 = 1), so that the largest proportion can never be bigger than one.

A percentage is simply a proportion multiplied by 100. So the formula for a percentage is

$$\text{percentage } (\%) = \frac{\text{frequency of cases in one category}}{\text{total number of cases}} \times 100$$

In our example, the percentage of singles in the sample is 14 per cent (0.14 × 100 = 14).

Comparing the frequency of one category against the frequency of another is called a *ratio* and gives an index of the relative frequency of two categories.

ratio = frequency of one category: frequency of another category

So, the ratio of married to divorced people in our example is 40:20 which may be simplified to 2:1, indicating that there are two married people to every divorced person in our sample.

Describing frequencies in proportions or percentages is particularly helpful when comparing some variable across samples of different sizes. For example, suppose we want to compare the number of married and non-married people in two samples. The number of married people is 40 in one sample of 70 and 30 in another sample of 50. It is easier to grasp and to compare these figures when they are converted into one of these two indices.

Frequencies	Proportions	Percentages
40 of 70	40/70 = 0.57	40/70 × 100 = 57
30 of 50	30/50 = 0.60	30/50 × 100 = 60

For example, the percentage of married people in the first sample is 57 compared with 60 in the second.

Note that percentages can be misleading when the total number of cases is small. For example, if we had a sample of only seven people, 14 per cent of them represents only one person. Similarly, if we expanded the size of our sample by one person from seven to eight people, then this is an increase of 14 per cent which seems large although it is an increase of only one person. Consequently, attention should be paid to what the numbers represent rather than to their absolute size.

Rounding numbers and number of decimals

When dividing one number by another we frequently obtain more numbers than the original one. To take an extreme example, if we divide one by three, the resulting number is 0.3333 recurring. When this happens two questions arise. The first is how many decimals in the number should we present and the second is how do we go about reducing or rounding the decimals. Some writers have suggested that generally we should have only one or two digits more than the original number. If we restricted ourselves to having two more digits than the original number, then dividing one by three would become 0.33. We would now have three digits instead of the original one.

The general rule for rounding numbers to the nearest whole number or to the nearest decimal place is that if the digit (reading from left to right) following the one to be rounded is less than five, it is dropped. So, in our example, the three (0.333) following the three to be rounded (0.333) is dropped since it is less than five. If the following digit is more than five (say, 0.336), then the digit to be rounded (0.336) is rounded up or increased by one (to 0.34).

The only complication arises when the following digit is five (0.335). The simple rule for handling this situation is to round up numbers that are equal to or greater than five and to drop numbers that are less than five. So, rounding to two decimal places, 0.335 becomes 0.34 while 0.334 becomes

0.33. Because of its simplicity and because this rule is employed by the statistical program we will be using, we shall adopt this method.

Different procedures for rounding numbers will lead to different results. One way of avoiding these differences (which may be large) is to follow the further rule that each number in a series of computations is rounded to one more decimal place than the number of places used in the final answer. The rules described in this section will generally be applied to the examples worked out by hand throughout this book to ensure that a consistent practice is adopted.

Measures of central tendency

When dealing with non-nominal variables which can have a large number of different values, it is useful to be able to summarise these scores in some way. One way of doing this is to describe these scores in terms of their typical or central value. These indices are known as *measures of central tendency*, of which the three most commonly discussed are the *mode*, the *median* and the *mean* or *arithmetic mean* (to distinguish it from other means such as the *geometric* and *harmonic* mean).

Mode

The least used and simplest of these three measures is the mode, which is the score that occurs most frequently.

mode = most frequent score

Suppose we have the following set of seven scores which may be number of hours of television watched by seven people:

    6   3   5   7   1   3   4

The most common score is 3, of which there are only two. Consequently, the mode is 3. Note that the mode is the most commonly occurring value (3) and not the frequency (2) of that value. If a number of the scores had the same frequency, then there would be more than one mode. For example, if there was another score of 5, then this set of scores would have two modes (3 and 5).

Median

The median is that point or number in a set of scores, arranged in ascending order of size from lowest to highest, which divides those scores into two equal parts. In some cases it is relatively easy to determine the median as in the above example of seven scores. To obtain the median, arrange these scores in ascending order of size from smallest to largest. This order is

1   3   3   4   5   6   7
        ↑

The median is 4 since the number of scores above it (3) is equal to the number below it (3) and all the scores above the median are higher than those below it. When the set of scores is an odd number, as it is here, the position of the median is the number of scores plus 1 and divided by 2 [(7 + 1)/2 = 4] since this is the position of the score that divides the sample into two equal halves.

When the set of scores is an even number as in the following group of eight ordered scores

1   3   3   4   5   6   7   7
          ↑

the position of the median lies midway between the two middle scores (4 and 5) and is the average of those two scores, i.e. 4.5 [(4 + 5)/2 = 4.5].

Calculating the median, however, becomes more complicated where there is an even number of scores and where the middle scores have the same values as in the following set of eight numbers

1   3   3   4   4   4   6   7
       ↑

Here the median lies between the first and second 4 but there is also a third 4 to take into account.

In this case the median is worked out by *linear interpolation* as follows. First, however, we have to realise that although all these scores are whole numbers or integers, they can vary anywhere between these numbers. In other words, they can take on fractional or non-integer values such as 1.7 or 8.53. Thus, an integer has *exact* or *real limits* which determine what fractional values it can have and these are set as 0.50 units below and above that number. The exact limits define the *interval* of any score which for 4, for example, ranges from 3.50 to 4.50 with the exact midpoint being 4 itself.

Since there are three 4's in this instance, we assume that the three values are equally spread between 3.50 and 4.50. This means that each value occupies a third or 0.333 of this interval (1/3 = 0.333). The limits of these three values, therefore, are 3.50, 3.83 (3.50 + 0.333 = 3.833), 4.17 (3.833 + 0.333 = 4.166) and 4.50 (4.166 + 0.333 = 4.499). Consequently, the median is midway between 3.50 and 4.17, which is 3.83.

    4   4   4
3.50   3.83   4.17   4.50
    ↑

In order to work out the median, it might be helpful to use the following formula, which may appear a little daunting at first sight and which is the usual one that is presented.

median = exact lower limit of the median interval (L) +
$$\left[\frac{\text{total number of scores/2} - \text{number of scores below } L}{\text{number of scores in median interval}} \times \text{size of median interval} \right]$$

In this formula, the position of the median is based on the total number of scores. If the number of scores is even, you may adjust it by adding 1 to the total number of scores, although when there are a large number of scores this adjustment will generally make little difference. 'L' is the symbol for the exact lower limit of the median interval.

We will illustrate how to apply this formula using our last example. To work out the median, carry out the following steps.

Step 1 Arrange the scores in ascending order, which we have already done and which is

1 3 3 4 4 4 6 7

Step 2 Count the total number of scores and divide by 2 to determine where the median score should roughly fall. There are 8 scores which divided by 2 gives 4 (8/2 = 4).

Step 3 Work out the size of the median interval. This is 1 since the exact limits of 4 are 0.50 units above and below it.

Step 4 Work out the exact lower limit of the median interval (L), which in this case is 3.5.

Step 5 Count the number of scores below the exact lower limit of the median limit (L). L is 3.5 and so the number of scores below it is 3.

Step 6 Count the number of scores in the median interval, which is 3.

Step 7 Put the appropriate values in the formula to calculate the median which is 3.83:

$$3.5 + \left[\frac{8/2 - 3}{3} \times 1 \right] = 3.5 + 0.333 = 3.83$$

We can also use this formula to work out the medians for the first two examples, which are 4 and 4.5 respectively:

$$3.5 + \left[\frac{7/2 - 3}{1} \times 1 \right] = 3.5 + 0.5 = 4.0$$

$$3.5 + \left[\frac{8/2 - 3}{1} \times 1 \right] = 3.5 + 1.0 = 4.5$$

Note that when following the calculations shown in this book, pay particular attention to the order in which the computations are done. In this last example, we first divide 8 by 2 and then subtract 3. We do not first subtract 3 from 2 and then divide 8 by this difference. To check the order of the calculations, repeat them yourself and see if you come up with the same results. If you find it easier to do this, use a cheap electronic calculator. Hopefully, there are no computational errors in this book, although these sometimes slip through.

Mean

The mean is the most commonly used measure of central tendency. To obtain it, add together or sum all the scores in a series and divide this sum by the number of scores. So, the formula for the mean is:

$$\text{mean} = \frac{\text{sum of scores}}{\text{number of scores}}$$

To illustrate its calculation, we will take the following set of seven scores which have already been used to work out the mode and the median:

1   3   3   4   5   6   7

To calculate the mean, carry out the following steps.

Step 1   Add the scores together to give the sum or total score, which is 29:

1 + 3 + 3 + 4 + 5 + 6 + 7 = 29

Step 2   Count the number of scores, which is 7.

Step 3   Divide the sum of scores by the number of scores to give the mean, which is 4.14:

29/7 = 4.14

Comparison of mode, median and mean

Which of these three measures of central tendency we should use to describe the typical value of a set of scores depends partly on the distribution of those scores when ordered according to size. When the distribution is *unimodal* (i.e. has one mode) and symmetrical, then the mode, median and mean will have very similar values. Take the following set of seven scores, whose distribution is unimodal and symmetrical:

1   2   3   3   3   4   5

The mode or most frequent score is 3, of which there are 3. The median or middle score is also 3 with two scores lower and two scores higher than it. The mean is also 3 [(1 + 2 + 3 + 3 + 3 + 4 + 5)/7 = 21/7 = 3]. What this means in practice is that when the distribution of scores has one mode and is approximately symmetrical, then the mode, median and mean will have roughly the same value so that it matters less which measure we use to describe the central tendency of the array of scores.

When the distribution of scores is symmetrical but *bimodal* (i.e. has two modes), then the median and the mean will have very similar values which will obviously differ from the modes since there are two of them. For example, in the following symmetrical and bimodal distribution of seven scores

1   2   2   4   5   5   6

the two modes are 2 and 5 while the median is 4 and the mean is 3.57 (25/7 = 3.57).

When the distribution of scores is asymmetrical, then all three measures of central tendency will differ. Examine the following asymmetrical distribution of seven scores:

1   2   2   3   7   8   9

The mode is 2, the median is 3 and the mean is 4.57 (32/7 = 4.57). When most of the scores in a set are relatively low, the mode will generally have the lowest value, the median the next lowest and the mean the highest.

Conversely, when most of the scores are relatively high, the mode will have the highest value, the median the next highest and the mean the lowest, as in the following example:

1   2   3   7   8   8   9

Here the mode is 8, the median is 7 and the mean is 5.43 (38/7 = 5.43).

Further complications arise when the data contain a few extreme scores (sometimes called *outliers*) since the mean is more strongly affected by such scores than either the mode or the median. We can see this if we substitute 90 for 9 in the preceding set of numbers. The mode and the median will remain the same (at 8 and 7 respectively) while the mean will be increased from 5.43 to 17 (119/7 = 17). In such situations, it may be more appropriate to use the median than the mean. Alternatively, the mean can be employed but calculated by either omitting the extreme values or making them less extreme. In this example, the mean would be 4.83 (29/6 = 4.83) if 90 was excluded or 5.43 if it was reduced to, say, the next highest score after 8 (i.e. 9).

Another possibility is to transform all the scores so that the differences between the extreme values and the other values are less. The two most common methods of doing this are to take either the square root or the (base 10) logarithm of the scores. These transformations are given below (to one decimal place) for the following set of scores which was previously used to illustrate the influence of an extreme value:

	1	2	3	7	8	8	90
Square root	1.0	1.4	1.7	2.6	2.8	2.8	9.5
Logarithm	0.0	0.3	0.5	0.8	0.9	0.9	2.0

For the untransformed scores, the difference between 8 and 90 (i.e. 81) is at least eleven times (81/7 = 11.6) as great as that between 1 and 8 (i.e. 7). For the square root transformations of the same scores, however, the difference between 2.8 and 9.5 (i.e. 6.7) is less than four times (6.7/1.8 = 3.7) as big as that between 1 and 2.8 (i.e. 1.8). While for the logarithm transformations, the difference between 0.9 and 2.0 (i.e. 1.1) is about the same size (1.1/0.9 = 1.2) as that between 0.0 and 0.9 (i.e. 0.9).

Measures of dispersion

Measures of central tendency only describe the typical value of a distribution of scores and do not indicate the spread or variation in those scores. Two distributions may have exactly the same mean but very different spreads of scores as the following two sets of scores illustrate:

    3   3   4   4   4   5   5
    1   2   3   4   5   6   7

The mean of both sets of scores is 4 but the spread of the first set is more restricted than the second. Indices of spread are called *measures of dispersion*, of which the three most often described are the *range*, the *interquartile range* and the *standard deviation*.

Range

The range is the simplest measure of dispersion and is simply the difference between the highest and the lowest value in a set of scores:

    range = highest score − lowest score

So, the range for the first set of scores above is 2 (5 − 3 = 2) while for the second set it is 6 (7 − 1 = 6). One disadvantage of the range is that, since it is only based on the two extreme scores, it gives little indication of what the distribution of the other scores is like. If either or both of these extreme scores differs greatly from the other scores, then the range will solely reflect the difference between the extreme scores. So, if in the following set of scores

1 2 3 4 5 6 7

the 7 is replaced with 17, then the range is 16 (17 − 1 = 16) rather than 6 (7 − 1 = 6).

Interquartile range

A measure of dispersion which is less dependent than the range on the two extreme scores is the interquartile range. To calculate it, the scores have to be arranged in ascending order and divided into four quarters (i.e. quartiles) containing equal numbers of scores. The *first quartile* is the value below which the lowest quarter of scores fall. The *second quartile* is the value below which half (or two quarters) of the lowest scores lie and corresponds to the median. While the *third quartile* is the value below which three-quarters of the lowest values congregate. The interquartile range is the difference between the third and first quartile.

interquartile range = third quartile − first quartile

To work out the number of scores which fall within the first quartile of a set of scores, we add one to the total number of scores and divide by four. Similarly, to calculate the number of scores which lie within the third quartile, we add one to the total number of scores and multiply by three-quarters. So, for the following set of seven scores

1 2 3 4 5 6 7
    ↑   ↑

the first quartile lies at the second score [(7 + 1)/4 = 2] which is 2. The third quartile falls on the sixth score [(7 + 1) × 3/4 = 6] which is 6. Consequently, the interquartile range of this set of scores is 4 (6 − 2 = 4).

Note that the interquartile range of the following set of scores (which includes the more extreme score of 17)

1 2 3 4 5 6 17
    ↑   ↑

is also 4 since the third quartile is still 6 [(7 + 1) × 3/4 = 6].

Sometimes the *semi-interquartile range* or *quartile deviation* is used instead of the interquartile range. This measure is simply the interquartile range divided by 2:

$$\text{semi-interquartile range} = \frac{\text{third quartile} - \text{first quartile}}{2}$$

In this example the semi-interquartile range is 2 $[(6 - 2)/2 = 2]$.

Calculating the first and third quartile is slightly more complicated where the quartiles fall between existing scores. Take the following sequence of nine numbers:

1   1   5   6   6   6   6   9   9

The first quartile falls at the 2.5th score $[(9 + 1)/4 = 2.5]$ while the third quartile lies at the 7.5th score $[(9 + 1) \times 3/4 = 7.5]$. In other words, the first quartile lies halfway between the second score (i.e. 1) and the third score (i.e. 5). The difference between these two scores is 4 $(5 - 1 = 4)$ which halved is 2 $(4/2 = 2)$. Therefore, the first quartile is the second score (1) plus half the distance between the second and third score (2) which comes to 3 altogether $(1 + 2 = 3)$. Similarly, the third quartile is the seventh score (i.e. 6) plus half the difference between the seventh and eighth score $[(9 - 6)/2 = 1.5]$ which makes 7.5 in total $(6 + 1.5 = 7.5)$.

The following procedure may be undertaken to calculate any *percentile* point for cutting off a specified percentage of the distribution below it, including the median (the 50th percentile point), the first quartile (the 25th percentile point) and the third quartile (the 75th percentile point). Although it appears complicated, we have presented it because it seems to be the procedure used by Minitab to calculate these three percentile points. We will illustrate the procedure by working out the 25th percentile point for the previous set of nine numbers.

Step 1   To find out the percentage point immediately above the required percentile point, add 1 to the number of values, multiply this sum by the desired percentile point and divide this product by the number of values. This value is 27.8 for our example:

$$\frac{(9 + 1) \times 25}{9} = \frac{250}{9} = 27.78$$

We shall call this point the cut-off percentage point.

Step 2   Work out the cumulative frequency and the cumulative per cent for the values above and below the cut-off percentage point. For our example these are:

Values	Frequency	Cumulative Frequency	Cumulative Per Cent
1	2	2	22.2
5	1	3	33.3

Step 3   From the cut-off percentage point, subtract the cumulative per cent for the value immediately below it. This difference is 5.6 (27.8 − 22.2 = 5.6) for our example.

Step 4   If this difference is equal to or greater than 100 divided by the number of values, use the following formula to calculate the percentile point:

$$\left[1 - \left[\frac{(N+1) \times p}{100} - cc_1\right] \times x_2\right] + \left[\left[\frac{(N+1) \times p}{100} - cc_1\right] \times x_2\right]$$

If this difference is less than 100 divided by the number of values, use the formula below to work out the percentile point:

$$\left[1 - \left[\frac{(N+1) \times p}{100} - cc_1\right] \times x_1\right] + \left[\left[\frac{(N+1) \times p}{100} - cc_1\right] \times x_2\right]$$

N stands for the number of values (i.e. 9 in this example), p the desired percentile point (i.e. 25), cc_1 the cumulative frequency below the cut-off percentage point (i.e. 2), x_1 the value corresponding to the cumulative frequency below the cut-off percentage point (i.e. 1) and x_2 the value corresponding to the cumulative frequency above the cut-off percentage point (i.e. 5).

Since the difference of 5.6 is less than 11.1 (100/9 = 11.11), we use the second formula. Inserting the appropriate figures into this formula we see that the 25th percentile point is 3:

$$\left[1 - \left[\frac{(9+1) \times 25}{100} - 2\right] \times 1\right] + \left[\left[\frac{(9+1) \times 25}{100} - 2\right] \times 5\right] =$$

$$\left[1 - \left[\frac{250}{100} - 2\right] \times 1\right] + \left[\left[\frac{250}{100} - 2\right] \times 5\right] =$$

$$[1 - [2.5 - 2] \times 1] + [[2.5 - 2] \times 5] =$$

$$[1 - (0.5 \times 1)] + (0.5 \times 5) = 0.5 + 2.5 = 3.0$$

Standard deviation

The most frequently used measure of dispersion is the standard deviation which is based on all the scores in a set. The standard deviation is the square root of the *variance*:

standard deviation = $\sqrt{\text{variance}}$

The variance and hence the standard deviation of a population is calculated in a slightly different way from that of a sample. The population variance is derived by subtracting each score of the population from its mean, squaring these differences or deviations, adding these squared deviations together and dividing this sum by the total number of scores:

$$\text{population variance} = \frac{\text{sum of (mean score} - \text{each score)}^2}{\text{total number of scores}}$$

The sample variance is calculated in the same way except that the sum of the squared deviations is divided by 1 subtracted from the total number of scores:

$$\text{sample variance} = \frac{\text{sum of (mean score} - \text{each score)}^2}{\text{total number of scores} - 1}$$

The sum of squared deviations is usually called the *sum of squares*.

The reason for using 1 less than the total number of scores in calculating the sample variance is to provide a less biased or *unbiased estimate* of the population variance and standard deviation. Consequently, the sample variance and standard deviation are sometimes respectively called the *estimated population variance* and the *estimated population standard deviation*. Because the sample variance of small samples in particular is less than that of the population, dividing the sum of squares by the total number of cases gives an underestimate of the population variance. Dividing the sum of squares by the total number of cases minus 1 provides a less biased estimate of the population variance. With large samples, the adjusted and unadjusted sample variances differ little. As we shall see the notion of variance is important since it forms the basis of the parametric tests described in this book. The sample variance is more commonly used than the population variance since we rarely have access to complete populations and are often primarily concerned with estimating the population variance from a sample.

We will illustrate this once we have shown how to calculate the sum of squares, the variance and the standard deviation for the following sample of eight scores:

    4   4   5   5   6   7   8   9

To calculate the sum of squares, we carry out the following steps.

Step 1   Find the mean score by adding the scores together and dividing by the total number of scores. The mean score for these eight scores is 6:

    (4 + 4 + 5 + 5 + 6 + 7 + 8 + 9)/8 = 48/8 = 6

Step 2 Subtract each score from the mean score, square the differences and sum them to form the sum of squares. The sum of squares for these eight scores is 24:

$$(6-4)^2+(6-4)^2+(6-5)^2+(6-5)^2+(6-6)^2+(6-7)^2+(6-8)^2+(6-9)^2$$
$$= 2^2 + 2^2 + 1^2 + 1^2 + 0^2 + (-1^2) + (-2^2) + (-3^2)$$
$$= 4 + 4 + 1 + 1 + 0 + 1 + 4 + 9 = 24$$

Note that if we simply added the differences together rather than squaring them first, we would have a sum of zero which would give no indication of the distribution of scores:

$$2 + 2 + 1 + 1 + 0 + (-1) + (-2) + (-3) = 0$$

We could, of course, have simply ignored the negative signs to give the sum of *absolute* deviations which for this set of eight scores is 12:

$$2 + 2 + 1 + 1 + 0 + (-1) + (-2) + (-3) = 12$$

There are various reasons why squared rather than absolute deviations are used but in general it is because they are easier to work with mathematically.

Note also that it does not matter whether we subtract each score from the mean score (mean score − each score), as shown above, or we subtract the mean score from each score (each score − mean score), as illustrated below, provided we use the same order for all scores:

$$(4-6)^2+(4-6)^2+(5-6)^2+(5-6)^2+(6-6)^2+(7-6)^2+(8-6)^2+(9-6)^2$$
$$= (-2)^2 + (-2)^2 + (-1)^2 + (-1)^2 + 0^2 + 1^2 + 2^2 + 3^2$$
$$= 4 + 4 + 1 + 1 + 0 + 1 + 4 + 9 = 24$$

Step 3 To calculate the sample variance or *mean square* (i.e. mean squared deviations), we divide the sum of squares by the total number of scores minus 1. The sample variance for our eight scores is 3.43:

$$24/(8-1) = 24/7 = 3.43$$

Step 4 To calculate the standard deviation, take the square root of the variance. The standard deviation for our eight scores is 1.85:

$$\sqrt{3.43} = 1.85$$

Note that the variance is expressed in mean squared units, which are not directly comparable to the original values. For example, if the eight scores represented the number of hours of television watched, then the variance would refer to 'mean squared hours'. The square root of the variance is used to convert the squared units into the original ones. The square root of the variance (3.43) of the eight scores above is 1.85, which describes more closely than the variance the *mean deviation* of the eight scores (12/7 = 1.71).

Because the standard deviation, like the mean, is based on all the scores in a sample, it is strongly affected by extreme scores. This point can be demonstrated with the following set of eight scores where 89 replaces the value of 9 in the previous example:

4   4   5   5   6   7   8   89

The mean of this set of scores is now 16 (128/8 = 16) instead of 6. The sum of squares is 6104 instead of 24:

$(16-4)^2 + (16-4)^2 + (16-5)^2 + (16-5)^2 + (16-6)^2 + (16-7)^2 + (16-8)^2 + (16-89)^2$
$= 12^2 + 12^2 + 11^2 + 11^2 + 10^2 + 9^2 + 8^2 + (-73)^2$
$= 144 + 144 + 121 + 121 + 100 + 81 + 64 + 5329 = 6104$

Consequently, the variance is 872 instead of 3.43 (6104/7 = 872) and the standard deviation is 29.53 ($\sqrt{872}$ = 29.53) instead of 1.85. Once again, we can see that the standard deviation (29.53) is closer than the variance (872) to the mean deviation, which is 20.86:

$(12 + 12 + 11 + 11 + 10 + 9 + 8 + 73)/7 = 146/7 = 20.86$

Because the above procedure for calculating the variance initially involves the arithmetic operation of division in arriving at the mean, it can result in greater rounding error than a process in which adding, subtracting and multiplying is done before dividing and taking the square root. Consequently, there is an alternative computational procedure which is generally used in deriving the variance where the division occurs at a later stage. This alternative computational formula for the variance is:

$$\text{variance} = \frac{\text{sum of squared scores} - \dfrac{\text{squared sum of scores}}{\text{number of scores}}}{\text{number of scores} - 1}$$

This procedure consists of the following steps which will be illustrated with the same set of numbers previously used to calculate the sample variance, i.e.

4   4   5   5   6   7   8   9

Step 1   Sum the scores and square the sum. The sum of scores for these numbers is 48:

$4 + 4 + 5 + 5 + 6 + 7 + 8 + 9 = 48$

which squared is 2304.

Step 2 Divide the squared sum of scores by the number of scores. Dividing 2304 by 8 gives 288:

2304/8 = 288

Step 3 Square each of the original scores and sum them. For our example the sum of squared scores is 312:

$4^2+4^2+5^2+5^2+6^2+7^2+8^2+9^2$ = 16+16+25+25+36+49+64+81 = 312

Step 4 To give the sum of squares, subtract the sum of squared scores (i.e. the results of Step 3) from the squared sum of scores divided by the number of scores (i.e. the results of Step 2). The sum of squares for our example is 24:

312 − 288 = 24

Step 5 To calculate the variance, divide the sum of squares by the number of scores minus 1. So, the variance for our example is 3.43 as previously calculated:

24/(8−1) = 3.43

Because the mean score in this example was a whole number (i.e. 6), both formulae gave the same result for the variance. However, when the mean score has a large number of decimal places which have been rounded to a few places, the results from the two formulae will differ. Take, for example, the following set of seven scores

4 4 5 5 6 7 8

which is the same as the previous set of eight scores except that the last score 9 is missing. The mean of these seven scores is 5.6 rounded to one decimal place (39/7 = 5.571).

Using the first computational formula, the variance is 2.33:

$[(5.6-4)^2 + (5.6-4)^2 + (5.6-5)^2 + (5.6-5)^2 + (5.6-6)^2 +$
$(5.6-7)^2 + (5.6-8)^2]/(7-1)$
$= [1.6^2 + 1.6^2 + 0.6^2 + 0.6^2 + (-0.4)^2 + (-1.4)^2 + (-2.4)^2]/6$
= (2.6 + 2.6 + 0.4 + 0.4 + 0.2 + 2.0 + 5.8)/6 = 14.0/6 = 2.33

With the second computational formula, the variance is 2.29:

$$\frac{231 - \dfrac{39^2}{7}}{7-1} = \frac{231 - \dfrac{1521}{7}}{6} = \frac{231 - 217.29}{6} = \frac{13.71}{6} = 2.29$$

As can be seen from these two examples, the numbers involved in the intermediate stages of the second more accurate computational procedure become large. Furthermore, the way in which this procedure is related to the idea of variance is less obvious. Consequently, this second computational procedure for calculating variance will not generally be followed in the book. If greater accuracy is required, then either this second procedure should be adopted or the first procedure in which a greater number of decimal places is used for the calculations.

One advantage of the standard deviation as a measure of dispersion is that if the scores of a sample are normally distributed, then the percentage of scores which fall between, say, one standard deviation above and below the mean, is known and is about 68.26. In other words, if the mean and standard deviation of a sample of normally distributed scores is known, then it is possible to work out what percentage of the scores lies within any set of two values. In such cases, the mean and standard deviation give a detailed summary of the distribution of scores. The procedure for determining whether a set of scores is normally distributed and for working out what percentage of values lies between any two values of a normal distributed variable is described in Chapter 4.

Now that we have shown how to calculate the sum of squares and the variance, let us return to the issue of demonstrating that dividing the sum of squares by the number of cases minus 1 rather than simply the number of cases gives a less biased estimate of the population variance. Let us assume that the population consists of the following three scores:

   0   1   2

The population mean of these three scores is 1 [(0 + 1 + 2)/3 = 3/3 = 1] and the population variance is 0.667:

$$[(1-0)^2 + (1-1)^2 + (1-2)^2]/3 = [1^2 + 0^2 + (-1)^2]/3 = 2/3 = 0.667$$

If we drew a sample of two scores from this population of three scores, then the maximum number of different samples that could be drawn is nine. These are shown in Table 2.1. Also presented in this table are the population and sample variances for the nine samples on their own and averaged across the nine samples. We can see that the sample variance averaged for the nine samples of two cases is 0.667 which is the same as the population variance for all three cases. However, the population variance averaged for the nine samples of two cases is 0.333 which is less than the population variance of the three cases. In other words, the population variance (i.e. dividing by the number of cases rather than the number of cases minus 1) for the two cases underestimates that for the three cases.

In calculating the estimated population variance, we divide the sum of squares by the number of cases minus 1 or what is known as the *degrees of freedom (df)*. This concept is an important and complex one which is explained more fully elsewhere (Walker 1940). The number of degrees of freedom is the number of independent observations, which is the number

Table 2.1 Population and sample variances for two cases

No	Two cases		Mean	Population variance (SS/2)	Sample variance (SS/1)
1	0	0	0.0	0.00	0.00
2	0	1	0.5	0.25	0.50
3	1	0	0.5	0.25	0.50
4	0	2	1.0	1.00	2.00
5	2	0	1.0	1.00	2.00
6	1	1	1.0	0.00	0.00
7	1	2	1.5	0.25	0.50
8	2	1	1.5	0.25	0.50
9	2	2	2.0	0.00	0.00
Sum				3.00	6.00
Average				0.333	0.667

of original observations minus the number of *parameters* estimated from them. A parameter is a measure which describes the distribution of the variable in the population such as its mean or variance.

Suppose we want to estimate the variance of a population of three scores from a sample of two scores, consisting of 0 and 2. In order to do this we need to estimate the mean of the population. Now the best estimate of the population mean is the sample mean which is 1 [(0 + 2)/2 = 1]. Once we have estimated the population mean, we have fixed it for estimating the population variance and so we have lost one degree of freedom. Since, in this case, we have two original observations and the one parameter of the population mean, we are left with one degree of freedom (2 − 1 = 1). If we had three original observations, we would have two degrees of freedom (3 − 1 = 2).

We can show that if we know the mean of a number of observations, then the value of one of those observations must be fixed and is not free to vary. Take the example of two observations. If the mean is 1 and one of the two observations is 0, then we know that the other observation must be 2 since 0 added to 2 makes 2 which divided by 2 is 1 [(0 + 2)/2 = 2/2 = 1]. One of these two observations is free to vary. So, for example, with the mean fixed at 1, 0 could be changed to, say, −10 in which case the other observation would become 8 since −10 added to 8 and then divided by 2 is 1 [(−10 + 8)/2 = 2/2 = 1]. Similarly, if the mean is known for three observations, one of the observations on which that mean is based must be fixed while the other two observations are free to vary. For instance, if the mean is 4 and two of the three observations are 2 and 3, then the third observation must be fixed at 7 since 7 added to 2 and 3 makes 12 which divided by 3 gives 4:

[(7 + 2 + 3)/3 = 12/3 = 4]

SUMMARY

Four levels or scales of measurement have been distinguished called nominal (or categorical), ordinal, interval and ratio. Ordinal scales are often treated as interval or ratio scales in the social sciences. The distribution of nominal or categorical data can only be quantified in terms of the frequency of each category, which can be further summarised as a proportion, percentage or ratio. The distribution of non-nominal or non-categorical data, on the other hand, can be described in terms of measures of central tendency (such as the mode, median and arithmetic mean) and dispersion (such as the range, interquartile range and standard deviation). The sum of squared deviations from the mean (i.e. the sum of squares) and the mean of that sum of squares (i.e. the mean square or variance) provides the basis of parametric tests of association and difference. Extreme scores can disproportionately affect the mean and standard deviation of a sample.

EXERCISES

1 Which is the highest level of measurement that socio-economic status represents?
2 Which is the highest level of measurement that number of persons in a household represents?
3 For this set of scores

    7   2   5   3   8   6   1   4   3   4

provide the following statistics: (a) mode; (b) range; (c) median; (d) interquartile range; (e) mean; (f) sum of squares; (g) variance; and (h) standard deviation (to two decimal places).

Chapter 3

Introducing Minitab

To understand the way in which statistical values are arrived at, it is necessary to work through the calculations ourselves since this practice will check our grasp of the steps involved. These calculations are relatively easily and quickly carried out by hand when the data consist of a small set of low whole numbers and when the statistics are comparatively straightforward like those presented in the previous chapter. However, with larger sets of numbers, the manual calculation of even these simple statistics can be time-consuming and may result in elementary mistakes being made. These two drawbacks become more serious when we need to employ more complicated statistics and/or when we want to examine the data in different ways, as is often the case. The advent of computers has led to the development of various computer programs for calculating statistics. These programs are not difficult to operate and carry out the required computations very quickly. With the ready accessibility of these packages, calculating statistics by computer is generally more efficient than doing so by hand, once the principles underlying the statistical tests have been grasped.

Knowing how to work one of these programs has three further advantages. First, our understanding of and ability to carry out these tests by hand on new sets of numerical data can be simply checked against the results given by the program. If our calculations are different from those of the program, then the reason for this discrepancy needs to be determined. Since the error may lie in either our calculations or the way in which we ran the program, this procedure will test our comprehension of both these processes. In other words, these programs can be used to assess the accuracy of our own efforts in conducting these tests by hand as well as by computer. Moreover, we can explore our knowledge of various statistical principles by generating and running examples of data which either confirm or disconfirm our expectations about what should happen. In this way we can try out our understanding of statistics on as many problems as we like, knowing that we can easily verify whether our work is correct.

Second, these programs can be employed for other aspects of data analysis such as selecting subsets of individuals for further investigation or creating new variables. For example, we may wish to examine the scores for females and males separately as well as together. Or, we may want to create a new variable which can be routinely worked out from information we possess. For example, we may wish to calculate for each person in a sample the total number of hours of television watched per week from the number of hours watched per day.

And third, we can write our own programs to perform tests we need to use repeatedly but which are not part of the package. In addition, provided that the necessary information is reported, we can construct programs which enable us to conduct tests on other people's data which have not been carried out or we can check the accuracy of what has been done by repeating them. For example, if we know the mean and standard deviation of two groups of participants, we can work out whether these measures differ significantly between the two groups. Needless to say, in order to do this we have to know how to run the test as well as the program. These programs are known as *macros*.

Consequently, there are considerable advantages in learning how to use a computer program for performing statistical tests. The aim of this chapter is to introduce you to one of the most widely used statistical programs in the social sciences which is called *Minitab* and which was initially written in 1972 at Penn State University for teaching introductory statistics to students. It is now readily available on both *mainframe* and *personal* computers. As Minitab is continuously being revised and the revisions take time to be implemented in different institutions, various versions of it may be accessible at any one time and these versions may be periodically replaced with new ones when these become available.

At present, there are two main kinds of *operating system* for computers. The traditional system, still employed by mainframe computers, requires *commands* to be typed in. The more recent system uses *menus* (see Figure 3.2 for an example) and *dialog boxes* (see Figure 3.3 for an example) from which commands can be selected by *keys* or a *mouse*, although commands can also be typed in. It was originally developed for Macintosh personal computers and is now available as a Windows environment on IBM-compatible personal computers having a 386 or higher processor. At the time of writing, the latest revision of Minitab is *Release 10Xtra for Windows and Macintosh* (Minitab 1995). *Release 9* is available for some kinds of mainframe (or multi-user) computers (Minitab 1992) and *Release 7* (Minitab 1989) for others. There is also a *Release 8* (Minitab 1991) for certain types of IBM-compatible personal computers and a *Release 7* for others.

Apart from the operating systems, the differences between these releases are few and relatively minor for the purposes of this book. Consequently, any differences are described as they arise. It is hoped that sufficient information has been presented in this book for you to operate this package without having to refer to the manuals produced by Minitab for instructing users. However, since the exact procedure for calling up Minitab varies according to the computer operating system, you will have to obtain this information elsewhere. If you want further details on Minitab or if you run into any problems, you could first try the *Help* system which is part of the package before turning to the appropriate volume for further help. Once you have learned the material presented in this book, you may wish to find out about the other statistical techniques included in Minitab.

The instructions or commands that Minitab follows consist of short English words. These commands and other information produced by Minitab will be printed in bold type in this book to distinguish them from the rest of the text. Although the commands themselves can be typed in small and capital letters, they will be printed in small letters throughout the book since these are easier to type for the inexperienced typist. The full words will be given initially although words longer than four letters can generally be shortened to the first four letters as the subsequent letters are ignored. So the word **retrieve** will work if shortened to **retr** or misspelt as **retrive**. A summary of these commands is provided in Appendix 1 for quick reference.

To use Minitab it is necessary to have access to it via a personal computer, or a *terminal* connected to a mainframe computer. Both a computer terminal and a personal computer consist of a *keyboard* on which we type in or put in (hence the term *input*) the instructions. They also usually have a video display unit (VDU) or television-like *screen* for presenting information. While the amount of information shown at any one moment on the screen is necessarily limited, further information can be brought into view with the appropriate use of the keys or the mouse. Furthermore, a *printer* is normally attached to the computer which allows us to print out a *hard copy* of any information we want to keep.

As previously mentioned, there are two main kinds of operating system. The first requires commands to be typed in after a *prompt* appears on the screen. Prompts in Minitab are short or abbreviated words written in capitals followed by a right facing arrow (e.g. **MTB >**). To call up this version of Minitab, we usually have to type its name and press the *Return* or *Enter* key. On many keyboards, the Return key is identified by having a ⌐ sign on it. After the title of the program has been shown, the prompt **MTB >** together with a flashing *cursor* will appear. The cursor is the sign which indicates your position on the screen where you may initiate an action such as typing in a command.

The second system allows commands to be selected from information presented as a menu or dialog box in a window on the screen. Commands can usually be selected by moving the cursor onto them with either the keys or the mouse, when they will become highlighted, and then pressing the

Return key or the left button on the mouse. Selecting options with the mouse is generally easier than doing so with keys since it simply involves moving the mouse appropriately. With keys, however, some options are chosen by pressing the relevant cursor keys while others are selected by pressing up to two keys other than the cursor keys. The cursor keys are usually on the right hand side of the keyboard and have arrows on them pointing in the direction in which the cursor is to be moved. You may prefer to use the mouse for some operations and the keys for others. The key strokes for carrying out actions are described in Appendix 3.1 at the end of this chapter.

However, in the Windows version of Minitab, commands can also be typed in if the window called **Session** is selected. To invoke the Windows version when in the windows environment, select the appropriate **Minitab** *icon*. In Release 10, two windows will appear as shown in Figure 3.1. The **Session** window occupies most of the upper half of the screen and the **Data** window most of the lower half. In Release 9, on the other hand, two overlapping or cascading windows will appear. The **Data** window is in front with the **Session** window immediately behind it. Move the cursor into the **Session** window and press the left button on the mouse when the **MTB** > prompt will be presented together with the cursor. The sign of the cursor

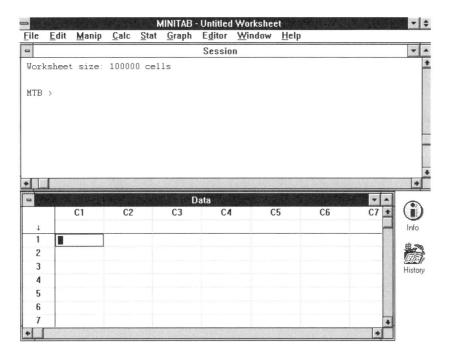

Figure 3.1 Opening **Session** and **Data** window in Release 10

varies according to the window it is in. In the **Session** window it is a capital I, in the **Data** window an upright cross and elsewhere it is a pointer.

The prompt or session method of running Minitab will always be described first since it is common to both operating systems and is more flexible in that it can be used to write commands for carrying out routines that are not available in menu format.

TABULATING DATA

When carrying out research, we normally collect data on more than one variable. For example, if we are interested in the relationship between aggressiveness and the frequency of viewing violent films, we would have at least two variables: (1) aggressiveness and (2) frequency of violent films seen. In addition, to describe some of the social characteristics of the people we studied, we usually obtain other information about them such as their age and gender. In this instance, therefore, we may have data on four variables: (1) aggressiveness; (2) frequency of violent films seen; (3) age; and (4) gender. Similarly, if we were interested in the effect of watching violence on aggressiveness, we would have data on at least two variables: (1) whether participants were in the condition that had watched the violent film or not; and (2) their post-test aggressiveness. In these or other studies we might also have data on the responses of participants to multi-item scales measuring some attitude or aspect of personality which consist of more than one item.

Before analysing data, we usually arrange them in the form of a table where the values for each variable are placed in the same column(s) and the value for each person or *case* is placed in a separate row. Cases are often people but can be any entity such as newspapers, schools or years. Suppose we had gathered information on the age, gender, aggressiveness and number of violent films watched for three children whom we wanted to remain anonymous. Aggressiveness was rated on a 4-point scale where 0 indicates not aggressive and 3 very aggressive. We could tabulate these data as shown in Table 3.1.

In many situations, the way in which the cases are ordered does not matter and they can be entered as the information becomes available. Although the cases do not have to be numbered, enumerating them is

Table 3.1 Tabulating data

Case no.	Age	Gender	Aggressiveness	Films
1	–	F	0	0
2	8	M	1	1
3	10	M	2	3

advantageous when we want to refer to any of them. Since numbers are read from left to right, single digits of a two or more digit number (such as age) should always be placed in the rightmost column for that variable. If this is not done, then it is possible when, say, adding 8 to 10 to add the 8 to the 1 rather than to the 0 making 90 instead of 18.

Incorrect	8	Correct	8
	10		10
	—		—
	90		18

Gender in this example was recorded as F for females and M for males. However, any code could be used such as 1 for females and 2 for males, or vice versa. Sometimes data for a particular variable will be missing. Someone may not have given their age or it may not have been clearly reported on the form. In such circumstances, the fact that this information is missing needs to be indicated in some way. In this example, the relevant column has simply been left empty or blank so that no age is given for the first child.

ENTERING DATA IN MINITAB

When using Minitab, however, it may not be necessary to tabulate the data first since this will, in effect, be done when the data are entered into the computer. When we have a large amount of data, this task can be very time-consuming. If your institution employs people for this purpose, then this job is best left to them since they will do it more efficiently and accurately than you can. The examples of data in this book have been kept deliberately small so that you should be able to quickly type in the data yourself. Although these are not physically displayed on the screen, the space into which the data are put consists of a potentially very large number of rows. Each row, however, is made up of a much more limited number of columns which, for example, is restricted to 1000 in Releases 7 to 10.

If we want to analyse a small set of data, like that shown in Table 3.1, then it is convenient to enter these data ourselves using Minitab. In doing this, the alphabetical characters need to be turned into numbers so that, for example, F is coded as 1 and M as 2. In addition, missing values should be represented with an asterisk (*) so that the age of the first case is denoted as an *. Numbers cannot contain commas.

Prompt system

With the prompt system, we can enter the data in Table 3.1 either row by row with the **read** command or column by column with the **set** command.

Columns in Minitab are specified by the letter **c** followed by their respective number so that the first column is called **c1**, the second **c2** and so on.

With the **read** command we need to list the columns for each case. Since in this example we have five columns of data, we can list the five columns on the **read** command by naming each one separately. Each column label needs to be separated by a blank space or a comma. Consequently, after the **MTB >** prompt, we can type either

MTB > read c1,c2,c3,c4,c5

or

MTB > read c1 c2 c3 c4 c5

Alternatively, as the columns are consecutive, we can list them implicitly by specifying only the first and last column (with a hyphen between the two), so that the **read** command becomes shortened to

MTB > read c1-c5

Note that Minitab commands have been printed in small letters throughout the book to distinguish them from Minitab prompts which are displayed on the screen in capital letters followed by a right facing arrow. The command is completed by pressing the Return key, when the **DATA>** prompt will appear.

If, before pressing the Return key, you type the wrong information (say, **a1** instead of **c1**), use the backspace delete key to delete back to and including the mistake (**a**) and type in the correct details. The backspace delete key usually has a leftward facing arrow sign [←] on it to identify it. If, after pressing the Return key, you realised you have made a mistake (say, **a1** instead of **c1**) type in the correct command when the **MTB >** prompt reappears. If, on the other hand, you typed in the wrong column (say, **c2** instead of **c1**), the **DATA>** prompt will appear in which case you need to type **end** after it when the **MTB >** prompt will be shown. You then type in the correct command.

After listing the appropriate column numbers, we type in the first row of data (separating each datum with either a blank space or a comma) as follows

DATA> 1,*,1,0,0

To enter this line of data, we press the Return key. We proceed in this way until we have typed in all three rows of data as follows

DATA> 1,*,1,0,0
DATA> 2,8,2,1,1
DATA> 3,10,2,2,3

If in a row you type in fewer values than the number of columns, you will receive the following error message

ERROR INCOMPLETE ROW -REENTER

whereas if you type in too many values, the error message will be

ERROR TOO MANY VALUES -REENTER ROW

Simply type in the values again after the **DATA>** prompt.

When we have finished typing in the data, we indicate this by typing **end** after the **DATA>** prompt

DATA> end

A message will appear which will state

3 ROWS READ

To display the data we have typed in, we simply type **print** after the **MTB >** prompt and the columns we want to see. So, to show all five columns, we need only type

MTB > print c1-c5

which will produce the following output

ROW	C1	C2	C3	C4	C5
1	1	*	1	0	0
2	2	8	2	1	1
3	3	10	2	2	3

Note that the output also gives the row number so that you may feel it unnecessary to input the case number if it is the same as the row number.

If you realise you have typed in a wrong value (say, 7 instead of 10 in column 2 for the age of case 3), you can correct this by typing

MTB > let c2 (3)=10

where the value in brackets refers to the row number and the value after the equals sign is the correct value. You can check that this has been done by printing **c2**

MTB > print c2

To type in data with the **set** command, we first specify the column (say, **c2**)

MTB > set c2

after which we press the Return key when the **DATA>** prompt appears. We then type in the values for that column, say

DATA> * 8 10

press the Return key, and type **end** after the **DATA>** prompt. So to type in the data in Table 3.1, we could use the following commands

MTB > set c1
DATA> 1 2 3
DATA> end
MTB > set c2
DATA> * 8 10
DATA> end
MTB > set c3
DATA> 1 2 2
DATA> end
MTB > set c4
DATA> 0 1 2
DATA> end
MTB > set c5
DATA> 0 1 3
DATA> end

You can name your columns with the **name** command which lists the column number and a name in single quotes of up to eight characters. So, the command for calling **c2** 'age' and **c4** 'agg' (for aggressiveness) is

MTB > name c2 'age' c4 'agg'

Once a column is named we can refer to it either by the name in single quotes or the column number. So, we can print **c2** and **c4** by typing

MTB > print 'age' 'agg'

If we do not save the set of data we have just typed in we will lose it when we leave Minitab and we will have to type it in again should we wish to carry out some further analyses on a later occasion. Since alternative ways of analysing data often come to us later on either as the result of our own thoughts or the suggestions of others, it is usually worthwhile saving the data. Information in computers is stored in *files* which we have to name in order to retrieve them. To save a set of data we use the **save** command followed by the name we wish to call it placed within single quotes. The name consists of a prefix or *stem* of up to eight characters followed by a full stop and a suffix or *extension* of up to three characters. To remind us of the content and the nature of the file, it is conventional practice to have the stem name refer to the content of the file and the extension name to the kind of file it is.

The **save** command stores the data as a *worksheet* which is written in binary code and which cannot be read as text. If we do not give this worksheet an extension name, then Minitab will automatically add the extension **.MTW** which is short for **M**initab **w**orksheet. Consequently, we shall follow this practice and use the extension **.mtw** for naming our worksheets. Since the data in our example refer to aggressiveness, the stem name could be **agg**. Alternatively, since the data are displayed in Table 3.1, the stem name could be **tab3.1**. We shall call it **'agg.mtw'**. The command for saving these data as a worksheet is

MTB > save 'agg.mtw'

If we are working on a personal computer, it is worthwhile storing a copy of the data file on a separate *floppy disk* in case the file stored in our computer is deleted or lost. The floppy disk is inserted into a slot called a *drive* after the computer has been switched on. The disk may first have to be *formatted* if it is new or if its present format is not compatible with the machine. It is preferable to do this before entering Minitab so that any files can be stored direct onto the floppy disk when you are using Minitab. To store a file onto a floppy disk, use the same **save** command but insert the letter of the drive followed by a colon after the opening quote of the name and before the stem. So, to store this file on the floppy disk in drive *a*, the command would be

MTB > save 'a:agg.mtw'

In a session of Minitab we may wish to work on a number of different data files. To call up a different file in the same session or to call a file in a new session we use the **retrieve** command followed by the name of the file (including the disk drive if it is on a floppy disk). So, to call up the file **agg.mtw** on the floppy disk in drive *a*, the command would be

MTB > retrieve 'a:agg.mtw'

Note that we can shorten the command **retrieve** to the first four letters **retr**.

Later on, we may wish to add one or more cases of data to our file. Suppose we wanted to add a fourth case to the data in the **agg.mtw** file who was a seven year old female who had a rating of 1 for aggressiveness and who had watched no violent films. It generally does not matter where we add the data for this case, so it is simpler to put it at the end of the file. To do this, we would use the **insert** command with the five columns listed as follows

MTB > insert c1-c5

After the **DATA>** prompt appears, we type in the data

DATA> 4 7 1 1 0

followed by **end** after the next **DATA>** prompt

DATA> end

So the three commands for reading the data for this case are

MTB > insert c1-c5
DATA> 4 7 1 1 0
DATA> end

We would then save this data file as **agg.mtw**.

On the other hand, we may wish to delete the data for a case such as the third and fourth case. To do this, we use the **delete** command as follows

MTB > delete 3 4 c1-c5

The row number(s) of cases to be removed are listed after the **delete** command.

If we wanted to add another column of data to our file such as the social class of the children's parent, we would use the **set** command as previously described, i.e.

MTB > set c6

To remove the values in a column such as those in the sixth column, we would use the **erase** command as follows

MTB > erase c6

If we wished to overwrite the values in any one column such as those in the sixth column, we would use the **set** command as follows

MTB > set c6

Data are often stored as a text or *ASCII* file. ASCII stands for American Standard Code for Information Interchange and is widely used for transferring information from one computer to another. If, for example, we had collected a large amount of data and if we had access to a service which typed in those data for us, then this information may be stored for us in a text file which we will transfer to the computer we are using. The conventional extension name of such files is often **dat** which is short for **dat**a. If the data in Table 3.1 had been stored as a text file, then we might call it **agg.dat**. To read such a file from our computer into a Minitab session, we would use the **read** command which lists the name of the file in single quotes together with the columns of data we want to read. So if we wanted to read all five columns, the command would be

MTB > read 'agg.dat' into c1-c5

Note that the word **into** can be omitted. If we find it easier, we can then name the column numbers as before and save the text file as a worksheet.

To leave Minitab, we use the command **stop**

MTB > stop

In the Windows version, the program will ask you if you wish to save the data as a worksheet if you have not already done so.

Menu system

When Release 10 of Minitab for Windows is called, two windows appear. The lower one is the **Data** window which consists of a matrix of numbered columns and rows. The cursor will be in the *cell* in the first row of the first column. The *frame* of this cell will be shown in bold to denote that it is the *active* cell. To enter a value in any one cell make that cell active by moving to it with either the cursor keys or the mouse, type in the value and then move to the next cell into which you want to put a value. To change any value already entered, move to the cell containing that value, remove that value with the backspace key and type in the new value. To leave that cell empty, delete the existing value with the delete key (which usually has Del on it). If you delete the entry with the backspace key and move to another cell, an * will be left denoting a missing value. To name any particular column move to the cell just below its column number and type in the name.

To increase the size of the **Data** (or any) window with the mouse, place the cursor on the triangle pointing upward in the right-hand corner of the window and press the left button. To return the window to its original size, place the pointer on the square in the right-hand corner containing the upward and downward facing triangle and press the left button.

To save the data as a worksheet, carry out the following steps.

Step 1   Select **File** from the bar on the **Worksheet** window when a menu will drop down. The options on this menu are shown in Figure 3.2. To cancel any *drop-down* menu, place the pointer anywhere outside the option and press the left button.

Step 2   Select **Save Worksheet As** when a dialog box will appear as illustrated in Figure 3.3.

Note that in Release 9 an intermediate dialog box is presented in which the **Minitab worksheet** option is ready to be selected. This is indicated by this option being encased in a rectangle drawn with a dashed line. So select it to produce the dialog box shown in Figure 3.3.

The ellipse or three dots after an option term (...) signifies a dialog box will appear if this option is chosen. A right facing arrowhead >, on the other hand, indicates that a further submenu will appear to the right of the drop-down menu. An option with neither of these signs means that there are no further drop-down menus to select.

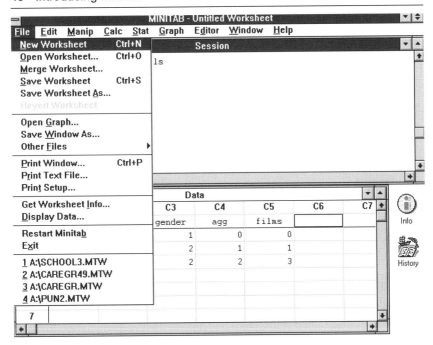

Figure 3.2 **File** menu options

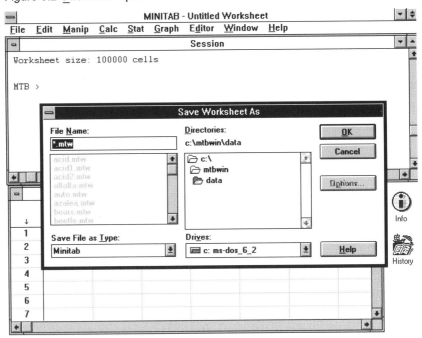

Figure 3.3 **Save Worksheet As...** dialog box

Step 3   In this dialog box the name ***.mtw** is highlighted in a rectangular box under the label **File Name:**. The asterisk or *wildcard* denotes any stem name.

Step 4   Type in the name of your file and press the Return key or select **OK**. When using the menu system you do not have to put single quotation marks around names. An exception to this is when forming mathematical expressions which will be described later on in this chapter.

To save the file on a floppy disk in a disk drive, select the appropriate drive (e.g. **a**) from those in the box below the label **Drives:** by putting the cursor on the downward button, pressing the left button and highlighting the **a** drive.

When carrying out procedures with the menu system, the prompt commands for performing the same procedure will be displayed in the **Session** window once the procedure has been executed. The first letter after the **MTB >** prompt is capitalised and the command ends with a full stop.

We will use a particular notation to describe the steps involved in using the menu system. The selection of a step or option will be indicated with a right facing arrow → pointing to the term(s) on the menu or dialog box to be chosen. Any explanations will be placed in square parentheses after the option shown. Thus, the notation for saving data as a worksheet using the menu system in Release 10 is

→**File** →**Save Worksheet As...** →box under **Drives** →drive [e.g. **a**] from options listed →box under **File Name** and in it type file name [e.g. **agg.mtw**] →**OK**

To retrieve this file at a later stage, when it is no longer the current file, carry out the following sequence

→**File** →**Open Worksheet...** →box under **Drives** →drive [e.g. **a**] from options listed →box under **File Name** →file name [e.g. **agg.mtw**] →press the left button once and select **OK** or press the left button twice

In Release 9 an intermediate **Open Worksheet** dialog box appears in which the **Type of Worksheet** is first selected before choosing **Select File**.

To read in a data text ASCII file, you need to use the prompt system in the **Session** window, as in the following example

MTB > read 'a:agg.dat' c1-c5

The data will be displayed in the **Data** window.

HELP SYSTEM

Minitab has a Help system which you may like to use to avoid having to refer to a book like this one or to find out more about the program. The

Help systems are meant to be self-explanatory and so you should be able to learn to use them yourself after a little experience. Consequently, only the way to access the Help system in the more recent releases of Minitab will generally be described.

In Release 7 of Minitab, type **help** after the **MTB >** prompt to find out how Help is organised. Basically, you can obtain general information about how Minitab works by typing **help overview** and details of the commands available by typing **help commands**. If you want help on a particular command such as **read**, type **help** followed by the name of the command.

In Release 8 you can obtain information about Minitab by typing these commands. For example, for information about the **read** command, type **help read**. The information will quickly *scroll* or move down the screen. To read it once it has stopped, move up it using either the cursor keys or the mouse. The cursor key with Pg Dn on it will take you down a page or a screenful at a time while the key with Pg Up on it will take you up a screenful at a time. To move through the text with the mouse, move the cursor to the bottom of the scroll bar on the right-hand side if you want to go down and to the top if you want to go up.

In the Windows version, there are three ways of accessing Help. In the **Session** window you may type **help** and the name of the command with which you want help. In a dialog box, select the **?** (Release 9) or **Help**

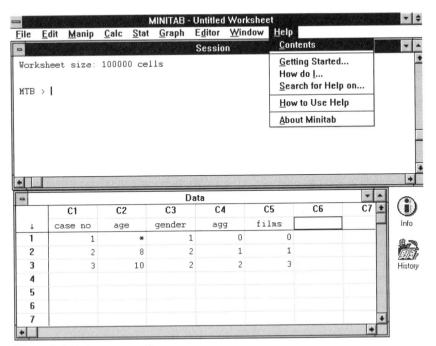

Figure 3.4 **Help** menu options

(Release 10) in the lower left corner for information about that procedure. When not in a dialog box, you may obtain help by pressing F1 when you will be presented with the **Contents** of the Help system. Alternatively, you may select the **Help** option from the menu bar, when you may then choose from a drop-down menu of **Contents**, **Getting Started...**, **How do I...**, **Search for Help on...** and **How to Use Help** as shown in Figure 3.4. Ignore **About Minitab** which simply displays the Minitab title page.

There are a number of different routes for selecting these options. The **Contents** option also contains **Using Help**, **Getting Started** and **How do I...** which are the same as **How to Use Help**, **Getting Started...** and **How do I....**. When you select any of these three options, a second horizontal menu bar will appear below the one containing the **Help** option. This menu bar will always offer **Contents**, **Search**, **Back** and **History**. In addition, when the **How to Use Help** option is chosen, a further **Glossary** menu bar option is offered as depicted in Figure 3.5. The **Search** option is the same as **Search for Help on....**

The **Search** or **Search for Help on...** option enables you to type in a topic you want help on or to choose one from those listed. The **Back** option takes you back to the **Contents** option when you have chosen the **Contents** option. The **History** option keeps a record of the **Help** options you have

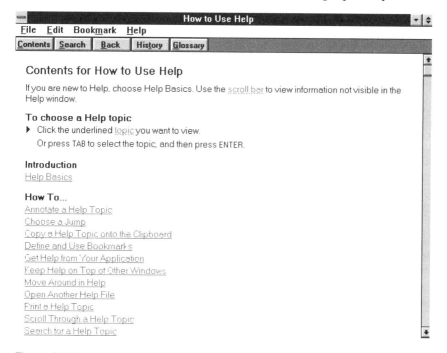

Figure 3.5 **Help** window with menu bar

selected. The **Glossary** option offers you information on a number of topics.

STATISTICAL ANALYSIS WITH MINITAB

To carry out a statistical analysis of the data in Table 3.1 we need to use the appropriate Minitab command. So far, we have only described the relatively simple descriptive statistical measures of central tendency and dispersion. One Minitab command which calculates the mean, median, standard deviation, and first and third quartile, among some other statistics, is **describe** followed by the column numbers or names of the variables for which these statistics are wanted. So, to provide these descriptive statistics for **c2** (or **'age'**) and **c4** (or **'agg'**), we type

MTB > describe c2 c4

Minitab output

The output from this command is displayed on the screen when this command is run and is shown in Table 3.2. This command gives the following information for each variable listed: the number of cases which have no missing values and on which the statistics are calculated (**N**); the number of cases which have missing values (**N***); the mean (**MEAN**); the median (**MEDIAN**); the trimmed mean (**TRMEAN**) which is the mean with the smallest 5 per cent and largest 5 per cent of the values removed; the standard deviation (**STDEV**); the standard error of the mean (**SEMEAN**) which is described in Chapter 7; the minimum (**MIN**) and the maximum (**MAX**) values; and the first (**Q1**) and third (**Q3**) quartile.

We can check the accuracy of these descriptive statistics by calculating these values by hand. Conversely, Minitab commands can be used to check the manual calculations in the previous and subsequent chapters. For

Table 3.2 **Describe** output

MTB > Describe c2 c4

	N	N*	MEAN	MEDIAN	TRMEAN	STDEV	SEMEAN
age	3	1	8.333	8.000	8.333	1.528	0.882
agg	4	0	1.000	1.000	1.000	0.816	0.408

	MIN	MAX	Q1	Q3
age	7.000	10.000	7.000	10.000
agg	0.000	2.000	0.250	1.750

MTB >

example, in Chapter 2 the mean was worked out by hand to be 17 for the following set of numbers

1   2   3   7   8   8   90

This value can be checked with the following Minitab commands:

MTB > set c1
DATA> 1 2 3 7 8 8 90
DATA> end
MTB > desc c1

The output for these commands shows that the mean is **17.0**.

To calculate statistics with the menu system, first select the **Stat** option from the menu bar when a drop-down menu will appear listing various statistics as shown by the first such drop-down menu in Figure 3.6. To carry out descriptive statistics, select the **Basic Statistics** option when another drop-down menu will be displayed alongside and to the right of the first one, which is the second drop-down menu depicted in Figure 3.6. Select the **Descriptive Statistics...** option when a dialog box will be displayed as illustrated in Figure 3.7.

Type in or select into the box on the right-hand side under the label **Variables:** the column numbers (**c2** and **c4**) or the names of the variables

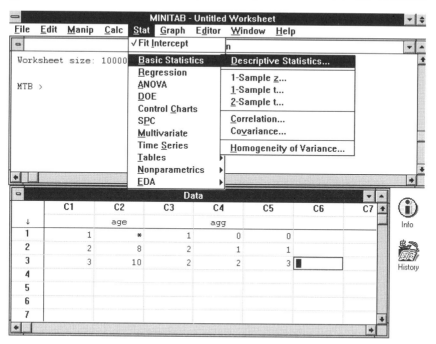

Figure 3.6 **Stat** menu options

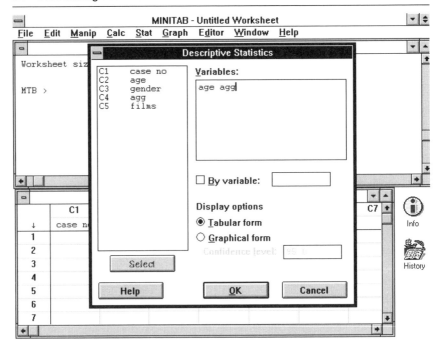

Figure 3.7 **Descriptive Statistics...** dialog box

(**age** and **agg**) on which you want the descriptive statistics. To select them, highlight in turn the appropriate variable in the box on the left-hand side and pick **Select**. To obtain the descriptive statistics, select **OK** or press Return. This sequence of steps can be summarised as follows:

→**Stat** →**Basic Statistics** →**Descriptive Statistics...** →**age** →**Select** [**age** will now appear in the **Variables:** box] →**agg** →**Select** [**agg** will now appear in the **Variables:** box below **age**] →**OK**

Keeping Minitab output

To keep a listing of what you will do in a session, type the command **outfile** followed by the name you want to call that file in single quotes at the point you want the record to begin. The default extension name is **.lis** which is short for **lis**ting. If we wished to call our output or listing file **'sess1.lis'**, we would use the following command

MTB > outfile='sess1.lis'

We can control the width of that output file from 30 to 132 spaces with the **ow** command (**o**utput **w**idth), although some commands cannot make their output narrower than 70. So, the command for requesting a width of 70 spaces is

MTB > ow=70

Output is saved in this file until the command **nooutfile** is typed. Output may be saved in different listing files if desired. If the same listing file is called up later in the session, then the output will be added to the end of that file.

In the Windows version of Minitab, the **Session** window keeps up to 25 half-full pages, after which it automatically discards the first half of the output. To save the output of an entire session with the menu system, execute the following steps:

→**File** →**Other Files** →**Start Recording Session...** →**Record output in file and display in Session window** →box to the left of **Set output width to** [optional e.g. →**70** in the box to its right] →**Select File** →box under **File Name** →filename [e.g. **sess1.lis**] →**OK**

To stop saving the output, carry out the following sequence

→**File** →**Other Files** →**Stop Recording Session**

DATA TRANSFORMATIONS

In addition to carrying out statistical tests, Minitab has commands which can transform variables (i.e. those within a row) by changing their value (e.g. taking their square root) and which can combine two or more variables (e.g. adding the value of one variable to that of another). These data transformation commands will be used to show how to carry out some of the computations needed to calculate a particular statistic.

The command for carrying out these kinds of arithmetic operations is **let** followed by the name (in single quotes) or column number for the new variable, an = sign and the set of operations to be conducted. The commands for arithmetic operations are as follows

+	addition
−	subtraction
/	division
*	multiplication
**	raise to a power
absolute(c...)	absolute values
sqrt(c..)	square root
loge(c..)	base e or natural logarithm
logten(c..)	base 10 logarithm

So, to take the square root of the following row of numbers

1   2   3   7   8   8   90

we could use the following commands:

MTB > read c1-c7
DATA> 1 2 3 7 8 8 90
DATA> end
MTB > let c8=sqrt(c1)
MTB > let c9=sqrt(c2)
MTB > let c10=sqrt(c3)
MTB > let c11=sqrt(c4)
MTB > let c12=sqrt(c5)
MTB > let c13=sqrt(c6)
MTB > let c14=sqrt(c7)

To display the square roots, type

MTB > print c8-c14

which will give the following output

ROW	C8	C9	C10	C11	C12	C13	C14
1	1	1.41421	1.73205	2.64575	2.82843	2.82843	9.48683

The command for adding the original set of numbers is

MTB > let c15=c1+c2+c3+c4+c5+c6+c7

which gives a sum or total of **119**. If any value of a row is missing (∗), the result is set to missing.

To calculate the mean of this set of numbers, divide the sum (**c15**) by the number of rows which is seven. The command for this is

MTB > let c16=c15/7

which gives a value of **17**. If an operation is impossible such as dividing by zero, the result is set to missing.

We could also calculate the mean with the following single command

MTB > let c17=(c1+c2+c3+c4+c5+c6+c7)/7

Note that without the parentheses, certain arithmetic operations are done before others. The operation of raising to a power (∗∗) is performed before that of multiplication (∗) and division (/), which are both executed before that of addition (+) and subtraction (−). Operations in parentheses [( )] are performed before those outside them. So, to sum a row of values before dividing them, we need to bracket the columns to be added first. If we omit the brackets as follows

MTB > let c17=c1+c2+c3+c4+c5+c6+c7/7

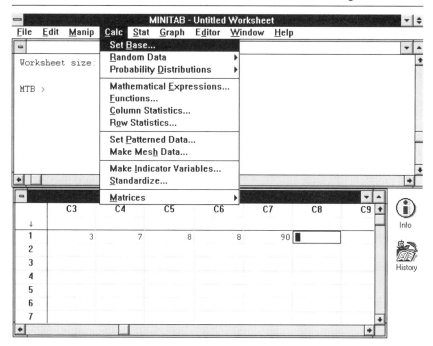

Figure 3.8 **Calc** menu options

the result or quotient of **c7/7** is added to the values in columns **c1** to **c6**, giving 41.86 rather than 17.

To transform values across rows with the menu system, first enter the data into the **Data** window. Then, carry out the following steps:

→**Calc** [the drop-down menu for this is presented in Figure 3.8] →**Mathematical Expressions...** [the dialog box for this step is shown in Figure 3.9] →variable column or name [e.g. **c15**] →**Select** [this puts **c15** in the box beside **Variable [new or modified]:**] →box under **Expression:** and in it type the desired expression [e.g. **c1+c2+c3+c4+c5+c6+c7**] →**OK**

Turn to the appropriate column (**c15**) in the **Data** window to see the new value.

Further details of transforming data can be found in Bryman and Cramer (1996).

Recoding values

You may wish to recode the values of a variable such as grouping the ages of the children in Table 3.1 into the two categories of those 5 to 9 years of

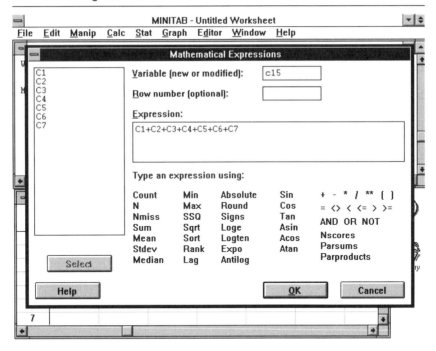

Figure 3.9 **Mathematical Expressions...** dialog box

age and those 10 to 15. To do this, we use the **code** command in the following way

MTB > code (5:9) 1 (10:15) 2 c2 c6

The ages between 5 and 9 inclusive [**(5:9)**] are to be recoded as **1** while those between 10 and 15 inclusive [**(10:15)**] are to be recoded as **2**. The colon (**:**) indicates that the values between and including those in the brackets are to be recoded. The recoded values of **c2** are to be put into **c6**. If we print **c2** and **c6** we see that **8** is now **1** and **10** is **2**.

The menu action for recoding is:

→**Manip** [this drop-down menu is presented in Figure 3.10] →**Code Data Values...** [the dialog box for this step is shown in Figure 3.11] →variable(s) to be changed [e.g. **c2**] →**Select** [this puts the variable(s) in the box beneath **Code data from columns:**] →box under **Into columns** and in it type new variable [e.g. **c6**] →first box under **Original values** [**eg, 1:4 12**]: and type first values to be changed [e.g. **5:9**] →first corresponding box under **New:** and in it type first new value [e.g. **1**] →second box under **Original** values [eg, 1:4 12]: and in it type second values to be changed [e.g. **10:15**] →second corresponding box under **New:** and in it type second new value [e.g. **2**] →**OK**

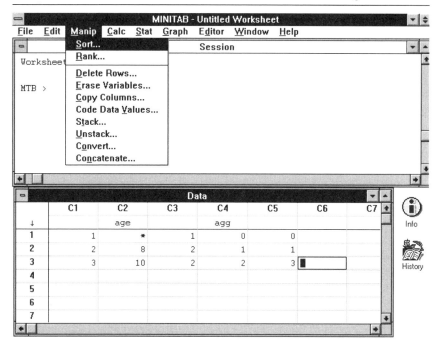

Figure 3.10 **Manip** menu options

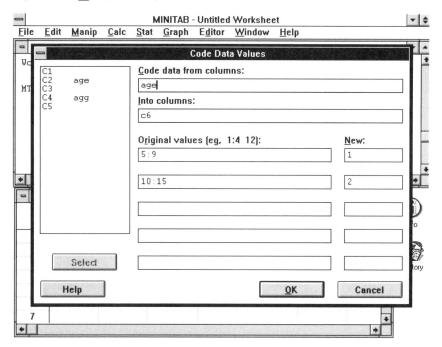

Figure 3.11 **Code Data Values...** dialog box

Selecting subgroups of cases

To select a subgroup of cases to work on such as the males in Table 3.1, we can copy the data of those cases into other columns with the **copy** command and select particular cases with the **use** subcommand. For example, if we wanted to find out the average age of the males in this study, we first copy **'age'** with the **copy** command into a new column **c6** which we shall call **'agem'** (for **age m**ales)

MTB > name c6 'agem'
MTB > copy 'age' 'agem';

Then with the **use** subcommand we would select **'gender'** (which contains the code for gender) and specify **2** which is the code for males

SUBC> use 'gender'=2.

Note that the line before a subcommand must end in a semi-colon (**;**) and the last subcommand must finish with a full stop (**.**).

The menu procedure for doing this is:

→**Manip** →**Copy Columns...** [this dialog box is illustrated in Figure 3.12] →variable or column to be copied [e.g. **age**] →**Select** [this puts the variable in the box under **Copy from columns:**] →box under **To**

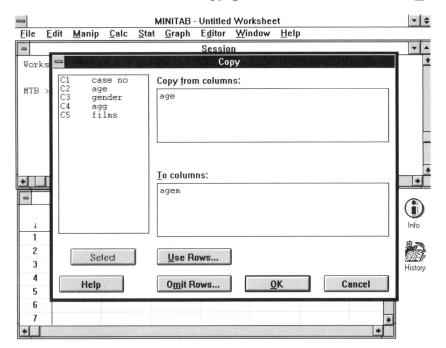

Figure 3.12 **Copy...** dialog box

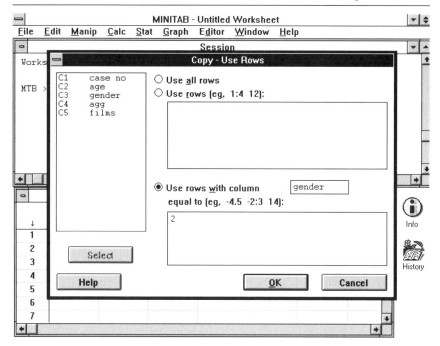

Figure 3.13 **Copy – Use Rows...** dialog box

columns: →type column or name of variable to be copied [e.g. **agem**]
→**Use Rows...** [this opens a second dialog box shown in Figure 3.13]
→**Use rows with column equal to [eg, -4.5 -2:3 14]:** →box beside it
→variable for selection [e.g. **gender**] →**Select** →type value for selection
[e.g. **2**] which goes in the box below →**OK** [this closes the second dialog
box] →**OK**

WRITING MACROS

Minitab is usually used *interactively*, which means that each command is
carried out once it is entered. However, if we need to execute a series of
commands on more than one occasion when analysing data, we may find it
useful to store this set of commands as a macro file which we can then run
with only a single command. The series of commands may be used, for
example, to compute an overall score for a number of variables or to
calculate a particular statistic such as skewness and kurtosis (described
in the next chapter) which only Release 10 carries out but which can be
computed with the relevant commands.

Although Minitab calculates the sample standard deviation, we will use
this statistic to illustrate the way in which we could write a macro to

produce this statistic. We will begin by showing which commands are needed to calculate the standard deviation for the following set of eight scores

4   4   5   5   6   7   8   9

These scores are the same as those used in the previous chapter to demonstrate the calculation of the standard deviation. The steps for working out the standard deviation are also the same as those carried out in the previous chapter so that you can check the results for the corresponding steps. Once we have shown the commands necessary for calculating the standard deviation, we will describe the procedure for writing and then running a macro file containing these commands.

Step 1 Enter the scores in **c1** with the following **set** command.

MTB > set c1
DATA> 4 4 5 5 6 7 8 9
DATA> end

Step 2 Count the number of non-missing values in **c1** and store them as a constant in **k1** using the following **n** command:

MTB > n c1 k1

Minitab will display that **N = 8**.

Step 3 Calculate the mean score of the scores in **c1** and save this mean as a constant in **k2** with the following **mean** command:

MTB > mean c1 k2

Minitab will show that the **MEAN = 6.0000**. This figure is the same as that found in Step 1 in the previous chapter of the corresponding procedure for calculating the standard deviation.

Step 4 Subtract each score in **c1** from the mean score stored as **k2**, square (****2**) the differences (**k2-c1**) and store these squared deviations in **c2** with the following **let** command:

MTB > let c2=(k2-c1)**2

If you want to check these computations, type **print c2**.

Step 5 Sum the squared deviations in **c2** and save them as a constant in **k3** with the following **sum** command:

MTB > sum c2 k3

Minitab displays that the **SUM = 24.000** which is the same figure as that shown in Step 2 of the corresponding procedure in the previous chapter.

Step 6 Calculate the sample variance by dividing the sum of squares (**k3**) by the number of scores minus 1 (**k1-1**) and store the result as a constant in **k4** with the following **let** command:

MTB > let k4=k3/(k1-1)

If you type **print k4**, you will see that **K4** equals **3.42857** which is the same as the figure of 3.43 (rounded to two decimal places) in Step 3 of the same procedure in the previous chapter.

Step 7 Compute the sample standard deviation by taking the square root (**sqrt**) of the sample variance (**k4**) with the following **let** command:

MTB > let k5=sqrt(k4)

To find out the sample standard deviation, type **print k5** and you will see that **K5** equals **1.85164** which is the same as the value of 1.85 (rounded to two decimal places) in Step 4 of the corresponding procedure in the previous chapter. In Release 9 and 10, you may label constants with the **name** command. So, to remind ourselves in these Releases that **k4** and **k5** are the variance and standard deviation respectively, we could call them **var** and **sd** with the following **name** command:

MTB > name k4 'var' k5 'sd'

Having shown that these commands give the same value for the standard deviation as we had previously worked out in Chapter 2, we will now save these commands as a macro file. Macros are written as a simple text (ASCII) file using an editor such as Word or WordPerfect. In Releases 7 and 8, macros have the default extension name of **MTB**, are run with the command **execute** and consist only of the commands which need to be carried out. So the macro for calculating the standard deviation may be called **sd.mtb** and consists of the following commands:

n c1 k1
mean c1 k2
let c2=(k2-c1)2**
sum c2 k3
let k4=k3/(k1-1)
let k5=sqrt(k4)
print k4 k5

After entering the data in **c1**, simply type **execute 'sd.mtb'** and the macro will give the same results as the individual commands do. Macros in Release 9 and 10 may be run with this prompt system command or with the menu system by selecting **File**, **Other _F_iles**, **_R_un an Exec...**, **_S_elect File** and the appropriate macro file.

In Release 9 and 10, *global* macros have the default extension name of **MAC** (short for **mac**ro) and are run with the command % followed by the appropriate directory and stem name of the macro. The first line of the file consists of the term **gmacro**, the second line the name of the macro (e.g. **sd.mac**) and the last line the term **endmacro**. So, the global macro for computing the standard deviation contains the following commands:

gmacro
sd.mac
n c1 k1
mean c1 k2
let c2=(k2-c1)**2
sum c2 k3
let k4=k3/(k1-1)
let k5=sqrt(k4)
name k4 'var' k5 'sd'
print 'var' 'sd'
endmacro

If you have stored this macro on a floppy disk in drive *a*, then to run it, simply type **%a:sd**.

SUMMARY

Statistical programs enable statistics to be calculated quickly and accurately. One of the most widely used and comprehensive statistical programs in the social sciences is Minitab, which is available on both mainframe and personal computers. Procedures are also available for selecting particular subsets of data and for creating new variables. The basic information needed to carry out a statistical analysis is a computer file containing the data and a command requesting the particular statistics required and specifying the column numbers or assigned names of the variables to be analysed. The data file contains a potentially large number of rows consisting of up to 100 000 columns. The values of variables are listed in columns and the data for each case or unit is put in one row. Values which are missing are coded as an *. The statistical results are usually displayed visually on a screen and can also be printed. Commands and variable names can either be typed in after a prompt or selected from menus and dialog boxes. Macro files comprising a series of commands to be run consecutively can be written and saved.

EXERCISES

1 How would you numerically code the variable of marital status which has the following five categories: single and never married; married; separated; divorced; and widowed?
2 How would you code someone who had said they were both single and widowed?
3 In your data file you have information on the year of birth of your respondents. What Minitab command or menu steps would you use to calculate their age in the year 2000?
4 For 10 respondents you have collected information on their age, gender and their responses to 10 dichotomous questions measuring aggressiveness. What Minitab command or menu sequence would you use to do the following:
   (a) Input this information in your Minitab data file;
   (b) Reverse the dichotomous scores for the even numbered items;
   (c) Add up the scores of the 10 questions to give a total score for each person;
   (d) Find the mean score for each person;
   (e) Find the mean of the total score for the whole sample of 10 individuals.
5 If some of the responses were missing what effect would this have on the total score?

APPENDIX 3.1 OPERATING WITHIN WINDOWS USING KEYS

To select the **Sessions** window, press the Tab key while holding down the Ctrl key. The Tab key is usually on the leftmost side of the keyboard and may have two arrows on it pointing leftwards and rightwards respectively.

To expand a window, press Alt and the key with the hyphen (-) on it which will produce a drop-down menu; select **Maximise**. To return the window to its original size, press the Alt and hyphen key and select either the **Restore** or **Minimise** option from the drop-down menu.

To save the data as a worksheet, carry out the following steps.

Step 1 Select **File** from the bar on the **Worksheet** window when a menu will drop down. To select any of these options, press the Alt key and the key of the letter underlined in the option, which is **F** in this case. To cancel the drop-down menu, press the Esc key.

Step 2 Select **Save Worksheet As** pressing either the downward cursor key or the key of the letter underlined in the option, which is **A**. A dialog box will appear.

In Release 9 an intermediate dialog box appears in which the **Minitab worksheet** option is ready to be, and should be, selected.

Step 3   In this dialog box the name ***.MTW** is highlighted in a rectangular box under the label **File Name:**.

Step 4   Type in the name of your file and press the Return key or select **OK**. To save it on a floppy disk in a disk drive, select the appropriate drive from those in the box below the label **Drives:**.

The cursor may be moved in a dialog box with the following keys. To move forwards to the box entitled **Drives:**, press the Tab key. To move backwards to it, press the Tab key while holding down the Shift key. Alternatively, press Alt and the letter underlined in the title which in this case is **v**. To move the cursor within a box, use the cursor keys.

To retrieve this file at a later stage when it is no longer the current file, select **File** from the bar of the window, **Open Worksheet**, the appropriate drive if it is not already present and either type in the name or select the name from the files listed. To select a file, use the downward cursor key until the right file has been underlined, press the upward cursor key and the Return key.

Chapter 4

Statistical significance and choice of test

As outlined in the first chapter, one of the main uses of statistics in the social sciences is to determine the probability of three different kinds of events or outcomes happening. The first kind is estimating whether a sample drawn from a population is representative of that population in terms of a specified characteristic. Suppose, for example, we know that the population of interest consists of an equal number of women and men and we draw a sample of five women and seven men. How likely are we to obtain this particular number of women and men by chance? The second kind is deciding whether one sample differs from another in terms of a particular variable. Assume, for instance, that ten people are randomly assigned to watching the same episode on television either with or without violence. Three of the five viewing the violent episode behave more aggressively than three of the five seeing the non-violent sequence, while there is no difference between the other two. What is the likelihood of finding this difference by chance? The third kind is estimating the probability of two events being associated by chance. Imagine, for example, that three of four people who watch violence on television behave aggressively whereas three of six people who do not view violence on television act aggressively. How likely are we to come across such a relationship by chance?

The probability of obtaining any particular event by chance on any occasion is one divided by the total number of possible events. So, the probability of randomly selecting a woman or man from a population containing an equal number of women and men is 0.5 (1/2 = 0.5). The probability of finding a person randomly assigned to watching a violent episode on television behaving more aggressively than another randomly assigned to viewing a non-violent episode is 0.33 (1/3 = 0.33) since that individual can be either more, less or equally aggressive as the other. While the probability of someone being by chance both aggressive and having watched violence on television is 0.25 (1/4 = 0.25). If the probability of being aggressive is independent of watching violence on television, then the probability of both events occurring is the product of their separate probability (0.5 × 0.5 = 0.25).

The probability of obtaining a particular sequence of independent events is the product of their separate probabilities. So, the probability of randomly choosing two women from a population consisting of the same number of women and men is 0.25 (0.5 × 0.5 = 0.25). The probability of finding two people randomly allocated to watching a violent sequence on television acting more aggressively than two individuals randomly assigned to seeing a similar non-violent episode is 0.11 (0.33 × 0.33 = 0.11). Whereas the probability of two people being by chance both aggressive and having watched violence on television is 0.06 (0.25 × 0.25 = 0.06).

Since the procedure for determining the probability of independent events is the same for the three kinds of situations described above, we will use the simplest case of randomly selecting women and men from a population containing an equal proportion of women and men. This situation is the same as tossing a number of unbiased coins once. If we select one person at random, then there are only two possible outcomes since that person can only be a woman or a man. Consequently, the probability of selecting a woman or a man is 0.5 (1/2 = 0.5). If we pick two people, there are four possible outcomes: (1) two women; (2) two men; (3) a woman followed by a man; and (4) a man followed by a woman. If these four outcomes are equiprobable, then the probability of any one of them occurring is 0.25 (1/4 = 0.25). Since there are two different orders in which a woman and a man can be selected, the probability of obtaining a woman and a man is the sum of the probability of these two orders which is 0.5 (0.25 + 0.25 = 0.5).

We can plot the distribution of the probability of choosing these three different numbers of women and men as shown in Figure 4.1. On the horizontal axis the varying proportions of women to men are ordered, ranging from two women and no men to no women and two men. The probabilities of these proportions are depicted on the vertical axis, ranging from zero to 0.75. Points are placed on the figure where the appropriate values on the horizontal and vertical axes meet. So we place a point, for example, where the vertical line drawn from the position on the horizontal axis representing the proportion of two women and no men meets the horizontal line drawn from the position on the vertical axis denoting a probability of 0.25. The points on the figure are then connected by straight lines. If we do this, we see that this distribution of proportions takes the form of an upturned 'V'.

If we select four people, there are sixteen possible outcomes as presented in Table 4.1. If these sixteen outcomes are equiprobable, then the probability of any one of them happening by chance is 0.0625 (0.5 × 0.5 × 0.5 × 0.5 = 0.0625). As there are four different ways in which either three

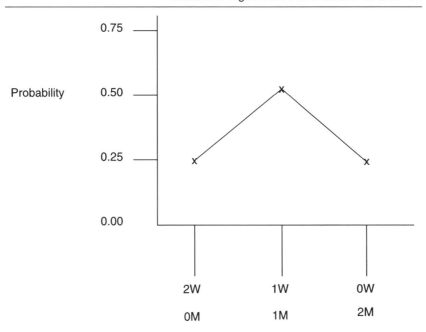

Figure 4.1 Two-case example of a probability distribution

Table 4.1 Four-case example of equiprobable gender outcomes

Possible outcomes	Probability
1 WWWW	0.0625
2 WWWM 3 WWMW 4 WMWW 5 MWWW	0.2500
6 WWMM 7 WMWM 8 WMMW 9 MWWM 10 MWMW 11 MMWW	0.3750
12 MMMW 13 MMWM 14 MWMM 15 WMMM	0.2500
16 MMMM	0.0625

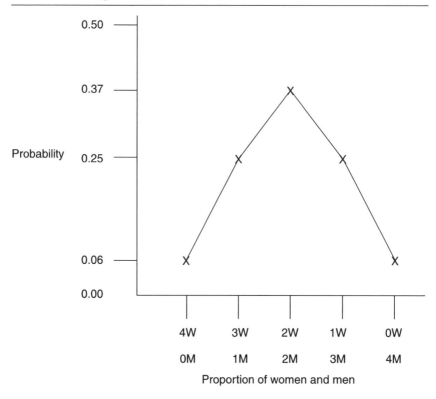

Figure 4.2 Four-case example of a probability distribution

women and one man or one woman and three men can be selected, the probability of obtaining either of these two outcomes is 0.25 (0.0625 + 0.0625 + 0.0625 + 0.0625 = 0.25). Similarly, as there are six different orders containing two women and two men, the probability of finding this outcome is 0.375 (0.0625 + 0.0625 + 0.0625 + 0.0625 + 0.0625 + 0.0625 = 0.375). If we plot the distribution of the probability of selecting these five different numbers of women and men, then this distribution takes the shape of an inverted 'V' once more, as drawn in Figure 4.2.

The distribution of the probability of only two outcomes (e.g. a woman and a man) occurring by chance on a specified number of occasions (e.g. for four people) is called a *binomial* distribution. The binomial distributions shown in Figures 4.1 and 4.2 are for two and four occasions respectively. The distribution of the probability of two outcomes occurring by chance on an infinite number of occasions takes the form of an inverted U or bell-shaped distribution usually called a *normal* or *z* distribution but also known as *DeMoivre*'s or a *Gaussian* distribution. Such a distribution is

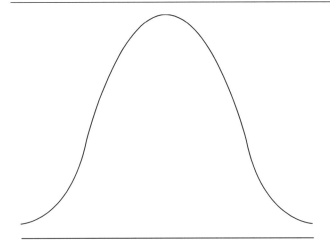

Figure 4.3 A normal distribution

illustrated in Figure 4.3. We can see that the binomial distribution approx-imates a normal one if we produce the binomial distribution for ten occasions as shown in Figure 4.4.

As can be worked out, the larger the number of people selected from a population, the less likely it is that the sample will consist of all women or men. For example, the probability of obtaining all five women from a population consisting of equal numbers of women and men is 0.031 (0.5 $\times$ 0.5 $\times$ 0.5 $\times$ 0.5 $\times$ 0.5 or $0.5^5 = 0.031$ rounded to three decimal places), while the probability of obtaining all six women is 0.016 ($0.5^6 = 0.016$ rounded to three decimal places). However, even with very large samples of people, there is always a very small probability that the sample will contain all women or all men. Consequently, the question arises as to when we decide that a sample is or is not representative of the population from which it is drawn. The same issue, of course, is also raised when determin-ing whether there is or is not a difference in the scores (e.g. aggression) between two groups (e.g. those watching the violent or non-violent episode on television) or whether there is or is not a relationship between two variables (e.g. being aggressive and having watched violence on television).

The conventional probability or *p* value for deciding that a result is not due to chance has been set as equal to or less than 0.05 or five times out of a hundred. If the probability level of an outcome is at or below 0.05, then the result is *statistically significant* in that it is thought unlikely to have been due to chance. If, on the other hand, the probability level of an outcome is above 0.05, then that result is *statistically non-significant* in the sense that

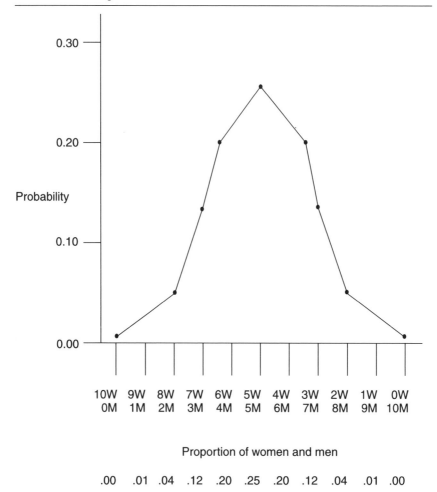

Figure 4.4 Ten-case example of a binomial probability distribution

it is considered likely that it could have been due to chance. Note that this result is *non*-significant and not *in*significant.

When analysing the probability of an outcome, we can either specify the direction of the results we expect to obtain or we can leave the direction unstated. In terms of the three kinds of situation outlined at the beginning of this chapter, we could predict that the sample will contain a greater proportion of women than that in the population, that the people watching the violent episode on television will show more aggression than those viewing the non-violent episode, and that aggressive people will have watched more violence on television than non-aggressive people. Take the case of expecting that the sample will consist of a greater proportion of women than that in the population. Suppose we obtain a sample of four women and no men. Since the probability of selecting such a sample is 0.0625 which is greater than 0.05, we would conclude that the sample does not differ significantly from the population. If, on the other hand, we had a sample of five women and no men, we would assume that the sample varied significantly from the population since the probability of finding such a sample is 0.031 which is below the 0.05 level. When the hypothesis is *directional*, we adopt the *one-tailed* probability level since only one end or tail of the probability distribution is used.

When, however, the hypothesis is *non-directional* in the sense that we do not predict what the results will be, we employ the *two-tailed* probability level which takes account of both ends or tails of the probability distribution. Suppose, for instance, we wanted to know whether the proportion of women in the sample differed from that in the population but did not have any expectations about the way in which it differed. Since the sample may contain either proportionately more or proportionately less women than that in the population, both these probabilities have to be included. Consequently, the criterion value of 0.05 for deciding whether the sample differs significantly from the population is made up of the 0.025 probability that the sample will contain proportionately more women than the population and the 0.025 probability that the sample will comprise proportionately less women than the population.

For example, if a sample of five women was obtained from a population containing equal numbers of women and men, then this sample could be interpreted as not differing from the population since the probability of obtaining five women (0.031) combined with the probability of obtaining five men (0.031) is 0.062 (0.031 + 0.031 = 0.062) which is greater than 0.05. If, on the other hand, a sample of six women was selected from the same population, then this sample could be said to differ from the population since the probability of selecting six women (0.016) added to the probability of selecting six men (0.016) is 0.032 (0.016 + 0.016 = 0.032) which is less than 0.05. Since the one-tailed probability level is half that of the two-tailed probability level, statistical significance is more likely to be obtained when the direction of the hypothesis is stated. However, the one-tailed probability level can only be used when the direction the results will take has been specified before the data are analysed. If the direction of the results is not predicted before the data are examined, then the two-tailed probability level has to be employed.

The convention of adopting the 0.05 probability level as the cut-off point for determining the statistical significance of a finding is arbitrary since there is always the probability that any result is due to chance. For example, although we assume that a sample containing only six women differs significantly from a population known to consist of an equal number

Table 4.2 Type I and Type II errors

		Real difference or relationship	
		Yes	No
Accept difference or relationship	Yes	Correct decision	Type I error α
	No	Type II error β	Correct decision

of women and men, there is a two-tailed probability of 0.032 that this result could have occurred by chance.

Because we can never be certain about whether a sample differs from its population, whether two groups differ from each other or whether a relationship exists between two variables, we can make one of two types of error as shown in Table 4.2. The first type of error, known as *Type I error* or *alpha error*, is when we accept that there is a difference or relationship when in reality there is none. For example, we may assume that the sample differs from its population when it does not. *Type II* or *beta error* is when we accept there is no difference or relationship when in actuality there is one.

We may reduce the possibility of making a Type I error by lowering the significance level from 0.05 to say, 0.01 (one in a hundred) or less. If, for example, we adopt the 0.01 probability level, then a sample of only six women would not differ significantly from a population containing equal numbers of women and men since the two-tailed probability of obtaining this result (0.032) is greater than 0.01. However, employing a more conservative probability level has the effect of increasing a Type II error. One way of decreasing the probability of making this kind of error is to increase the size of the sample. For instance, the two-tailed probability of finding that a sample contains all women is 0.062 for a sample of five but 0.032 for a sample of six.

DIFFERENT KINDS OF STATISTICAL TESTS

What particular statistical test we use for deciding whether a result is statistically significant depends on five main considerations. First, are we interested in determining whether two variables are related or whether one or more groups differ on some variable? Tests of association assess the size and often the direction of a relationship between two variables, whereas tests of difference ascertain whether one or more groups differ on some variable. Second, are the data categorical or non-categorical? With categorical data, the number or frequency of cases in each category is simply counted whereas with non-categorical data, the data can be described in terms of measures of central tendency and dispersion. Third, do we need to make assumptions about the way the values of the variables are distributed? *Non-parametric* tests generally depend less than *parametric* tests on the distribution of variables in the population and are, therefore, sometimes known as *distribution-free* tests. Fourth, when two or more groups are being compared, do they consist of different (*unrelated*) cases or ones which are the same or have been matched (*related*)? And fifth, is there one, two or more groups being compared? *Omnibus* tests for comparing three or more groups are listed in Table 4.3 which determine whether a difference exists between the groups but do not tell which groups differ. To find this out we need to compare two groups at a time. When we have predicted beforehand where the differences lie, we determine whether any differences are significant with what is called an *a priori* or *planned* test. Whereas when we have not previously predicted any differences, we test for what appear to be differences using what has been variously called an *a posteriori*, *post hoc* or *unplanned* test.

The major tests of difference and association covered in this book are displayed in Tables 4.3 and 4.4 respectively, together with the considerations for their application. Each of these tests has its own test statistic (such as *t* and *r*) and the probability of that statistic arising by chance. In other words, the way in which a particular test calculates the probability of a certain outcome occurring by chance depends on the five considerations outlined above. The test for determining, for example, whether people who watched the violent programme were more aggressive than those who viewed the non-violent programme will be different from the test that assesses whether, say, there is a statistically significant association between being aggressive and the amount of violence watched on television.

PARAMETRIC AND NON-PARAMETRIC TESTS

One of the unresolved issues in statistics is the question of when parametric rather than non-parametric tests should be used. Some writers have argued that parametric tests should only be applied when the data fulfil the following three conditions: (1) the variables are measured with an equal interval or ratio scale; (2) the samples are drawn from populations whose variances are equal or *homogeneous* and (3) whose distributions are normal. A normal distribution is a theoretical or idealised one which is based on a population of an infinite number of cases and which takes the form of a bell or an inverted-U as shown in Figure 4.3. The extent to which a normal distribution looks like a bell depends upon the values of its parameters. Greater variances will create flatter distributions. The term *parameter* refers to a measure which describes the distribution of the variable in the population such as its mean or variance. Parametric tests

Table 4.3 Tests of difference

Nature of variable	Type of test	Kind of data	Number of groups	Name of test	Page numbers
Categorical (nominal or frequency)	Non-parametric	Unrelated	1	Binomial	112–16
			1	Chi-square	117–28
			2	Fisher's exact	133–6
			2+	Chi-square	128–33, 136–40
		Related	2	McNemar	140–2
			3+	Cochran Q	142–5
Non-categorical	Non-parametric	Unrelated	1	Kolmogorov-Smirnov	149–51
			2	Kolmogorov-Smirnov	151–3
			2	Mann-Whitney U	153–7
			2+	Median	157–9
			3+	Kruskal-Wallis H	159–62
		Related	2	Sign	163–5
			2	Wilcoxon	165–7
			3+	Friedman	167–71
	Parametric	Unrelated	1	t	174–80
			2	t	180–9
			2+	One-way and two-way analysis of variance	189–99 199–209
		Related	2	t	213–18
			3+	Single factor repeated measures	218–25
		Related and unrelated	2+	Two-way analysis of variance with repeated measures on one factor	225–32
				One-way analysis of covariance	232–47

are so called because they are based on assumptions about the parameters of the population from which the sample has been drawn (i.e. that the variances should be equal and that the distributions should be normal).

Whether these three conditions have to be satisfied before parametric

Table 4.4 Tests of association

Nature of variable	Type of test	Name of test	Page numbers
Categorical (nominal or frequency)	Non-parametric	Phi coefficient	251–2
		Contingency coefficient	252–3
		Cramer's *V*	253
		Goodman and Kruskal's lambda	254–5
		Goodman and Kruskal's tau	255–6
Non-categorical	Non-parametric	Kendall's tau *a*	257
		Kendall's tau *b*	257–60
		Kendall's tau *c*	260–1
		Goodman and Kruskal's gamma	261
		Somer's *d*	261–3
		Spearman's rank-order correlation	263–6
		Mantel–Haenszel's chi-square	266
		Kendall's partial rank-order correlation	271–3
		Partial gamma	273–4
	Parametric	Pearson's product-moment correlation	277–82
		Pearson's partial correlation	290–7
		eta	297–8
		Unstandardised regression coefficient	305–11
		Standardised regression coefficient	311–12
		Part correlation	321–6

tests can be employed has been seriously questioned. Concerning the first condition, it has been suggested that parametric tests can also be used with ordinal variables since tests apply to numbers and not to what those numbers refer (Lord 1953). Suppose, for example, we compare the number of violent films watched during the last year by three individuals judged to be aggressive and three people thought to be non-aggressive. The number of violent films seen by the three aggressive individuals is 5, 7 and 8 respectively and is 1, 3 and 6 for the three non-aggressive ones as shown in Table 4.5. Consequently, the aggressive group has viewed 20 violent films in all while the non-aggressive group has seen 10. The variable of the number of violent films watched is a ratio scale since it has a zero point and

Table 4.5 Ratio and ordinal measures of frequency of violent films watched by three aggressive and three non-aggressive individuals

	Aggressive		Non-aggressive	
	Ratio	Ordinal	Ratio	Ordinal
	5	3	1	1
	7	3	3	2
	8	4	6	2
Total	20	10	10	5

the numbers indicate equal intervals. Indeed, the aggressive group has seen twice as many violent films as the non-aggressive group.

Now, assume that instead of asking people how many violent films they had seen, we had them rate how often they watched violent films on a 4-point scale where 1 signifies 'not at all', 2 'rarely', 3 'occasionally' and 4 'often'. This measure would be an ordinal scale since someone scoring 4 would not necessarily have seen twice as many violent films as someone scoring 2. As indicated in Table 4.5, the three aggressive individuals rated themselves as 3, 3 and 4 and the three non-aggressive ones as 1, 2 and 2. Therefore, the total score is 10 for the aggressive group and 5 for the non-aggressive one. Since the measure is an ordinal one, we cannot say that the aggressive group saw twice as many violent films as the non-aggressive one. However, we can state that the aggressive group viewed more films with violence than the non-aggressive group. Since a parametric test applied to these two measures simply determines whether the mean scores of the two groups differ, the measure can be ordinal, equal interval or ratio.

With respect to the second and third conditions, a number of studies have been conducted to see what effect samples drawn from populations with non-normal distributions and unequal variances have on the values of parametric tests. Some authors have suggested that violation of these two assumptions generally has little effect on the values of these tests (e.g. Boneau 1960). One exception to this general finding was where both the size of the samples and the variances were unequal although some have argued that this exception applies even with equal sample sizes (Wilcox 1987). Another exception was where both distributions of scores were non-normal. In such circumstances, it may be prudent to compare the results of a non-parametric test with those of a parametric test. Where the distributions of scores are not normal, it may also be worth running a parametric test on the scores as they are and after they have been transformed closer to normality. For more details on transforming scores to normality, see Mosteller and Tukey (1977). Tests for determining normality of distribution and equality of variances are described next.

SKEWNESS

The extent to which a set of scores deviates from a normal or bell-shaped distribution is estimated by two statistics called *skewness* and *kurtosis*. Skewness is a measure of the extent to which the distribution is not symmetrical while kurtosis is an index of the degree to which there are either too many or too few cases in the middle of the distribution.

The formula for skewness (Bliss 1967) is:

$$\text{skewness} = \frac{[\text{sum of (each score} - \text{mean) cubed]} \times N}{\text{standard deviation cubed} \times (N - 1) \times (N - 2)}$$

where N is the total number of cases.

We will demonstrate the steps involved in using this formula to calculate skewness with the following set of 4 scores which are symmetrically distributed:

1   3   3   5

Step 1   Compute the mean, which for these four scores is 3 [(1 + 3 + 3 + 5)/4 = 12/4 = 3].

Step 2   Subtract the mean from each score, which gives the following differences.

−2   0   0   2

Step 3   Cube these differences, which become

−8   0   0   8

Step 4   Sum the cubed differences for each of the scores, which is 0 (−8 + 0 + 0 + 8 = 0).

Step 5   Multiply this sum by the number of cases, which is also 0 (0 × 4 = 0).

Step 6   Compute the standard deviation. To compute the standard deviation of the four scores, the mean is first subtracted from each score to give

−2   0   0   2

and then squared to give

4   0   0   4

These squared differences are summed and divided by one less than the number of cases to give a variance of 2.66 [(4 + 0 + 0 + 4)/(4 − 1) = 8/3 =

2.66]. The square root of the variance is the standard deviation which is 1.63 ($\sqrt{2.66} = 1.63$).

Step 7   Cube the standard deviation and multiply it by the number of cases less one and the number of cases less two. The standard deviation cubed ($1.63^3 = 4.33$) and multiplied by the number of cases less one ($4 - 1 = 3$) and the number of cases less two ($4 - 2 = 2$) is 25.98 ($4.33 \times 3 \times 2 = 25.98$).

Step 8   Divide the result of Step 5 by that of Step 7 to give the value for skewness, which is 0 ($0/25.98 = 0$).

The value of skewness is zero when a set of scores is symmetrically distributed because the sum of the cubed differences below the mean is equal to the sum of the cubed differences above the mean. The need to cube the differences will become apparent when the two examples of asymmetrical distributions are presented. When most of the scores are to the left of the mean, the distribution is said to be *positively skewed* as the value of skewness is positive. This point can be illustrated with the following set of four scores which is positively skewed:

2   2   2   6

To show the steps involved in the calculation of skewness for this set of scores, the scores will be arranged in a column as displayed in Table 4.6. The sum of these scores is given at the bottom of this column followed by the mean. The difference (d) between these scores and their mean is presented in a second column while the differences squared (d^2) and cubed (d^3) are displayed in a third and fourth column. The result for Step 5 of the calculation, which involves multiplying the sum of the cubed differences (24) by the number of cases (4), gives 96 ($24 \times 4 = 96$). The variance is 4 [$12/(4 - 1) = 4$] which yields a standard deviation of 2 ($\sqrt{4} = 2$). Consequently, the value for Step 7 is 48 ($2^3 \times 3 \times 2 = 48$). Dividing the result for Step 5 by that for Step 7 gives a skewness value of 2 ($96/48 = 2$).

Table 4.6 Positively skewed scores: initial computations

	Scores	d	d^2	d^3
	2	−1	1	−1
	2	−1	1	−1
	2	−1	1	−1
	6	3	9	27
Sum	12	0	12	24
N	4			
Mean	3			

Table 4.7 Negatively skewed scores: initial computations

	Scores	d	d^2	d^3
	1	−2	4	−8
	3	0	0	0
	4	1	1	1
	4	1	1	1
Sum	12	0	6	−6
N	4			
Mean	3			

The reasons for cubing the difference between each score and the mean should be clearer from this example. First, since the mean is the central point in any distribution, the sum of differences below the mean is equal to the sum of differences above the mean regardless of the shape of the distribution. Second, as negative signs become positive when squared but remain negative when cubed, cubing the difference indicates the direction of any asymmetry in the distribution.

When most of the scores are clustered to the right of the mean, the distribution is *negatively skewed* and takes on a negative value as shown by the following set of negatively skewed scores:

1   3   4   4

Once again, to make it easier to follow the steps in calculating skewness, the scores and the three indices of their difference from the mean will be displayed in columns as shown in Table 4.7. Multiplying the sum of the cubed differences by the number of cases gives −24 (−6 × 4 = −24) for Step 5. The square root of the variance is 1.414 ($\sqrt{6/3}$ = 1.4142) which when cubed (1.4142^3) and multiplied by the number of cases less one (4 − 1) and the number of cases less two (4 − 2) becomes 16.97 in Step 7 (1.4142^3 × 3 × 2 = 16.97). Consequently, skewness equals −1.414 (−24/16.97 = −1.414).

To determine whether the distribution is significantly asymmetrical, the value of skewness is divided by the *standard error of skewness* and the resulting value looked up in the table of the *standard normal distribution* in Appendix 2 (Bliss 1967). The standard error of skewness is a measure of the extent to which skewness may vary as a function of the size of the sample. It is most conveniently described in terms of the following formula where N is the total number of cases:

$$\text{standard error of skewness} = \sqrt{\frac{6 \times N \times (N-1)}{(N-2) \times (N+1) \times (N+3)}}$$

To calculate the standard error of skewness for a sample containing four cases, we substitute 4 for N in the formula:

$$\sqrt{\frac{6 \times 4 \times (4 - 1)}{(4 - 1) \times (4 + 1) \times (4 + 3)}} = \sqrt{\frac{6 \times 4 \times 3}{3 \times 5 \times 7}} = \sqrt{\frac{72}{70}} =$$

$$\sqrt{1.028} = 1.01$$

To find out, for example, whether a skewness value of -1.41 for a sample of 4 differs significantly from normality, we divide this value by 1.01 which gives a figure of -1.40 ($-1.41/1.01 = -1.40$). We look up this figure in the table in Appendix 2. To use this table, we need to know what the standard normal distribution or curve is.

The standard normal distribution is a theoretical distribution which has a mean of 0 and a standard deviation of 1. Since the distribution is perfectly symmetrical, 50 per cent or 0.50 of the values lie above the mean and 0.50 of the values fall below it. Furthermore, because the shape of the distribution is fixed and known, the proportion of values falling between any two points on its base can be easily calculated. For example, the proportion of values lying between the mean and one, two and three standard deviations on one side of the distribution is about 0.341, 0.477 and 0.499 respectively. The values given in the table represent that proportion of the distribution which lies between the mean and a cut-off point called z on the horizontal axis. In the left-hand margin of the table are the z values to one decimal place which range from 0.0 to 3.9. Along the top row of the table are the z values given to the second decimal place which vary from 0.00 to 0.09. In the extreme case where the z value is zero (0.00), the proportion of the area between z and the mean is zero which makes the proportion beyond z 0.5 ($0.5 - 0.0 = 0.5$). The value of z becomes larger as it moves away from the centre of the distribution towards either tail. As it does so, the proportion of the area between it and the mean increases while the proportion beyond it decreases. For example, the proportion of the area between a z value of 3.0 (which corresponds to a standard deviation of 3) and the mean is 0.4987 while the proportion beyond it is 0.0013 ($0.5000 - 0.4987 = 0.0013$). Since the tails of the standard normal curve never touch the horizontal axis (i.e. the distribution is *asymptotic*), z increases to infinity.

In effect, dividing skewness by its standard error provides a statistic which can be seen to be comparable to z. When this statistic has a value of 0, the distribution will be perfectly symmetrical. The further this statistic departs from zero, the more asymmetrical the distribution will be. To look up how far a z value of -1.40 is from the midpoint of a distribution, we ignore its negative sign since the z values describe either the left- or the right-hand side of the distribution. In the table of Appendix 2, the relevant portion of which has been reproduced in Table 4.8, we see that the

Table 4.8 Part of the table of the standard normal distribution

z	0.00	0.01	0.02	. . .
.				
.				
.				
1.3	0.4032	0.4049	0.4066	
1.4	0.4192	0.4207	0.4222	
1.5	0.4332	0.4345	0.4357	
.				
.				
.				

proportion of the area between a z value of 1.40 and the mean is 0.4192 of the distribution. This indicates that the proportion of the area beyond z is 0.0808 (0.5000 − 0.4192 = 0.0808).

Now, the proportion of the area beyond z can be interpreted as representing the probability of an outcome occurring at the one-tailed level so that a z of −1.40 indicates a one-tailed probability of 0.0808. However, to determine whether a distribution is asymmetrical, we have to use a two-tailed probability level since the asymmetry can be either positive or negative. As the two-tailed probability level reflects the possibility that the value of 1.40 may have been either positive or negative, it is simply twice the one-tailed level which makes it 0.1616 (2 × 0.0808 = 0.1616). Since this figure is larger than 0.05, we would conclude that this distribution was not significantly asymmetrical. On the other hand, the z value for the example of the positively skewed distribution is 1.98 (2.00/1.01 = 1.98). From the table in Appendix 2, it can be seen that this value has a one-tailed probability of 0.0239 which may be converted into a two-tailed one of 0.0478 (0.0239 × 2 = 0.0478) by doubling it. As the two-tailed probability level of this value is less than 0.05, we would assume that this distribution is significantly asymmetrical. Note that the larger the value of z is, the further away it is from the centre of the distribution and, so, the more likely it is to be statistically significant.

The standard error of skewness and its z value are not given by Minitab. Since these are useful statistics, we could write a macro to compute them as well as skewness. We will use the above example of the symmetrically distributed data to illustrate the operation of the commands for this macro.

Step 1   Enter these data in **c1** with the following **set** command:

MTB > set c1
DATA> 1 3 3 5
DATA> end

Step 2   Count the number of non-missing values in **c1** and store them as a constant in **k1** using the following **n** command:

MTB > n c1 k1

Minitab will show that **N = 4**.

Step 3   Calculate the mean of the scores in **c1** and save this mean as a constant in **k2** with the following **mean** command:

MTB > mean c1 k2

Minitab will display that the **MEAN = 3.0000**.

Step 4   Compute the standard deviation of the scores in **c1** and store this standard deviation as a constant in **k3** with the following **stdev** command:

MTB > stdev c1 k3

Minitab will indicate that the **ST.DEV. = 1.6330**.

Step 5   Subtract the mean (**k2**) from each score in **c1** and cube (****3**) this difference and keep these cubed deviations in **c2** with the following **let** command:

MTB > let c2=(c1−k2)**3

Step 6   Sum the cubed deviations in **c2** and store them as a constant in **k4** with the following **sum** command:

MTB > sum c2 k4

Minitab shows the **SUM = 0.000000000**.

Step 7   Multiply the sum of the cubed deviations (**k4**) by the number of non-missing scores (**k1**) and save this value as a constant in **k5** with the following **let** command:

MTB > let k5=k4*k1

Step 8   Cube (****3**) the standard deviation (**k3**), multiply it by the number of values minus 1 (**k1−1**) and the number of values minus 2 (**k1−2**) and retain this figure as a constant in **k6** with the following **let** command:

MTB > let k6=(k3**3)*(k1−1)*(k1−2)

If we display **k6**, we see that it is **26.1279** which is slightly different from our previously calculated figure of 25.98 due to differences in rounding.

Step 9   To obtain skewness, we divide **k5** by **k6** and store the result in **k7** with the following **let** command:

MTB > let k7=k5/k6

If we show **k7**, we see that it is **0** as previously calculated.

Step 10   To compute the standard error of skewness, we first multiply 6 by the number of values (**6*k1**) and the number of values minus 1 (**k1−1**) and store this figure as **k8** with the following **let** command:

MTB > let k8=6*k1*(k1-1)

Step 11   Next, we multiply the number of values minus 2 (**k1−2**) by the number of values plus 1 (**k1+1**) and the number of values plus 3 (**k1+3**) and save this product in **k9** with the following **let** command:

MTB > let k9=(k1−2)*(k1+1)*(k1+3)

Step 12   Finally, we divide **k8** by **k9** (**k8/k9**), take the square root (**sqrt**) of the result and keep this value (which is the standard error of skewness) in **k10** with the following **let** command:

MTB > let k10=sqrt(k8/k9)

If we display **k10**, we see that it is **1.01419**, which rounded to two decimal places, is the same as the figure of 1.01 we calculated earlier.

Step 13   To determine the *z* value of skewness, we divide skewness (**k7**) by its standard error (**k10**) and save the resulting *z* value in **k11** with the following **let** command:

MTB > let k11=k7/k10

If we display **k11**, we see that it is **0**. To check the statistical significance of this value, we can look it up in the table in Appendix 2.

So, the macro for calculating skewness, its standard error and its *z* value consists of the following commands:

n c1 k1
mean c1 k2
stdev c1 k3
let c2=(c1−k2)**3
sum c2 k4
let k5=k4*k1
let k6=(k3**3)*(k1−1)*(k1−2)
let k7=k5/k6
let k8=6*k1*(k1−1)

```
let k9=(k1−2)*(k1+1)*(k1+3)
let k10=sqrt(k8/k9)
let k11=k7/k10
print k7 k10 k11
```

KURTOSIS

Distributions can be symmetrical but not normal if there are either too many or too few cases in the middle of the distribution. A normal distribution may be called *mesokurtic* (derived from the Greek 'meso' meaning middle and 'kurtic' meaning curve) and has a kurtosis value of 0. A distribution with too many cases in the centre of the distribution is known as *leptokurtic* ('lepto' meaning narrow) and has a positive kurtosis value while a distribution with too few cases at its centre is referred to as *platykurtic* ('platy' meaning flat) and has a negative kurtosis value. The formula for kurtosis (Bliss 1967) is:

$$\text{kurtosis} = \frac{[(d^4 \text{ summed})(N)(N+1)] - [(d^2 \text{ summed})(d^2 \text{ summed})(3)(N-1)]}{(SD^4)(N-1)(N-2)(N-3)}$$

where d is the difference of each score from the mean, SD is the standard deviation, N is the total number of cases, and values in adjacent parentheses are multiplied by each other [e.g. $(3)(N-1) = (3) \times (N-1)$].

We will illustrate the steps involved in using this formula to work out kurtosis for the following set of 6 scores which approximate a mesokurtic distribution

1   2   3   3   4   5

Step 1   Calculate the mean, which for these six scores is 3 [(1 + 2 + 3 + 3 + 4 + 5)/6 = 18/6 = 3].

Step 2   Subtract the mean from each score, which gives the following differences

−2   −1   0   0   1   2

Step 3   Square each of these differences, which become

4   1   0   0   1   4

Then sum these squared differences (d^2 summed), which gives 10 (4 + 1 + 0 + 0 + 1 + 4 = 10).

Step 4   Raise each of these differences to the power of 4 (i.e. multiply them by themselves four times), giving

16   1   0   0   1   16

Then sum these differences to the power of 4 (d^4 summed), making 34 (16 + 1 + 0 + 0 + 1 + 16 = 34).

Step 5 Calculate the standard deviation by dividing the sum of squared differences in Step 3 by one less the number of cases and then take the square root of the result, which is 1.41

$$[\sqrt{(4 + 1 + 0 + 0 + 1 + 4)/(6 - 1)} = \sqrt{10/5} = \sqrt{2} = 1.41]$$

Step 6 Multiply the standard deviation by itself four times (SD^4), giving 3.95 ($1.41^4 = 3.953$).

Step 7 Multiply the sum of differences to the power of 4 (d^4 summed) in Step 4 by the number of cases (N) and the number of cases plus one ($N + 1$). This is 1428 [34 × 6 × (6 + 1) = 1428].

Step 8 Multiply the sum of squared differences (d^2 summed) in Step 3 by itself, by 3 and by the number of cases minus one ($N - 1$). This becomes 1500 [10 × 10 × 3 × (6 - 1) = 1500].

Step 9 Multiply the standard deviation to the power of 4 (SD^4) in Step 6 by the number of cases minus one ($N - 1$), the number of cases minus two ($N - 2$) and the number of cases minus three ($N - 3$). This becomes 237 [3.95 × (6 - 1) × (6 - 2) × (6 - 3) = 237].

Step 10 Subtract the result of Step 8 from that of Step 7 and divide the difference by the result of Step 9 to give kurtosis. This is −0.30 [(1428 − 1500)/237 = −72/237 = −0.30]. In other words, kurtosis for this set of scores is slightly negative.

To clarify the computations for this last example, we will arrange these scores in a column with the relevant difference indices in adjacent columns as presented in Table 4.9. The standard deviation is 1.41 ($\sqrt{10/5} = 1.41$). Substituting the appropriate figures in the above formula, we obtain a kurtosis of −0.30:

$$\frac{[(34)(6)(6+1)]-[(10)(10)(3)(6-1)]}{(1.41^4)(6-1)(6-2)(6-3)} = \frac{1428-1500}{237} = \frac{-72}{237} = -0.30$$

We will illustrate the calculation of kurtosis for a leptokurtic distribution represented by the five scores shown in the first column of Table 4.10. The standard deviation of these scores is 0.71 ($\sqrt{2/4} = 0.71$). Placing the relevant numbers in the formula produces a kurtosis of 2:

Table 4.9 A mesokurtic distribution: initial computations

	Scores	d	d^2	d^3
	1	−2	4	16
	2	−1	1	1
	3	0	0	0
	3	0	0	0
	4	1	1	1
	5	2	4	16
Sum	18	0	10	34
N	6			
Mean	3			

Table 4.10 A leptokurtic distribution: initial computations

	Scores	d	d^2	d^3
	1	−1	1	1
	2	0	0	0
	2	0	0	0
	2	0	0	0
	3	1	1	1
Sum	10	0	2	2
N	5			
Mean	2			

$$\frac{[(2)(5)(6)]-[(2)(2)(3)(4)]}{(0.71^4)(4)(3)(2)} = \frac{60-48}{6} = \frac{12}{6} = 2$$

Kurtosis for this group of scores is positive, indicating a leptokurtic curve.

Finally, we will show the calculation of kurtosis for a platykurtic distribution exemplified by the five scores presented in the first column of Table 4.11. The standard deviation of these scores is 1.00 ($\sqrt{4/4} = 1.00$). Inserting the pertinent values in the same formula gives a kurtosis of −3.00:

$$\frac{[(4)(5)(6)]-[(4)(4)(3)(4)]}{(1^4)(4)(3)(2)} = \frac{120-192}{24} = \frac{-72}{24} = -3.00$$

The negative value for kurtosis signifies that the distribution is platykurtic.

To determine whether a distribution differs significantly from a mesokurtic curve, we divide the kurtosis value by its standard error and look up in the table of the standard normal distribution in Appendix 2 how probable

Table 4.11 A platykurtic distribution: initial computations

Scores	d	d^2	d^3
1	−1	1	1
1	−1	1	1
2	0	0	0
3	1	1	1
3	1	1	1
Sum 10	0	4	4
N 5			
Mean 2			

the resulting figure is (Bliss 1967). The standard error of kurtosis is most conveniently described in terms of the following formula:

$$\text{standard error of kurtosis} = \sqrt{\frac{(\text{variance of skewness}) (4) (N^2 - 1)}{(N-3) (N+5)}}$$

The use of this formula can be illustrated by calculating the standard error of kurtosis for the example of the mesokurtic distribution.

First, we need to work out the variance of skewness according to the following formula:

$$\text{variance of skewness} = \frac{6 \times N \times (N-1)}{(N-2) \times (N+1) \times (N+3)}$$

Inserting the appropriate figures in this formula, variance of skewness is found to be 0.71

$$\frac{(6)(6)(6 - 1)}{(6 - 2)(6 + 1)(6 + 3)} = \frac{(6)(6)(5)}{(4)(7)(9)} = \frac{180}{252} = 0.71$$

Putting the variance of skewness in the formula for calculating the standard error of kurtosis gives a standard error of 1.74:

$$\sqrt{\frac{(0.71) (4) (6^2 - 1)}{(6 - 3) (6 + 5)}} = \sqrt{\frac{(0.71) (4) (35)}{(3) (11)}} = \sqrt{\frac{99.4}{33}} = \sqrt{3.01} = 1.74$$

Dividing the kurtosis by its standard error results in a value of −0.17 (−0.30/1.74 = −0.17) which, looked up in the table in Appendix 2, has a one-tailed probability of 0.4325 and a two-tailed one of 0.8650 (2 × 0.4325). Consequently, we would conclude that this distribution is meso-kurtic.

Since the standard error of kurtosis and its z value are not provided by Minitab, a macro comprising the following commands would compute these statistics together with kurtosis. Comments, beginning with a #, can be and have been inserted between these commands to remind us what some of the steps are doing:

```
n c1 k1
mean c1 k2
stdev c1 k3
let c2=(c1−k2)**2
sum c2 k4
# k4 is the sum of d squared
let c3=(c1−k2)**4
sum c3 k5
# k4 is the sum of d to the power of 4
let k6=k5*k1*(k1+1)
let k7=(k4*k4)*3*(k1−1)
let k8=(k3**4)*(k1-1)*(k1−2)*(k1−3)
let k9=(k6−k7)/k8
# k9 is the kurtosis
let k10=(6*k1*(k1−1))/((k1−2)*(k1+1)*(k1+3))
# k10 is the variance of skewness
let k11=k10*4*(k1**2−1)
let k12=(k1−3)*(k1+5)
let k13=sqrt(k11/k12)
# k13 is the standard error of kurtosis
let k14=k9/k13
# k14 is the z value
print k9 k13 k14
```

If we run this macro on the example of the mesokurtically distributed data, we see that **k9** (kurtosis) is **−0.300000**, **k13** (kurtosis standard error) is **1.74078**, and **k14** (z value) is **−0.172337**. When rounded to two decimal places, the respective values of −0.30, 1.74 and −0.17 are the same as those previously calculated.

NORMAL AND STANDARD NORMAL DISTRIBUTION

If we know that the data for a variable are normally distributed, then we can work out what proportion or percentage of scores lies between any two values of that variable and also what the probability is of obtaining a score between those two values. To do this, we first need to transform the original or *raw* scores into *standard* or z scores by subtracting from the individual score the mean score and then dividing this *deviation* score by the standard deviation of the scores.

$$\text{standard score} = \frac{\text{individual score - mean score}}{\text{standard deviation of scores}}$$

Assume, for instance, that the following data in Table 4.9 are normally distributed.

1 2 3 3 4 5

Subtracting the mean score of 3 from each of these values gives deviation scores of

−2 −1 0 0 1 2

Dividing by the standard deviation of 1.41 produces standard scores of

−1.42 −0.71 0 0 0.71 1.42

Note that dividing the standard deviation of the raw scores (1.41) by itself (1.41) gives 1 (1.41/1.41 = 1) which is why the standard deviation of the standard normal distribution is always 1. The mean of the standard normal distribution is always 0 since the sum of the negative standard scores below it (−1.42 + −0.71 = −2.13) equals the sum of the positive standard scores above it (1.42 + 0.71 = 2.13). So, a standard normal distribution always has a mean of 0 and a standard deviation of 1.

With the Minitab prompt system, we can standardise scores (say, in **c1**) and store them (say, in **c2**) with the following **center** command:

MTB >center c1 c2

The menu system for doing this is

→**Calc** →**Standardize...** →variable column or name [e.g. **c1**] →**Select** [this puts **c1** in the box under **Input column(s):**] →box under **Store results in:** and in it type the desired column [e.g. **c2**] →**OK**

A standard score is a score measured in standard deviation units. So, a standard score of −1.42 is a score that is 1.42 standard deviation units below the mean while a standard score of 1.42 is 1.42 standard deviation units above the mean. We can illustrate how these standard scores can be used to work out what proportion of them lie between certain values. Because the number of scores is small, we will look up in the table in Appendix 2 the z values of both the non-zero scores (1.42 and 0.71) which, rounded to two decimal places, are 0.42 and 0.26 respectively. Below we have ordered the distribution of the raw scores, their standard scores and the z values they represent.

			3		
Raw scores	1	2	3	4	5
Standard scores	−1.42	−0.71	0	0.71	1.42
z values	−0.42	−0.26	0	0.26	0.42

If we take the raw score of 3 which is the midpoint of the distribution, we see that it has a z value of 0. This means that half or 0.50 of the scores lie at and below the midpoint and 0.50 lie at and above it. In other words, there will be three scores ($6 \times 0.50 = 3$) at and below the standard score of 0 (i.e. 1, 2 and 3) and three scores at and above it (i.e. 3, 4 and 5). If we turn to the raw score of 1, we see that it has a value of -0.42. This means that 0.42 of the scores lie between it and 0 inclusive, 0.08 ($0.50 - 0.42 = 0.08$) lie at and below it and 0.92 ($1.00 - 0.08$ or $0.42 + 0.50 = 0.08$) lie at and above it. Since there is only one score of 1, half of this score lies at and below the z value of -0.42 while the other half lies at and above it. We can see that, of the six scores, half a score represents a proportion of 0.08 ($0.5/6 = 0.083$) while the remaining five and a half scores reflect a proportion of 0.92 ($5.5/6 = 0.916$). We can also work out that two and a half scores ($0.42 \times 6 = 2.5$) lie between the z values of -0.42 and 0 inclusive. In the same way, we can calculate the proportion of scores that fall between any two standard scores.

Proportions of scores falling between any two standard scores can also be thought of as the probability of obtaining a score between those two standard scores. So, the probability of obtaining a standard score between -1.42 and 0 is 0.42. The probability of getting a standard score between -1.42 and -0.71 is 0.16 ($0.42 - 0.26 = 0.16$).

It may also be worth pointing out here that it is possible to compare the relative standing of an individual or case on two or more normally distributed measures when the values on these measures differ widely. Suppose, for example, we wanted to compare the performance of Ann on an English and Maths test in relation to that of other people who also took these tests. The marks (out of 10) for these people are shown in Table 4.12. The mean score for the English test (1) is considerably lower than that for the Maths test (8). In effect, the mean mark of 1 on the English test is the equivalent of the mean mark of 8 on the Maths test. Because of the different range of marks used in these two tests, it is difficult to compare the relative performance of Ann. To do so, we need to convert her raw

Table 4.12 Raw scores on an English and Maths test

People	English	Maths
Ann	2	7
Mary	0	8
Jane	1	9
Susan	1	8
Helen		6
Emily		10
Mean	1	8

Table 4.13 Deviation and standard scores on an English and Maths test

People	Deviation scores		Standard scores	
	English	Maths	English	Maths
Ann	1	−1	1.22	−0.71
Mary	−1	0	−1.22	0
Jane	0	1	0	0.71
Susan	0	0	0	0
Helen		−2		−1.41
Emily		2		1.41
SD	0.82	1.41		

scores into standard ones which are shown in Table 4.13 together with those for the other people. We can see that Ann's mark in English was 1.22 standard deviation units above the mean $[(2 - 1)/0.82 = 1.22]$ while her mark in Maths was 0.71 standard deviation units below the mean $[(7 - 8)/1.41 = −0.71]$.

PLOTTING FREQUENCY DISTRIBUTIONS

The shape of a distribution can be visualised more clearly if it is displayed graphically as either a *histogram* or *polygon*. A histogram contains a horizontal line (called the *x* axis or *abscissa*) and a vertical line (called the *y* axis or *ordinate*). The values of the distribution are shown on the horizontal axis while the frequencies of the values are depicted on the vertical axis. The frequency of each value is represented by a vertical bar or box which is centred on the midpoint of the value. The height of the box corresponds to the frequency of the value. A histogram of the above example of a mesokurtic distribution is shown in Figure 4.5. In a polygon, on the other hand, the frequency of each value is represented by a point which lies directly above its value and whose height corresponds to its frequency. Adjacent points are connected by straight lines. The line extends to meet the horizontal axis where the frequency of the adjacent value is zero so that the whole area of the distribution is bounded by straight lines. Figure 4.6 presents a polygon of the mesokurtic distribution. One advantage of the polygon over the histogram is that it is easier to read when two distributions are plotted along the same axis for comparison. For instance, in Figure 4.7 the polygon for a mesokurtic and a leptokurtic distribution is shown. In both histograms and polygons the frequency of each value can also be plotted as a percentage or proportion of the total number of values. This has the advantage that, where the sizes of two samples differ, the area covered by the two distributions will be the same.

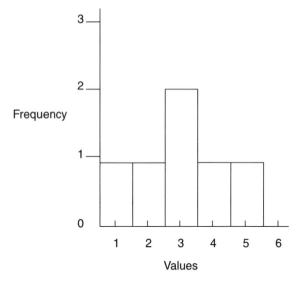

Figure 4.5 A histogram

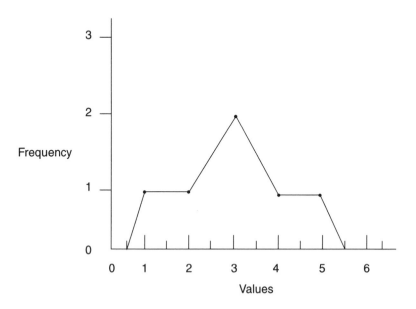

Figure 4.6 A polygon

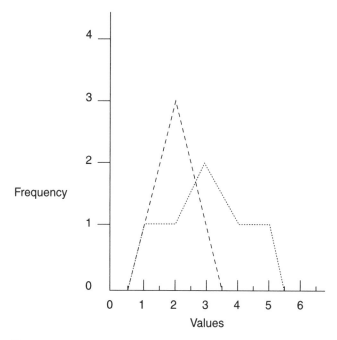

Figure 4.7 Two polygons

Histograms can be plotted with the Minitab prompt system using the **histogram** command. To produce a histogram of the mesokurtic distribution in Table 4.9, execute the following commands:

MTB > set c1
DATA> 1 2 3 3 4 5
DATA> end
MTB > histogram c1

In Releases 7 and 8, Minitab will produce a histogram like that shown in Figure 4.8. Note that the histogram is displayed vertically and not horizontally as in Figure 4.4. The number of asterisks represents the height of each box. In Release 8, a histogram like that shown in Figure 4.9 is produced with the **ghistogram** command.

In Releases 9 and 10, Minitab will generate a histogram like that depicted in Figure 4.10 in the **Graph** window.

The menu sequence for producing a histogram is:

→**Graph** →**Histogram...** →variable name or column [e.g. **c1**] →**Select** [this puts **c1** into the **Graph variables:** box; in the **Data display:** box you should have **Bar** in the cell by **Item 1** in the column labelled

Histogram of C1   N = 6

Midpoint	Count	
1	1	*
2	1	*
3	2	**
4	1	*
5	1	*

Figure 4.8 **Histogram** output (Releases 7 and 8)

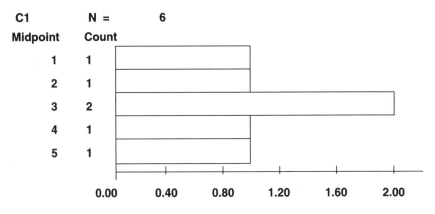

Figure 4.9 **Ghistogram** output (Release 8)

Display and in the cell to its right you should have **Graph** in the column labelled **For each] →OK**

F TEST FOR EQUAL VARIANCES

One test for determining whether the variances of two groups of scores differ is the *F* test or ratio, named in honour of Sir Ronald Fisher who developed analysis of variance. Since this test is affected by non-normality

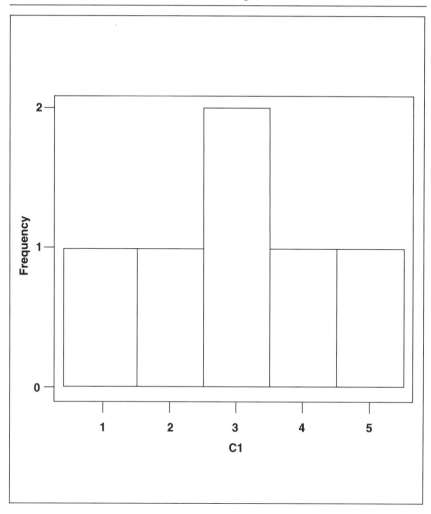

Figure 4.10 **Histogram** output (Releases 9 and 10)

of data (Box 1953), it should only be used when the data are normally distributed. As described in Chapter 2, the sample variance or estimated population variance is calculated by subtracting each score from the mean score for the group, squaring these differences, adding the squared differences together and dividing this total by the number of scores minus one. The *F* test for two groups is simply the greater variance of one group divided by the smaller variance of the other:

$$F = \frac{\text{greater variance}}{\text{smaller variance}}$$

Table 4.14 Number of violent films seen by an aggressive and non-aggressive
group

Group 1 (aggressive)	Group 2 (non-aggressive)
3	1
8	2
9	2
4	2
	3

In other words, it compares the greater variance against the lesser variance. Since the greater variance is always divided by the smaller variance, F values cannot be smaller than 1. To find out if the two variances differ significantly, we look up the statistical significance of the F value in a table like that in Appendix 3. Note that the minimum value of F in this table (in the bottom right-hand corner) is 1.000. The larger the value of F is, the bigger the greater variance is in relation to the smaller variance and, therefore, the more likely it is to be statistically significant.

Suppose we have the two sets of scores shown in Table 4.14 which, for example, reflect the number of violent films watched by four aggressive and five non-aggressive individuals during the past year. The values needed for computing the F ratio are shown in Table 4.15. The mean of the aggressive group is 6 [(3 + 8 + 9 + 4)/4 = 24/4 = 6] and of the non-aggressive group is 2 [(1 + 2 + 2 + 2 + 3)/5 = 10/5 = 2]. The variance of the aggressive group is 8.667 [$(3^2 + 2^2 + 3^2 + 2^2)/(4 - 1) = 26/3 = 8.667$] and of the non-aggressive group is 0.5 [$(1^2 + 0 + 0 + 0 + 1^2)/(5 - 1) = 2/4 = 0.5$]. Consequently, the F value or ratio is 17.33 (8.667/0.5 = 17.334).

We look up the statistical significance of this ratio in the table of F values in Appendix 3, the relevant proportion of which has been reproduced in Table 4.16. In this example, the number of people in the group with the larger variance (the *numerator*) is 4 while the number in the group with the smaller variance (the *denominator*) is 5. The *degrees of freedom* (*df*) for each group are the number of people in that group minus one which is 3 for the aggressive group and 4 for the non-aggressive one.

According to this table, for an F ratio to be significant at the 0.05 per cent two-tailed probability level with 3 degrees of freedom for the numerator and 4 degrees of freedom for the denominator, the F ratio must be equal to or larger than the *critical* value of 6.5914. The critical value of a test statistic is that value on its distribution which represents the cut-off point at and beyond which a result is considered to be statistically significant. Since an F ratio of 17.33 is larger than 6.5914, we can assume that the variances of the two groups are not equal. If the F ratio had been less than the critical

Table 4.15 Computations for the F ratio

	Aggressive group			Non-aggressive group		
	Scores	d	d^2	Scores	d	d^2
	3	−3	9	1	−1	1
	8	2	4	2	0	0
	9	3	9	2	0	0
	4	−2	4	2	0	0
				3	1	1
Sum	24		26	10		2
N	4			5		
Mean	6			2		
df			3			4
Variance			8.667			0.5

$$F = \frac{8.667}{0.5} = 17.33$$

Table 4.16 Part of the table of two-tailed 0.05 critical values of F

df_1	. . .	2	3	4	. . .
df_2					
.					
.					
.					
3		9.5521	9.2766	9.1172	
4		6.9443	6.5914	6.3882	
5		5.7861	5.4095	5.1922	
.					
.					
.					

value of 6.59, then we would have inferred that the variances of the two groups were equal.

The *F* distribution table, like many of the tables for the other test statistics described in this book, differs from the table for the standard normal distribution. It would be possible to present a table similar to the standard normal distribution for these other test statistics. However, since these distributions vary according to their degrees of freedom, we would have to present separate tables for different degrees of freedom. As we often need to look up the test statistic for various degrees of freedom, we would need to include a large number of such tables. However, since we are usually only interested in the critical values of a test statistic, most of this information would not be used. Consequently, to conserve space, we have only provided tables of certain critical values for these other test statistics. Note that if we had wanted to have a table containing only the 0.05 two-tailed critical value of z, then this table would have consisted of the sole value of 1.96 since a z of 1.96 cuts off a proportion of 0.025 (0.5 − 0.4750 = 0.025) at either end of the distribution, representing a two-tailed probability of 0.05 (0.025 × 2 = 0.05).

The F test statistic represents the probability of obtaining that statistic by chance for a specified pair of degrees of freedom. All distributions of F are skewed to the right but as the degrees of freedom increase, they begin to approximate the shape of the normal distribution. With 1 degree of freedom in the numerator (i.e. two groups) and infinite degrees of freedom in the denominator (i.e. an infinite number of cases), F is equal to z^2. We can illustrate this by selecting a z value of 1.96 which denotes a two-tailed probability of 0.05. The square of this value is 3.8416 (1.96 × 1.96 = 3.8416) which is virtually identical to that of 3.8415 shown in the table in Appendix 3 for a two-tailed 0.05 critical value of F with 1 degree of freedom in the numerator and infinite (∞) degrees of freedom in the denominator.

To compute with Minitab an F test for comparing the variances of the four aggressive and five non-aggressive individuals, we need to carry out the four steps below:

Step 1   Calculate for the two groups the standard deviations of the number of violent films seen with the following Minitab commands:

MTB > set c1
DATA > 3 8 9 4
DATA > end
MTB > set c2
DATA > 1 2 2 2 3
DATA > end
MTB > describe c1 c2

To do this with the menu system, first enter the data in columns 1 and 2 of the **Data** window. Then carry out these steps

→**Stat** →**Basic Statistics** →**Descriptive Statistics...** →**c1** →**Select** [**c1** will now appear in the **Variables:** box] →**c2** →**Select** [**c2** will now appear in the **Variables:** box below **c1**] →**OK**

The standard deviation for **c1** is **2.9439** and for **c2** is **0.70711**.

Step 2   Work out the variance by squaring the standard deviation, which is 8.667 for **c1** (**2.9439** × **2.9439** = 8.6667) and 0.50 for **c2** (**0.70711** × **0.70711** = 0.5000).

Step 3 Divide the larger variance by the smaller variance, which is 17.33 (8.667/0.50 = 17.334).

Step 4 Find the critical value of the *F* distribution with the requisite degrees of freedom by using the **invcdf** (**inv**erse **c**umulative **d**istribution function) command and the **f** subcommand. On the **invcdf** command the level of statistical significance is specified by subtracting that level from 1.00. So, for the 0.05 probability level the appropriate figure is 0.95 (1.00 − 0.05 = 0.95).

MTB > invcdf .95;

On the **f** subcommand, which provides critical values for the *F* distribution, the degrees of freedom for the numerator and denominator need to be respectively listed after the **f**. Therefore, the subcommand for finding the 0.05 two-tailed critical value of *F* with 3 and 4 degrees of freedom in the numerator and denominator respectively is

SUBC> f 3 4.

The output from this command first gives the inverse cumulative distribution function of **0.9500** followed by the critical *F* value of **6.5914**.

Since the critical *F* value cannot be produced with the menu system in Release 9, use the prompt system in the **Session** window. In Release 10 the critical *F* can be obtained as follows

→**Calc** →**Probability Distributions** →**F...** →**Inverse cumulative probability** →box beside **Numerator degrees of freedom:** and type **1** →box beside **Denominator degrees of freedom:** and type **1** →**Input constant:** →box beside it and in it type **.95** →**OK**

It may be more convenient to write a macro for carrying out the *F* test which could consist of the following commands:

stdev c1 k1
stdev c2 k2
let k3=k1*k1
let k4=k2*k2
let k5=k3/k4
let k6=k4/k3
print k5 k6
 # choose the larger value
invcdf .95;
f 3 4.

The value for **k5** is displayed as **17.3333**, which (to two decimal places) is the same as the 17.33 previously calculated.

In Releases 9 and 10, **if** conditional commands can be used in **gmacros** so that the command can request that if the variance in **k3** is greater than or equal to (**ge**) the variance in **k4**, **k3** is divided by **k4**; whereas if (**elseif**) **k3** is less than (**lt**) **k4**, **k4** is divided by **k3**. **If** procedures need to end with an **endif** command. Thus, the **gmacro** for conducting an *F* test could consist of the following commands:

```
gmacro
ftest.mac
stdev c1 k1
stdev c2 k2
let k3=k1*k1
let k4=k2*k2
if k3 ge k4
let k5=k3/k4
elseif k3 lt k4
let k5=k4/k3
endif
print k5
invcdf .95;
f 6 7.
endmacro
```

LEVENE'S TEST FOR EQUAL VARIANCES

When the data are not normally distributed, a more appropriate test for equality of variances is Levene's (1960) test. Levene's test is the *F* test of a *one-way analysis of variance* of the absolute deviation scores rather than the raw scores. Analysis of variance, often referred to by its abbreviated name ANOVA (*analysis of variance*), is used to compare the means of two or more groups and is essentially an *F* test in which estimates of variance are compared. In a one-way analysis of variance the *F* test compares the estimate of the variance between the groups (i.e. the *between-groups* estimated variance) against the estimate of the variance within the groups (i.e. the *within-groups* estimated variance) by dividing the former by the latter:

$$F = \frac{\text{between-groups estimated variance}}{\text{within-groups estimated variance}}$$

The between-groups estimated variance is based on the extent to which the means of the groups vary from the overall or *grand* mean of the groups, while the within-groups estimated variance reflects the degree to which the scores within each group differ from the mean of that group for all the groups. The between-groups estimated variance is often referred to as the *explained* variance since it is more likely to reflect the variance of the variable being investigated. The within-groups estimated variance, on the other hand, is often called the *error* variance (or sometimes the *residual* variance) as it is more likely to correspond to the variance of other factors which have not been measured or controlled. Consequently, if the between-groups variance is considerably greater than the within-groups variance, then this implies that the differences between the means are less likely to be due to chance error or variation. Note that this F ratio may also have values between 1 and 0 because the between-groups variance may be less than the within-groups variance. If the means of three groups were identical, then the F ratio would be zero.

We will begin by showing how to compute a one-way analysis of variance. We will then demonstrate how to calculate Levene's test. The steps in both procedures will be illustrated with the data in Table 4.14 of the number of violent films seen by four aggressive and five non-aggressive individuals.

One-way analysis of variance

A one-way analysis of variance may be computed with the following steps.

Step 1   Compute the between-groups estimated variance.

Step 1.1   Calculate the mean of each group, which is 6 for the aggressive group and 2 for the non-aggressive group.

Step 1.2   Calculate the overall or grand mean by adding the sum for each group and dividing by the total number of scores. Adding the sum for the aggressive group (24) to that for the non-aggressive group (10) gives a grand sum of 34 (24 + 10 = 34), which divided by the total number of scores (4 + 5 = 9) is 3.78 (34/9 = 3.777).

Step 1.3   Subtract the grand mean from each of the group means, square this difference, multiply this squared difference by the number of cases within that group and sum these products for all the groups (giving what is known as the between-groups *sum of squares* or *SS*). For our example, doing this gives a between-groups sum of squares of 35.57:

$$[(6-3.78)^2 \times 4] + [(2-3.78)^2 \times 5] =$$
$$(2.22^2 \times 4) + (1.78^2 \times 5) = (4.93 \times 4) + (3.17 \times 5) =$$
$$19.72 + 15.85 = 35.57$$

Step 1.4   Divide the between-groups sum of squares by its degrees of freedom, which is the number of groups minus 1 (to form the between-groups *mean square* or *MS*). Since the between-groups degrees of freedom is 1 (2 − 1 = 2), the between-groups mean square remains 35.57 (35.57/1 = 35.57).

Step 2   Compute the within-groups mean square.

Step 2.1   To calculate the within-groups sum of squares, subtract the group mean from the individual score in the group, square this difference and add these squared differences across all the groups. Doing this for our data gives a within-groups sum of squares of 28:

$$(3\text{-}6)^2+(8\text{-}6)^2+(9-6)^2+(4-6)^2+(1-2)^2+(2-2)^2+(2-2)^2+$$
$$(2-2)^2+(3-2)^2 = 3^2+2^2+3^2+2^2+1^2+0^2+0^2+0^2+1^2 =$$
$$9+4+9+4+1+0+0+0+1 = 28$$

Step 2.2   Divide the within-groups sum of squares by its degrees of freedom, which is 1 from the number of cases within each group for each group summed across all groups. The within-groups degrees of freedom are 7:

$$(4 - 1) + (5 - 1) = 3 + 4 = 7$$

Therefore, the within-groups mean square is 4 (28/7 = 4).

Step 3   Compute the *F* ratio by dividing the between-groups mean square by the within-groups mean square, which gives an *F* ratio of 8.89 (35.57/4 = 8.89).

Step 4   Look up the statistical significance of this *F* ratio in the table in Appendix 3. As already mentioned, the degrees of freedom for the between-groups mean square are the number of groups minus 1 while for the within-groups mean square they are the number of cases within each group minus 1 summed across all groups. The degrees of freedom are 1 for the between-groups mean square (or the numerator of the *F* ratio) and 7 for the within-groups mean square (or the denominator of the *F* ratio). With these degrees of freedom the *F* value has to be 5.5914 or greater to be significant at the 0.05 level which it is. Consequently, in this case we would conclude that there was a statistically significant difference in the mean number of violent films watched by the two groups and that the mean number of violent films watched by the aggressive group was significantly greater than that seen by the non-aggressive group.

The results of this one-way analysis of variance can be summarised in the table shown in Table 4.17.

With the Minitab prompt system a one-way analysis of variance is computed with the **aovoneway** command. To analyse the data for this example, put the data of the aggressive and the non-aggressive group in **c1** and **c2** respectively and type the following command:

MTB > aovoneway c1 c2

The menu sequence for a one-way analysis of variance is

Table 4.17 One-way analysis of variance table

Sources of variation	df	SS	MS	F
Between-groups	1	35.57	35.57	8.89
Within-groups	7	28.00	4.00	
Total	8	63.57		

→**Stat** →**ANOVA** →**Oneway (Unstacked)...** →**c1** →**Select** [this puts **c1** in the box below **Responses (in separate columns):**] →**c2** →**Select** [this puts **c2** below **c1** in the same box] →**OK**

The output for this procedure is displayed in Table 4.18. In the analysis of variance table produced by Minitab the between-groups source of variation is called **FACTOR** and the within-groups source **ERROR**. The Minitab output also gives the exact probability (**p**) for the F value, which is **0.020**. In other words, the means of these two groups are significantly different.

Levene's test

In carrying out Levene's test, we first find the absolute deviation of scores by subtracting the group mean from the individual scores in that group. We then perform a one-way analysis of variance on these absolute deviations. We will illustrate the calculation of Levene's test with the data on the number of violent films watched by the aggressive and non-aggressive people previously used. The raw scores, absolute deviations and some of the computations needed for calculating a one-way analysis of variance are shown in Table 4.19.

Table 4.18 **Aovoneway** output

ANALYSIS OF VARIANCE

SOURCE	DF	SS	MS	F	p
FACTOR	1	35.56	35.56	8.89	0.020
ERROR	7	28.00	4.00		
TOTAL	8	63.56			

```
                                  INDIVIDUAL 95 PCT CI'S FOR
                                  MEAN BASED ON POOLED STDEV
LEVEL   N   MEAN   STDEV   -+-------+-------+-------+---
C1      4   6.000  2.944                    (-------*-------)
C2      5   2.000  0.707    (------*------)
                           -+-------+-------+-------+---

POOLED STDEV =  2.000       0.0     2.5     5.0     7.5
```

Table 4.19 Computations for Levene's test

	Aggressive group				Non-aggressive group			
	Scores	d	dd	dd²	Scores	d	dd	dd²
	3	3	0.5	0.25	1	1	0.6	0.36
	8	2	0.5	0.25	2	0	0.4	0.16
	9	3	0.5	0.25	2	0	0.4	0.16
	4	2	0.5	0.25	2	0	0.4	0.16
					3	1	0.6	0.36
Sum		10				2		
N		4				5		
Mean		2.5				0.4		
df				3				4

Step 1   Compute the between-groups estimated variance.

Step 1.1   Calculate the mean of the absolute deviations in each group, which is 2.5 for the aggressive group and 0.4 for the non-aggressive group.

Step 1.2   Calculate the grand mean by adding the sum of absolute deviations for each group and dividing by the total number of scores. Adding the sum for the aggressive group (10) to that for the non-aggressive group (2) gives a grand sum of 12 (10 + 2 = 12), which divided by the total number of scores (4 + 5 = 9) is 1.33 (12/9 = 1.333).

Step 1.3   Subtract the grand mean from each of the group means, square this difference, multiply this squared difference by the number of cases within that group and sum these products for all the groups (giving what is known as the between-groups *sum of squares* or *SS*). For our example, doing this gives a between-groups sum of squares of 9.78:

$$[(2.5-1.33)^2 \times 4 + (0.4-1.33)^2 \times 5)] =$$
$$(1.17^2 \times 4) + (-0.93^2 \times 5) = (1.37 \times 4) + (0.86 \times 5) =$$
$$5.48 + 4.30 = 9.78$$

Step 1.4   Divide the between-groups sum of squares by its degrees of freedom, which is the number of groups minus 1 (to form the between-groups *mean square* or *MS*). Since the between-groups degrees of freedom is 1 (2 − 1 = 2), the between-groups mean square remains 9.78 (9.78/1 = 9.78).

Step 2   Compute the within-groups mean square.

Step 2.1   To calculate the within-groups sum of squares, subtract the mean absolute deviation of the group from each individual absolute deviation (*dd*) within this group, square this difference (*dd²*) and add these squared differences across all the groups. Doing this for our data gives a within-groups sum of squares of 2.2:

$$(3-2.5)^2+(2-2.5)^2+(3-2.5)^2+(2-2.5)^2+(1-0.4)^2+$$
$$(0-0.4)^2+(0-0.4)^2+(0-0.4)^2+(1-0.4)^2 =$$
$$0.5^2+0.5^2+0.5^2+0.5^2+0.6^2+0.4^2+0.4^2+0.4^2+0.6^2 =$$
$$0.25+0.25+0.25+0.25+0.36+0.16+0.16+0.16+0.36 = 2.2$$

Step 2.2   Divide the within-groups sum of squares by its degrees of freedom, which is 1 from the number of cases within each group for each group summed across all groups. The within-groups degrees of freedom are 7:

$$(4 - 1) + (5 - 1) = 3 + 4 = 7$$

Therefore, the within-groups mean square is 0.314 (2.2/7 = 0.314).

Step 3   Compute the F ratio by dividing the between-groups mean square by the within-groups mean square, which gives an F ratio of 31.15 (9.78/0.314 = 31.146).

Step 4   Look up the statistical significance of this F ratio in the table in Appendix 3. As already mentioned, the degrees of freedom for the between-groups mean square are the number of groups minus 1 while for the within-groups mean square they are the number of cases within each group minus 1 summed across all groups. The degrees of freedom are 1 for the between-groups mean square (or the numerator of the F ratio) and 7 for the within-groups mean square (or the denominator of the F ratio). With these degrees of freedom the F value has to be 5.5914 or greater to be significant at the 0.05 level which it is. Consequently, we would conclude that the variances of the two groups were unequal since they were significantly different.

The results of this Levene's test are summarised in Table 4.20.

Minitab Release 8 and 9 does not have a specific command for carrying out Levene's test, so we first have to create the absolute deviation scores. If the data of the aggressive and the non-aggressive group are put in **c1** and **c2** respectively, we can find their absolute deviation scores with the following commands:

Table 4.20 One-way analysis of variance table for Levene's test

Sources of variation	df	SS	MS	F
Between-groups	1	9.78	9.78	31.15
Within-groups	7	2.20	0.31	
Total	8	11.98		

Table 4.21 **Aovoneway** output using absolute deviation scores

ANALYSIS OF VARIANCE

SOURCE	DF	SS	MS	F	p
FACTOR	1	9.800	9.800	31.18	0.000
ERROR	7	2.200	0.314		
TOTAL	8	12.000			

				INDIVIDUAL 95 PCT CI'S FOR MEAN BASED ON POOLED STDEV			
LEVEL	N	MEAN	STDEV	-+-------+-------+-------+---			
C3	4	2.5000	0.5774				(-------*-------)
C4	5	0.4000	0.5477	(----*----)			
				-+-------+-------+-------+---			
POOLED STDEV = 0.5606				0.0	1.0	2.0	3.0

mean c1 k1
mean c2 k2
let c3=absolute(c1 −k1)
let c4=absolute(c2 −k2)

We then carry out a one-way analysis of variance on **c3** and **c4** with the following command:

aovoneway c3 c4

The output from this analysis is shown in Table 4.21. The **p** level of **0.000** means that the *p* value of obtaining an *F* value of **31.18** is less than 0.0005.

Levene's test can be performed with Release 10 using the **%vartest** command. To carry out this test, first create two new columns. The first new column **c3** consists of **c1** stacked on top of **c2** and consists of the number of violent films seen by both groups

MTB > stack c1 c2 c3

The menu action for stacking is:

→**Manip** →**Stack...** →**c1** →**Select** [this puts **c1** in the first box below **Stack the following blocks:**] →second box under **Stack the following blocks:** →**c2** →**Select** [this puts **c2** in this box] →box under **Store results in blocks:** and in it type **c3** →**OK**

The second new column **c4** is set up to identify which of the values in **c3** come from the aggressive group (coded **1**) and which come from the non-aggressive group (coded **2**). There are four **1**'s and five **2**'s:

MTB > set c4
DATA> 1 1 1 1 2 2 2 2 2
DATA> end

Table 4.22 **%vartest** output showing the results of Levene's test

---

Executing from file: C:\MTBWIN10\MACROS\vartest.MAC
Macro is running . . . please wait
Homogeneity of Variance

Response C2
Factors C1
ConfLvl 95.0000

Bonferroni confidence intervals for standard deviations

Lower	Sigma	Upper	n	Factor Levels
1.54720	2.94392	13.9424	4	1
0.39588	0.70711	2.4463	5	2

Bartlett's Test (normal distribution)
Test Statistic: 5.230
p value   : 0.022

Levene's Test (any continuous distribution)
Test Statistic: 31.182
p value   : 0.001

The command for executing Levene's test on these two new columns is:

MTB > %vartest c3 c4

The dependent variable **c3** is listed first followed by the independent variable **c4**.

The menu sequence for doing this is

→**S**tat →**B**asic Statistics →**H**omogeneity of Variance...→**c3** →**Select** [this puts **c3** in the box beside **R**esponse:] →**c4** →**Select** [this puts **c4** in the box beside **F**actors:] →**OK**

The output from this command is shown in Table 4.22. The value of Levene's test is **31.182** which is statistically significant at the **0.001** or less.

SUMMARY

One of the principal uses of statistics in the social sciences is to determine the probability of a finding occurring by chance. Results having a probability of happening at or less than 0.05 (i.e. 1 out of 20) are considered to be statistically significant and are thought to be unlikely to be due to chance. Where the direction of the results has been predicted before the data have been analysed a one-tailed probability level is used and where the direction of the results has not been predicted beforehand a two-tailed probability level is employed. A number of different statistical tests exist for determining the size and often the probability of an association between two or more variables and the probability of a difference between two or more groups. Which test to use depends primarily on whether the data are categorical or not, and if the data are not categorical whether their variances are equal and their distributions normal. Non-parametric or distribution-free tests are used for analysing categorical data or non-categorical data whose variances are unequal and whose distributions are non-normal. Parametric tests are applied to non-categorical data whose variances are equal and whose distributions are normal. Tests of skewness and kurtosis assess whether distributions are normal. To find out whether variances are equal, the F test should be used with normal distributions and Levene's test with non-normal distributions. The F test is the greater variance of one group divided by the smaller variance of the other. Levene's test is the F test of a one-way analysis of variance of the absolute deviation scores.

EXERCISES

1 Toss a coin six times. What is the probability of finding the particular outcome obtained?

2 There are 10 women and 10 men in a room. The first 3 people selected are women. What is the probability of this outcome?

3 There are 15 women and 5 men in a room. The first 3 people selected are women. What is the probability of this outcome?

4 A test of general knowledge consists of 50 statements, half of which are true and half of which are false. One point is awarded for each correct answer. What is the most likely score on this test for someone who has no general knowledge?

5 The probability value of a finding was 0.15. Is the finding statistically significant?

6 It is predicted that two groups in a study will differ significantly. Should a one- or a two-tailed probability level be used?

7 Does the skewness and kurtosis of this distribution of scores differ from normality?

 5   3   1   2   1   2   3   4   2

(a) What is the value of its skewness (to three decimal places)?
(b) What is the standard error of its skewness (to three decimal places)?
(c) What is its z value?
(d) What is the one-tailed probability of this value?
(e) What is the two-tailed probability of this value?
(f) Is the distribution symmetrical, positively or negatively skewed?
(g) What is the value of its kurtosis?

(h) What is the standard error of its kurtosis?
(i) What is its z value?
(j) What is the one-tailed probability of this value?
(k) What is the two-tailed probability of this value?
(l) Is the kurtosis mesokurtic, leptokurtic or platykurtic?

8 Determine for these two groups of scores whether their variances differ significantly using the F test and Levene's test.

Group A	Group B
2	1
3	9
2	2
2	8
3	

(a) What is the F ratio (to two decimal places)?
(b) What are the degrees of freedom for the numerator?
(c) What are the degrees of freedom for the denominator?
(d) What is its probability level?
(e) Do the two variances differ significantly?
(f) What is the F value of Levene's test?
(g) What is its probability level?
(h) Do the two variances differ significantly?

Chapter 5

Tests of difference for categorical data

The statistical tests covered in this chapter only apply to data in which the number of cases falling into various categories is simply counted. The tests determine whether the frequency of cases in the different categories varies across one or more groups or from some expected distribution. We would use these tests to answer the following kinds of questions. Is the number of women who have watched a violent film in the past week significantly less than the number of men who did so? Is the number of people who have watched a violent film in the past week significantly greater in the United States than in the United Kingdom? Are people who have watched a violent film in one week also significantly more likely to have viewed a violent film in the following week? Note that the variable of whether or not a person has seen a violent film in the past week is categorical in the sense that a person either has or has not seen such a film. This variable is not the number of violent films a person has seen in the past week which would be a ratio scale measure.

BINOMIAL TEST FOR ONE SAMPLE

The binomial test determines whether the number of cases that fall into one of only two categories differs significantly from some expected proportion. Suppose, for instance, we know that there are equal numbers of women and men in the population and that of a small sample of five people all five were women. On the basis of these figures, can we assume that in terms of gender our sample represents the population? The binomial test can be used to answer this question, the only two categories being women and men.

The following formula can be used for calculating the probability of obtaining a particular number of cases in categories A and B:

$$\frac{\text{total number of cases } (N)!}{\text{number of A } (n)! \times \text{number of B } (N-n)!} \times \text{probability of A}^n \times \text{probability of B}^{N-n}$$

where the exclamation mark (!) signifies a *factorial* expression. For example, $N!$ means $N \times (N - 1) \times (N - 2) \ldots N \times [N - (N - 1)]$.

We can illustrate the use of this formula to find out what the probability is of obtaining five females ($n = 5$) in a sample of five ($N = 5$) when the probability of obtaining a woman is 0.5 and the probability of obtaining a man is therefore also 0.5. Inserting the relevant values into the above formula, we see that the probability of obtaining a sample of five women and no men is 0.031:

$$\frac{5!}{5! \times (5-5)!} \times 0.5^5 \times 0.5^{5-5} =$$

$$\frac{5!}{5!} \times 0.03125 \ (\times \ 0) = \frac{5 \times 4 \times 3 \times 2 \times 1}{5 \times 4 \times 3 \times 2 \times 1} \times 0.03125 =$$

$$1 \times 0.03125 = 0.03125$$

The probability of obtaining a sample of four women and one man is 0.156:

$$\frac{5!}{4! \times (5-4)!} \times 0.5^4 \times 0.5^{5-4} =$$

$$\frac{5!}{4! \times 1!} \times 0.0625 \times 0.5 = \frac{5 \times 4 \times 3 \times 2 \times 1}{4 \times 3 \times 2 \times 1 \times 1} \times 0.03125 =$$

$$5 \times 0.03125 = 0.15625$$

Consequently, the probability of obtaining five women and no men as well as four women and one man is the sum of their separate probabilities which is the cumulative probability of 0.188 (0.03125 + 0.15625 = 0.1875).

If the size of the sample is less than 26 and the probability of obtaining either outcome is 0.5, we can look up the cumulative probability of finding a particular outcome in the table in Appendix 4. To use the table we need to know the size of the sample (which is represented by N and which in this case is 5) and the smaller of the two frequencies (which is indicated by n and which is 0 for men). The size of the sample being investigated is given in the left-hand column of the table and varies from 1 to 25, while the smaller frequency is presented along the top row of the table and ranges from 0 to 15.

Reading from the table, the relevant part of which has been reproduced in Table 5.1, we can see that the probability of obtaining five women and no men is 0.031. Incidentally, this figure is identical to that worked out in the previous chapter for the same problem. The probability values in this

Table 5.1 Part of the binomial test one-tailed probabilities table

N\n	0	1	2	. . . 15
4	0.062	0.312	0.687	
5	*0.031*	0.188	0.500	
6	0.016	0.109	0.344	
.				
.				
.				
25				

table are one-tailed. Since we have not specified the direction of the results we expected to find, a two-tailed probability level is more appropriate. To obtain this, we simply double the one-tailed level which gives a two-tailed probability of 0.062 ($0.031 \times 2 = 0.062$). Since the figure of 0.062 is larger than 0.05, we would conclude that our sample of five women does not differ significantly from the expected proportion of women in the population which is 0.5. Note also that the probability of a sample of five women and one or no men is 0.188, which is the same as the figure previously calculated.

If the size of our sample is larger than 25 and the probability of obtaining either outcome is near to 0.5, then the binomial distribution tends to be similar to the normal distribution which may be used instead. So, to determine the probability of a particular outcome under these circumstances, we calculate the z value of finding this result by using the following formula:

$$z = \frac{\text{smaller frequency} - (\text{number of cases} \times \text{expected probability of one category})}{\sqrt{(\text{number of cases} \times \text{expected probability of one category} \times \text{expected probability of other category})}}$$

Suppose that 30 of the 40 people in our sample were female. On the basis of these figures, could we argue that with respect to gender our sample was representative of the population? To work out whether this is the case, we need to substitute the following numbers into the formula:

$$\frac{10 - (40 \times 0.5)}{\sqrt{40 \times 0.5 \times 0.5}} = \frac{-10}{3.162} = -3.16$$

The category with the smaller frequency is men, of which there are 10. The expected probability of sampling either a man or a woman is 0.5 and the total number of people in the sample is 40. To determine the statistical significance of this z value, we ignore its sign and look it up in the table in Appendix 2 where we see that the probability of this value occurring by chance is 0.0009.

The normal distribution is based on a continuous variable (consisting of non-whole numbers) whereas the binomial distribution assumes a discrete variable (comprising whole numbers). The binomial distribution can be made more similar to the normal distribution when a correction for continuity is included. This is done by presupposing that the frequency of cases in the smaller category (e.g. 10) occupies an interval, the lower limit of which is half a unit (0.5) below its observed value (10 − 0.5 = 9.5) while its upper limit is half a unit (0.5) above it (10 + 0.5 = 10.5). The correction for continuity consists of reducing by 0.5 the difference between the observed value of the smaller category (10) and its expected value (40 × 0.5 = 20). So, in this case, where the observed frequency (10) is less than the expected frequency (20), we would add 0.5 to 10. If we substitute this new value in the formula for calculating z, we would obtain a z value of −3.00:

$$\frac{10.5 - 20}{3.162} = \frac{-9.5}{3.162} = -3.00$$

Looking up this figure in the table in Appendix 2, we see that the probability of obtaining this result at the one-tailed level is slightly higher at 0.0013 which when doubled gives a two-tailed level of 0.0026. Consequently, we would conclude that the proportion of women in our sample was significantly greater than that in the population.

With the Minitab prompt system, the binomial test can be calculated with the **cdf** command (which stands for **c**umulative **d**istribution **f**unction) and the **binomial** subcommand. On the **cdf** command specify the smaller of the two frequencies, which is **0** men for our first example, followed by a semicolon:

MTB > cdf 0;

On the **binomial** subcommand, type **binomial** followed by the total number of cases in the sample (which is **5** in this example), the expected probability of obtaining the more frequent value (which is **.5**) and a full stop:

SUBC> binomial 5 .5.

The menu sequence for running a binomial test is:

→**Calc** →**Probability** **Distributions** →**Binomial** . . . →**Probability** [as this is the default it is already selected] →box beside **Number of trials:** and type in the sample size [e.g. 5] →box beside **Probability of success:** and type in probability of obtaining the less frequent category [e.g. .5] →**Input constant:** →box beside it and in it type the frequency of that category [e.g. 0] →**OK**

The output displays the value of the smaller frequency (**K**) and the probability of obtaining that outcome (**P**) as follows:

K   P(X LESS OR = K)
0.00   0.0313

The commands for determining the probability of a sample of five having one or no men are:

MTB > cdf 1;
SUBC> binomial 5 .5.

and the output is:

K   P(X LESS OR = K)
1.00   0.1875

The commands for calculating the probability of a sample of 40 containing 10 or fewer men are:

MTB > cdf 10;
SUBC> binomial 40 .5.

and the resulting output is:

K   P(X LESS OR = K)
10.00   0.0011

Note that the binomial probability of **0.0011** is similar to the previously determined z values of 0.0013 (corrected for continuity) and 0.0009 (uncorrected for continuity).

CHI-SQUARE TEST FOR ONE OR MORE UNRELATED SAMPLES

The Pearson chi-square (pronounced 'ky-square' and symbolised as χ^2) test compares the observed frequency of cases against the expected frequency for one or more unrelated samples on a variable which may have two or more categories. It does this for each category of the sample. The closer the expected number is to the observed number across all categories, the less likely it is that any difference between the observed and expected frequency is statistically significant. The general formula for calculating chi-square is:

$$\text{chi-square} = \text{sum of} \quad \frac{(\text{observed frequency} - \text{expected frequency})^2}{\text{expected frequency}} \quad \text{for each category}$$

Note, however, that many textbooks on statistics suggest that chi-square should only be used when the expected frequency is not too small. The reason for this restriction is that the distribution of the chi-square statistic, like the normal distribution, is a smooth, continuous curve. Observed frequencies, however, change in discrete steps, such as from 1 to 2 and 2 to 3. Discrepancies between the smooth distribution of chi-square and the steplike distribution of frequencies are likely to be bigger when the frequencies are small.

Based on the recommendations of Cochran (1954), Siegel in his influential text on non-parametric statistics (Siegel 1956; Siegel and Castellan 1988) suggested that, with two categories from one sample, the minimum expected frequency in either category should be 5. If one or both of the expected frequencies is less than 5, the binomial test should be used. In the case of one sample with three or more categories, chi-square should not be used when any expected frequency is less than 1 or when more than 20 per cent of the expected frequencies are smaller than 5. This restriction also applies to the following two situations: (1) two samples with a variable of three or more categories; and (2) three or more samples with a variable of only two categories. In all three of these cases, it may be possible to increase the expected frequencies in a category by combining it with those of another. Siegel's suggestions for the special case of two samples with a variable of two categories will be discussed when we present this case later on.

CHI-SQUARE TEST FOR ONE SAMPLE

Because it is the simplest, we will begin by describing the calculation of chi-square for two categories from one sample. Suppose, for instance, we wish to determine whether a sample of 20 women and no men differs significantly from an expected proportion of 0.5 for women. This question is the same as wanting to know whether gender in this sample is representative of that in a population in which the proportion of women is known to be 0.5. Computing chi-square involves carrying out the following six steps:

Step 1 Calculate the expected frequency for each cell. Since the expected proportion of women is 0.5 and the total number of cases in the sample is 20, then the expected frequency of women should be 10 (0.5 × 20 = 10). Similarly, the expected frequency of men is 10 (0.5 × 20 = 10). The observed and expected frequencies for this example are shown in Table 5.2.

Step 2 Subtract the expected frequency from the observed frequency for each cell and square the difference. The differences are squared to remove the minus values. If this was not done the sum of differences would equal zero since the sum of negative differences is equal to the sum of positive differences.

Table 5.2 Observed and expected frequency for one sample of two categories

Frequencies	Women	Men
Observed	20	0
Expected	10	10

Step 3   Divide the squared difference by the expected frequency of that cell (to take account of the expected size of that cell). Note that in this case the expected frequencies are the same although this is often not the case.

Step 4   Add together the results for all the cells.

Applying Steps 2 to 4, we see that chi-square is 20:

$$\frac{(20-10)^2}{10} + \frac{(0-10)^2}{10} = \frac{10^2}{10} + \frac{-10^2}{10} = \frac{100}{10} + \frac{100}{10} = 10 + 10 = 20$$

Note that if we had not squared the difference between the observed and expected difference, chi-square would be equal to 0 since the sum of the negative differences equals the sum of the positive differences:

$$\frac{(20-10)}{10} + \frac{(0-10)}{10} = \frac{10}{10} + \frac{-10}{10} = 1 + -1 = 0$$

Note also that it does not matter whether we subtract the expected frequency from the observed frequency (observed frequency − expected frequency), as shown in the above formula, or the observed frequency from the expected frequency (expected frequency − observed frequency) provided that we adopt one or other order for the test:

$$\frac{(10-20)^2}{10} + \frac{(10-0)^2}{10} = \frac{-10^2}{10} + \frac{10^2}{10} = \frac{100}{10} + \frac{100}{10} = 10 + 10 = 20$$

Step 5   Calculate the degrees of freedom for a one sample chi-square which is the number of categories minus 1. In this case the degree of freedom is 1 ($2 - 1 = 1$).

Step 6   Look up the value of chi-square against the appropriate degrees of freedom in the table in Appendix 5, part of which has been reproduced in Table 5.3. We see that for chi-square with 1 degree of freedom to be statistically significant at the two-tailed 0.05 level, it has to be 3.84 or bigger. Since our chi-square value of 20 is larger than 3.84, we would conclude that the number of women in this sample is significantly greater than the expected proportion of 0.5.

A number of other points should be noted about chi-square at this stage.

Table 5.3 Part of the chi-square two-tailed critical values table

	Level of significance		
df	0.10	0.05	0.01
1	2.71	3.84	6.64
2	4.60	5.99	9.21
3	6.25	7.82	11.34
.			
.			
.			
30	40.26	43.77	50.89

Chi-square is 0 when the observed frequency is exactly the same as the expected frequency.

$$\frac{(10-10)^2}{10} + \frac{(10-10)^2}{10} = \frac{0^2}{10} + \frac{0^2}{10} = \frac{0}{10} + \frac{0}{10} = 0 + 0 = 0$$

The larger chi-square is for the same number of categories, the more likely it is to be statistically significant since this means that the difference between the observed and expected frequencies is bigger.

Other things being equal, the larger the sample, the bigger chi-square is and so the more likely it is to statistically significant. This can be illustrated with the three samples of data shown in Table 5.4. If there is a real difference in the observed frequency between two categories, then this difference as a proportion of the total frequency should remain the same for different sized samples. In Table 5.4 the proportional difference has been set at 0.2 for Sample 1 (4/20 = 0.2), Sample 2 (8/40 = 0.2) and Sample 3 (16/80 = 0.2). If we calculate chi-square for the three samples of data, we see that as the sample size doubles from 20 to 40 to 80, so chi-square doubles from 0.8 to 1.6 to 3.2. As the size of the sample increases, so the exact probability of finding such a difference by chance decreases from 0.37 to 0.20 to 0.07. In other words, this proportional difference would be statistically significant at the one-tailed level in Sample 3

Table 5.4 Chi-square and sample size

	Sample 1		Sample 2		Sample 3	
Obs freq	12	8	24	16	48	32
Exp freq	10	10	20	20	40	40
Sample size		20		40		80
Proportional difference	4/20 = 0.2		8/40 = 0.2		16/80 = 0.2	
Chi-square		0.80		1.60		3.20
Exact *p*		0.37		0.20		0.07

(0.07/2 = 0.035) where it is not significant at either the one- or two-tailed level for Samples 1 (0.37/2 = 0.185) and 2 (0.20/2 = 0.10).

Because chi-square sums the squared difference between the observed and the expected frequencies, it is likely to be bigger with more categories. Consequently, the critical values of chi-square are adjusted for the number of categories which is done through the degrees of freedom.

The distribution of chi-square, like the distribution of most of the other test statistics described in this text, is determined by the degrees of freedom and is unique for each such number. In chi-square the degrees of freedom refer to the number of categories and not the number of cases. With only two categories, chi-square has one degree of freedom because if the total frequency is known and the frequency of one of the categories (which is free to vary) is also known, then the frequency of the other category is fixed. For example, if the total frequency is 20 and the frequency of one of the categories is 15, then the frequency of the other category must be 5 (20 − 15 = 5). With three categories, chi-square has two degrees of freedom because if the total frequency and the frequency of two of the categories are known, then the frequency of the third category is fixed. For instance, if the total frequency is 60, and the frequencies of the two categories free to vary are 10 and 20, then the frequency of the third category is fixed at 30 (60 − 10 − 20 = 30).

Chi-square with one degree of freedom is related to the standard normal curve in that it is equal to z^2. For example, looking at the table in Appendix 2, we see that a z value of 1.96 cuts off a proportion of 0.025 (0.5 − 0.4750 = 0.025) at either end of the distribution which means that this z value represents a two-tailed probability of 0.05. The square of 1.96 is 3.84 which is the same value as a two-tailed chi-square with one degree of freedom.

Up to 30 degrees of freedom, the chi-square distribution is skewed to the right. As the degrees of freedom increase, it becomes more symmetrical and begins to look like the normal curve with more than 30 degrees of freedom.

The chi-square test is, in effect, non-directional because all differences between observed and expected frequencies are squared making them all positive. In other words, any negative differences (e.g. fewer men than expected) are made positive by squaring. Consequently, observed frequencies which lie in one direction (e.g. fewer men than expected) are combined with observed frequencies which lie in the other direction (e.g. more women than expected) so that it is not possible to distinguish the direction of any difference. The critical values for chi-square are two-tailed in the sense that the test is non-directional. However, in the case of one sample with only two categories it is possible to determine whether the difference obtained is in the predicted direction because there are only two cells. So, for example, we can tell whether there are more women than men. Con-

Table 5.5 Expected frequency of marital status in a sample based on observed proportion in the population

Marital status	Frequency		
	Population proportion	Sample	
		Observed n	Expected n
Never married	0.20	30	0.20 × 100 = 20
Married	0.70	50	0.70 × 100 = 70
Divorced/ separated	0.05	10	0.05 × 100 = 5
Widowed	0.05	10	0.05 × 100 = 5
Total	1.00	100	100

sequently, in this case it is possible to use a one-tailed level by dividing the two-tailed critical value by 2. If we do this for our example above, we can conclude that the statistical significance of our finding at the one-tailed level has a probability of less than 0.025 (0.5/2 = 0.025). The chi-square test may also be directional (and hence one-tailed) in two samples with only two categories in each, as we shall explain when we discuss this case.

When a sample has three or more categories, the chi-square test is non-directional. Suppose, for example, that we were interested in whether the distribution of marital status of our sample of 100 adults differed from that of the population. As shown in Table 5.5, the proportion of the never married, the married, the divorced/separated and the widowed in the population was 0.20, 0.70, 0.50 and 0.50 respectively while our sample consisted of 30 never married, 50 married, 10 divorced/separated and 10 widowed individuals. If the distribution of marital status in the sample is the same as that in the population, then we can work out that the expected number of people in our sample who are single, married, divorced/separated and widowed is 20 (0.20 × 100 = 20), 70 (0.70 × 50 = 70), 5 (0.05 × 100 = 5) and 5 (0.05 × 100 = 5) respectively.

Since the expected frequency of both the divorced/separated and widowed in our sample is less than 10, it would be inappropriate to apply chi-square. To carry out chi-square we could either omit them from the analysis or, if we can justify this, group them either together or with other categories so that no category would have an expected frequency of less than 10. To demonstrate this procedure, we have grouped the divorced/separated and the widowed categories together into the formerly married. The expected frequency of this combined category is 10 (0.10 × 100 = 10) and its observed frequency 20 (10 + 10 = 20). Chi-square for these three groups is 20.71:

$$\frac{(30-20)^2}{20} + \frac{(50-70)^2}{70} + \frac{(20-10)^2}{10} = \frac{10^2}{20} + \frac{-20^2}{70} + \frac{10^2}{10} =$$

$$\frac{100}{20} + \frac{400}{70} + \frac{100}{10} = 5 + 5.71 + 10 = 20.71$$

We can use this example, where the expected frequencies for categories differ, to illustrate the reason for and the effect of dividing the squared difference between the observed and expected frequencies by the expected frequency. What this does is to weight the squared difference by the expected frequency so that the same squared difference has a smaller effect on chi-square when the expected frequency is greater. For instance, the squared difference between the observed and expected frequency for the never married is 100 $[(30-20)^2 = 10^2 = 100]$ which is the same size as the squared difference between the observed and expected frequency for the formerly married $[(20-10)^2 = 10^2 = 100]$. However, since the expected frequency of the never married (20) is greater than that of the formerly married (10), the contribution to chi-square of the difference for the never married (100/20 = 5) is less than that for the formerly married (100/10 = 10). If we had not weighted the differences according to expected frequency, both differences would have made the same contribution.

Looking at the table in Appendix 5, we can see that the 0.01 two-tailed critical value of chi-square with 2 (3 − 1 = 2) degrees of freedom is 9.21. Since the chi-square value of 20.71 for our sample is greater than this critical value, we can conclude that the distribution of marital status in our sample differs significantly from that in the population. Note that we cannot use a one-tailed test in this case where there are more than two categories because, even if we had predicted that there would be proportionately more never married people in our sample than in the population, the test compares the distribution of the observed and expected frequency across all three categories and so does not tell us which differences are significant.

Minitab does not perform a one-way chi-square. However, we could calculate a one-way chi-square test for two or more categories (such as in our last example) in the following way.

Step 1 Put the observed values in one column (e.g. **c1**) and the expected values in another column (e.g. **c2**).

MTB > set c1
DATA> 30 50 20
DATA> end
MTB > set c2
DATA> 20 70 10
DATA> end

Step 2 Calculate the squared difference between the observed and expected frequency as a proportion for each cell, sum these squared differences and store the sum in the first row of another column (e.g. **c1**):

MTB > let c1=sum((c1-c2)**2/c2)

Step 3 To work out the statistical significance of the obtained chi-square at the 0.05 two-tailed level, use the **invcdf** command followed by the **chisquare** subcommand. On the **invcdf** command the level of statistical significance is specified by subtracting that level from 1.00. So, for the 0.05 probability level the appropriate figure is 0.95 (1.00 − 0.05 = 0.95):

MTB > invcdf .95;

On the **chisquare** subcommand, which gives critical values for the chi-square distribution, the appropriate degrees of freedom are listed after the keyword **chisquare**. Therefore, the subcommand for finding the 0.05 two-tailed critical value of chi-square with 2 degrees of freedom is

SUBC> chisquare 2.

The output from this command first gives the inverse cumulative distribution function of **0.9500** followed by the critical chi-square value of **5.9915**. As the chi-square value we obtained, which was **20.7143**, is larger than the critical value of **5.9915**, we would conclude that the frequencies differed significantly from those expected by chance at less than the two-tailed 0.05 level.

The menu action for finding the critical value of chi-square is

→**Calc** →**Probability** **Distribution** →**Chisquare** . . . →**Inverse cumulative probability** →box beside **Degrees of freedom** and type degrees of freedom [e.g. **2**] in it →box beside **Input constant:** and in it type the cumulative probability level [e.g. **.95**] →**OK**

MULTIPLE COMPARISON TESTS FOR THREE OR MORE GROUPS

With three categories or groups, we can compare three pairs of groups (i.e. 1 *vs* 2, 1 *vs* 3 and 2 *vs* 3). The major problem with this approach is that the more pairwise comparisons we make on the same set of data, the more likely it is that one of these comparisons will be statistically significant. In other words, the probability of making a Type I error (finding a difference when there is none) increases with the number of comparisons. For example, if we make one comparison, the probability of finding a statistically significant difference at the 0.05 critical level by chance is 5 out of 100 or 1 out of 20. The rate of making this type of error is known as the *per comparison error rate*. If we make two comparisons on the same set of data

Table 5.6 Differences in percentage frequencies of three pairwise comparisons

Pairwise comparisons	Differences in percentage frequencies
Never married *vs* married	30 − 50 = −20
Never *vs* formerly married	30 − 20 = 10
Married *vs* formerly married	50 − 20 = 30

and the comparisons are independent of one another, the probability of obtaining a statistically significant difference at the same critical level by chance is 10 out of 100 or 1 out of 10. This error rate is known as the *familywise* or *experimentwise* error rate. The relationship between these two error rates is given by the following formula

familywise error rate $= 1 - (1 -$ per comparison error rate$)^c$

where c represents the number of independent or orthogonal comparisons.

Note that with three groups, only two of the possible three pairwise comparisons are orthogonal while the third is not orthogonal. We can illustrate this by comparing the differences in the observed percentage of cases in our example shown in Table 5.6. The observed frequencies in the three categories of the never married, the married and the formerly married are also observed percentages since the total number of cases is 100 (e.g. $30/100 \times 100 = 30$). If we know the difference in percentage frequencies of any two comparisons, we can work out the absolute difference for the third comparison by subtracting one of the differences from the other. For instance, if we know that the difference between the never married and the married is -20 and the difference between the never married and the formerly married is 10, then if we subtract one from the other we obtain the absolute difference between the married and the formerly married, which is 30 $[(-20) - 10$ or $10 - (-20) = 30]$. Similarly, if we know that the difference between the never married and the formerly married is 10 and the difference between the married and the formerly married is 30, then the absolute difference between the never married and the married is 20 ($10 - 30 = -20$ or $30 - 10 = 20$).

BONFERRONI'S TEST

Some authors suggest that we do not need to correct the per comparison error rate when we carry out planned or *a priori* orthogonal comparisons to test for predicted differences between particular groups because this was the reason for conducting the study in the first place (e.g. Keppel 1991). Others recommend that *Bonferroni's* test or procedure, also known as *Dunn's* test or the *Dunn–Bonferroni* test, should be used to adjust the per comparison error rate (Marascuilo and McSweeney 1977).

Table 5.7 Observed frequencies and expected percentages and frequencies for the two comparisons

| | Comparisons | | | |
	First		Second	
Observed frequencies	30	50	50	20
Expected percentages	22.22	77.78	87.50	12.50
Expected frequencies	17.78	62.22	61.25	8.75

Suppose, for example, that prior to conducting our study we had predicted that there would be proportionately more never married and formerly married people than married ones. To carry out Bonferroni's test on these two orthogonal comparisons, we would first conduct a chi-square test for each of them. The observed frequencies and expected percentages for these two comparisons is presented in Table 5.7. Note that the expected percentages for each of the categories have had to be slightly adjusted so that, for example, what was 20 per cent for the never married is now 22.22 per cent (i.e. $20/90 \times 100 = 22.22$) in the first comparison. Chi-square for comparing the proportion of the never married with the married is about 10.80:

$$\frac{(30-17.78)^2}{17.78} + \frac{(50-62.22)^2}{62.22} = \frac{12.22^2}{17.78} + \frac{-12.22^2}{62.22} =$$

$$\frac{149.33}{17.78} + \frac{149.33}{62.22} = 8.40 + 2.40 = 10.80$$

Chi-square for comparing the proportion of the formerly married with the married is 16.53:

$$\frac{(50-61.25)^2}{61.25} + \frac{(20-8.75)^2}{8.75} = \frac{-11.25^2}{61.25} + \frac{11.25^2}{8.75} =$$

$$\frac{126.56}{61.25} + \frac{126.56}{8.75} = 2.07 + 14.46 = 16.53$$

Inspecting the table in Appendix 5, we can see that for 1 degree of freedom chi-squares at or greater than 6.64 are statistically significant at the 0.01 two-tailed or the 0.005 one-tailed level. Looking at the observed and expected frequencies for the first comparison in Table 5.7 and as predicted, the observed frequency of the never married (30) is greater than their expected frequency (17.78) while the observed frequency of the married (50) is less than their expected frequency (62.22). The prediction for the second comparison was also confirmed, with the observed frequency of the formerly married (20) being bigger than their expected frequency (8.75) and the observed frequency of the married (50) being smaller than their expected frequency (61.25).

The last column in the table of Appendix 6 presents the 0.05 critical values of the Bonferroni test for different numbers of comparisons when used with the z distribution. The 0.05 critical value of z for two comparisons is 2.24. Since z^2 equals chi-square with one degree of freedom, values of chi-square at or greater than 5.08 ($2.24^2 = 5.08$) are statistically significant at the 0.05 level with Bonferroni's test. Since both our chi-square values exceed this figure, both comparisons are statistically significant when adjusted for the number of orthogonal comparisons made.

MODIFIED SCHEFFÉ'S TEST

If we had not predicted any differences before carrying out the study, Marascuilo and McSweeney (1977) recommend that we apply the Scheffé test to the chi-square distribution. This will enable us to compare the observed proportions across all three categories. This test may be thought of as calculating the 100 per cent confidence limit of finding a particular difference in the observed proportions between two categories. When the confidence interval fails to include 0, the comparison is said to be significant (Hays 1994). To execute this test, perform the following 11 steps which are illustrated with the example of the three categories of marital status. The statistics for Steps 1 to 3 are shown in Table 5.8. The statistics for Steps 4, 5, 8, 9 and 10 are displayed in Table 5.9.

Step 1 Calculate the proportion of cases in each category by dividing the number of cases in that category with the total number of cases. The observed proportions of the never married, married and formerly married are 0.30 (30/100 = 0.30), 0.50 (50/100 = 0.50) and 0.20 (20/100 = 0.20) respectively.

Step 2 Work out the remaining proportion of cases in each category by subtracting the observed proportion of cases from 1. The remaining pro-

Table 5.8 Observed proportion of cases in three categories of marital status and their squared standard error

	Never married	Married	Formerly married
Observed frequency	30	50	20
Observed proportion	0.30	0.50	0.20
Remaining proportion	0.70	0.50	0.80
Squared standard error of proportion	0.0021	0.0025	0.0016

Table 5.9 Confidence limits for differences in proportions for three categories

Comparisons	Difference	Estimated variance	Confidence interval	Lower limit	Upper limit
Never married vs married	−0.20*	0.0046	0.166	−0.366	−0.034
Never vs formerly married	0.10	0.0037	0.149	−0.049	0.249
Married vs formerly married	0.30*	0.0041	0.157	0.143	0.457

* $p < .0.05$

portions for the three categories are 0.70 (1 − 0.30 = 0.70), 0.50 (1 − 0.50 = 0.50) and 0.80 (1 − 0.20 = 0.80) respectively.

Step 3   Calculate the squared standard error of the observed proportion by multiplying the observed proportion in a category by its remaining proportion and dividing by the number of cases. The squared standard errors of the observed proportion for the three categories are 0.0021 (0.30 × 0.70/100 = 0.0021), 0.0025 (0.50 × 0.50/100 = 0.0025) and 0.0016 (0.20 × 0.80/100 = 0.0016).

For each comparison, perform the following eight steps:

Step 4   Work out the difference in the observed proportion of cases in the two categories by subtracting one from the other. The difference in the observed proportion of cases is −0.20 (0.30 − 0.50 = −0.20) for the never married *vs* the married, 0.10 (0.30 − 0.20 = 0.10) for the never married *vs* the formerly married and 0.30 (0.50 − 0.20 = 0.30) for the married *vs* the formerly married.

Step 5   Calculate the estimated variance by adding together the squared standard error for each category. The estimated variance for the three comparisons is 0.0046, 0.0037 and 0.0041 respectively.

Step 6   Work out the required degrees of freedom for chi-square which is the number of comparisons minus 1. This is 2 (3 − 1 = 2) for this example.

Step 7   Find the value of chi-square for these degrees of freedom. In the table in Appendix 5, we see that at the 0.05 two-tailed critical level, this value is 5.99.

Step 8 Calculate the confidence interval for the comparison by multiplying chi-square by the estimated variance and taking the square root of the product:

$$\text{confidence interval} = \sqrt{\text{chi-square} \times \text{estimated variance}}$$

The confidence interval for the three comparisons is 0.166 ($\sqrt{5.99 \times 0.0046} = \sqrt{0.0276} = 0.166$); 0.149 ($\sqrt{5.99 \times 0.0037} = \sqrt{0.0222} = 0.149$); and 0.157 ($\sqrt{5.99 \times 0.0041} = \sqrt{0.0246} = 0.157$) respectively.

Step 9 Work out the lower limit of the confidence interval by subtracting it from the difference for that comparison. The lower limit for the three comparisons is -0.366 (-0.20 $-$ 0.166 = -0.366), -0.049 (0.10 $-$ 0.149 = -0.049) and 0.143 (0.30 $-$ 0.157 = 0.143) respectively.

Step 10 Work out the upper limit of the confidence interval by adding it to the difference for that comparison. The upper limit for the three comparisons is -0.034 (-0.20 + 0.166 = -0.034), 0.249 (0.10 + 0.149 = 0.249) and 0.457 (0.30 + 0.157 = 0.457) respectively.

Step 11 If the confidence interval fails to include 0, the comparison is statistically significant. We can see that the confidence interval for the second comparison includes a 0 (-0.049 to 0.249) so this difference is not statistically significant at the 0.05 two-tailed critical level. The confidence interval does not include a 0 for both the first (-0.366 to -0.034) and the third (0.143 to 0.457) comparison, so both these comparisons are statistically significant at the 0.05 two-tailed critical level.

CHI-SQUARE TEST FOR TWO UNRELATED SAMPLES

We can extend chi-square to more than one sample. The simplest case is one with two samples and where the variable is *dichotomous* (i.e. has only two categories). Imagine, for example, that we wanted to find out whether the number of people who have watched a violent film in the past week was significantly greater in the United States than in the United Kingdom. Illustrative data for this question are displayed in Table 5.10 in what is called a *contingency* table. A contingency table consists of a number of rows and columns which show the contingency or relationship between two variables, where the variables have been classified into mutually exclusive categories and where the data consist of frequencies. The two samples in our example may be thought of as a second variable which consists of two categories (the United States and the United Kingdom). A contingency table is also called a *cross-tabulation* table since the frequencies in the

Table 5.10 Contingency table of number of people having watched a violent film in the past week in the United States and the United Kingdom

| | Country | | Row |
	US	UK	total
Watched	30	5	35
Not watched	10	15	25
Column total	40	20	60

categories of one variable are tabulated across the frequencies in the categories of the other variable.

The table shown in Table 5.10 is known as a 2×2 contingency table since it has 2 rows to represent the 2 categories of the first variable and 2 columns to reflect the 2 categories of the second variable. It has four *cells*. If the second variable comprised three categories, then it would be a 2×3 contingency table as it would consist of 2 rows and 3 columns comprising six cells. The number of people who have watched a film in the past week is shown in the upper left-hand cell for the United States (30) and in the upper right-hand cell for the United Kingdom (5). The number of people who have not watched a violent film in the past week is displayed in the lower left-hand cell for the United States (10) and in the lower right-hand cell for the United Kingdom (15). The total number of cases in each row, called the *row total* or the *row marginal total*, is presented in the right-hand column of the table. The row total is 35 for those who have watched a violent film in the past week and 25 for those who have not. The total number of cases in each column, called the *column total* or *column marginal total*, is given in the bottom row. The column total is 40 for the United States and 20 for the United Kingdom. Finally, the total number of cases in the sample, called the *grand total*, is shown in the bottom right-hand corner of the table and is 60.

As before, to calculate chi-square for these data we begin by working out the expected frequency of cases in each cell assuming that the two variables are unrelated. We can do this using probability theory. The probability that a person has watched a violent film in the past week regardless of whether they were in the United States or the United Kingdom is 0.58 (35/60 = 0.583). The probability that a person comes from the United States is 0.67 (40/60 = 0.667). Therefore, the probability that a person has watched a violent film in the past week and comes from the United States is the product of their separate probabilities and is 0.39 (0.583 $\times$ 0.667 = 0.389). The expected frequency that a person has watched a violent film in the past week and comes from the United States is the product of that joint probability and the total number of cases and is 23.4 (0.39 $\times$ 60 = 23.4). We can translate this procedure for obtaining the expected frequency for any cell into the following general formula:

$$\text{expected frequency} = \frac{\text{row total}}{\text{grand total}} \times \frac{\text{column total}}{\text{grand total}} \times \text{grand total}$$

Since the grand total appears in one of the numerators and both the denominators, we can simplify this formula by cancelling out the grand total in the numerator and one of the denominators as follows:

$$\text{expected frequency} = \frac{\text{row total} \times \text{column total}}{\text{grand total}}$$

If we use this formula, the expected frequency for having watched a violent film in the past week and coming from the United States is 23.3. The expected frequency for each of the four cells is presented in Table 5.11.

Applying the chi-square formula to these data, we see that chi-square is 13.87:

$$\frac{(30-23.3)^2}{23.3} + \frac{(5-11.7)^2}{11.7} + \frac{(10-16.7)^2}{16.7} + \frac{(15-8.3)^2}{8.3} =$$

$$\frac{6.7^2}{23.3} + \frac{-6.7^2}{11.7} + \frac{-6.7^2}{16.7} + \frac{6.7^2}{8.3} =$$

$$\frac{44.89}{23.3} + \frac{44.89}{11.7} + \frac{44.89}{16.7} + \frac{44.89}{8.3} =$$

$$1.93 + 3.84 + 2.69 + 5.41 = 13.87$$

The formula for calculating the degrees of freedom (df) for chi-square is:

chi-square df = (number of rows − 1) × (number of columns − 1)

Since we have two rows and two columns, the appropriate degree of freedom is 1 [(2 − 1) × (2 − 1) = 1]. Note that if we know the total row and column frequencies and the frequency of one of the cells, then the frequencies in the other three cells are fixed. For example, if as in Table 5.12 we know that the frequency of cell a is 30, then we can work out that

Table 5.11 Expected frequencies of people having watched a violent film in the past week in the United States and the United Kingdom

| | Country | | Row |
	US	UK	total
Watched	23.3	11.7	35
Not watched	16.7	8.3	25
Column total	40	20	60

Table 5.12 Cell frequencies in a 2 × 2 contingency table

| | Country | | Row |
	US	UK	total
Watched	a 30	b	35
Not watched	c	d	25
Column total	40	20	60

the frequency of cell *b* is 5 (35 − 30 = 5), of cell *c* is 10 (40 − 30 = 10) and of cell *d* is 15 (20 − 5 = 15 or 25 − 10 = 15).

Looking at the table in Appendix 5, we see that chi-square to be statistically significant with one degree of freedom has to be 3.84 or larger at the 0.05 two-tailed level. As the chi-square value of 13.87 is larger than 3.84, we can conclude that there is a statistically significant difference between the United States and the United Kingdom in the number of people who have watched a violent film in the past week. Inspecting the relationship between the observed frequencies in Table 5.10 and the expected frequencies in Table 5.11, we can see that in the United States more people (30) than expected (23.3) viewed a violent film in the past week while in the United Kingdom fewer people (5) than expected (11.7) did so, which was what we predicted. Since it is possible to specify the direction of the results in a 2 × 2 table and since we did so, we could use a one-tailed probability level.

Siegel (1956), on the basis of Cochran (1954), recommended that in the case of a 2 × 2 contingency table the general formula for chi-square should be corrected for continuity either when the number of cases is greater than 40 or when the number of cases is between 20 and 40 and all four expected frequencies are 5 or more. On the other hand, *Fisher's exact test* should be used either when the number of cases is between 20 and 40 and the smallest expected frequency is less than 5 or when the number of cases is less than 20.

The correction for continuity is known as *Yates's correction* (Yates 1934) and consists of subtracting 0.5 from each of the absolute differences (i.e. ignoring the sign of the differences – indicated by the vertical bars in the equations below) between the observed and expected frequencies before squaring them. This has the effect of reducing the size of chi-square which was thought to decrease the probability of making a Type I error (i.e. assuming there is a difference when none exists).

Since the number of cases in our example is greater than 40, we could follow Siegel's recommendation and apply Yates's correction. If we do

Table 5.13 Observed frequencies (and expected frequencies in brackets) for a smaller sample

	Country US	UK	Row total
Watched	6 (4.1)	1 (2.9)	7
Not watched	1 (2.9)	4 (2.1)	5
Column total	7	5	12

this, chi-square corrected for continuity is 11.87 which is slightly smaller than an uncorrected chi-square of 13.87:

$$\frac{(|30-23.3|-0.5)^2}{23.3} + \frac{(|5-11.7|-0.5)^2}{11.7} + \frac{(|10-16.7|-0.5)^2}{16.7} +$$

$$\frac{(|15-8.3|-0.5)^2}{8.3} =$$

$$\frac{6.2^2}{23.3} + \frac{6.2^2}{11.7} + \frac{6.2^2}{16.7} + \frac{6.2^2}{8.3} =$$

$$\frac{38.44}{23.3} + \frac{38.44}{11.7} + \frac{38.44}{16.7} + \frac{38.44}{8.3} =$$

$$1.65 + 3.29 + 2.30 + 4.63 = 11.87$$

Based on this reasoning, earlier texts on statistics used to suggest that Yates's correction should be made when the frequency of one or more of the cells in a 2×2 contingency is less than 5. Since none of the expected frequencies in Table 5.11 is less than 5, we will use the data in Table 5.13 for computing chi-square uncorrected and corrected for continuity. The expected frequencies are given in brackets. We can see that the expected frequency for people in the United Kingdom who had not watched a violent film in the previous week is 2.1. Chi-square uncorrected for continuity is 5.07:

$$\frac{(6-4.1)^2}{4.1} + \frac{(1-2.9)^2}{2.9} + \frac{(1-2.9)^2}{2.9} + \frac{(4-2.1)^2}{2.1} =$$

$$\frac{1.9^2}{4.1} + \frac{-1.9^2}{2.9} + \frac{-1.9^2}{2.9} + \frac{1.9^2}{2.1} = \frac{3.6}{4.1} + \frac{3.6}{2.9} + \frac{3.6}{2.9} + \frac{3.6}{2.1} =$$

$$0.88 + 1.24 + 1.24 + 1.71 = 5.07$$

Looking at the table in Appendix 5, we see that for chi-square to be statistically significant it has to be 3.84 or larger at the two-tailed 0.05 level, which it is. Chi-square corrected for continuity, however, is 2.82:

$$\frac{(|6-4.1|-0.5)^2}{4.1} + \frac{(|1-2.9|-0.5)^2}{2.9} +$$

$$\frac{(|1-2.9|-0.5)^2}{2.9} + \frac{(|4-2.1|-0.5)^2}{2.1} =$$

$$\frac{1.4^2}{4.1} + \frac{-1.4^2}{2.9} + \frac{-1.4^2}{2.9} + \frac{1.4^2}{2.1} = \frac{2.0}{4.1} + \frac{2.0}{2.9} + \frac{2.0}{2.9} + \frac{2.0}{2.1} =$$

$$0.49 + 0.69 + 0.69 + 0.95 = 2.82$$

This figure is not statistically significant at the 0.05 two-tailed level.

Subsequent research, however, has suggested that Yates's correction may be too conservative in that it increases the probability of making a Type II error (i.e. assuming there is no difference when one exists) when the expected frequencies are small (e.g. Bradley, Bradley, McGrath and Cutcomb 1979; Camilli and Hopkins 1978, 1979; Overall 1980). Consequently, making this adjustment may no longer be necessary.

FISHER'S EXACT TEST

Siegel (1956) suggested that Fisher's exact probability test should be used either when the number of cases is between 20 and 40 and the smallest expected frequency is less than 5 or when the number of cases is less than 20. Since the data in Table 5.13 correspond to the former condition, we will use it to illustrate the computation of this test.

The frequency data in a 2×2 contingency table can be represented more generally by the table shown in Table 5.14 where the letters a, b, c and d signify the frequencies in the four cells. The probability of obtaining a

Table 5.14 2×2 contingency table for calculating Fisher's exact test

	Sample		Row total
	1	2	
Category 1	a	b	a + b
2	c	d	c + d
Column total	a + c	b + d	a + b + c + d

particular set of frequencies in such a table is given by the *hypergeometric distribution* which is determined by the following formula

$$p = \frac{(a+b)!(c+d)!(a+c)!(b+d)!}{(a+b+c+d)!a!b!c!d!}$$

The hypergeometric distribution reflects the probability of finding a particular outcome (i.e. the frequency of cases in Category 1) in a sample when an outcome, once chosen, is not replaced and when the marginal totals remain fixed (Berenson and Levine 1992).

Determining the probability of an outcome with or without replacement is like estimating the probability of obtaining, say, two aces on two draws of a well shuffled standard deck of 52 cards. The probability of drawing the first ace is the same in both situations and is 4/52 or 0.077. If the first card drawn is replaced and the deck of cards is reshuffled, then the probability of obtaining a second ace is 4/52 × 4/52 or 0.006. If the first card is an ace and if this ace is not replaced, then the probability of drawing a second ace is 4/52 × 3/51 or 0.0045.

To calculate the probability of obtaining the particular outcome shown in Table 5.13, we substitute the appropriate values in the formula for the hypergeometric distribution which gives us a probability of 0.04419:

$$\frac{(6+1)!(1+4)!(6+1)!(1+4)!}{(6+1+1+4)!6!1!1!4!} = \frac{7!5!7!5!}{12!6!1!1!4!} =$$

$$\frac{7 \times 5 \times 5 \times 4 \times 3 \times 2 \times 1}{12 \times 11 \times 10 \times 9 \times 8} = \frac{7 \times 5}{11 \times 9 \times 8} = \frac{35}{792} = 0.04419$$

However, to this probability we need to add the probability of obtaining distributions which deviate more extremely from the expected distribution. With the marginal totals remaining fixed, there is only one distribution which is more extreme than that shown in Table 5.13 and that is presented in Table 5.15. Two points should be noted about the data in this table. First, the expected frequencies are the same as those in Table 5.13 because the

Table 5.15 Observed frequencies (and expected frequencies in brackets) for a more extreme distribution

	Country US	UK	Row total
Watched	7 (4.1)	0 (2.9)	7
Not watched	0 (2.9)	5 (2.1)	5
Column total	7	5	12

marginal totals are fixed. And second, in order to ensure the marginal totals are the same, we need to change the frequency in both the upper right-hand cell and the lower left-hand cell. The probability of obtaining this more extreme distribution is 0.00126:

$$\frac{(7+0)!(0+5)!(7+0)!(0+5)!}{(7+0+0+5)!7!0!0!5!} = \frac{7!5!7!5!}{12!7!0!0!5!} =$$

$$\frac{5 \times 4 \times 3 \times 2 \times 1}{12 \times 11 \times 10 \times 9 \times 8} = \frac{1}{11 \times 9 \times 8} = \frac{1}{792} = 0.00126$$

Consequently, the probability of finding a distribution as and more extreme than that depicted in Table 5.13 is 0.04545 (0.04419 + 0.00126 = 0.04545). Since both these distributions deviate in the same direction of there being more people in the United States who have watched a violent film in the past week, this probability represents the one-tailed level.

To determine the two-tailed probability level, we need to add the one-tailed probability level to the probability level of distributions which have a lower probability than that shown in Table 5.13 and which deviate in the other direction (Siegel and Castellan 1988). Such a distribution is displayed in Table 5.16 which has a probability of 0.02652:

$$\frac{(2+5)!(5+0)!(2+5)!(5+0)!}{(2+5+5+0)!2!5!5!0!} = \frac{7!5!7!5!}{12!2!5!5!0!} =$$

$$\frac{7 \times 6 \times 5 \times 4 \times 3}{12 \times 11 \times 10 \times 9 \times 8} = \frac{7}{11 \times 3 \times 8} = \frac{7}{264} = 0.02652$$

So, the two-tailed probability of obtaining the distribution presented in Table 5.13 is 0.07197 (0.04419 + 0.00126 + 0.02652 = 0.07197).

As the calculations become more cumbersome with larger frequencies and less extreme distributions, the table in Appendix 7 can be employed to determine whether an observed distribution differs significantly from its expected one. Part of this table has been reproduced in Table 5.17 to illustrate its use. To look up the one-tailed 0.05 critical value of the

Table 5.16 Observed frequencies for a more extreme distribution in the opposite direction

| | Country | | Row |
	US	UK	total
Watched	2	5	7
Not watched	5	0	5
Column total	7	5	12

Table 5.17 Part of the table of one-tailed 0.05 critical values of *d* (or *c*) in Fisher's Test

Row totals		Cells					
a+b	*c+d*	*b* (or *a*)	*d* (or *c*)	*b* (or *a*)	*d* (or *c*)	*b* (or *a*)	*d* (or *c*)
.							
.							
7	7	7	3	5	0	4	0
		6	2				
	6	7	2	5	0	4	0
		6	1				
	5	7	2	6	1	5	0
	4	7	1	6	0	5	0
	3	7	0	6	0		
	2	7	0				
.							
.							
.							

frequencies in cell *d* for the data in Table 5.13, we first select the line which has an *a+b* row total of 7, a *c+d* row total of 5 and a cell *b* frequency of 1. Since there is not a cell *b* frequency of 1 in the table, we have to choose the corresponding cell *a* frequency of 6. If there is a frequency of 1 or less in cell *c*, we would conclude that our observed distribution differs significantly from the expected one at or less than the 0.05 one-tailed level. Since the cell *c* frequency is 1, we would draw this conclusion.

For another example, we could see whether the distribution in Table 5.16 differs significantly from the expected one. Once again, we would select the line which has an *a+b* row total of 7 and a *c+d* row total of 5 but this time we would choose a cell *b* frequency of 5, which is listed in the table. In order for this distribution to differ significantly from the expected one at or less than the 0.05 one-tailed level, the cell *d* frequency has to be 0 which it is. Consequently, we would presume that the distribution differs significantly from the expected one at this level.

CHI-SQUARE TEST FOR THREE OR MORE UNRELATED SAMPLES

Analysing frequency data from three or more unrelated samples with chi-square follows the same procedure as a one-sample chi-square for three or more categories. We will use the 3×4 contingency table presented in Table 5.18 to demonstrate this. People were classified into the three categories of having in the past week either watched a violent film,

Table 5.18 A 3 × 4 contingency table

	Country				Row total
	US	UK	Canada	Australia	
Watched a violent film	14	3	5	1	23
Watched a non-violent film	6	5	15	3	29
Not watched a film	20	12	10	6	48
Column total	40	20	30	10	100

Table 5.19 Expected frequencies in a 3 × 4 table

	Country				Row total
	US	UK	Canada	Australia	
Watched a violent film	9.2	4.6	6.9	2.3	23
Watched a non-violent film	11.6	5.8	8.7	2.9	29
Not watched a film	19.2	9.6	14.4	4.8	48
Column total	40	20	30	10	100

watched a non-violent film or not watched any film. The four samples were people from the United States, the United Kingdom, Canada and Australia. Assuming that we wanted to carry out a chi-square on this table, the first step would be to see if any expected frequency is less than 1 or more than 20 per cent of the expected frequencies are smaller than 5. The expected frequencies for this table are displayed in Table 5.19. There are no expected frequencies of less than 1, but 4 of the 12 cells (or 33.3 per cent) have expected frequencies of less than 5.

One way of reducing the percentage of cells with an expected frequency of less than 5 would be to omit the sample from Australia. If we do this, only 1 of the 9 cells (or 11.1 per cent) has an expected frequency of less than 5, as shown in Table 5.20. Chi-square for this 3 × 3 contingency table is 12.64:

Table 5.20 Expected frequencies in a 3 × 3 table

	Country			Row total
	US	UK	Canada	
Watched a violent film	9.8	4.9	7.3	22
Watched a non-violent film	11.6	5.8	8.7	26
Not watched a film	18.7	9.3	14.0	42
Column total	40	20	30	90

$$\frac{(14-9.8)^2}{9.8} + \frac{(3-4.9)^2}{4.9} + \frac{(5-7.3)^2}{7.3} + \frac{(6-11.6)^2}{11.6} + \frac{(5-5.8)^2}{5.8} +$$

$$\frac{(15-8.7)^2}{8.7} + \frac{(20-18.7)^2}{18.7} + \frac{(12-9.3)^2}{9.3} + \frac{(10-14.0)^2}{14.0} =$$

$$\frac{4.2^2}{9.8} + \frac{-1.9^2}{4.9} + \frac{-2.3^2}{7.3} + \frac{-5.6^2}{11.6} + \frac{-0.8^2}{5.8} + \frac{6.3^2}{8.7} + \frac{1.3^2}{18.7} + \frac{2.7^2}{9.3} +$$

$$\frac{-4.0^2}{14.0} =$$

$$\frac{17.64}{9.8} + \frac{3.61}{4.9} + \frac{5.29}{7.3} + \frac{31.36}{11.6} + \frac{0.64}{5.8} + \frac{39.69}{8.7} + \frac{1.69}{18.7} +$$

$$\frac{7.29}{9.3} + \frac{16.00}{14.00} =$$

$$1.80 + 0.74 + 0.72 + 2.70 + 0.11 + 4.56 + 0.09 + 0.78 + 1.14 = 12.64$$

Next, we determine the degrees of freedom which are the product of the number of rows minus 1 and the number of columns minus 1. Since we have 3 rows and 3 columns, the degrees of freedom for this 3 $\times$ 3 table are 4 [(3 − 1) $\times$ (3 − 1) = 2 $\times$ 2 = 4]. In other words, if we know the total row and column frequencies and the frequencies of four of the nine cells (provided that three of these are not in the same row or column), then the frequencies of the other five cells are fixed. Suppose, for example, that we know the frequencies of the four cells (*a*, *b*, *d* and *e*) in the 3 $\times$ 3 contingency table shown in Table 5.20 are 14, 3, 6 and 5 respectively. Then the frequency must be 5 for cell *c* (22 − 14 − 3 = 5), 15 for cell *f* (26 − 6 − 5 = 15), 20 for cell *g* (40 − 14 − 6 = 20), 12 for cell *h* (20 − 3 − 5 = 12) and 10 for cell *i* (42 − 20 − 12 = 10 or 30 − 5 − 15 = 10).

Turning to the table in Appendix 5, we see that with 4 degrees of freedom, chi-square has to be 9.49 or larger to be significant at the 0.05 two-tailed level which, with a value of 12.64, it is. Consequently, we would conclude that the frequencies in the nine cells differ significantly from those that would be expected by chance. To determine which of the cells differ significantly, we need to carry out the appropriate multiple comparison tests as described earlier.

Minitab carries out a chi-square test on two or more unrelated samples. Yates's correction for 2 $\times$ 2 tables is not used. Fisher's exact test is also

Table 5.21 Cell frequencies in a 3 × 3 contingency table

	Country			Row total
	US	UK	Canada	
Watched a violent film	a	b	c	
	14	3		22
Watched a non-violent film	d	e	f	
	6			26
Not watched a film	g	h	i	
				42
Column total	40	20	30	90

not provided. The number of cells having an expected frequency of less than 5 is shown at the bottom of the output.

The Minitab prompt system for conducting a chi-square is the command **chisquare** followed by a maximum of 7 columns. So to perform a chi-square on the first three columns in Table 5.18, we would first read in these data as follows:

MTB > read c1−c3
DATA> 14 3 5
DATA> 6 5 15
DATA> 20 12 10
DATA> end

We would then type

MTB > chisquare c1−c3

The output from this command is shown in Table 5.22.

To work out the statistical significance of obtaining a chi-square of **12.699** at the 0.05 two-tailed level, use the **invcdf** command followed by the **chisquare** subcommand. On the **invcdf** command the level of statistical significance is specified by subtracting that level from 1.00. So, for the 0.05 probability level the appropriate figure is 0.95 (1.00 − 0.05 = 0.95):

MTB > invcdf .95;

On the **chisquare** subcommand, which gives critical values for the chi-square distribution, the appropriate degrees of freedom are listed after the keyword **chisquare**. Therefore, the subcommand for finding the 0.05 two-tailed critical value of chi-square with 4 degrees of freedom is:

SUBC> chisquare 4.

The output from this command first gives the inverse cumulative distribution function of **0.9500** followed by the critical chi-square value of **9.4877**.

Table 5.22 **Chisquare** output for a 3 × 3 contingency table

Expected counts are printed below observed counts

	C1	C2	C3	Total
1	14	3	5	22
	9.78	4.89	7.33	
2	6	5	15	26
	11.56	5.78	8.67	
3	20	12	10	42
	18.67	9.33	14.00	
Total	40	20	30	90

ChiSq = 1.823 + 0.730 + 0.742 +
2.671 + 0.105 + 4.628 +
0.095 + 0.762 + 1.143 = 12.699

df = 4

1 cells with expected counts less than 5.0

As the chi-square value we obtained, which was 12.699, is larger than the critical value of 9.4877, we would conclude that the frequencies differed significantly from those expected by chance at less than the two-tailed 0.05 level.

The menu sequence for finding chi-square is

→**Stat** →**Tables** →**Chisquare Test . . .** →**c1** →**Select** [this puts **c1** in the box under **Columns containing the table:**] →**c2** →**Select** →**c3** →**Select** →**OK**

In Release 10 the probability of obtaining chi-square is given, which for our example is displayed as **p = 0.013**.

In Releases 8 and 9, the critical value of chi-square is found by:

→**Calc** →**Probability Distribution** →**Chisquare . . .** →**Inverse cumulative probability** →box beside **Degrees of freedom** and type degrees of freedom [e.g. **4**] in it →box beside **Input constant:** and in it type the cumulative probability level [e.g. **.95**] →**OK**

McNEMAR TEST FOR TWO RELATED SAMPLES

The McNemar test compares the frequencies of a dichotomous variable from two related samples of cases. These two samples may consist of the same or *matched* cases tested on two occasions or receiving two treatments. Matching involves selecting samples of cases to be the same in certain respects such as age, gender and socio-economic status and is used to make

Table 5.23 Number of people having seen two particular violent films

		Second film	
		Seen	*Not seen*
First	Seen	6	4
film	Not seen	8	12

the samples as similar as possible. We could employ the McNemar test, for example, to determine whether people who had seen a particular violent film were also significantly more likely to have seen another particular one. The dichotomous variable in this instance would be whether the person had seen or not seen the film and the two related samples would be the two films.

Suppose that of a group of 40 people, 6 watched both films, 12 saw neither, 4 saw the first violent film but not the second one and 8 saw the second one but not the first. Do these results suggest that people who saw the first violent film are also more likely to see the second one? To visualise the data, it may be helpful to arrange it in the form of a table as displayed in Table 5.23. With the McNemar test, we are only interested in whether the number of cases who have changed in one direction on the two occasions (say, those seeing the first violent film but not the second) are different from the number who have changed in the other direction (say, those seeing the second violent film but not the first). In other words, we are only concerned with the number of cases who have changed from one occasion to the next (i.e. those in the top right and bottom left cell). If there was no difference between the number of cases who saw the first violent film only and those who saw the second violent film only, then the expected frequency of cases in each of these two cells should be 6 [i.e. $(4 + 8)/2 = 6$]. If the expected frequency is less than 5, the binomial test should be used.

The McNemar test is like the chi-square test in that it compares the observed with the expected frequency of cases and the statistic that is computed is chi-square but, unlike the chi-square test, it only does this for the cases who have changed from one occasion (or condition) to the next. The formula for the McNemar test is:

$$\text{chi-square} = \frac{(|\text{cell}_1 \text{ frequencies} - \text{cell}_2 \text{ frequencies}| - 1)^2}{\text{cell}_1 + \text{cell}_2}$$

where the two cells (cell_1 and cell_2) refer to the two cells which indicate change. This test has one degree of freedom.

The steps involved in calculating chi-square for the McNemar test are as follows:

Step 1   Find the absolute difference between the observed frequency of cases for the two cells representing a change from one occasion or condition to the next. Since the two cells in our example which reflect this change are the top right and the bottom left cells, the absolute difference is 4 ($|4 - 8| = 4$).

Step 2   Subtract 1 from this absolute difference to correct for continuity, which gives 3 ($4 - 1 = 3$).

Step 3   Square this difference, making 9 ($3^2 = 9$).

Step 4   Divide this squared difference by the sum of the observed frequencies in the two cells reflecting change. As the sum of the frequencies in these two cells is 12 ($4 + 8 = 12$), this result is 0.75 ($9/12 = 0.75$) which can be obtained by substituting the appropriate figures in the above formula:

$$\frac{(|4 - 8| - 1)^2}{4 + 8} = \frac{9}{12} = 0.75$$

We look up the statistical significance of this value in the table in Appendix 5. Because we specified the direction of the results we expected to find, we can use the one-tailed level of significance which simply involves halving the significance value. With one degree of freedom, the critical value at the 0.05 one-tailed level is 2.71. Since our value is less than this, we would conclude that people who saw the first film were not significantly more likely to have seen the second one.

Minitab does not compute a McNemar test but it is relatively easy to write a macro for carrying one out if necessary.

COCHRAN Q FOR THREE OR MORE RELATED SAMPLES

If we wanted to compare the frequencies of a dichotomous variable from three or more related samples of cases, we would use the Cochran Q test. We would apply this test if we wished to determine, for example, whether people who saw one particular violent film were also likely to have seen two other particular violent films. The data for 8 such people are presented in Table 5.24 where 1 represents having seen the film and 0 not having seen it.

The values of the Q test approximate those of chi-square when the number of rows is not too small, although Cochran does not specify what the minimum number is. To calculate Q, we first need to sum each of the rows (RT) and columns (CT) and then square them (RT^2 and CT^2) as shown in Table 5.25. So, from this table we can see that 4 people watched the first film, 5 the second and zero the third, giving a total number of 9

Table 5.24 Number of people having seen three particular violent films

Cases	Film 1	Film 2	Film 3
1	0	0	0
2	1	1	0
3	0	1	0
4	0	0	0
5	1	0	0
6	1	1	0
7	1	1	0
8	0	1	0

Table 5.25 Cochran Q test: Initial computations

Cases	Film 1	Film 2	Film 3	RT	RT^2
1	0	0	0	0	0
2	1	1	0	2	4
3	0	1	0	1	1
4	0	0	0	0	0
5	1	0	0	1	1
6	1	1	0	2	4
7	1	1	0	2	4
8	0	1	0	1	1
CT	4	5	0	9	15
CT^2	16	25	0	41	

over all three films. The number of violent films seen by any one individual is zero for the first person, 2 for the next one and so on, giving a total of 9 for all 8 people.

The formula for computing Q is:

$$Q = \frac{[(\text{number of groups} \times \text{sum of CT}^2) - \text{squared sum of RT}] \times (\text{number of groups} - 1)}{(\text{number of groups} \times \text{sum of RT}) - \text{sum of RT}^2}$$

To compute the Q value, we carry out the following steps:

Step 1   Take the sum of the row totals (which is 9 and which is the total number of 1's in this example) and square this to give the squared sum of row totals (i.e. 81).

Step 2   Multiply the sum of the squared column totals (i.e. 41) by the number of groups (i.e. 3).

Step 3   Subtract from this figure (i.e. 41 × 3 = 123) the squared sum of row totals (i.e. 81).

Step 4   Multiply this difference (i.e. 123 − 81 = 42) by the number of groups minus 1 (i.e. 3 − 1 = 2). This figure (i.e. 42 × 2 = 84) which we will call the numerator is divided by another figure which we shall call the denominator and which is calculated in the following way.

Step 5   Multiply the sum of row totals (i.e. 9) by the number of groups (i.e. 3) and subtract from this the sum of the squared row totals (i.e. 15) to give the denominator (i.e. (9 × 3) − 15 = 12).

Step 6   Divide the numerator (i.e. 84) by the denominator (i.e. 12) to produce the Q value (i.e. 7.0).

Substituting the appropriate values in the formula, we see that Q is 7.0:

$$\frac{[(3 \times 41) - 81)] \times 2}{(3 \times 9) - 15} = \frac{(123 - 81) \times 2}{27 - 15} = \frac{84}{12} = 7.0$$

To check the statistical significance of this value, we look it up in the table in Appendix 5. Since, with 2 degrees of freedom, the value of 7.0 is larger than the critical value of 5.99 at the two-tailed 0.05 level, we would conclude that people differed significantly in terms of which films they saw.

This test does not, of course, tell us where this difference arises. To find this out, Marascuilo and McSweeney (1977) recommend using either the Bonferroni or the modified Scheffé test which involve the following preliminary steps:

Step 1   Determine the number of comparisons between pairs of samples or groups. With three samples, we can compare three pairs of groups (i.e. 1 *vs* 2, 1 *vs* 3 and 2 *vs* 3).

Step 2   Calculate the difference in proportions for these comparisons as shown in Table 5.26.

Table 5.26 Differences in proportions for the three pairwise comparisons

Pairwise comparisons	Differences in proportions
Film 1 *vs* Film 2	4/8 − 5/8 = −0.125
Film 1 *vs* Film 3	4/8 − 0/8 = 0.500
Film 2 *vs* Film 3	5/8 − 0/8 = 0.625

Step 3   Work out the estimated variance of the comparisons according to the following formula:

$$\frac{(\text{number of groups} \times \text{sum of CT}) - \text{sum of RT}^2}{\text{squared number of cases} \times \text{number of groups} \times (\text{number of groups} - 1)} \times 2$$

Substituting the figures from our example into the formula, we see that the estimated variance is 0.0626:

$$\frac{(3 \times 9) - 15}{8^2 \times 3 \times 2} \times 2 = \frac{27 - 15}{64 \times 6} \times 2 = \frac{12}{384} \times 2 = 0.0313 \times 2 = 0.0626$$

To perform the Bonferroni test, carry out the following additional steps:

Step 1   With three groups there are three comparisons. Look up in the last column of the table in Appendix 6 the critical value for the 0.05 probability level for three comparisons, which is 2.39.

Step 2   Multiply this figure by the square root of the estimated variance, which gives 0.598:

$$2.39 \times \sqrt{0.0626} = 2.39 \times 0.25 = 0.598$$

The difference between any two groups must be bigger than 0.598 to be statistically significant. The difference between the proportion of people seeing Film 2 and Film 3 is the only one which is greater than this figure.

To conduct a modified Scheffé test, carry out the following steps:

Step 1   The degrees of freedom for chi-square with three groups are 1 minus the total number of groups which is two. Look up in the table in Appendix 5 the critical value for the 0.05 probability level with 2 degrees of freedom, which is 5.99.

Step 2   Multiply the square root of this value by the square root of the estimated variance, which is 0.612:

$$\sqrt{5.99} \times \sqrt{0.0626} = 2.447 \times 0.25 = 0.612.$$

The difference between any two groups must be larger than 0.612 to be statistically significant. Once again, the difference between the proportion of people seeing Film 2 and Film 3 is the only one which is bigger than this figure.

SUMMARY

The computation of non-parametric tests for assessing whether the number of cases in different categories varies across one or more groups or from some expected distribution is described. The binomial test determines whether the number of cases falling into one of only two categories differs significantly from some expected number or proportion. The Pearson chi-square test compares the observed frequency of cases against the expected frequency for one or more unrelated samples on a variable with two or more categories. When there are only two categories the binomial test should be used when the minimum expected frequency for one of the two categories is less than 5. With three or more categories chi-square should not be used when the expected frequency is less than 1 or when more than 20 per cent of the expected frequencies are less than 5. Expected frequencies may be increased by dropping or combining appropriate categories. Applying Yates's correction may no longer be necessary when each variable has only two categories and when the number of cases is greater than 40 or when the number of cases is between 20 and 40 and all four expected frequencies are 5 or more. Fisher's exact test is used when each variable has only two categories and either the number of cases is between 20 and 40 and the smallest expected frequency is less than 5 or the number of cases is less than 20. The McNemar test compares the frequencies of a dichotomous variable which have changed values in two related samples of cases whereas the Cochran Q test compares them in three or more related samples. The *a priori* or planned test for determining which pair of three or more unrelated or related groups differ is the Bonferroni test whereas the *post hoc* test is the modified Scheffé test.

EXERCISES

1 Of a sample of 80 women, 20 are single, 40 are married, 10 are separated or divorced and 10 are widowed. The percentages of women in the population falling into these four categories are known to be 10, 70, 10 and 10.
   (a) What test would you use to determine if the distribution of marital status in the sample is similar to that of the population?
   (b) What is the value of this test?
   (c) What are the degrees of freedom?
   (d) Would you use a one- or two-tailed probability level to evaluate the significance of this value?
   (e) What is the probability value of the test?
   (f) Is the distribution of marital status in the sample significantly different from that in the population?

2 Of 90 married couples, 10 of the women compared to 25 of the men said

that they fell in love with their partner at first sight.

(a) What test would you use to determine whether this difference was significant?

(b) What is the value of this test?

(c) What are the degrees of freedom?

(d) Would you use a one- or two-tailed probability level to evaluate the significance of this value?

(e) What is the probability value of the test?

(f) Do significantly more men than women fall in love with their future spouse at first sight?

3 Of 30 members who are supposed to meet twice, 5 attend both meetings, 5 attend neither meeting, 15 attend the first but not the second meeting and 5 attend the second but not the first meeting.

(a) What test would you use to determine whether of the people attending the first meeting significantly fewer were present at the second meeting?

(b) What is the value of this test?

(c) What are the degrees of freedom?

(d) Would you use a one- or two-tailed probability level to evaluate the significance of this value?

(e) What is the probability value of the test?

(f) Of the people attending the first meeting did significantly fewer attend the second?

## Chapter 6

Tests of difference for ordinal data

The statistical tests described in this chapter are used to analyse ordinal data from one or more groups of cases. These tests determine whether the distribution of cases differs significantly from chance across the groups or from some theoretical distribution. Suppose we are interested in finding out whether watching a film of someone being rewarded for behaving aggressively increases aggressiveness. To measure how aggressive people are observers rate their aggressiveness on a 5-point scale where 0 indicates 'not at all aggressive', 1 'slightly aggressive', 2 'fairly aggressive' and 3 'considerably aggressive' and 4 'very aggressive'. This measure is an ordinal scale since the intervals between the four points do not necessarily represent equal increments or intervals in the level of aggressiveness. We could use some of the tests discussed in this chapter to find out whether seeing a film of someone being rewarded for being aggressive produces significantly more aggressiveness than watching a film of the same person being punished for being aggressive. We could use the other tests contained in this chapter to see whether there is a significant increase in aggressiveness after watching this film as compared to before seeing it and whether any increase which occurs is maintained after, say, three months.

In this example, which we will use throughout this chapter, 9 girls and 9 boys are randomly assigned to one of three conditions in which they watch a film of the same boy being aggressive. In the first condition this boy is rewarded for being aggressive (reward condition), while in the second condition he is punished for being aggressive (punishment condition). The third condition is a control condition in which he is neither rewarded nor punished for being aggressive. The purpose of this control condition is to find out whether seeing a person being rewarded or punished for being aggressive actually changes the level of aggressiveness shown compared to not being rewarded or punished. Participants are rated for aggressiveness on the 5-point scale immediately before receiving treatment (pre-test), immediately after treatment has ended (post-test) and three months later

Table 6.1 Pre-test, post-test and follow-up aggressiveness ratings for the
reward, punishment and control conditions

Gender	Condition	Pre-test	Post-test	Follow-up
Girls	Reward	0	1	1
		1	2	0
		2	3	2
	Punishment	1	0	1
		2	1	0
		3	2	2
	Control	1	0	0
		2	2	1
		0	1	2
Boys	Reward	1	2	2
		2	4	3
		3	3	4
	Punishment	0	1	3
		1	2	2
		2	3	1
	Control	3	3	2
		1	1	1
		2	2	0

(follow-up). There are three girls and three boys in each of the three
conditions. The ratings for the groups are shown in Table 6.1.

KOLMOGOROV–SMIRNOV TEST FOR ONE SAMPLE

The Kolmogorov–Smirnov test for one sample determines whether the
distribution of an ordinal variable differs significantly from some theoretical distribution. We could use this test to find out whether the distribution
of, for example, pre-test aggressiveness for the nine boys in our study
differed from the distribution of the population or some expected distribution such as that shown in Table 6.2 in which 20 per cent obtained a rating
of 0 or 3 and 30 per cent had one of 1 or 2. To perform this test, we carry
out the following steps:

Table 6.2 Proportions of expected or theoretical distribution of pre-test
aggressiveness

	Ratings			
	0	*1*	*2*	*3*
Proportions	0.20	0.30	0.30	0.20

Table 6.3 Cumulative frequency table of pre-test aggressiveness ratings for the sample

	0	1	2	3
Sample	1	4	7	9

Step 1   Draw up a cumulative frequency table of the pre-test aggressiveness ratings for the sample in which the frequency of the previous category is added to the frequency of the subsequent category as shown in Table 6.3. For instance, one boy has a rating of 0 and three boys have a rating of 1 so that the cumulative frequency of boys having a rating of either 0 or 1 is 4 (1 + 3 = 4).

Step 2   Calculate the cumulative frequency proportion for each rating by dividing each cumulative frequency by the total number of cases in the sample as shown in Table 6.4.

Step 3   Work out the cumulative frequency proportion for the population (or expected) distribution and for each rating calculate the difference between the population (or expected) distribution and the sample value as depicted in Table 6.5.

Step 4   Select the largest absolute difference between these two distributions and look up the probability of obtaining this difference in the table in Appendix 8. As we can see from Table 6.5 the largest absolute difference is 0.09. From the table in Appendix 8, for a sample of 9 cases this difference to be significant must be equal to or bigger than 0.388 at the 0.05 one-tailed

Table 6.4 Cumulative frequency proportions of pre-test aggressiveness ratings for the sample

	0	1	2	3
Sample	1/9	4/9	7/9	9/9
	0.11	0.44	0.78	1.00

Table 6.5 Differences between the cumulative frequency proportions of the sample and the population

	0	1	2	3
Sample	0.11	0.44	0.78	1.00
Expected	0.20	0.50	0.80	1.00
Difference	0.09	0.06	0.02	0.00

level and 0.432 at the 0.05 two-tailed level which it is not. Consequently, we would conclude that the sample distribution does not differ significantly from the population (or expected) distribution.

KOLMOGOROV–SMIRNOV TEST FOR TWO UNRELATED SAMPLES

The Kolmogorov–Smirnov test determines whether the distribution of an ordinal variable differs significantly between two unrelated samples. We could apply this test if we wanted to compare the distribution, for example, of aggressiveness ratings for any two of the groups, such as pre-test aggressiveness for girls and boys. To do this, we would carry out the following steps:

Step 1   Draw up a cumulative frequency table for the two groups in which the frequency of the previous category is added to the frequency of the subsequent category as shown in Table 6.6.

Step 2   Calculate the cumulative frequency proportion for each rating by dividing each cumulative frequency by the total number of cases in each sample as illustrated in Table 6.7.

Step 3   Compute the difference between the cumulative proportions within each rating as displayed in Table 6.7.

Step 4 for small samples   When the number of cases in both samples is 25 or less as it is in this example, take the largest absolute difference which is

Table 6.6 Cumulative frequency table of pre-test aggressiveness ratings for girls and boys

	0	1	2	3
Girls	2	5	8	9
Boys	1	4	7	9

Table 6.7 Cumulative frequency proportions of pre-test aggressiveness ratings for girls and boys

	0	1	2	3
Girls	2/9	5/9	8/9	9/9
	0.22	0.55	0.88	1.00
Boys	1/9	4/9	7/9	9/9
	0.11	0.44	0.77	1.00
Difference	0.11	0.11	0.11	0.00

0.11. Multiply this difference by the number of cases in each sample which gives a value of 8.91 (0.11 $\times$ 9 $\times$ 9 = 8.91). Turn to the table in Appendix 9 for the one-tailed level and the table in Appendix 10 for the two-tailed level. As we did not predict the direction of any difference, we would use the two-tailed level in Appendix 10. When the size of both samples is 9 this absolute difference must be 54 or bigger to be statistically significant at the 0.05 level which it is not. Consequently, we would conclude that there is no significant difference in the distribution of pre-test aggressiveness between the girls and boys.

Step 4: two-tailed level for large samples   When either sample is larger than 25, we would have to carry out the computation shown in the table in Appendix 11 to determine the two-tailed significance level. If we multiplied the numbers within each rating by 50, we would have 450 cases in each sample. To determine the value which an absolute difference of 0.11 from 450 cases would have to be larger than to be significant, we proceed as follows. We have to add the two sample sizes together (450 + 450 = 900), divide by the product of the two sample sizes [900/(450 $\times$ 450) = 2/450 = 0.004], take the square root of the resulting figure ($\sqrt{0.004}$ = 0.06) and multiply by 1.36 which gives a value of 0.08 (0.06 $\times$ 1.36 = 0.08).

Since the absolute difference of 0.11 is larger than 0.08, we would conclude in this instance that the two distributions differed significantly at less than the 0.05 two-tailed level and that boys had significantly higher pre-test aggressiveness than girls. We could go on to calculate that the absolute difference of 0.11 was just smaller than the 0.001 two-tailed value (i.e. 0.06 $\times$ 1.95 = 0.117) and so was not significant at this level.

Step 4: one-tailed level for large samples   To calculate the one-tailed probability level when either sample is larger than 25, we compute a chi-square according to the following formula where n_1 is the number of cases in one sample and n_2 is the number of cases in the other sample:

$$\text{chi-square} = \frac{n_1 \times n_2}{n_1 + n_2} \times 4 \times \text{largest absolute difference squared}$$

If we substitute the appropriate figures into this formula we see that chi-square is 10.8:

$$\frac{450 \times 450}{450 + 450} \times 4 \times 0.11^2 = \frac{202500}{900} \times 4 \times 0.012 = 225 \times 0.048 = 10.8$$

We look up this figure in the table in Appendix 5. Since this test has two degrees of freedom and since a chi-square of 10.8 is larger than 9.21 at the 0.01 two-tailed level, we can conclude that boys had significantly higher pre-test aggressiveness than girls at less than the 0.005 one-tailed level.

Minitab does not carry out a one- or two-sample Kolmogorov–Smirnov test.

MANN–WHITNEY *U* TEST FOR TWO UNRELATED SAMPLES

The Mann–Whitney *U* test determines the number of times a score from one of the samples is ranked higher than a score from the other sample. If the two sets of scores are similar, then the number of times this happens should be similar for the two samples. To calculate the Mann–Whitney test to find out if the sum of ranked scores for follow-up aggressiveness in boys is greater for the reward than for the punishment condition, we would carry out the following steps:

Step 1   Rank the scores of both the samples together, using rank 1 for the lowest score, rank 2 for the next lowest score and so on. If two or more scores have the same value, each of the tied scores has the same rank which is equal to the average rank of those scores for the combined samples. For example, if two scores are equal and would have occupied second and third place, the two positions are added together $(2 + 3 = 5)$ and divided by the number of scores (2) to give a ranking of 2.5 (5/2), which is then assigned to the two scores. The ranking of the follow-up aggressiveness ratings for the two conditions is shown in Table 6.8.

Step 2   Sum the ranks for the smaller sample. Since in our example both samples are of the same size, it does not matter which sample we work with. We will use the second sample (the punishment condition) as indicated in Table 6.9.

Step 3   The Mann–Whitney *U* is calculated by the following formula where n_1 represents the smaller sample and n_2 the larger sample:

Table 6.8 Ranking of follow-up aggressiveness in boys for the reward and punishment conditions

| | | Scores | | | |
	Original	Reordered	Position	Ranked	Ranks of originals
Reward	2	1	1	1.0	2.5
	3	2	2	2.5	4.5
	4	2	3	2.5	6.0
Punishment	3	3	4	4.5	4.5
	2	3	5	4.5	2.5
	1	4	6	6.0	1.0

Table 6.9 Ranked aggressiveness ratings in boys for the punishment condition

3	4.5
2	2.5
1	1.0
Total	8.0

$$U = (n_1 \times n_2) + \frac{n_1 \times (n_1 + 1)}{2} - \text{summed ranks of } n_1$$

Substituting the appropriate values into this formula, we find that U is 7:

$$(3 \times 3) + \frac{3 \times (3 + 1)}{2} - 8 = 9 + \frac{12}{2} - 8 = 9 + 6 - 8 = 7$$

Step 4   Calculate the U value for the second sample using the following formula:

U of second sample $= n_1 \times n_2 - U$ of first sample

Putting the relevant figures into this formula, we see that the U of the second sample is 2:

$(3 \times 3) - 7 = 9 - 7 = 2$

Note that if we know the U value of one sample (e.g. 7) and the two sample sizes (i.e. 3 and 3), we can work out the U value for the other sample (9 − 7 = 2) since the two U values combined equal the product of the number of cases in the two samples.

Step 5 for samples up to 20   If the samples are 20 or less, as they are in this case, we look up the significance of the smaller of the two U values (i.e. 2) in the appropriate table in Appendix 12 or 13. If the value of the smaller U is greater than the critical value of U in the table, we conclude that there is no significant difference between the summed ranks of the two samples. Since we specified the direction of the difference we expected to find, we would use the 0.05 one-tailed level shown in the table in Appendix 12. As the U value of 2 is greater than the critical value of 0 when the size of one sample is 3 and the other 3, we would argue that there is no significant difference in follow-up aggressiveness between the two conditions.

Step 5 for samples larger than 20   If the samples are greater than 20, we convert our U value into an approximate z value by using the following formula:

$$z = \frac{U - [(n_1 \times n_2)/2]}{\sqrt{[(n_1 \times n_2)(n_1 + n_2 + 1)]/12}}$$

We can change our U value into a z value by substituting the appropriate numbers into the formula which gives a z of 1.09:

$$\frac{7 - [(3 \times 3)/2]}{\sqrt{[(3 \times 3)(3 + 3 + 1)/12]}} = \frac{7 - 4.5}{\sqrt{(9 \times 7)/12}} = \frac{2.5}{\sqrt{5.25}} = \frac{2.5}{2.29} = 1.09$$

Since we ignore the sign of the U value, it does not matter which U value is put into the formula. If we subtracted 4.5 from 2 instead of 7 the absolute difference is still 2.5.

We look up the significance of this z value in the table in Appendix 2. The area between the middle of the curve and a z value of 1.09 is 0.3621, indicating that the area beyond the z value on one side of the curve is 0.1379 (0.5000 − 0.3621 = 0.1379). Since 0.1379 is larger than 0.05, we would conclude that there is no significant difference in follow-up aggressiveness in boys between the reward and punishment condition. If we had wanted the two-tailed probability level we would double 0.1379 to give 0.2758 (0.1379 × 2 = 0.2758).

When ties occur between the scores of the two samples, the U value is affected although this effect is usually slight. To correct for tied ranks in calculating z, we carry out the following steps:

Step 1   Count the number of ties for each score. So, in our example, we have two scores or ties of 2 and two ties of 3.

Step 2   For each tied score, subtract the number of ties from the number of ties cubed and divide by 12. So, two ties becomes 0.5 [$(2^3 − 2)/12 = 0.5$].

Step 3   Sum these values for each tied score, which in our example would give a figure of 1:

$$\frac{2^3 - 2}{12} + \frac{2^3 - 2}{12} = \frac{8 - 2}{12} + \frac{8 - 2}{12} = \frac{6}{12} + \frac{6}{12} = \frac{12}{12} = 1$$

Step 4   This value (which we shall call ST for sum of ties) is used in the following formula to calculate z, where N stands for the total number of cases in both samples:

$$z = \frac{U - \frac{(n_1 \times n_2)}{2}}{\sqrt{\frac{n_1 \times n_2}{N \times (N - 1)} \times \left(\frac{N^3 - N}{12} - ST\right)}}$$

Inserting the values of our example, we find that z is 1.1072:

$$\frac{7 - \dfrac{(3 \times 3)}{2}}{\sqrt{\dfrac{(3 \times 3)}{6 \times (6 - 1)} \times \left(\dfrac{6^3 - 6}{12} - 1\right)}} =$$

$$\frac{7 - 4.5}{\sqrt{\dfrac{9}{30} \times \left(\dfrac{216}{12} - 1\right)}} = \frac{2.5}{\sqrt{0.3 \times (18 - 1)}} = \frac{2.5}{\sqrt{0.3 \times 17}} = \frac{2.5}{\sqrt{5.1}} =$$

$$\frac{2.5}{2.258} = 1.1072$$

Looking up the significance of this value of 1.11 in the table in Appendix 2, we find that we obtain a one-tailed probability value of 0.1335 (0.5000 − 0.3665 = 0.1335). Since this value is larger than 0.05, we would conclude that there was no significant difference in follow-up aggressiveness in boys between the reward and punishment condition.

To carry out a Mann–Whitney test (also sometimes called the Wilcoxon Rank Sum W Test) we would use the following **mann-whitney** command where follow-up aggressiveness rating for **boys** was stored in the column labelled '**rewb**' for the **rew**ard condition and '**punb**' for the **pun**ishment condition:

MTB > mann-whitney 'rewb' 'punb';
SUBC> alternative 1.

Since we expected that aggressiveness would be greater in the reward than in the punishment condition we put **1** on the **alternative** subcommand to obtain the one-tailed level of significance. For the two-tailed level simply omit this subcommand and the semi-colon on the previous line.

The menu sequence for doing this is:

→**Stat** →**Nonparametrics** →**Mann-Whitney...** →**rewb** →**Select** [this puts **rewb** in the box beside **First Sample:**] →**punb** →**Select** [this puts **punb** in the box beside **Second Sample:**] →the down button on the box beside **Alternative:** →**greater than** [for the two-tailed level →**not equal**] →**OK**

The output for this command is presented in Table 6.10. This shows the Wilcoxon W rather the Mann–Whitney U. Wilcoxon W is the sum of the ranks of the first group listed which is the reward condition. From Table 6.8 we can work out that this sum is **13.0** (2.5 + 4.5 + 6.0 = 13.0). If we had put

Table 6.10 **Mann–Whitney** *U* test output comparing follow-up aggressiveness in boys for the reward and punishment conditions

Mann-Whitney Confidence Interval and Test

rewb	N = 3	Median = 3.000
punb	N = 3	Median = 2.000

Point estimate for ETA1-ETA2 is   1.000

91.9 Percent C.I. for ETA1-ETA2 is (−1.001, 2.999)

W = 13.0

Test of ETA1 = ETA2 vs. ETA1 > ETA2 is significant at 0.1914
The test is significant at 0.1843 (adjusted for ties)

Cannot reject at alpha = 0.05

the smaller group first (the punishment condition), **W** would have been **8.0**. The one-tailed probability of obtaining this result by chance adjusted for ties is **0.1843** (which is close to our calculated figure of 0.1335 for large samples). Since **0.1843** is larger than 0.05 we would conclude that there is no significant difference in follow-up aggressiveness in boys between the reward and punishment condition. In other words, we **cannot reject** the null hypothesis of no difference **at** the **alpha** or probability level of **0.05**.

MOOD'S MEDIAN TEST FOR TWO OR MORE UNRELATED SAMPLES

Mood's median test is used to determine if the distribution of values either side of a common median differs for two or more unrelated samples. To calculate Mood's median test to discover if the scores for follow-up aggressiveness in boys are higher for the reward than for the punishment condition, we would carry out the following steps.

Step 1   Combine the scores for the two groups and find the median for this combined group. The median for this example is 2.50:

1   2   2   3   3   4

Step 2   Form a contingency table where the columns represent the conditions, the first row the frequencies of values above the median and the second row the frequencies of values at or below the median as shown in Table 6.11.

Table 6.11 2 × 2 contingency table of frequencies of follow-up aggressiveness in boys in the reward and punishment condition above the median and at or below the median

	Reward	Punishment
Above the median	2	1
At or below the median	1	2

Step 3 Carry out a chi-square test on the observed frequencies in this contingency table. Doing this gives a chi-square of 0.67:

$$\frac{(2 - 1.5)^2}{1.5} + \frac{(1 - 1.5)^2}{1.5} + \frac{(1 - 1.5)^2}{1.5} + \frac{(2 - 1.5)^2}{1.5} =$$

$$\frac{0.5^2}{1.5} + \frac{-0.5^2}{1.5} + \frac{-0.5^2}{1.5} + \frac{0.5^2}{1.5} = \frac{0.25}{1.5} + \frac{0.25}{1.5} + \frac{0.25}{1.5} + \frac{0.25}{1.5} =$$

$$0.167 + 0.167 + 0.167 + 0.167 = 0.668$$

Step 4 We look up this value which has 1 degree of freedom in the table in Appendix 5 where we see that chi-square has to be 2.71 or bigger to be significant at the one-tailed 0.05 level which it is not. Note, however, that because of the small expected frequencies, it would not be suitable to use a chi-square test in this instance and a Fisher's exact test would be more appropriate.

To conduct Mood's median test with Minitab first code numerically the condition for each boy (e.g. **1** for the reward condition and **2** for the punishment condition) and store this code in a column called **'cond'**. Then put in a column called **'agg'** the follow-up aggressiveness rating for each boy so the data are as follows:

1 2
1 3
1 4
2 3
2 2
2 1

The prompt command for performing Mood's median test comparing aggressiveness (**'agg'**) in the two conditions (**'cond'**) is:

MTB > mood 'agg' 'cond'

Note that the variable to be compared (**'agg'**) is listed first followed by the variable which provides the categories (**'cond'**).

The menu action for doing this is:

Table 6.12 **Mood**'s median test output comparing follow-up aggressiveness in boys for the reward and punishment conditions

Mood Median Test

Mood median test of agg

Chisquare = 0.67   df = 1   p = 0.414

```
                                  Individual 95.0% CIs
cond     N<=     N>    Median Q3-Q1 -------+-------+-------+-----
  1       1       2     3.00  2.00        (-------+-------)
  2       2       1     2.00  2.00  (-----+-----)
                                  -------+-------+-------+-----
                                    2.0     3.0     4.0
```

Overall median = 2.50

* NOTE * Levels with < 6 obs. have confidence < 95.0%

A 89.8% C.I. for median(1) − median(2): (−1.00, 3.00)

→**Stat** →**Nonparametrics** →**Mood's Median Test...** →**agg** →**Select** [this puts **agg** in the box beside **Response:**] →**cond** →**Select** [this puts **cond** in the box beside **Factor:**] →**OK**

The output for this command is shown in Table 6.12. The number of scores greater than (**N>**) and less than or equal (**N<=**) to the median is shown as well as the chi-square value and its exact probability level. When there are relatively few scores above the median, Minitab counts scores equal to the median as those above it.

When three or more groups are being compared we can conduct *post hoc* comparisons between any two groups using the same procedure (Marascuilo and McSweeney 1977). However, we need to adjust the 0.05 significance level by dividing it by the number of comparisons being made. For example, for three comparisons the appropriate significance level would be 0.0167 (0.05/3 = 0.0167).

KRUSKAL–WALLIS ONE-WAY ANALYSIS OF VARIANCE OR *H* TEST FOR THREE OR MORE UNRELATED SAMPLES

The Kruskal–Wallis *H* test is similar to the Mann–Whitney *U* test in that the cases in the different samples are ranked together in one series except that this test can be used with more than two unrelated samples. If there is little difference between the sets of scores, then their mean ranks should be similar. We would use the Kruskal–Wallis *H* test to determine if follow-up aggressiveness in boys differed between the three conditions of reward,

Table 6.13 Follow-up aggressiveness ratings for boys in the reward, punishment and control conditions

Reward	Punishment	Control
2	3	2
3	2	1
4	1	0

Table 6.14 Ranking of follow-up aggressiveness ratings for boys in the reward, punishment and control conditions

	Reward	Punishment	Control
	5.0	7.5	5.0
	7.5	5.0	2.5
	9.0	2.5	1.0
Total	21.5	15.0	8.5

punishment and control. To apply this test to these data, we would carry out the following steps:

Step 1   Rank the scores of the conditions taken together, giving rank 1 to the lowest score. Where two or more scores are tied, allocate the average rank to those scores. The follow-up aggressiveness ratings for the three conditions are presented in Table 6.13 where they have been rearranged in three parallel columns. The ranking of these data is shown in Table 6.14.

Step 2   Sum the ranks for each group which, in this example, gives 21.5, 15.0 and 8.5 respectively.

Step 3   For each group, square the sum of ranks and divide by the number of cases. This in turn yields 154.08 (462.25/3 = 154.08), 75 (225/3 = 75) and 24.08 (72.25/3 = 24.08).

Step 4   Sum these values which, in this case, is 253.16.

Step 5   Place this figure (which we shall call SR for sum of ranks) in the following formula which gives *H*:

$$H = \frac{12 \times SR}{N \times (N + 1)} - [3 \times (N + 1)]$$

Substituting the appropriate values, *H* is 3.75:

$$\frac{12 \times 253.16}{9 \times (9 + 1)} - [3 \times (9 + 1)] = \frac{3037.92}{90} - 30 = 33.75 - 30 = 3.75$$

When there are more than 5 cases in each of the conditions, the significance of H may be determined from the chi-square table in Appendix 5. The degrees of freedom is one less than the number of samples which in this case is 2 ($3 - 1 = 2$). Since with 2 degrees of freedom an H value of 3.75 is not greater than 5.99 at the two-tailed 0.05 level, we would conclude that there was no significant difference in follow-up aggressiveness between the three conditions.

To correct for tied scores, we carry out the following steps:

Step 1   Count the number of ties for each score. In this example, we have two ties of 1, three ties of 2 and two ties of 3.

Step 2   For each tied score, subtract the number of ties from the number of ties cubed. So, three ties becomes 6 ($3^3 - 3 = 24$).

Step 3   Sum these values for each tied score, which in this case gives 28:

$$(2^2 - 2) + (3^3 - 3) + (2^2 - 2) = 2 + 24 + 2 = 28$$

Step 4   Divide this value by the total number of cases subtracted from the total number of cases cubed, which in this instance produces a figure of 0.039:

$$\frac{28}{9^3 - 9} = \frac{28}{729 - 9} = \frac{28}{720} = 0.0388$$

Step 5   Subtract this number from one, which gives 0.961 ($1 - 0.039 = 0.961$).

Step 6   Divide the uncorrected value of H by this figure to give the value corrected for ties, which in this example is 3.91 ($3.76/0.961 = 3.91$). We look up this value in the chi-square table in Appendix 5. Since with 2 degrees of freedom this figure is not greater than 5.99 at the two-tailed 0.05 level, we would conclude that there was no significant difference in follow-up aggressiveness between the three conditions.

To conduct a Kruskal–Wallis H test with Minitab first code numerically the condition for each boy (e.g. **1** for the reward condition, **2** for the punishment condition and **3** for the control condition) and store this code in a column called **'cond'**. Then put in a column called **'agg'** the follow-up aggressiveness rating for each boy so the data are as follows:

1 2
1 3
1 4
2 3
2 2
2 1
3 2
3 1
3 0

The prompt command for performing a Kruskal–Wallis test comparing aggressiveness ('agg') across the three conditions ('cond') is:

MTB > kruskal-wallis 'agg' 'cond'

Note that the variable to be compared ('agg') is listed first followed by the variable which provides the categories ('cond').

The menu action for doing this is:

→**Stat** →**Nonparametrics** →**Kruskal-Wallis. . .** →**agg** →**Select** [this puts **agg** in the box beside **Response:**] →**cond** →**Select** [this puts **cond** in the box beside **Factor:**] →**OK**

The output for this command is shown in Table 6.15. The number of observations or cases (**NOBS**) for the conditions or **LEVEL**s is displayed in the second column and their average rank (**AVE. RANK**) in the fourth column. The H and its significance both unadjusted and adjusted for ties is also displayed. Since the significance level is greater than 0.05 on both tests (unadjusted **p = 0.153** and adjusted **p = 0.139**), we would conclude that there was no difference in boys in follow-up aggressiveness between the three conditions.

This test only tells us whether three or more groups differ but not which

Table 6.15 **Kruskal–Wallis** *H* test output comparing follow-up aggressiveness for boys in the reward, punishment and control conditions

Kruskal–Wallis Test

Level	NOBS	MEDIAN	AVE.RANK	Z VALUE
1	3	3.000	7.2	1.68
2	3	2.000	5.0	0.00
3	3	1.000	2.8	−1.68
Overall	9		5.0	

H = 3.76   d.f. = 2   p = 0.153
H = 3.95   d.f. = 2   p = 0.139 (adjusted for ties)

* NOTE * One or more small samples

of any two groups differ. Marascuilo and McSweeney (1977) suggest that the Mann–Whitney test can be used to make *post hoc* comparisons between all pairs of groups adjusting the significance level of 0.05 by dividing it by the number of comparisons. For example, with three comparisons the appropriate significance level would be 0.0167 (0.05/3 = 0.0167).

SIGN TEST FOR TWO RELATED SAMPLES

The sign test compares the number of positive and negative differences between scores from the same or matched samples. If the two samples do not differ, then the number of positive and negative differences should be similar. We could use the sign test to determine if there had been for one or more conditions any change in aggressiveness between any two occasions when aggressiveness had been measured such as at pre-test and post-test.

To apply the sign test to determine whether aggressiveness had increased from pre-test to post-test for boys in the reward condition, we would carry out the following steps:

Step 1 Record the direction of change between the two occasions, giving a plus (+) if the second score is larger than the first, a minus (−) if it is smaller and a zero (0) if there is no difference. These differences have been noted in Table 6.16 for the pre-test and post-test aggressiveness scores for boys in the reward condition.

Step 2 Count the number of pluses and minuses. Let *n* represent the less frequent sign and *N* the total number of pluses and minuses. In this example, *n* is 0 since there are no pluses and *N* is 2.

Step 3 for less than 26 differences For samples containing less than 26 differences (number of pluses and minuses), look up the significance of the results in the binomial table in Appendix 4. The one-tailed probability of obtaining this value is 0.250 which is greater than the 0.05 criterion. In other words, aggressiveness did not increase significantly from pre-test to post-test for the reward condition.

Table 6.16 Pre-test and post-test aggressiveness ratings for boys in the reward condition

Pre-test	Post-test	Sign of Difference
1	2	−
2	4	−
3	3	0

Step 3 for greater than 25 differences For samples having more than 25 differences, the less frequent difference can be converted into a z value using the following formula:

$$z = \frac{(n + 0.5) - N/2}{0.5 \times \sqrt{N}}$$

where n and N have the same meaning as before. Substituting the appropriate values in this formula, z is -0.70:

$$\frac{(0 + 0.5) - 2/2}{0.5 \times \sqrt{2}} = \frac{-0.5}{0.5 \times 1.41} = \frac{-0.5}{0.71} = -0.70$$

We look up the significance of this z value of 0.70 in the normal distribution table in Appendix 2, where we see that it has a one-tailed probability value of less than 0.2420 ($0.5000 - 0.2580 = 0.2420$).

To perform a sign test with Minitab first put the aggressiveness ratings of the boys in the reward condition for the pre-test in one column called, say, **'pre'** and for the post-test in another column called, for example, **'post'**. Then subtract the post-test scores from the pre-test scores using the following **let** command and store the difference in a third column called **c3**:

MTB > let c3='pre'-'post'

The menu procedure for doing this is:

→**C**alc →**M**athematical **E**xpressions... →**c3** →**Select** [this puts **c3** in the box beside **V**ariable [new **o**r modified]:] →box under **E**xpression: and in it type **'pre'-'post'** →**O**K

To determine if the number of positive differences differs from the number of negative differences, we carry out the sign test on the differences stored in **c3** with the following **stest** command:

MTB > stest c3;
SUBC> alternative -1.

Since we expect the difference between the pre- and post-test scores to be

Table 6.17 Sign test output comparing pre- and post-test aggressiveness for boys in the reward condition

Sign Test for Median

Sign test of median = 0.00000 versus L.T. 0.00000

	N	BELOW	EQUAL	ABOVE	P-VALUE	MEDIAN
C3	3	2	1	0	0.2500	−1.000

negative, we put −1 on the **alternative** subcommand to obtain the one-tailed level of significance. Omit this subcommand and the semi-colon on the previous line if the two-tailed probability is required.

The menu procedure for doing this is:

→**Stat** →**Nonparametrics** →**1-Sample Sign...** →**c3** →**Select** [this puts **c3** in the box under **Variables:**] →the down button on the box beside **Alternative:** →**less than** [for the two-tailed level →**not equal**] →**OK**

The output for this procedure is presented in Table 6.17. The number of negative (**BELOW**), positive (**ABOVE**) and zero (**EQUAL**) differences are shown together with the probability value.

WILCOXON MATCHED-PAIRS SIGNED-RANKS TEST FOR TWO RELATED SAMPLES

Whereas the sign test only makes use of the sign of the difference between the two samples, the Wilcoxon matched-pairs signed-ranks test (or Wilcoxon test for short) takes some account of the size of the difference by ranking the size of the differences and summing ranks of the same sign.

To conduct a Wilcoxon test to determine whether aggressiveness had increased from pre-test to post-test for boys in the reward condition, we would carry out the following steps:

Step 1 Calculate the difference between each pair of scores and rank these in size, ignoring the sign of the difference. Give a rank of 1 to the smallest difference (regardless of its sign) and omit pairs where there is no difference. For example, 2 would receive a higher rank than either 1 or −1, which would be given the same rank. The size and rank of the differences between pre-test and post-test aggressiveness scores for the boys in the reward condition are presented in Table 6.18.

Where two or more differences are the same size, they are given the average of the ranks they would have received if they had differed. The smallest difference in our data is 1 and there is only one such value, so its rank is 1.

Table 6.18 Ranked differences between pre-test and post-test aggressiveness ratings for boys in the reward condition

Pre-test	Post-test	Difference	Rank
1	2	−1	1.0
2	4	−2	2.0
3	3	0	

Step 2   Sum the ranks of the difference with the less frequent sign. In this case, the less frequent sign is plus. Since there are no positive differences, the sum of ranks is zero.

Step 3 for less than 26 differences   For data having fewer than 26 differences, look up the significance of the smaller sum of ranks with the same sign in the table in Appendix 14. We can use the one-tailed significance level as we are testing for an increase rather than a change in aggressiveness. The smaller sum of ranks has to be the same as or smaller than the values shown in the table in order to be significant at the stated level. The significance level for samples with fewer than 5 differences is not given. However, if the sample had been 6, we can see that a sum of ranks of 0 is smaller than 2 at the two-tailed 0.10 level (and therefore at the one-tailed 0.05 level), and so we would have concluded that aggressiveness had decreased significantly from pre-test to post-test for boys in the reward condition.

Step 3 for more than 25 differences   For data with more than 25 differences, the following formula is used to transform the smaller sum of ranks (denoted as SR) into a z score where N stands for the number of differences:

$$z = \frac{SR - \dfrac{N \times (N + 1)}{4}}{\sqrt{\dfrac{N \times (N + 1) \times [(2 \times N) + 1]}{24}}}$$

To illustrate the use of this formula, we will substitute the values of our example which gives a z of -1.34:

$$\frac{0 - \dfrac{2 \times (2 + 1)}{4}}{\sqrt{\dfrac{2 \times (2 + 1) \times [(2 \times 2) + 1]}{24}}} = \frac{0 - \dfrac{6}{4}}{\sqrt{\dfrac{6 \times 5}{24}}} = \frac{-1.5}{\sqrt{1.25}} =$$

$$\frac{-1.5}{1.12} = -1.339$$

We look up the significance of this z value of 1.34 in the normal distribution table in Appendix 2, where we see that it has a one-tailed probability of less than 0.0901 ($0.5000 - 0.4099 = 0.0901$).

To run this test on Minitab we would use the following **wtest** command on the difference between pre- and post-test aggressiveness for boys in the punishment condition stored in **c3**:

Table 6.19 Wilcoxon test output comparing pre- and post-test aggressiveness for boys in the reward condition

Wilcoxon Signed Rank Test

TEST OF MEDIAN = 0.000000 VERSUS MEDIAN L.T. 0.000000

	N	N FOR TEST	WILCOXON STATISTIC	P-VALUE	ESTIMATED MEDIAN
C3	3	2	0.0	0.186	−1.000

MTB > wtest c3;
SUBC> alternative -1.

As we expected the difference between the pre- and post-test scores to be negative, we put −1 on the **alternative** subcommand to obtain the one-tailed probability. Omit this subcommand and the semi-colon on the previous line if the two-tailed probability is needed.

The menu procedure for doing this is:

→**Stat** →**Nonparametrics** →**1-Sample Wilcoxon...** →**c3** →**Select** [this puts **c3** in the box under **Variables:**] →the down button on the box beside **Alternative:** →**less than** [for the two-tailed level →**not equal**] →**OK**

The output for these commands is shown in Table 6.19. The Wilcoxon statistic reported is the sum of the ranks for the positive differences. As the one-tailed p value is greater than 0.05 we would conclude that aggressiveness for boys in the reward condition did not increase significantly from pre- to post-test.

FRIEDMAN TWO-WAY ANALYSIS OF VARIANCE TEST FOR THREE OR MORE RELATED SAMPLES

The Friedman two-way analysis of variance test (or Friedman test for short) compares the mean ranks of three or more related samples. If the samples do not differ, the mean ranks should be similar. The Friedman test approximates a chi-square distribution where the degrees of freedom are the number of columns minus 1. This test was developed by the Nobel prize-winning economist Milton Friedman.

To calculate the Friedman test to determine whether pre-test, post-test and follow-up aggressiveness differs for boys in the reward condition, we would carry out the following steps.

Step 1   Arrange the scores in a table where the columns represent the conditions and the rows the cases. This has been done for the pre-test, post-

Table 6.20 Pre-test, post-test and follow-up aggressiveness ratings for boys in the reward condition

Pre-test	Post-test	Follow-up
1	2	2
2	4	3
3	3	4

Table 6.21 Ranked pre-test, post-test and follow-up aggressiveness ratings for boys in the reward condition and initial computations

	Pre-test	Post-test	Follow-up	
	1.0	2.5	2.5	
	1.0	3.0	2.0	
	1.5	1.5	3.0	
Sum	3.5	7.0	7.5	
Sum^2	12.25	49.0	56.25	117.5

test and follow-up aggressiveness scores for boys in the reward condition in Table 6.20.

Step 2 Rank the scores in each row across all the conditions, ranking the lowest score as 1. Where two or more scores are tied, allocate the average rank to those scores. The scores in Table 6.20 have been ranked in this way in Table 6.21. For example, in the first row 1 would be ranked 1 and the two 2s would receive the average rank of 2.5 [(2 + 3)/2 = 2.5].

Step 3 Sum the ranks for each condition, as shown in Table 6.21, which gives 3.5, 7.0 and 7.5 respectively.

Step 4 Square the sum of ranks for each condition, as indicated in Table 6.21, producing 12.25, 49.0 and 56.25 respectively.

Step 5 Add together the squared sum of ranks to form the total squared sum of ranks which we shall abbreviate as TSSR and which is 117.5.

Step 6 To obtain chi-square unadjusted for ties (referred to by Hollander and Wolfe 1973 as S), insert this value into the following formula where C represents the number of columns and N the number of rows or cases:

$$S = \frac{12 \times \text{TSSR}}{N \times C \times (C + 1)} - 3 \times N \times (C + 1)$$

Substituting the appropriate figures in our example, we find that S is 3.17:

$$\frac{12 \times 117.5}{3 \times 3 \times (3 + 1)} - 3 \times 3 \times (3 + 1) =$$

$$\frac{117.5}{3} - 36 = 39.167 - 36 = 3.167$$

We look up the significance of this value, which has 2 degrees of freedom, in the table in Appendix 5. The two-tailed probability level is used because with three conditions, we cannot specify the direction of any differences. Chi-square has to be 5.99 or larger to be significant which it is not. Consequently, we could conclude that there is no significant difference between pre-test, post-test and follow-up aggressiveness for the reward condition when no adjustment is made for tied ranks.

To obtain chi-square adjusted for ties (called by Hollander and Wolfe 1973 S'), we would insert the TSSR into the following formula:

$$S' = \frac{(12 \times \text{TSSR}) - [3 \times N^2 \times C \times (C + 1)^2]}{[N \times C \times (C + 1)] - [\text{sum of adjustments for each row}]/(C - 1)]}$$

where the adjustment for each row is the number of ties cubed for any rank added to 1 cubed (i.e. 1) for every untied rank minus the number of columns.

Rows 1 and 3 have two ties of the same rank and 1 untied rank, so the adjustment for rows with tied ranks would be 12:

$$[(2^3 + 1^3) - 3] + [(2^3 + 1^3) - 3] = (9 - 3) + (9 - 3) = 6 + 6 = 12$$

Consequently, chi-square adjusted for ties would be 3.80

$$\frac{(12 \times 117.5) - [3 \times 3^2 \times 3 \times (3 + 1)^2]}{[3 \times 3 \times (3 + 1) - [12/(3 - 1)]} =$$

$$\frac{1410 - (3 \times 9 \times 3 \times 16)}{36 - 6} = \frac{1410 - 1296}{30} = \frac{114}{30} = 3.80$$

From the table in Appendix 5, we can see that this value with 2 degrees of freedom is smaller than the two-tailed 0.05 critical value of 5.99 and so we would conclude that there is no significant difference in aggressiveness between the three occasions when an adjustment is made for tied ranks.

To run this Friedman test on Minitab, we need to create three columns of data. The first will contain the aggressiveness ratings in the three columns of data in Table 6.15 stacked on top of each other, starting with the pre-test and ending with the follow-up column. The second column will consist of a numerical code to denote which of the values in the first column correspond to which of the three treatments. We could use **1** for the pre-test, **2** for the post-test and **3** for the follow-up. The third column contains the number to identify the aggressiveness rating for the same person in the three groups. We will call these three columns **'agg'**, **'cond'** and **'cases'**. The three columns of data should look like this:

1 1 1
2 1 2
3 1 3
2 2 1
4 2 2
3 2 3
2 3 1
3 3 2
4 3 3

Note that the second column can be quickly created with the following **set** prompt command:

MTB > set c2
DATA> (1:3)3
DATA> end

The numbers to be repeated are placed within parentheses. The colon represents consecutive numbers between **1** and **3**. The number **3** after the closing parenthesis means the first number **1** is repeated 3 times after which the second number **2** is repeated 3 times and so on. There must be no space between this number and the closing bracket.

The third column can be most efficiently created with the following **set** command:

MTB > set c3
DATA> 3(1:3)
DATA> end

The numbers to be repeated are placed within parentheses. The colon represents consecutive numbers between **1** and **3**. The number **3** before the opening parenthesis means the sequence 1 to 3 is repeated 3 times. There must be no space between this number and the opening bracket.

With the menu system, one can first type in the numbers **1** to **3** in the appropriate column. Move the cursor to the first cell, press the left button on the mouse and holding it down move the mouse so that all three numbers are highlighted and then release the button. Select **Edit** and **Copy Cells**. With the cursor in the first cell, select **Edit** and **Paste/Insert Cells** (putting the numbers 1 to 3 in cells 4 to 6) and then select **Edit** and **Paste/Insert Cells** again (putting the numbers 1 to 3 in cells 4 to 6 and moving the previous set of numbers to cells 7 to 9).

Table 6.22 **Friedman** test output comparing pre-test, post-test and follow-up aggressiveness for boys in the reward condition

Friedman Test

Friedman test of agg by cond blocked by cases

S = 3.17   d.f. = 2   p = 0.206
S = 3.80   d.f. = 2   p = 0.150 (adjusted for ties)

		Est.	Sum of
cond	N	Median	RANKS
1	3	2.0000	3.5
2	3	3.0000	7.0
3	3	3.0000	7.5

Grand median = 2.6667

We would use the following prompt command to run the Friedman test on these data:

MTB > friedman 'agg' 'cond' 'cases'

where the variable to be compared (**'agg'**) is listed first followed by the variable forming the categories (**'cond'**) and then by the variable which identifies the same or matched participant (**'cases'**). Using the same or similar cases to control for individual variation within experimental designs is known as *blocking*. The same or matched cases are arranged in *blocks* which is the term used by Minitab. In this situation each block consists of one participant.

The menu procedure for doing this is:

→**Stat** →**Nonparametrics** →**Friedman...** →**agg** →**Select** [this puts **agg** in the box beside **Response:**] →**cond** →**Select** [this puts **cond** in the box beside **Treatment:**] →**cases** →**Select** [this puts **cases** in the box beside **Blocks:**] →**OK**

The output for this procedure is shown in Table 6.22 which includes the *S* statistic adjusted and unadjusted for ties, the degrees of freedom and the sum of ranks.

The Friedman test only tells us whether three or more groups differ but not which of any two groups differ. Marascuilo and McSweeney (1977) suggest that the Wilcoxon matched-pairs signed-ranks test can be used to make planned comparisons between pairs of groups adjusting the significance level of 0.05 by dividing it by the number of comparisons. For example, with three comparisons the appropriate significance level would be 0.0167 (0.05/3 = 0.0167).

SUMMARY

The computation of non-parametric tests for assessing whether the distribution of ordinal data from two or more samples differs significantly across the samples has been described. The Kolmogorov–Smirnov test determines whether the largest absolute difference between two unrelated samples is significant. The Mann–Whitney U test ascertains the number of times a score from one of the samples is ranked higher than a score from the other sample whereas the Kruskal–Wallis H test does this for three or more unrelated samples. If the different sets of scores are similar, then the number of times this happens should be similar for the samples being compared. A *post hoc* test for determining which pairs of samples differ is the Mann–Whitney U test. The Mood median test compares the distribution of scores of two or more unrelated groups around a common median. The sign test compares the number of positive and negative differences between scores from two related samples. If the two samples do not differ, then the number of positive and negative differences should be similar. The Wilcoxon test takes account of the size of the difference between the two unrelated samples by ranking the size of the differences and summing ranks of the same sign. The Friedman test compares the mean ranks of three or more related samples. If the samples do not differ, the mean ranks should be similar. The planned test for finding out which pairs of samples differ is the Wilcoxon test.

EXERCISES

The data presented in Table 6.23 will be used for the exercises in Chapters 6 to 11. The data consist of type of school (with single-sex schools coded as

Table 6.23 Type of school, gender, socio-economic status and educational interest at 9, 12 and 15

Case	School	Gender	SES	Age 9	Age 12	Age 15
1	1	1	1	2	3	4
2	1	1	2	2	3	4
3	1	1	3	2	4	3
4	1	2	1	3	4	2
5	1	2	2	1	2	3
6	1	2	3	1	2	2
7	2	1	1	3	3	4
8	2	1	2	2	2	3
9	2	1	3	2	1	3
10	2	2	1	3	2	3
11	2	2	2	2	2	1
12	2	2	3	2	1	1

1 and mixed-sex schools as 2), gender of pupil (with girls coded as 1 and boys as 2), socio-economic status (with higher status coded as 1, middle as 2 and lower as 3) and educational interest rated on a 4-point scale (with 1 for 'not interested', 2 for 'slightly interested', 3 for 'fairly interested' and 4 for 'very interested') at ages 9, 12 and 15 for the same pupils.

1 Use the Mann–Whitney U test to compare educational interest at 12 between single- and mixed-sex schools.
   (a) What is the U value of this test?
   (b) What is its two-tailed probability level?
   (c) Is educational interest at 12 significantly greater at single- than at mixed-sex schools?

2 Use the Mood median test to compare educational interest at 12 between single- and mixed-sex schools.
   (a) What is the value of this test?
   (b) What are the degrees of freedom?
   (c) What is the two-tailed probability level?
   (d) Is educational interest at 12 significantly greater at single- than at mixed-sex schools?

3 Use the Kruskal-Wallis H test to compare educational interest at 12 for pupils of different socio-economic status.
   (a) What is the value of this test adjusted for ties?
   (b) What are the degrees of freedom?
   (c) What is the two-tailed probability level?
   (d) Does educational interest at 12 differ significantly between pupils of different socio-economic status?

4 Use the sign test to compare educational interest at 12 and 15 for pupils from mixed-sex schools.
   (a) What is the two-tailed probability level?
   (b) Is educational interest significantly greater at 12 than at 15 for pupils from mixed-sex schools?

5 Use the Wilcoxon test to compare educational interest at 12 and 15 for pupils from mixed-sex schools.
   (a) What is the two-tailed probability level?
   (b) Is educational interest significantly greater at 12 than at 15 for pupils from mixed-sex schools?

6 Use the Friedman test to compare educational interest at 9, 12 and 15 pupils from single-sex schools?
   (a) What is the value of this test?
   (b) What are the degrees of freedom?
   (c) What is the two-tailed probability level?
   (d) Does educational interest differ significantly between 9, 12 and 15 for pupils from mixed-sex schools?

Chapter 7

Tests of difference for interval/ratio data in unrelated samples

The statistical tests covered in this chapter determine whether the means and variances of interval or ratio measures differ between two or more unrelated samples of cases. However, as discussed in Chapter 4, these tests can also be employed with ordinal data and the example used in the previous chapter of the effect on aggressiveness of watching aggressiveness being rewarded or punished will also be used in this chapter to illustrate the way in which these parametric tests are calculated. In addition, some of the tests discussed in this chapter can examine the effect of more than one variable. So, for example, the effect of gender as well as the effect of different treatments can be looked at in the same analysis. For instance, it is possible that watching aggressiveness being punished may reduce aggressiveness more in, say, girls than in boys while watching aggressiveness being rewarded may increase aggressiveness more in boys than in girls.

t TEST FOR ONE SAMPLE

This test is used to determine if the mean of a sample is similar to that of the population. We could use this test to find out whether the mean of, for example, follow-up aggressiveness for the nine boys in our study differed from the mean of the population. Suppose we knew that the population mean for self-rated aggressiveness in boys of that age group was 1.5. The formula for the t test is the difference between the population and the sample mean, divided by the *standard error of the mean*:

$$t = \frac{\text{population mean} - \text{sample mean}}{\text{standard error of the mean}}$$

It is important to outline what the standard error of the mean is since this important idea also forms the basis of other parametric tests such as the analysis of variance. One of the assumptions of many parametric tests is that the population of the variable to be analysed should be normally distributed. The errors of most distributions are known to take this form. For example, if a large group of people were asked to guess the mean height of an adult woman in Britain, the distribution of their guesses would approximate that of a normal distribution, even if the height of individual women did not represent a normal distribution.

If we draw sufficiently large samples of the same size from a population of values (which need not be normally distributed), then the means of those samples will also be normally distributed. In other words, most of the means will be very similar to that of the population, although some of them will vary quite considerably. This proposition is known as the *central limit theorem* and was formulated by LaPlace. The standard error of the mean represents the standard deviation of the means of samples of that size divided by the square root of the number of cases in the sample:

$$\text{standard error of the mean} = \frac{\text{standard deviation of the sample means}}{\sqrt{\text{number of cases in the sample}}}$$

However, it may be more convenient to re-express this formula as the square root of the division of the variance of the sample means by the number of cases in the sample

$$\text{standard error of the mean} = \sqrt{\frac{\text{variance of the sample means}}{\text{number of cases in the sample}}}$$

This formula is the same as the previous one. What we have done is simply to square the two terms in the first formula

$$\frac{(\text{standard deviation of the sample means})^2}{(\sqrt{\text{number of cases in the sample}})^2} = \frac{\text{variance of the sample means}}{\text{number of cases in the sample}}$$

and then taken the square root of the result.

We can check this using 1 as the standard deviation of the sample means and 4 as the number of cases in the sample. The standard deviation of the sample means divided by the square root of the number of cases in the sample is 0.5 ($1/\sqrt{4} = 1/2 = 0.5$) which is the same as the square root of the division of the variance of the sample means ($\sqrt{1} = 1$) by the number of cases in the sample ($\sqrt{1/4} = 0.5$).

Finally, in order to compare the formula for the standard error of the mean with the formula for the standard error of the difference in means used in the *t* test for two samples outlined below, we should note that

$$\text{standard error of the mean} = \sqrt{\frac{\text{variance of the sample means}}{\text{number of cases in the sample}}}$$

can be re-written as:

$$\text{standard error of the mean} = \sqrt{\text{variance of the sample means} \times \frac{1}{\text{number of cases in the sample}}}$$

It is worth noting that the standard deviation of the individual scores in a sample is the square root of the variance of the individual scores comprising that sample divided by the number of individual scores. The standard error of the means, however, is the standard deviation of the variance of the means of samples of a particular size. Since we do not know what the variance of the means of samples of that size is, we assume that it is the same as the variance of the sample. However, in order to calculate the standard deviation of the means we have to take account of the size of that sample by dividing the sample variance by the size of the sample (or, what amounts to the same thing, by multiplying by 1 over the size of the sample).

The bigger the sample is, the closer the sample mean will be to the population mean. If, for example, the number of cases in the sample is 100 and its variance is 1, then the standard error of the mean will be 0.10 ($\sqrt{1/100} = \sqrt{0.01} = 0.10$). Note, however, that if you quadruple the size of the sample, the standard error of the mean is a half ($\sqrt{1/400} = \sqrt{0.0025} = 0.05$) and not a quarter of its original size. In other words, very large samples are often unnecessary since they do not produce a sufficient decrease in standard error to be worthwhile.

The one-sample t test compares the mean of a sample with that of the population in terms of how likely that difference has arisen by chance. The smaller this difference is, the more likely it is to have resulted from chance.

To work out a one-sample t test for, say, comparing the mean pre-test aggressiveness of the nine boys in our example, we would carry out the following six steps:

Step 1   Work out the mean of the sample which is 1.67:

$(1+2+3+0+1+2+3+1+2)/9 = 15/9 = 1.67$

Step 2   Calculate the variance of the sample which is 1.0:

$[(1-1.67)^2 + (2-1.67)^2 + (3-1.67)^2 + (0-1.67)^2 + (1-1.67)^2 +$
$(2-1.67)^2 + (3-1.67)^2 + (1-1.67)^2 + (2-1.67)^2]/(9-1) =$
$[-0.67^2 + 0.33^2 + 1.33^2 + -1.67^2 + -0.67^2 +$
$0.33^2 + 1.33^2 + -0.67^2 + 0.33^2]/8 =$
$[0.45 + 0.11 + 1.77 + 2.79 + 0.45 +$
$0.11 + 1.77 + 0.45 + 0.11]/8 = 8.01/8 = 1.0$

Step 3   Work out the standard error of the mean which is the square root of the division of the variance of the sample by the number of cases in the sample. The standard error of the mean for this example is 0.33 ($\sqrt{1/9} = \sqrt{0.11} = 0.33$).

Step 4   Work out the *t* value by subtracting the sample mean from the population mean and dividing the difference by the standard error of the mean. The *t* value for this example is −0.52 [(1.5 − 1.67)/0.33 = −0.17/0.33 = −0.515].

Step 5   The degrees of freedom for this test are the number of cases minus 1 since, if we know the sample mean, one of the sample scores will be fixed while the rest will be free to vary.

Step 6   Look up the significance of the *t* value in the table in Appendix 15. With 8 degrees of freedom *t* has to be 2.306 or bigger to be significant at the two-tailed 0.05 level which it is not. Consequently, we would conclude that the sample mean does not differ significantly from the population mean.

The distribution of *t* values is symmetrical like the normal or *z* distribution except it is flatter. As the number of cases increases, the *t* distribution begins to approximate the normal distribution. We can see this if we compare the one-tailed *t* values in the table in Appendix 15 with the one-tailed *z* values in the table in Appendix 2. The one-tailed 0.05 *z* value is 1.65 which, rounded up, is the same as the one-tailed 0.05 critical *t* value of 1.645 with infinite degrees of freedom. As the degrees of freedom decrease from infinity to 1 so the one-tailed 0.05 critical *t* value increases from 1.645 to 6.314.

To compare the population mean with the sample mean using Minitab, we would use the following **ttest** command in which the population mean is listed before the column number or name of the variable analysed called here **'preb'** (for **pre**-test aggressiveness scores in **b**oys):

MTB > ttest 1.5 'preb'

The menu action for doing this is:

→**Stat** →**Basic Statistics** →**1-Sample t...** →**preb** →**Select** [this puts **preb** in the box beside **Variables:**] →**Test mean:** →box beside it and in it type **1.5** →**OK**

The output for this procedure is presented in Table 7.1. The sample mean is **1.667**. We see that the sample mean is not significantly different from the population mean of 1.5 since the two-tailed probability level is greater than 0.05.

If we expected the sample mean to be greater than the population mean we would put **1** in the **alternative** subcommand to obtain the one-tailed probability level:

MTB > ttest 1.5 'preb';
SUBC> alternative=1.

Table 7.1 Two-tailed **ttest** output comparing a sample and population mean

T-Test of the Mean

Test of mu = 1.500 vs mu not = 1.500

Variable	N	Mean	StDev	SE Mean	T	P-Value
preb	9	1.667	1.000	0.333	0.50	0.63

The menu sequence for doing this is:

→**Stat** →**Basic Statistics** →**1-Sample t...** →**preb** →**Select** →**Test mean:** →box beside it and in it type **1.5** →down button on the box beside **Alternative:** →**greater than** →**OK**

The output from this procedure is displayed in Table 7.2. The one-tailed probability value (**0.32**) is half that of the two-tailed level (**0.63**).

It should be pointed out that since we often do not know the population mean, the one-sample test is more likely to be used to estimate the population mean from the sample. The formula for the estimated population mean is:

estimated population mean = sample mean $\pm$ sampling error

This formula does not tell us what the population mean is but tells us within what range of values the population mean will fall. The population mean can fall either above, below or on the sample mean. The difference between the sample mean and the estimated population mean is known as the *sampling error* while the range of values within which the population mean can fall is known as the *confidence interval*. The formula for calculating the sampling error is:

sampling error = standard error of the mean $\times$ *t*

The lower confidence limit is the sample mean minus the sampling error:

lower confidence limit = sample mean $-$ sampling error

while the upper confidence limit is the sample mean plus the sampling error:

Table 7.2 One-tailed **ttest** output comparing a sample and population mean

T-Test of the Mean

Test of mu = 1.500 vs mu > 1.500

Variable	N	Mean	StDev	SE Mean	T	P-Value
preb	9	1.667	1.000	0.333	0.50	0.32

upper confidence limit = sample mean + sampling error:

What t value we choose to calculate the sampling error depends on how confident we want to be about the range within which the population mean is likely to fall. If we wanted to be 95 per cent confident that the population mean will fall within a certain range we would use the two-tailed 0.05 critical t value whereas if we wanted to be 99 per cent confident we would use the two-tailed 0.01 critical t value. We need to use the two-tailed rather than the one-tailed level since the population mean can fall either side of the sample mean. The t value and therefore the sampling error depends on the size of our sample. The bigger the sample, the bigger the t value and the smaller the sampling error.

To calculate the estimated population mean we carry out the following steps:

Step 1   Calculate the standard error of the mean by taking the square root of the division of the variance of the sample by the number of cases. As we have worked out above, the standard error of the mean for our example is 0.33 ($\sqrt{1/9} = \sqrt{0.11} = 0.33$).

Step 2   Look up in the table in Appendix 15 the critical value of t we need to use for the size of our sample and for the degree of confidence we want. With a sample of 9 and to be 95 per cent confident of the range within which the population mean is likely to fall, we would choose the critical t value that corresponds to the two-tailed 0.05 level with 8 degrees of freedom, which is 2.306.

Step 3   Work out the sampling error by multiplying the standard error of the mean by the appropriate t value. For our example, the sampling error is 0.76 ($0.33 \times 2.306 = 0.761$).

Step 4   The lower confidence interval is the sample mean minus the sampling error while the upper confidence interval is the sample mean plus the sampling error. For our example, the lower confidence limit is 0.91 ($1.67 - 0.76 = 0.91$) while the upper confidence limit is 2.43 ($1.67 + 0.76 = 2.43$). In other words, we can be 95 per cent confident that the population mean of pre-test aggressiveness in boys lies between 0.91 and 2.43.

To calculate the one-sample t confidence limit with Minitab we use the following **tinterval** prompt command in which the desired confidence level is listed before the variable name or column:

MTB > tinterval 95 'preb'

The menu action for doing this is

Table 7.3 **1-sample t confidence interval** output

Confidence Intervals

Variable	N	Mean	StDev	SE Mean	95.0 % C.I.
preb	9	1.667	1.000	0.333	(0.898, 2.436)

→**Stat** →**Basic Statistics** →**1-Sample t . . .** →**preb** →**Select** →**Confidence interval** if not already selected →in box beside **Level:** type **95** if not already given →**OK**

The output from this procedure is displayed in Table 7.3. The 95 per cent confidence interval (**95.0 % C.I.**) ranges from **0.898** to **2.436**.

t TEST FOR TWO UNRELATED SAMPLES

The *t* test for unrelated or independent samples determines if the means of two such samples differ. For example, we may wish to find out if mean aggressiveness in boys at follow-up is significantly higher in the reward than in the punishment condition. The *t* test compares the difference between the means of the two samples with the probability of those two means differing by chance. To determine the probability of two means differing by chance, we would draw a large number of samples of a certain size from some given population, subtract the means of these samples from each other and plot the distribution of these differences. If we did this, these differences would be normally distributed. Since the means of most of the samples will be close to the mean of the population and therefore similar to one another, most of the differences will be close to zero. The *t* test compares the means of the two samples with what is known as the *standard error of the difference in means* which is the standard deviation of the sampling distribution of differences between pairs of means:

$$t = \frac{\text{mean of one sample} - \text{mean of other sample}}{\text{standard error of the difference in means}}$$

Before applying the *t* test, we need to know whether the variances of the two samples differ significantly since the way in which the standard error of the difference in means is calculated varies slightly according to whether the variances are equal or not.

If the variances are unequal, they are treated separately according to the following formula:

$$\text{standard error of the difference in means} = \sqrt{\frac{\text{variance}_1}{n_1} + \frac{\text{variance}_2}{n_2}}$$

where variance$_1$ and variance$_2$ are the variances of the two samples 1 and 2 and where n_1 and n_2 are the numbers of cases in each sample.

This formula can be re-expressed in the same way as the last formula we gave for the standard error of the means which then becomes:

$$\text{standard error of the difference in means} = \sqrt{(\text{variance}_1 \times 1/n_1) + (\text{variance}_2 \times 1/n_2)}$$

If, on the other hand, the variances are equal, they are averaged or *pooled* together to take account of their differing degrees of freedom according to the following formula:

$$\sqrt{\left[\frac{((\text{variance}_1 \times (n_1 - 1)) + ((\text{variance}_2 \times (n_2 - 1)))}{n_1 + n_2 - 2}\right] \times \left[\frac{1}{n_1} + \frac{1}{n_2}\right]}$$

Note that this formula gives the same result as the previous one when the size of the samples are equal.

The pooled variance is calculated by multiplying the variance of one group by its degrees of freedom, doing the same for the other group, adding the two products together and dividing the result by the total degrees of freedom. This is like working out the mean of two groups of differing size from the group means. Say, the mean of the first group of four people is 1 while the mean of the second group of three people is 2. To calculate the mean of the two groups we multiply the first mean by the number of people in that group (4) which gives 4 ($1 \times 4 = 4$). We multiply the second mean by the number of people in that group (3) which gives 6 ($2 \times 3 = 6$). We add these two products together to give 10 ($4 + 6 = 10$) and divide this result by the total number of people in both groups (7) to give 1.43 ($10/7 = 1.43$). In effect, the standard error of the difference in means for unequal variances is the square root of the product of the pooled variance and the sum of one over the number of cases in one sample and one over the number of cases in the other group:

$$\text{standard error of the difference in means} = \sqrt{\text{pooled variance} \times (1/n_1 + 1/n_2)}$$

To determine whether the variances of two samples differ, we apply the F test if the distributions are normal and Levene's test if they are not, as described in Chapter 4.

Consequently, to apply the t test to determine whether the mean follow-up aggressiveness for boys is significantly higher in the reward than in the punishment condition we would carry out the following steps:

Step 1   Calculate the means of the two samples by adding the scores for each sample and dividing by the number of cases in that sample. The individual follow-up aggressiveness scores for the reward and punishment conditions for boys as well as their means are shown in Table 7.4.

Table 7.4 Follow-up aggressiveness ratings for boys in the reward and punishment conditions and initial computations for the unrelated *t* test

	Reward			Punishment		
	Original	Difference	Squared	Original	Difference	Squared
	2	−1	1	3	1	1
	3	0	0	2	0	0
	4	1	1	1	−1	1
Total	9		2	6		2
No of cases	3			3		
Mean	3			2		
Variance			1.0			1.0

Step 2 Calculate the variance for each of the samples by subtracting each score from the mean score for the sample, squaring these differences, adding the squared differences together and dividing this total by the number of scores minus one.

If we do this, we obtain a variance of 1.0 for both the reward and punishment condition.

Step 3 To apply the *F* test, we divide the larger by the smaller variance and look up the significance of the resulting *F* value in the table in Appendix 3.

Dividing 1.0 by 1.0 gives an *F* value of 1.0 which, with 2 degrees of freedom for the numerator and 2 degrees of freedom for the denominator, needs to be greater than 19.000 to be statistically significant at the 0.05 level which it is not. Consequently, the variances of the two samples in this instance do not differ significantly and the variances need to be pooled.

Step 4 for pooled variances Substitute the appropriate values in the formula for calculating the standard error of the difference in the means for pooled variances, which in our example is 0.82:

$$\sqrt{\left[\frac{[1.0 \times (3 - 1)] + [1.0 \times (3 - 1)]}{3 + 3 - 2}\right] \times \left[\frac{1}{3} + \frac{1}{3}\right]} =$$

$$\sqrt{\frac{2.0 + 2.0}{4}} \times 0.5833 = \sqrt{1.0 \times 0.667} = \sqrt{0.667} = 0.816$$

Step 5 for pooled variances To calculate *t*, subtract the mean of one sample from that of the other and divide by the standard error of the difference in the means. Substituting the relevant values from our example, t is 1.22:

$$\frac{3 - 2}{0.82} = \frac{1}{0.82} = 1.22$$

Step 6 for pooled variances   The degrees of freedom are found by using the following formula:

$$df = (n_1 - 1) + (n_2 - 1) = n_1 + n_2 - 2$$

Consequently, the degrees of freedom for this example are 4 (3 + 3 − 2 = 4).

Step 7 for pooled variances   To determine the significance of this t value, look it up in the table in Appendix 15. Since we specified the direction of the difference in aggressiveness between the two groups, we would use a one-tailed test. With 4 degrees of freedom, the t value would have to be greater than 2.132 to be statistically significant at or less than the 0.05 one-tailed level. As a t value of 1.22 is smaller than 2.132, we would conclude that there was no significant difference in follow-up aggressiveness between the two conditions.

Step 4 for separate variances   Substitute the appropriate values in the formula for calculating the standard error of the difference in means for separate variances, which for our example would be 0.82:

$$\sqrt{\frac{1.0}{3} + \frac{1.0}{3}} = \sqrt{0.333 + 0.333} = \sqrt{0.666} = 0.816$$

Step 5 for separate variances   To calculate t, subtract the mean of one sample from that of the other and divide by the standard error of the difference in the means. Substituting the relevant values from our example, t is 1.22:

$$\frac{3 - 2}{0.82} = \frac{1}{0.82} = 1.22$$

Step 6 for separate variances   The degrees of freedom are calculated using the following formula:

$$df = \frac{[(\text{variance}_1/n_1) + (\text{variance}_2/n_2)]^2}{\dfrac{(\text{variance}_1/n_1)^2}{(n_1 - 1)} + \dfrac{(\text{variance}_2/n_2)^2}{(n_2 - 1)}}$$

Substituting the appropriate figures from our example, the degrees of freedom are 3 when the decimal places are omitted which makes the test more conservative:

$$\frac{[(1.0/3) + (1.0/3)]^2}{\dfrac{(1.0/3)^2}{3-1} + \dfrac{(1.0/3)^2}{3-1}} = \frac{(0.333 + 0.333)^2}{\dfrac{0.333^2}{2} + \dfrac{0.333^2}{2}} = \frac{0.666^2}{\dfrac{0.111}{2} + \dfrac{0.111}{2}} =$$

$$\frac{0.444}{0.056 + 0.056} = \frac{0.444}{0.112} = 3.96$$

Step 7 for separate variances   Look up the significance of the *t* value in the table in Appendix 5. With 3 degrees of freedom, a *t* value of 1.42 has to be 2.353 or greater to be statistically significant at the 0.05 one-tailed level which it is not.

It should be clear that if we know the means, standard deviations (the square root of the variances) and numbers of cases of any two samples, we should be able to compute *t* tests by inserting the relevant information in the appropriate formulae.

One way of carrying out an unrelated *t* test with Minitab is to use the **twosample** command in which the scores for one sample are in one column (e.g. **'folrewb'** for **fol**low-up aggressiveness in the **rew**ard condition for **b**oys) and the scores for the other sample is in another column (e.g **folpunb**):

MTB > twosample 'folrewb' 'folpunb'

If we expected aggressiveness to be greater in the first than in the second condition we would have to add a semi-colon to the above command and to add the following subcommand:

SUBC> alternative 1.

which gives us the one-tailed level for this result. To run a one-tailed *t* test with pooled variances, replace the full stop of the last subcommand with a semi-colon and add the following subcommand:

SUBC> pooled.

The menu procedure for doing this is:

→**Stat** →**Basic Statistics** →**2-Sample t...** →**Samples in different columns** →box beside **First:** →**folrewb** →**Select** [this puts **folrewb** in this box] →**folpunb** →**Select** [this puts **folpunb** in the box beside **Second:**] →box beside **Assume equal variances** [omit this for separate variances] →down button on the box beside **Alternative:** →**greater than** for the one-tailed *p* level →**OK**

Table 7.5 **Twosample** one-tailed unrelated *t* test with pooled variances

Two Sample T-Test and Confidence Interval

Twosample T for folrewb vs folpunb

	N	Mean	StDev	SE Mean
folrewb	3	3.00	1.00	0.58
folpunb	3	2.00	1.00	0.58

95% C.I. for mu folrewb − mu folpunb: (−1.27, 3.27)
T-Test mu folrewb = mu folpunb (vs >): T= 1.22 P=0.14 DF= 4
Both use Pooled StDev = 1.00

Table 7.6 **Twosample** one-tailed unrelated *t* test with separate variances

Two Sample T-Test and Confidence Interval

Twosample T for folrewb vs folpunb

	N	Mean	StDev	SE Mean
folrewb	3	3.00	1.00	0.58
folpunb	3	2.00	1.00	0.58

95% C.I. for mu folrewb − mu folpunb: (−1.27, 3.27)

T-Test mu folrewb = mu folpunb (vs >): T= 1.22 P=0.14 DF= 4

Table 7.5 shows the output for the *t* test with pooled variances while Table 7.6 displays that for separate variances which in this case is the same apart from the phrase **Both use Pooled StDev = 1.00** in Table 7.5. The *t* value in both cases is **1.22** with an exact one-tailed *p* value of **0.14**.

Another way of conducting an unrelated *t* test with Minitab is to use the following **twot** command where the variable listed first contains the scores for the two conditions stacked on top of one another (**'folb'** for **fol**low-up aggressiveness in **b**oys) and the variable listed second has the code which identifies the two conditions (**'conrp'** for the **con** of **r**eward and **p**unishment):

MTB > twot 'folb' 'conrp'

The subcommands for requesting the one-tailed *p* value and pooled variances are the same as for the **twosample** command.

The menu sequence for carrying this out is:

→**S̲tat** →**B̲asic Statistics** →**2̲-Sample t...** →**Samples in o̲ne column** [this is automatically selected] →box beside **S̲amples:** →**folb** [this puts **folb** in this box] →**Select** →**conrp** →**Select** [this puts **conrp** in the box beside **S̲ubscripts:**] →box beside **Assume e̲qual variances** [omit this for

Table 7.7 **Twot** one-tailed unrelated *t* test with pooled variances

Two Sample T-Test and Confidence Interval

Twosample T for folb

conrp	N	Mean	StDev	SE Mean
1	3	3.00	1.00	0.58
2	3	2.00	1.00	0.58

95% C.I. for mu 1 − mu 2: (−1.27, 3.27)
T-Test mu 1 = mu 2 (vs >): T= 1.22 P= 0.14 DF= 4
Both use Pooled StDev = 1.00

separate variances] →down button on the box beside **Alternative:** →**greater than** for the one-tailed *p* level →**OK**

The output from both the **twosample** and **twot** procedures is the same apart from the names of the variables. Output from the **twot** procedure for a one-tailed unrelated *t* test with pooled variances is shown in Table 7.7.

Means, standard deviations and numbers of cases are often presented in social science papers. Having this information enables you to determine whether the means and variances differ. Minitab, however, does not compute *t* tests with these descriptive statistics as data. However, if you wish to carry out a number of these tests, then you might find it quicker to write a program using Minitab commands which will allow you to do this.

First, it is useful to name the columns we are going to put the data in. The mean, standard deviation and number of cases for the group entered first have been called '**m1**', '**s1**' and '**n1**' respectively and '**m2**', '**s2**' and '**n2**' for the group entered second. It is also helpful to name the other columns we are going to use to store the computed statistics. We will call them as follows: '**v1**' and '**v2**' for the variances of groups **1** and **2**; '**f**' for the **F**-ratio; '**df1**' for the degrees of freedom for the numerator; '**df2**' for the degrees of freedom for the denominator; '**ses**' for the standard error of the separate variances; '**ts**' for the **t** value for separate variances; '**dfs**' for the degrees of freedom for separate variances; '**sep**' for the standard error of the pooled variances; '**tp**' for the **t** value for pooled variances; and '**dfp**' for the degrees of freedom for pooled variances. We can do this using either the prompt or menu system.

We then write a macro as described in Chapter 3. Since we have to know whether we need to use pooled or separate variances, the first step in this macro will be to compute the *F* test which involves dividing the greater variance by the smaller variance. Consequently, we calculate the variance by squaring the standard deviation using the following commands where the symbols ** refer to exponentiation which in this case is to the power of 2:

let 'v1'='s1'**2
let 'v2'='s2'**2

To ensure that the larger variance is always divided by the smaller variance, we will use the following **if** command which specifies that if the first variance ('**v1**') is greater than or equal to (**ge**) the second variance ('**v2**'), the value of '**f**' will be '**v1**' divided by '**v2**' otherwise (**else**) the value of '**f**' will be the second variance ('**v2**') divided by the first variance ('**v1**'):

if 'v1' ge 'v2'
    let 'f'='v1'/'v2'
else
    let 'f'='v2'/'v1'
endif

Note that this **if** sequence ends with an **endif** command and will only run as part of a macro.

We need to look up the statistical significance of the F value in the appropriate table. Where the number of cases in each group differs, it would be useful if we also calculated and listed the degrees of freedom which can be done with the following Minitab commands:

if 'v1' ge 'v2'
    let 'df1'='n1'−1
else
    let 'df1'='n2'−1
endif
if 'v1' ge 'v2'
    let 'df2'='n2'−1
else
    let 'df2'='n1'−1
endif

To display the results of running these commands in a macro, we can use the **print** command, specifying the variables we want to see which in this case will be '**v1**', '**v2**', '**f**', '**df1**' and '**df2**':

MTB > print 'v1' 'v2' 'f' 'df1' 'df2'

If we do this, the following output will be presented:

Row	v1	v2	f	df1	df2
1	1	1	1	2	2

With the menu system, we could look them up in the appropriate columns in the **Data** window.

When writing a command for a fairly complex computation such as the pooled variances *t* test, it might be advisable to begin by breaking down the computation into a series of simpler steps to ensure that the correct sequence of calculations is carried out. Each step in the calculation can be checked by printing or examining the relevant values. Without any further information, Minitab will perform the following mathematical operations in order of priority: (1) square root (**sqrt**); (2) exponentiation (******); (3) multiplication (*****) and division (**/**); and (4) addition (**+**) and subtraction (**−**). However, you can control the order in which operations are carried out by enclosing in brackets the operation you first want to perform. So, for example, if you want to add or subtract two variables before multiplying or dividing them by another variable, you would bracket the first operation.

Since the calculation for the separate variance *t* test is simpler than that for the pooled variance one, we will begin by showing the commands that can be used for working out this test. The computation can be broken down into two steps, the first which calculates the standard error for separate variances (**'ses'**) and the second which gives the *t* value for separate variances (**'ts'**):

let 'ses'=sqrt(('v1'/'n1')+('v2'/'n2'))
let 'ts'=('m1'−'m2')/'ses'

The operations in brackets will be performed before those outside them so, for example, **'m2'** will be subtracted from **'m1'** before being divided by **'ses'**. These two commands could be collapsed into one as follows:

let 'ts'=('m1'−'m2')/(sqrt(('v1'/'n1')+('v2'/'n2')))

To calculate the appropriate degrees of freedom for separate variances (**'dfs'**), we could use the following two commands where the first command computes the denominator of the formula:

let 'dfs'=((('v1'/'n1')**2)/('n1'−1))+((('v2'/'n2')**2)/('n2'−1))
let 'dfs'=((('v1'/'n1')+('v2'/'n2'))**2)/'dfs'

Since the total length of a **let** command is 78 characters we cannot reduce these two commands to one.

If we run these commands as a macro and print **'ts'** and **'dfs'**, the following output is produced:

Row	ts	dfs
1	1.22474	4

For the pooled variance test, we could break down the computation into the following five steps:

let 'sep'=('v1'*('n1'−1))+('v2'*('n2'−1))
let 'sep'='sep'/('n1'+'n2'−2)

let 'sep'='sep'*(1/'n1'+1/'n2')
let 'sep'=sqrt('sep')
let 'tp'=('m1' − 'm2')/'sep'

Calculating the degrees of freedom for the pooled variance t test can be done with this simple command:

let 'dfp'='n1'+'n2'-2

The following output is displayed if we run these commands and print **'tp'** and **'dfp'**:

Row	tp	dfp
1	1.22474	4

Once we have checked that this set of commands for calculating the F test, t test and degrees of freedom for pooled and separate variances from means, standard deviations and number of cases is accurate, we can keep them as a file for future use.

ONE-WAY ANALYSIS OF VARIANCE FOR TWO OR MORE UNRELATED SAMPLES

One-way analysis of variance compares the means of two or more unrelated samples such as the mean follow-up aggressiveness ratings of boys for the three treatment conditions in our example. Analysis of variance (often abbreviated and referred to as ANOVA) is essentially an F test in which an estimate of the variance between the groups (i.e. the between-groups estimated variance usually known as the *between-groups* or *between-treatments mean-square*) is compared with an estimate of the variance within the groups (i.e. the within-groups estimated variance known as the *within-groups* or *within-treatments mean-square*) by dividing the former with the latter:

$$F = \frac{\text{between-groups estimated variance or mean-square}}{\text{within-groups estimated variance or mean-square}}$$

The mean-square refers to the mean of the squared deviations which is the sum of squared deviations divided by the appropriate degrees of freedom.

The between-groups mean square is based on the extent to which the means of the groups vary from the overall or total mean of the groups, while the within-groups mean square reflects the degree to which the scores within each group differ from the mean of that group combined across all the groups. If the variance between the groups is considerably greater than the overall variance within the groups, then this implies that the differences between the means are less likely to be due to chance. This situation is illustrated in Figure 7.1 where the means of the three groups (M_1, M_2, and

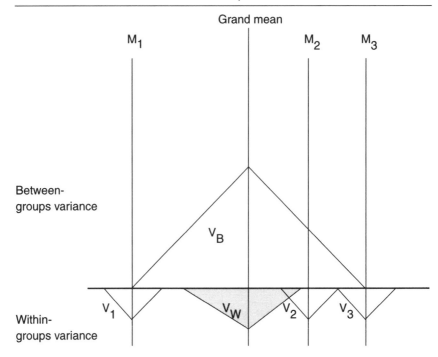

Figure 7.1 Schematic representation of a significant one-way effect

M_3) are quite widely separated causing a greater spread of between-groups variance (V_B) while the variance within the groups (V_1, V_2, and V_3) is considerably less when combined (V_W). The between-groups mean square is often referred to as the *explained* variance and the within-groups mean square as the *error* or *residual* variance since the between-groups mean square is more likely to represent the variance of the variable being investigated whereas the within-groups mean square is more likely to correspond to the variance of other factors which have not been measured or controlled.

The procedures described in this book for calculating analysis of variance will be based on the *fixed model* where the results apply only to the particular categories of the variables chosen by the investigator. The fixed model is distinguished from the *random model* where the categories of the variables have been randomly selected to be representative of those variables and where, therefore, the results can be generalised to the variables as a whole.

To compute a one-way analysis of variance we first need to work out the between- and within-groups sum of squares (*SS*) and their respective degrees of freedom (*df*) from which we can calculate the between- and within-groups mean-squares (*MS*) and *F* ratio. It is helpful to display these

Table 7.8 A one-way analysis of variance table

Source of variance	Sum of squares SS	Degrees of freedom df	Mean square MS	F ratio	F probability
Between-groups					
Within-groups/Error					
Total					

statistics in an analysis of variance table as shown in Table 7.8. Note that the total sum of squares equals the sum of the between- and within-groups sum of squares. Similarly, the total degrees of freedom equal the sum of the between- and within-groups degrees of freedom.

In many experimental designs which require analysis of variance, the number of cases in cells is unequal. However, this situation is more problematical in that there are three different procedures for analysing or partitioning the variance. All three methods produce the same result when there are equal numbers of participants in cells which is why we have done this. When numbers are unequal we could equalise them by randomly omitting cases from conditions. However, this procedure would waste valuable data and so is not recommended. Consequently, one of these three methods has to be selected as the preferred method since the results they give differ. The first method, referred to as the *regression* or *unweighted means* approach, assigns equal weight to the means in all cells regardless of their size. In other words, interaction effects have the same importance as main ones in designs with more than one factor. This is the approach to be recommended in a true experimental design such as this one where subjects have been randomly assigned to treatments. The second method, known as the *classic experimental* or *least squares* approach, places greater weight on cells with larger numbers of subjects and is recommended for non-experimental designs in which the number of sub-jects in each cell may reflect its importance. This approach gives greater weight to main effects than to interaction ones in designs with more than one factor. The third method, called the *hierarchical* approach, allows the investigator to determine the order of the effects. If one factor is thought to precede another, then it can be placed first. This approach should be used in non-experimental designs where the factors can be ordered in some sequential manner. If, for example, we are interested in the effect on aggressiveness of gender and watching violent films, then gender may be entered first since watching violent films cannot determine gender. Note that with these other approaches the component sums of squares will not necessarily add up to the total sum of squares because the effects may not be independent of one another.

We will illustrate the calculation of a one-way analysis of variance using the follow-up aggressiveness ratings of the boys in the three treatment conditions.

Step 1 To compute the between-groups mean square: (1) calculate the mean of each group; (2) subtract the overall (or *grand*) mean from the group mean; (3) square this difference; (4) multiply this squared deviation by the number of cases in that group; (5) sum these products for all the groups (giving what is known as the between-groups *sum of squares*); and (6) divide by the degrees of freedom which are the number of groups minus 1 (forming what is known as the between-groups *mean square*):

$$\text{between-groups mean square} = \frac{\text{sum of } [(\text{group mean} - \text{grand mean})^2 \times \text{number of cases in group}] \text{ for all groups}}{\text{number of groups} - 1}$$

When we multiply the squared deviation (of the grand mean from the group mean) by the number of cases in that group we are saying this is what the overall variation in that group would be if everyone in that group had that group's mean score.

The individual follow-up aggressiveness scores for boys in the three treatments are shown in Table 7.9 together with the group and overall (or grand) sum and mean. Therefore, the between-groups sum of squares is 6:

$$[(3 - 2)^2 \times 3] + [(2 - 2)^2 \times 3] + [(1 - 2)^2 \times 3] =$$
$$(1^2 \times 3) + (0^2 \times 3) + (-1^2 \times 3) = (1 \times 3) + (0 \times 3) + (1 \times 3) =$$
$$3 + 0 + 3 = 6$$

The between-groups sum of squares divided by the between-groups degrees of freedom $(3 - 1 = 2)$ gives a between-groups mean-square of 3 (6/2= 3).

Table 7.9 Follow-up aggressiveness ratings for boys in the reward, punishment and control conditions and initial computations

	Reward			Punishment			Control				
	O	D	D^2	O	D	D^2	O	D	D^2		
	2	−1	1	3	1	1	2	1	1		
	3	0	0	2	0	0	1	0	0		
	4	1	1	1	−1	1	0	−1	1		
Sum	9		2	6		2	3		2	Grand sum	18
N	3			3			3				9
Mean	3			2			1			Grand mean	2
Variance			1			1			1		

Step 2   We can calculate the within-groups mean square either directly or indirectly by computing the total sum of squares, subtracting from it the between-groups sum of squares and dividing the result by the within-groups degrees of freedom. To compute the within-groups degrees of freedom subtract 1 from the number of cases in each group and sum the results across all the groups:

$$\text{within-groups mean square} = \frac{\text{total sum of squares} - \text{between-groups sum of squares}}{\text{within-groups } df}$$

To calculate the total sum of squares subtract each score from the grand mean, square them, and add them together. The total sum of squares is 12:

$$(2 - 2)^2 + (3 - 2)^2 + (4 - 2)^2 + (3 - 2)^2 + (2 - 2)^2 +$$
$$(1 - 2)^2 + (2 - 2)^2 + (1 - 2)^2 + (0 - 2)^2 =$$
$$0^2 + 1^2 + 2^2 + 1^2 + 0^2 + -1^2 + 0^2 + -1^2 + -2^2 =$$
$$0 + 1 + 4 + 1 + 0 + 1 + 0 + 1 + 4 = 12$$

To work out the within-groups mean square subtract the between-groups sum of squares from the total sum of squares and divide by the within-groups degrees of freedom. For our example, the within-groups mean square is 1.0:

$$\frac{12 - 6}{(3 - 1) + (3 - 1) + (3 - 1)} = \frac{6}{2 + 2 + 2} = \frac{6}{6} = 1.0$$

To compute the within-groups mean square directly, add together the sum of squares for each group and divide this sum by the within-groups degrees of freedom. Calculated this way, the within-groups mean square is 1.0:

$$[(2-3)^2 + (3-3)^2 + (4-3)^2 + (3-2)^2 + (2-2)^2 + (1-2)^2 + (2-1)^2 +$$
$$(1-1)^2 + (0-1)^2]/[(3-1) + (3-2) + (3-2)] =$$
$$(-1^2 + 0^2 + 1^2 + 1^2 + 0^2 + -1^2 + 1^2 + 0^2 + -1^2)/(2 + 2 + 2) =$$
$$(1 + 0 + 1 + 1 + 0 + 1 + 1 + 0 + 1)/6 = 6/6 = 1.0$$

Step 3   To calculate the *F* ratio, simply divide the between-groups mean square by the within-groups mean square. In this case the *F* ratio is 3 (3/1 = 3).

Step 4   Look up the statistical significance of this *F* ratio in the table in Appendix 3. The degrees of freedom for the between-groups mean square are the number of groups minus 1 while for the within-groups mean square they are the sum of the number of cases within each group minus 1. So, the degrees of freedom are 2 for the between-groups mean square (or the numerator of the *F* ratio) and 6 for the within-groups mean square (or the denominator of the *F* ratio). With these degrees of freedom the *F* value

Table 7.10 A one-way analysis of variance table for follow-up aggressiveness in boys

Source of variance	SS	df	MS	F	p
Between-groups	6.0	2	3.0	3.0	ns
Within-groups/Error	6.0	6	1.0		
Total	12.0	8			

has to be 5.1433 or greater to be significant at the 0.05 level which it is not. Consequently, we would conclude that there were no significant differences in follow-up aggressiveness in boys between the three conditions. The one-way analysis of variance table of the results is shown in Table 7.10.

However, before we can draw such a conclusion we need to know whether the variances are homogeneous. Levene's test should be used to test this if the data are not normally distributed and the F ratio when the data are normally distributed. If the variances are unequal, then depending on the exact conditions there is a greater or lesser possibility that the F ratio will be significant. When the number of cases in each group is the same or nearly the same, there is a greater tendency for F to be significant. In these circumstances the *Hartley* and *Cochran* tests can be used for comparing variances.

Hartley's test (F_{max}) is simply the largest of the group variances divided by the smallest. In our example the variances for the reward, punishment and control condition are all 1.0. So F_{max} is 1.0 (1.0/1.0 = 1.0). We check the significance of F_{max} in the table in Appendix 16 where the parameters of the distribution are the number of conditions in the numerator and the number of cases in a group minus 1 in the denominator (or where the number of cases in each group vary slightly, the number of cases in the largest group minus 1). The parameters for our example are 3 and 2 respectively. The smallest degrees of freedom for the denominator in this table are 4. With these degrees of freedom in the denominator, for the variances to be significantly different at the 0.05 level, F_{max} would have to be 15.5 or larger which it is not. Consequently, we would conclude that the variances were equal.

In Cochran's C test the largest variance is divided by the sum of the variances. In this case, C is 0.33 [1.0/(1.0 + 1.0 + 1.0) = 1.0/3.0 = 0.33]. We look up the C value in the table in Appendix 17 where the parameters of the distribution are the number of groups in the numerator and the number of cases in a group minus 1 in the denominator (or where the number of cases in each groups vary slightly, the number of cases in the largest group minus 1). For the variances to be significantly different at the 0.05 level, C has to be 0.8709 or bigger which it is not. Therefore, we would conclude that the variances were homogeneous.

Where the number of cases vary considerably and where no group is smaller than 3 and most groups are larger than 5, the *Bartlett-Box F* test can be used for comparing variances. The procedure for computing this test will be illustrated with our example and is as follows:

Step 1 Calculate the value called M based on the following formula:

M = {(N - no. of groups) × log of [(n_1 − 1 × variance$_1$) + (n_2 − 1 × variance$_2$) +.../(N − no. of groups)]} − [(n_1 − 1 × log of variance$_1$) + (n_2 − 1 × log of variance$_2$) + ...]

where log is the natural logarithm, N is the total number of cases, n_1, n_2 and so on are the number of cases in each of the groups in the analysis and variance$_1$, variance$_2$ the variances.

For our example, M is 0:

{(9 − 3) × log of [(3 − 1 × 1.0) + (3 − 1 × 1.0) + (3 − 1 × 1.0)/(9 − 3)]} − [(3 − 1 × log of 1.0) + (3 − 1 × log of 1.0) + (3 − 1 × log of 1.0)] = {[6 × log of [(2 × 1.0) + (2 × 1.0) + (2 × 1.0)/6]} − [(2 × 0) + (2 × 0) + (2 × 0) = {6 × log of [(2.0 + 2.0 + 2.0)/6} − (0 + 0 + 0) = (6 × log of 0/6) − 0 = (6 × log of 0) − 0 = (6 × 0) − 0 = 0 − 0 = 0

Step 2   Calculate the value called A based on the following formula:

$$A = \frac{1}{3 \times (\text{no. of groups} - 1)} \times \left[\frac{1}{n_1-1} + \frac{1}{n_2-1} +... - \frac{1}{N - \text{no. of groups}} \right]$$

where n_1, n_2 and so on are the number of cases in each of the groups in the analysis.

For our example, A is 0.22:

$$\frac{1}{3 \times (3 - 1)} \times \left[\frac{1}{3 - 1} + \frac{1}{3 - 1} + \frac{1}{3 - 1} - \frac{1}{9 - 3} \right] =$$

$$\frac{1}{6} \times \left[\frac{1}{2} + \frac{1}{2} + \frac{1}{2} - \frac{1}{6} \right] = 0.167 \times (0.5 + 0.5 + 0.5 - 0.167) =$$

$$0.167 \times 1.33 = 0.222$$

Step 3   Calculate the value f_2 from the following formula:

$$f_2 = (\text{no. of groups} + 1)/A^2$$

For our example, f_2 is 80:

$$(3 + 1)/0.22^2 = 4/0.05 = 80$$

Step 3   Calculate the value f_1 from the following formula:

$f_1 = 1 - A + (2/f_2)$

For our example, f_1 is 0.76:

$1 - 0.22 + (2/80) = 1 - 0.22 + 0.025 = 0.755$

Step 4   Calculate the Bartlett-Box F from the following formula:

$$F = \frac{f_2 \times M}{(\text{no. of groups} - 1) \times (f_2/f_1 - M)}$$

For our example, F is 0:

$$\frac{100 \times 0}{(3 - 1) \times (80/0.76 - 0)} = \frac{0}{2 \times (105.26 - 0)} =$$

$$\frac{0}{2 \times 105.26} = \frac{0}{210.52} = 0$$

Step 5   We look up the significance of this F value in the table in Appendix 3 where the degrees of freedom are the number of groups minus 1 in the numerator and f_2 in the denominator. With 2 and 80 degrees of freedom respectively, F would have to be 3.0718 or larger to be statistically significant which it is not. Consequently, we would conclude that the variances did not differ significantly among the three groups. If the variances were found to be unequal, then it may be possible to make them similar through transforming the scores by, for example, taking their log or square root. Alternatively, a non-parametric test could be used for analysing the data.

Note that as the F test or ratio is a proportion, its minimum value is zero indicating no variation in the data. Since it cannot take on a negative value, the F test is non-directional. Therefore, the critical values for F are two-tail in the sense that the test is non-directional. However, when comparing the variances of two groups or in an analysis of variance with two conditions, it is possible to determine whether the difference obtained is in the predicted direction. Consequently, in these cases, it is possible to use a one-tailed level by dividing the two-tailed critical value by 2.

To carry out a one-way analysis of variance on follow-up aggressiveness in boys in the three conditions, we could use the following command:

MTB > oneway 'folb' 'con'

The variable to be compared is listed first (**'folb'** for **fol**low-up aggressive-ness in **b**oys) followed by the grouping variable (**'con'** for **con**ditions).

The menu sequence for doing this is:

Table 7.11 **Oneway** analysis of variance output for follow-up aggressiveness in boys

One-Way Analysis of Variance

Analysis of Variance on folb

Source	DF	SS	MS	F	p
con	2	6.00	3.00	3.00	0.125
Error	6	6.00	1.00		
Total	8	12.00			

				INDIVIDUAL 95% CIS FOR MEAN BASED ON POOLED STDEV			
LEVEL	N	MEAN	STDEV	-+-------+-------+-------+---			
1	3	3.000	1.000	(--------*------)			
2	3	2.000	1.000	(------*------)			
3	3	1.000	1.000	(------*------)			
				-+-------+-------+-------+---			

POOLED STDEV =	1.000			0.0	1.5	3.0	4.5

→**Stat** →**ANOVA** →**Oneway...** →**folb** →**Select** [this puts **folb** in the box beside **Response:**]→**con** →**Select** [this puts **con** in the box beside **Factors:**] →**OK**

The output for this procedure is displayed in Table 7.11. The *F* ratio of **3.00** has an exact two-tailed probability of **0.125** and so fails to be statistically significant at the 0.05 level.

INTERPRETING A SIGNIFICANT ANALYSIS OF VARIANCE *F* RATIO

The *F* ratio in the analysis of variance only tells us whether there is a significant difference between one or more of the means. It does not let us know where that difference lies. To find this out, we have to carry out further statistical tests. Some authors argue that these tests should be carried out even if the *F* ratio is not significant. Which tests we use depends on whether we predicted where the differences would be. If we had predicted, for example, that mean follow-up aggressiveness would be higher in the control condition than in either the reward or the punishment condition and had the *F* ratio been significant, then we would employ unrelated *t* tests to determine whether these predictions were confirmed. If, on the other hand, we had not anticipated any differences but discovered that the *F* ratio was significant, we could use one of a number of *post hoc* or *a posteriori* tests to find out where any differences lay. These tests take into account the fact that the more comparisons we make, the more likely we are to find that some of these comparisons would differ significantly by chance. For example, at the 5 per cent level of significance, of twenty comparisons one would be expected to differ significantly by chance while this figure would rise to five if a hundred comparisons had been made. The *Scheffé* test will be described as it provides an exact value for groups of unequal size and is more conservative in the sense that the probability of a Type I error is less (i.e. accepting a difference when there is no difference).

Scheffé test

The formula for the Scheffé test is:

$$\text{Scheffé test} = \sqrt{\text{within-groups mean square} \times (\text{no. of gps} - 1) \times F \times \left(\frac{1}{n_1} + \frac{1}{n_2}\right)}$$

where n_1 and n_2 are the number of cases in the two groups being compared and where F refers to the desired probability level (e.g. 0.05) with the appropriate degrees of freedom (i.e. those for the between-groups variance as the numerator and those for the within-groups variance as the denominator).

If the difference between the two means being compared is greater than the value given by the Scheffé test, then the two means differ significantly at the specified probability level.

To calculate the Scheffé test for our example, we substitute into the formula the following values, which will be the same for all three comparisons as the number of cases in each of the three groups is the same. The Scheffé test value for these comparisons is 2.62:

$$\sqrt{1.0 \times (3 - 1) \times 5.1433 \times (1/3 + 1/3)} =$$
$$\sqrt{1.0 \times 2 \times 5.1433 \times 0.6666} = \quad \sqrt{6.86} = 2.62$$

According to the table in Appendix 5, the F value at the 0.05 per cent level with 2 and 6 degrees respectively as the numerator and denominator is 5.1433.

The differences in means for the three comparisons are:

Group 1 (reward) vs Group 2 (punishment)
$3.0 - 2.0 = 1.0$
Group 1 (reward) vs Group 3 (control)
$3.0 - 1.0 = 2.0$
Group 2 (punishment) vs Group 3 (control)
$2.0 - 1.0 = 1.0$

Since none of these differences is greater than the Scheffé test value of 2.62, none of the group means differs significantly from each other.

Analysis of variance and the *t* test

It is worth noting that an unrelated analysis of variance for two conditions gives the same results as an unrelated *t* test since F is equal to t^2. We can readily see this if we compare the two-tailed 0.05 critical *t* values in the table in Appendix 15 with the two-tailed 0.05 critical F values with 1 degree of freedom in the numerator in the table in Appendix 3. For example, with 1 degree of freedom the critical *t* value is 12.706 which squared is 161.44 and which (within rounding error) is the same as the critical F value of 161.45 ($12.70629^2 = 161.4498$).

TWO-WAY ANALYSIS OF VARIANCE

Two-way analysis of variance compares the means of groups made up of two variables or *factors*. The two factors in our example are gender and treatment. With two categories or *levels* of gender and three of treatment (reward, punishment and control), we have what is known as a 2×3 analysis of variance. If we just had two levels of treatment (e.g. reward and control), we would have a 2×2 analysis of variance. The variable being compared is often called the *dependent* variable because it is usually assumed that the values of this variable *depend* on, or are affected by, the factors being investigated. As a consequence, the factors being investigated are frequently referred to as *independent* variables since they are not thought to be affected by the dependent variable. Furthermore, their statistical association with the dependent variable is called an *effect*.

There are two main advantages of analysing two factors at a time. The first is that it enables us to determine whether the two factors affect each other or *interact*. An interaction is when the effect of one variable is not the same under all conditions of the other variable. An example of an interaction would be if follow-up aggressiveness in the punishment condition was lower for girls than for boys while in the control condition there was no difference between girls and boys. Interactions are often more readily grasped when they are portrayed in the form of a graph. This example is shown in Figure 7.2. The vertical axis represents the mean follow-up aggressiveness while the horizontal axis can depict either of the other two variables. In this case it is used to show the two treatments. The effects of the other variable are indicated by points on the graph and lines joining them. Girls are represented by a circle and a broken line and boys by a cross and a continuous line.

An interaction is likely when the lines representing the variable are not parallel. Another example of an interaction is illustrated in Figure 7.3 where follow-up aggressiveness is lower for girls in both treatments but the difference between girls and boys is greater in the punishment treatment.

The absence of an interaction is likely when the lines representing the

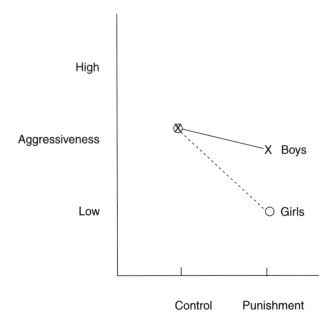

Figure 7.2 An example of an interaction

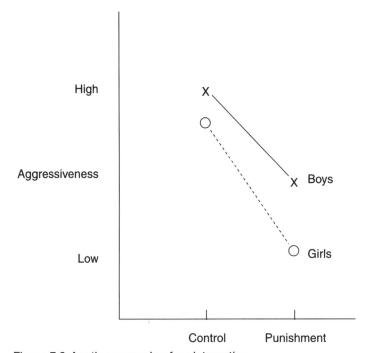

Figure 7.3 Another example of an interaction

second independent variable are more or less parallel as shown in Figures 7.4 and 7.5. In Figure 7.4 girls are less aggressive than boys in both treatments but the two treatments do not differ from one another. In Figure 7.5 girls are also less aggressive than boys but the two treatments also differ. Although interactions are more easily conveyed graphically, whether an interaction actually exists needs to be determined statistically and not graphically.

The second advantage of a two-way over a one-way analysis of variance is that it provides a more sensitive or powerful test of the effect of either factor than evaluating them singly, provided that the two factors do not interact substantially. The variance of the dependent variable is made up of variance attributed to the independent variable (explained variance) and variance that is unaccounted for (error or residual variance). When two variables are being analysed separately, the residual error is likely to be greater than when the two variables are being examined together since part of the residual error may be due to the other variable and to their interaction. Since the F ratio is derived by dividing the explained variance by the error variance, the F ratio is likely to be smaller and hence less likely to be significant when variables are analysed separately. This point will be illustrated after the procedure for computing a two-way analysis of variance has been described.

In a two-way analysis of variance there are four sources of variance as

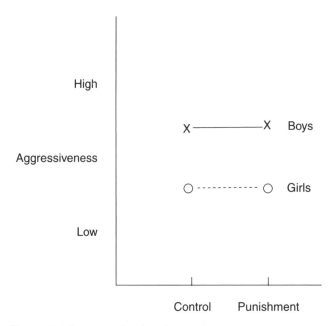

Figure 7.4 An example of no interaction

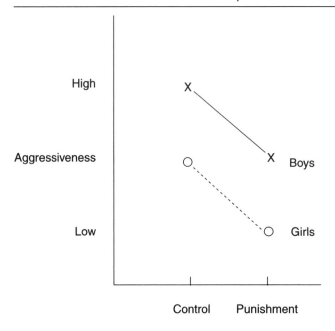

Figure 7.5 Another example of no interaction

shown in Table 7.12: (1) the between-groups variance of the first factor; (2) the between-groups variance of the second factor; (3) the between-groups variance of the interaction of the two factors; and (4) the within-groups variance. Consequently, three main F ratios have to be calculated which respectively compare the variance of the first and second factor and their interaction with the within-groups variance.

To simplify matters a little, we will illustrate the computation of a two-way analysis of variance with the follow-up aggressiveness scores from only two of the three treatment conditions, namely the reward and control conditions. The individual scores together with the group sums and means (rounded to two decimal places) are presented in Table 7.13. In addition,

Table 7.12 A two-way analysis of variance table

Source of variance	SS	df	MS	F	p
Between-groups					
First main effect					
Second main effect					
Two-way interaction					
Within-groups/Residual					
Total					

Table 7.13 Follow-up aggressiveness of girls and boys in the reward and control conditions together with initial computations

Gender	Treatment		Row sum and mean
	Reward	Control	
Girls	1	0	
	0	1	
	2	2	
Sum	3	3	6
N	3	3	6
Mean	1	1	1
Boys	2	2	
	3	1	
	4	0	
Sum	9	3	12
N	3	3	6
Mean	3	1	2
Column sum	12	6	Grand sum 18
Column N	6	6	Grand N 12
Column mean	2	1	Grand mean 1.5

the sum and mean for girls and boys (across treatments) is shown as the row sum and mean while the sum and mean for the two treatments (ignoring gender) is presented as the column sum and mean, together with the grand sum and mean.

Step 1   To compute the between-groups sum of squares for the first factor: (1) calculate the mean of each group of this factor (ignoring the other factor); (2) subtract the grand mean from the group mean of this factor; (3) square this difference; (4) multiply this squared difference by the number of cases within that group; and (5) sum these products for all the groups of that factor.

The sum of squares for the treatment factor is 3.0:

$$[(2 - 1.5)^2 \times 6] + [(1 - 1.5)^2 \times 6] =$$
$$(0.5^2 \times 6) + (-0.5^2 \times 6) = (0.25 \times 6) + (0.25 \times 6) =$$
$$1.5 + 1.5 = 3.0$$

Step 2   We repeat the same procedure for the second factor except that we use the group means of the second factor (ignoring the first factor).

The sum of squares for the gender factor is also 3.0:

$$[(1 - 1.5)^2 \times 6] + [(2 - 1.5)^2 \times 6] =$$
$$(-0.5^2 \times 6) + (0.5^2 \times 6) = (0.25 \times 6) + (0.25 \times 6) =$$
$$1.5 + 1.5 = 3.0$$

Step 3 To compute the between-groups sum of squares for the interaction we calculate the overall between-groups sum of squares and subtract from it the sum of squares for the first and second factor:

between-groups interaction sum of squares $=$ overall between-groups sum of squares $-$ first factor between-groups sum of squares $-$ second factor between-groups sum of squares

The overall between-groups sum of squares is calculated using the means of the groups formed by the two factors. We subtract the grand mean from the mean of each of these groups, square this difference, multiply this squared difference by the number of cases within that group and sum these products for all the groups:

overall between-groups sum of squares $=$ sum of [(first group mean $-$ grand mean)^2 $\times$ no. of cases in first group for each group]

In this example, there are four such groups so the overall between-groups sum of squares is 9.0:

$$[(1 - 1.5)^2 \times 3] + [(3 - 1.5)^2 \times 3] +$$
$$[(1 - 1.5)^2 \times 3] + [(1 - 1.5)^2 \times 3] =$$
$$(-0.5^2 \times 3) + (1.5^2 \times 3) + (-0.5^2 \times 3) + (-0.5^2 \times 3) =$$
$$(0.25 \times 3) + (2.25 \times 3) + (0.25 \times 3) + (0.25 \times 3) =$$
$$0.75 + 6.75 + 0.75 + 0.75 = 9.0$$

Subtracting the sum of squares for the two factors from the overall between-groups sum of squares gives the sum of squares for the interaction which is 3.0:

$$9.0 - 3.0 - 3.0 = 3.0$$

Step 4 Calculate the within-groups or residual sum of squares by adding together the sum of squares for each group. The within-groups sum of squares is 8:

$$(1-1)^2+(0-1)^2+(2-1)^2+(0-1)^2+(1-1)^2+(2-1)^2+$$
$$(2-3)^2+(3-3)^2+(4-3)^2+(2-1)^2+(1-1)^2+(0-1)^2 =$$
$$(-0)^2+(-1)^2+1^2+(-1)^2+0^2+1^2+(-1)^2+0^2+1^2+1^2+0^2+(-1)^2 =$$
$$0+1+1+1+0+1+1+0+1+1+0+1 = 8$$

Note that to complete the two-way analysis of variance table the total sum of squares can be obtained by subtracting each score from the grand mean, squaring them, and adding them together.

The total sum of squares for our example is 17.0:

$$(1.5 - 1)^2 + (1.5 - 0)^2 + (1.5 - 2)^2 + (1.5 - 0)^2 +$$
$$(1.5 - 1)^2 + (1.5 - 2)^2 + (1.5 - 2)^2 + (1.5 - 3)^2 +$$
$$(1.5 - 4)^2 + (1.5 - 2)^2 + (1.5 - 1)^2 + (1.5 - 0)^2 =$$
$$0.5^2 + 1.5^2 + -0.5^2 + 1.5^2 + 0.5^2 + -0.5^2 +$$
$$-0.5^2 + -1.5^2 + -2.5^2 + -0.5^2 + 0.5^2 + 1.5^2 =$$

$0.25 + 2.25 + 0.25 + 2.25 + 0.25 + 0.25 + 0.25 +$
$2.25 + 6.25 + 0.25 + 0.25 + 2.25 = 17.0$

Step 5   Calculate the residual mean square by dividing the residual sum of squares by its degrees of freedom. To compute the residual degrees of freedom subtract 1 from the number of cases in each group and sum the results across all the groups.

The residual mean square for our example is 1.0:

$$\frac{8}{(3-1) + (3-1) + (3-1) + (3-1)} = \frac{8}{2+2+2+2} = \frac{8}{8} = 1.0$$

Step 6   To derive the mean square for the first factor or main effect, divide the sum of squares for this factor by its degrees of freedom, which are the number of groups making up this factor minus 1.

The mean square for the treatment factor is 3.0:

$$\frac{3.0}{2-1} = \frac{3.0}{1} = 3.0$$

Step 7   To calculate the F ratio for the first main effect, divide its mean square by the residual mean square.

The F ratio for the treatment effect is 3.0:

$$\frac{3.0}{1.0} = 3.0$$

Look up the statistical significance of this F ratio in the table in Appendix 3. With 1 degree of freedom in the numerator and 9 degrees in the denominator, the F ratio has to be 5.1174 or larger to be statistically significant at the 0.05 level which it is not. Consequently, we would conclude that follow-up aggressiveness was not significantly greater in the reward than in the control condition. If there were more than two conditions in this factor, we would use tests such as the unrelated t or Scheffé to determine which if any pair of conditions differed significantly.

Step 8   Repeat this procedure for working out the mean square and F ratio for the second main effect.

The mean square for the gender effect is 3.0:

$$\frac{3.0}{2-1} = \frac{3.0}{1} = 3.0$$

The F ratio for the gender effect is also 3.0:

$$\frac{3.0}{1.0} = 3.0$$

Since this F ratio is also smaller than 5.1174, we would conclude that follow-up aggressiveness was not significantly lower in girls than in boys.

Step 9   Repeat this procedure for calculating the mean square and F ratio for the interaction effect. The degrees of freedom for the interaction effect are calculated by subtracting 1 from the number of groups in each factor and multiplying the resulting values.

The mean square for the interaction effect is 3.0:

$$\frac{3.0}{(2 - 1) \times (2 - 1)} = \frac{3.0}{1} = 3.0$$

The F ratio for the interaction effect is 3.0:

$$\frac{3.0}{1.0} = 3.0$$

Since this F ratio is smaller than 5.1174, we would conclude that there was no significant interaction between treatment and gender on follow-up aggressiveness. The results of this two-way analysis of variance are presented in Table 7.14.

If we had predicted an interaction effect, we could use the t tests for unrelated samples to determine whether our predictions were confirmed. If, on the other hand, we had not anticipated an interaction effect, we could use a *post hoc* test such as the Scheffé test.

The formula for computing the Scheffé test for a two-way analysis of variance is modified by multiplying the degrees of freedom for the first factor by those for the second:

Table 7.14 A two-way analysis of variance table for follow-up aggressiveness for girls and boys in the reward and control condition

Source of variance	SS	df	MS	F	p
Between-groups					
Treatment main effect	3.0	1	3.0	3.0	ns
Gender main effect	3.0	1	3.0	3.0	ns
Treatment × gender					
interaction	3.0	1	3.0	3.0	ns
Within-groups/Residual	8.0	8	1.0		
Total	17.0	11			

$$\sqrt{\frac{\text{within-groups}}{\text{mean square}}} \times \left(\begin{array}{c}\text{no. of groups} \\ \text{in factor A}\end{array} - 1\right) \times \left(\begin{array}{c}\text{no. of groups} \\ \text{in factor B}\end{array} - 1\right) \times F \times \left(\frac{1}{n_1} + \frac{1}{n_2}\right)$$

where n_1 and n_2 are the number of cases in the two groups being compared and where F refers to the desired probability level (e.g. 0.05). The appropriate degrees of freedom for F in the numerator are the product of the number of groups in the first factor (A) minus 1 times the number of groups in the second factor (B) minus 1, and in the denominator the total number of cases minus the product of the number of groups in the first and second factor.

With four groups, as in our example, we would have to make six comparisons:

1 Girls in reward group vs Girls in control group;
2 Boys in reward group vs Boys in control group;
3 Girls in reward group vs Boys in reward group;
4 Girls in control group vs Boys in control group;
5 Girls in reward group vs Boys in control group;
6 Boys in reward group vs Girls in control group.

We will illustrate the computation of this Scheffé test with the second comparison where the absolute difference between the two group means is 2 ($3 - 1 = 2$). The 0.05 F ratio with 1 degree of freedom in the numerator [$(2 - 1) \times (2 - 1) = 1$] and 10 in the denominator ($13 - 3 = 10$) is 4.9646. Substituting the appropriate values in the formula for the Scheffé test, this difference would have to exceed 1.52 to be statistically significant which it does not:

$$\sqrt{0.8 \times (2-1) \times (2-1) \times 4.9646 \times (1/3 + 1/4)} =$$
$$\sqrt{0.8 \times 1 \times 1 \times 4.9646 \times 0.583} = \sqrt{2.32} = 1.52$$

The proportion of variance in the dependent variable that is explained by the independent variables can be described by a statistic called *eta squared*. Eta squared is defined as the ratio of the between-groups sum of squares to the total sum of squares:

$$\text{eta squared} = \frac{\text{between-groups sum of squares}}{\text{total sum of squares}}$$

To calculate the amount of variance explained by the treatment factor we divide the between-groups sum of squares for this factor by the total sum of squares which gives 0.176:

$$\frac{3.0}{17.0} = 0.176$$

In this instance, 17.6 per cent of the variance in follow-up aggressiveness is explained by the treatment factor. To work out the proportion of variance explained by two factors, we would add together the two eta squared values. Since the between-groups sum of squares for gender is also 0.176, the percentage of variance explained by both treatment and gender is 35.2 (17.6 + 17.6 = 35.2).

To conduct with Minitab a two-way analysis of variance on the effect of treatment, gender and their interaction on follow-up aggressiveness for equal or unequal numbers of cases in cells, we need to use the **glm** command which would take the following form:

MTB > glm folrc = conrc genrc conrc*genrc;
SUBC> means conrc genrc conrc*genrc;
SUBC> brief 1.

Glm is short for **g**eneral **l**inear **m**odel. Note that the quotation marks around the variable names can be omitted from the **glm** command. The column labelled **folrc** contains the **fol**low-up scores for the **r**eward and **c**ontrol conditions; the column called **conrc** holds the code for the two **con**ditions of **r**eward and **c**ontrol; while the column named **genrc** stores the code for **gen**der for the **r**eward and **c**ontrol conditions. The **means** subcommand provides means and standard deviations for subjects grouped according to treatment, gender and their interaction. Specifying 1 on the **brief** subcommand restricts the output to the analysis of variance table.

The menu procedure for doing this is:

→**Stat** →**ANOVA** →**General Linear Model...** →**folrc** →**Select** [this puts **folrc** in the box beside **Response:**] →box under **Model:** →**conrc** →**Select** [this puts **conrc** in this box] →**genrc** →**Select** →type **conrc*genrc** →**Options...** →box under **Display means for (list of terms):** →**conrc** →**Select** [this puts **conrc** in this box] →**genrc** →**Select** →type **conrc*genrc** →**OK**

The menu system does not have the **brief 1** output option, so the default output option (**brief 2**) is produced which includes the table of factor levels.

The **brief 2** output is presented in Table 7.15. Because the number of cases is the same in each cell, the sequential sums of squares (**Seq SS**) are the same as the adjusted ones (**Adj SS**). The adjusted sums of squares are based on the regression approach and the F ratios are produced by dividing the adjusted mean square of an effect by the adjusted mean square of the error. For example, the F ratio for the treatment effect (**conrc**) is **3.00** which is derived by dividing the adjusted mean square (**Adj MS**) of the treatment effect (**3.000**) by the adjusted mean square of **Error** (**1.000**). This effect is not significant ($p = 0.122$).

To illustrate that a two-way analysis is a more sensitive test of the effect of a variable than a one-way analysis of variance, we will run a one-way analysis on follow-up aggressiveness for the reward and control conditions for the whole sample using Minitab. The output for this analysis is

Table 7.15 **Glm brief 2** output for a two-way analysis of variance of the effect of treatment (**conrc**), gender (**genrc**) and their interaction (**conrc*genrc**) on follow-up aggressiveness (**folrc**) in the reward and control conditions

General Linear Model

Factor	Levels	Values	
genrc	2	1	2
conrc	2	1	2

Analysis of Variance for folrc

Source	DF	Seq SS	Adj SS	Adj MS	F	P
genrc	1	3.000	3.000	3.000	3.00	0.122
conrc	1	3.000	3.000	3.000	3.00	0.122
genrc*conrc	1	3.000	3.000	3.000	3.00	0.122
Error	8	8.000	8.000	1.000		
Total	11	17.000				

Means for folrc

genrc*conrc		Mean	StDev
1	1	1.000	0.5774
1	2	1.000	0.5774
2	1	3.000	0.5774
2	2	1.000	0.5774

displayed in Table 7.16. As we can see from comparing the information in this table with that of Table 7.15, while the sum of squares for the treatment factor is the same in the two analyses (**3.000**), the residual sum of squares is smaller in the two-way analysis (**8.000**) than in the one-way analysis (**14.000**). The treatment mean square is also **3.000** in the two analyses while the error sequential mean square is **1.000** for the two-way analysis and **1.400** for the one-way analysis. Consequently, the F ratio for the treatment main effect is larger (and hence more likely to be significant) for the two-way analysis (**3.00**) than the one-way analysis (**2.14**). As shown in the two-way analysis in Table 7.15, when the gender effect is taken into account, the residual error is reduced.

SUMMARY

The computation of parametric tests for assessing whether the means and variances of interval or ratio data from two or more unrelated samples differ significantly across samples has been described. The unrelated t test compares the difference between the means of the two samples with the standard error of the difference in means which takes into account the

Table 7.16 **Glm brief 2** output for a one-way analysis of variance of the effect of treatment (**conrc**) on follow-up aggressiveness (**folrc**) in the reward and control conditions

General Linear Model

Factor   Levels   Values
conrc   2   1   2

Analysis of Variance for folrc

Source	DF	Seq SS	Adj SS	Adj MS	F	P
conrc	1	3.000	3.000	3.000	2.14	0.174
Error	10	14.000	14.000	1.400		
Total	11	17.000				

Means for folrc

conrc	Mean	Stdev
1	2.000	0.4830
2	1.000	0.4830

variances of the two samples. The variances are pooled if they are equal and treated separately if they are unequal. The F test, which is the greater variance of one group divided by the smaller variance of the other, should be used to determine whether the variances differ when the data are normally distributed and Levene's test when they are not. The two means differ significantly if their difference is substantially larger than the standard error of the difference in means. The one-sample t test compares a sample mean with the population mean and is more commonly used to determine within what range the population mean is likely to fall.

One-way analysis of variance compares the means of two or more unrelated samples and is essentially an F test in which the between-groups mean square is divided by the within-groups mean square. Differences between means are less likely to be due to chance when the between-groups variance is considerably greater than the within-groups variance provided that the variances are equal. The Hartley, Cochran C and Bartlett-Box F test assess whether the variances differ when the data are normally distributed and Levene's test when they are not. To test for significant differences between pairs of means, the t test should be employed when differences are predicted, otherwise a range test such as the Scheffé test should be performed. Two-way analysis of variance compares the means of groups made up of two variables or factors and enables the interaction between those two factors to be examined. It is a more sensitive test of the effect of either factor than evaluating them singly provided that the two factors do not interact substantially. The proportion of variance explained by one or more factors is estimated by eta squared.

EXERCISES

The data for these exercises are available in Table 6.23.

1 Use the unrelated t test to compare educational interest at 12 between single- and mixed-sex schools.
   (a) What is the value of the F test?
   (b) What are its degrees of freedom?
   (c) What is its probability level?
   (d) Do the variances differ significantly?
   (e) Should the variances be pooled?
   (f) What is the value of the t test?
   (g) What are its degrees of freedom?
   (h) What is its two-tailed probability level?
   (i) Is educational interest at 12 significantly greater in single- than in mixed-sex schools?
2 Use a one-way analysis of variance to compare educational interest at 12 between single- and mixed-sex schools.
   (a) What is the value of this test?
   (b) What are the degrees of freedom?
   (c) What is the two-tailed probability level?
   (d) Is educational interest at 12 significantly greater in single- than in mixed-sex schools?
   (e) What proportion of variance of educational interest at 12 is explained by type of school?
3 Use a one-way analysis of variance to compare educational interest at 12 for pupils of different socio-economic status.
   (a) What is the value of this test?
   (b) What are the degrees of freedom?
   (c) What is the probability level?
   (d) Does educational interest at 12 differ significantly between pupils of different socio-economic status?
   (e) What is the Scheffé range which the means of the three socio-economic status groups have to exceed to be significantly different?
   (f) Which group means differ according to this range?
4 Use a two-way analysis of variance to determine the effect of socio-economic status and type of school on educational interest at 12.
   (a) What is the F ratio for the effect of socio-economic status?
   (b) What are its degrees of freedom?
   (c) What is its probability?

(d) Does educational interest at 12 differ significantly between pupils of different socio-economic status?

(e) What is the F ratio for the effect of type of school?

(f) What are its degrees of freedom?

(g) What is its probability?

(h) Is educational interest at 12 significantly greater in single- than in mixed-sex schools?

(i) What is the F ratio for the interaction between socio-economic status and type of school?

(j) What are its degrees of freedom?

(k) What is its probability?

(l) Is there a significant interaction between socio-economic status and type of school on educational interest at 12?

Chapter 8

Tests of difference for interval/ratio data in related and mixed samples

The statistical tests described in this chapter ascertain whether the means of two or more related samples differ. For example, we may wish to know whether aggressiveness is lower immediately after watching it being punished compared with immediately before seeing it being punished and whether any decrease in aggressiveness is maintained later on at follow-up. We may also be interested in whether aggressiveness in the punishment group is lower than in the reward condition. Furthermore, we may want to find out whether there is any difference in post-test aggressiveness between the reward and punishment condition when differences at pre-test have been controlled.

t TEST FOR TWO RELATED SAMPLES

The *t* test for related samples determines if the means of two such samples differ. The means of related samples are less likely to differ than the means of unrelated samples because the scores come from the same or similar cases. Consequently, the *t* test for related samples takes into account the extent to which the scores of the two samples are correlated by modifying the way the standard error of the difference in means is computed. This standard error can be calculated with the following formula:

$$\text{standard error of the difference in means} = \sqrt{\frac{\text{variance}_1 + \text{variance}_2 - (2 \times \text{covariance}_{1,2})}{N}}$$

where N is the total number of pairs of cases. The covariance is defined as the mean cross product of two sets of deviation scores and is calculated by: (1) subtracting each of a pair of scores from their respective means; (2) multiplying the deviations together; (3) summing the product for all pairs of scores; and (4) dividing this sum by the number of pairs of cases. If the two sets of scores were perfectly related the standard error of the difference in means would be zero since twice the covariance would be the same as the sum of the two variances. If, at the other extreme, the two sets of scores were totally unrelated, the covariance would be zero.

To illustrate the computation of the t test for related samples, we will compare pre-test aggressiveness with post-test aggressiveness for the boys in the reward condition. The individual scores for these boys are shown in Table 8.1 together with the results of the computational procedure needed to calculate the variance and covariance of pre-test and post-test aggressiveness. To calculate a t test for related samples, carry out the following steps:

Step 1   Calculate the variance for each of the samples by subtracting each score from the mean score for that sample, squaring these differences, adding the squared differences together and dividing this total by the number of scores minus 1.

When this is done, we obtain a variance of 1.0 for both pre- and post-test aggressiveness.

Step 2   Compute the covariance for the two samples by subtracting each score from the mean score for that sample, multiplying this difference with the difference from the corresponding score, summing the products for all pairs of scores and dividing this sum by the number of cases minus 1. Ignore the sign of the covariance.

The covariance for these scores is 0.5.

Step 3   Work out the standard error of the difference in means by multiplying the covariance by 2, subtracting this product from the sum of the variances, dividing this result by the number of cases and taking the square root of this value.

The standard error of the difference in means for our example is 0.577:

$$\sqrt{\frac{1.0 + 1.0 - (2 \times 0.5)}{3}} = \sqrt{\frac{2.0 - 1.0}{3}} = \sqrt{\frac{1.0}{3}} = \sqrt{0.333} = 0.577$$

Step 4   Subtract one sample mean from the other and divide by the standard error of the difference in the mean to give the t value.

In this case, t is -1.73:

$$\frac{2 - 3}{0.577} = \frac{-1}{0.577} = -1.73$$

Step 5   Look up the t value in the table in Appendix 15 where the degrees of freedom are the number of cases minus 1.

For t to be significant at the 0.05 one-tailed level with 2 degrees of

Table 8.1 Pre-test and post-test aggressiveness ratings for the boys in the reward condition together with initial computations

	Pre-test			Post-test			Pre-test × Post-test
	Original	Difference	Squared	Original	Difference	Squared	Difference
	1	−1	1	2	−1	1	1
	2	0	0	4	1	0	0
	3	1	1	3	0	1	0
Sum	6		2	9		2	1
N	3			3			
Mean	2			3			
Variance			1.0			1.0	
Covariance							0.5

freedom it would have to be 2.920 or bigger which it is not. Consequently, we would conclude that aggressiveness in the reward condition is not significantly lower at post-test than at pre-test.

A simpler procedure for calculating t uses the following formula which is mathematically the same as the previous one:

$$t = \frac{\text{difference between sample means}}{\sqrt{\dfrac{\text{sum of D}^2 - \dfrac{(\text{sum of D})^2}{N}}{N \times (N - 1)}}}$$

where D stands for the difference between pairs of scores and N refers to the number of pairs of scores. It is also more accurate since it involves less rounding error.

The pairs of scores for our example are shown in Table 8.2 together with the difference between these pairs (D) and the square of this difference (D^2).

Substituting the appropriate values in the computational formula gives a t of -1.73:

$$\frac{2 - 3}{\sqrt{\dfrac{5 - \dfrac{(-3)^2}{3}}{3 \times (3 - 1)}}} = \frac{-1}{\sqrt{\dfrac{5 - 3}{6}}} =$$

$$\frac{-1}{\sqrt{\dfrac{2}{6}}} = \frac{-1}{\sqrt{0.333}} = \frac{-1}{0.577} = -1.73$$

To carry out a one-tailed related t test with Minitab comparing pre- with

Table 8.2 Pre-test and post-test aggressiveness ratings together with their differences and squared differences

	Pre-test	Post-test	D	D^2
	1	2	−1	1
	2	4	−2	4
	3	3	0	0
Sum	6	9	−3	5
N	3	3		
Mean	2	3	3	

Table 8.3 Related *t* test output comparing the difference between pre- and post-test aggressiveness in boys in the reward condition

T-Test of the Mean

Test of mu = 0.000 vs mu < 0.000

Variable	N	Mean	StDev	SE Mean	T	P-Value
diff	3	−1.000	1.000	0.577	−1.73	0.11

post-test aggressiveness in boys in the reward condition, we first subtract the post-test scores from the pre-test ones and store them in a new column called, say, **diff** for difference. We then simply specify this new column (**diff**) on the **ttest** command:

MTB > ttest diff;
SUBC> alternative=−1.

Since we expect the difference to be negative we put −**1** on the **alternative** subcommand. If we had expected the difference to be positive we would have put **1** on the **alternative** subcommand, while if we had wanted the two-tailed probability we would have omitted this subcommand.

The menu sequence for a related *t* test is:

→**Stat** →**Basic Statistics** →**1-Sample t...** →**diff** →**Select** [this puts **diff** in the box beside **Variables**] →**Test mean:** →down button on the box beside **Alternative:** →**less than** →**OK**

The output from this procedure is shown in Table 8.3. Since the **P VALUE** is larger than 0.05, we would conclude that post-test aggressiveness is not significantly lower than pre-test aggressiveness in boys in the reward condition.

t TEST FOR TWO RELATED VARIANCES

If we want to determine whether the variances of two related samples are significantly different from one another, we have to calculate it using the following formula (McNemar 1969) since it is not available on Minitab:

$$t = \frac{(\text{larger variance} - \text{smaller variance}) \times \sqrt{(\text{number of cases} - 2)}}{\sqrt{\begin{array}{l}(1 - \text{correlation of 2 sets of} \quad \times \quad (4 \times \text{larger variance} \times \\ \text{scores squared}) \qquad\qquad\qquad \text{smaller variance})\end{array}}}$$

To compare the pre- and post-test aggressiveness variances of boys in the reward condition, we would first have to work out Pearson's product moment correlation (*r*) which is described in Chapter 10 and which can be computed with the following formula:

$$r = \frac{\text{sum of products of pre- and post-test scores}}{\sqrt{\text{pre-test sum of squares} \times \text{post-test sum of squares}}}$$

The correlation between the pre- and post-test scores is 0.5 ($1/\sqrt{2 \times 2} = 1/2 = 0.5$).

Substituting the appropriate values in the above equation, we find that t is 0:

$$\frac{(1.0 - 1.0) \times \sqrt{3 - 2}}{\sqrt{(1 - 0.5^2) \times (4 \times 1.0 \times 1.0)}} = \frac{0 \times \sqrt{1}}{\sqrt{(1 - 0.25) \times 4}} = \frac{0 \times 1.0}{\sqrt{0.75 \times 4}} =$$

$$\frac{0}{1.73} = 0$$

We look up the significance of this value in the table in Appendix 15 where the degrees of freedom are the number of cases minus 1. At the 0.05 two-tailed level t would have to be 4.303 or bigger to be statistically significant which it obviously is not. Consequently, we would conclude that the variances do not differ significantly.

SINGLE FACTOR REPEATED MEASURES

Analysis of variance also determines whether the means of three or more related samples differ. Since measures from the same or similar cases are taken more than once, this analysis is often known as a *repeated measures* analysis. In this analysis the total variation in the scores consists of three sources of variation: (1) the variation within the conditions of the factor being investigated called the *within-factor* or *between-treatments* variation; (2) the variation between cases usually called the *between-subjects* variation; and (3) the residual variation. The between-subjects and residual variation constitute the *within-treatments* or *within-subjects* variation. The sources of variation for a single factor repeated measures analysis of variance are shown in Table 8.4 together with their associated degrees of freedom. The F ratio for determining whether the three or more means differ is the mean square for the factor or treatments divided by the residual mean square. Note that in an independent measures analysis of variance the within-treatments mean square acts as the error term. In a repeated measures analysis of variance, however, subjects act as their own controls. Consequently, in this analysis the variance due to subjects is removed from the within-treatments variance to form the error term which will, as a result, be smaller than that in an independent measures analysis of variance.

The procedure for calculating a single factor repeated measures analysis of variance will be illustrated by comparing the pre-test, post-test and

Table 8.4 Sources of variation and degrees of freedom in a single factor repeated measures analysis

Sources of variation	Degrees of freedom
Between-treatments/within-factor	No. of conditions −1
Within-treatments/within-subjects	No. of cases × (no. of conditions −1)
Between-subjects	No. of cases −1
Residual	(No. of cases −1) × (no. of conditions −1)
Total	(No. of cases × no. of conditions) −1

follow-up aggressiveness scores for the boys in the reward condition. Their individual scores are shown in Table 8.5. The total and mean score are presented in the last two columns of the table while the total and mean score for the three periods are displayed in the last two rows. The overall total and mean score (grand mean) are in the bottom right-hand corner of the table. Means have been calculated to two decimal places.

Step 1 Work out the between-treatments sum of squares by subtracting the grand mean from the mean score for each of the conditions, squaring them, multiplying them by the number of cases and summing them:

between-treatments sum of squares = sum of [(condition mean − grand mean)^2 × no. of cases] for all conditions

The between-treatments sum of squares for our example is 2.01:

$[(2.00−2.67)^2 × 3] + [(3−2.67)^2 × 3] + [(3.00−2.67)^2 × 3] =$
$(−0.67^2 × 3) + (0.33^2 × 3) + (0.33^2 × 3) =$
$(0.45 × 3) + (0.11 × 3) + (0.11 × 3) = 1.35 + 0.33 + 0.33 =$
2.01

Step 2 Calculate the between-treatments degrees of freedom which are the number of conditions minus 1. For this example it is 2 (3 − 1 = 2).

Table 8.5 Pre-test, post-test and follow-up individual, total and mean aggressiveness ratings in boys in the reward condition

	Pre-test	Post-test	Follow-up	Sum	Mean
	1	2	2	5	1.67
	2	4	3	9	3.00
	3	3	4	10	3.33
Sum	6	9	9	24	
N	3	3	3		
Mean	2	3	3		2.67

Step 3 Compute the between-treatments mean square which is the between-treatments sum of squares divided by its degrees of freedom. In this instance it is 1.01 (2.01/2 = 1.01).

Step 4 Calculate the between-subjects sum of squares by subtracting the grand mean from the mean score for each subject, squaring them, multiplying them by the number of conditions and adding them together:

between-subjects sum of squares =

sum of [(subject mean − grand mean)^2 × number of conditions] for all subjects

The between-subjects sum of squares for our example is 4.65:

$[(1.67−2.67)^2 \times 3] + [(3.00−2.67)^2 \times 3] + [(3.33−2.67)^2 \times 3] =$
$(−1.00^2 \times 3) + (0.33^2 \times 3) + (0.66^2 \times 3) =$
$(1.00 \times 3) + (0.11 \times 3) + (0.44 \times 3) =$
$3.00 + 0.33 + 1.32 = 4.65$

Step 5 Derive the within-treatments sum of squares by subtracting the condition mean from the subject score for that condition for each condition, and then squaring and summing the results:

within-treatments sum of squares =

sum of (subject score − condition mean)^2 for all conditions

The within-treatments sum of squares for our example is 6.

$(1−2)^2 + (2−2)^2 + (3−2)^2 + (2−3)^2 + (4−3)^2 + (3−3)^2 + (2−3)^2 +$
$(3−3)^2 + (4−3)^2 =$
$−1^2 + 0^2 + 1^2 + −1^2 + 1^2 + 0^2 + −1^2 + 0^2 + 1^2 =$
$1 + 0 + 1 + 1 + 1 + 0 + 1 + 0 + 1 = 6$

Step 6 Calculate the residual sum of squares by subtracting the between-subjects sum of squares from the within-treatments sum of squares:

residual sum of squares = within-treatments sum of squares − between-subjects sum of squares

The residual sum of squares for our example is 1.35 (6 − 4.65 = 1.35).

Step 7 Work out the residual degrees of freedom which is the number of cases minus 1 multiplied by the number of conditions minus 1. For our example the residual degrees of freedom are 4 [(3 − 1) × (3 − 1) = 2 × 2 = 4].

Step 8 Compute the residual mean square which is the residual sum of squares divided by its degrees of freedom. In this case, the residual mean square is 0.338 (1.35/4 = 0.338).

Step 9   The F ratio is the between-treatments mean square divided by the residual mean square. For our example the F ratio is 2.99 ($1.01/0.338 = 2.988$).

We look up the significance of this F ratio in the table in Appendix 3. We see that with 2 degrees of freedom in the numerator and 4 degrees of freedom in the denominator, F has to be 6.9443 or larger to be significant at the 0.05 level which it is not. Consequently, we would conclude that there is no significant difference in aggressiveness across the three tests.

Finally, to calculate the total sum of squares, we subtract the grand mean from each score, square them and add them together.

If we do this for our example, the total sum of squares is 8.01:

$$(1 - 2.67)^2 + (2 - 2.67)^2 + (3 - 2.67)^2 +$$
$$(2 - 2.67)^2 + (4 - 2.67)^2 + (3 - 2.67)^2 +$$
$$(2 - 2.67)^2 + (3 - 2.67)^2 + (4 - 2.67)^2 =$$
$$-1.67^2 + -0.67^2 + 0.33^2 + -0.67^2 + 1.33^2 +$$
$$0.33^2 + -0.67^2 + 0.33^2 + 1.33^2 =$$
$$2.79 + 0.45 + 0.11 + 0.45 + 1.77 +$$
$$0.11 + 0.45 + 0.11 + 1.77 = 8.01$$

The results of these steps are presented in Table 8.6 which shows the sums of squares, the degrees of freedom, the mean squares and the F ratio. Note that the total sum of squares is the sum of the between- and the within-treatments sum of squares.

As was the case for the one-way analysis of variance test, the F test only tells us whether there is a significant difference between the three related scores but does not inform us where this difference lies. To determine which pair of means differ significantly, we would need to carry out some supplementary analyses. If we had predicted a difference between two scores, we determine if this prediction was confirmed by conducting a related t test as described above. If we had not predicted a difference, then Maxwell (1980) recommends the Bonferroni inequality test. The Bonferroni test is based on the related t test but modifies the significance

Table 8.6 Single factor repeated measures analysis of variance table comparing pre-test, post-test and follow-up aggressiveness in boys in the reward condition

Sources of variation	SS	df	MS	F	p
Between-treatments	2.01	2	1.01	2.99	ns
Within-treatments	6.00				
Between-subjects	4.65				
Residual	1.35	4	0.338		
Total	8.01				

Table 8.7 Original and absolute difference score for pre-test, post-test and follow-up aggressiveness ratings in boys in the reward condition

	Pre-test		Post-test		Follow-up	
	Original	Absolute difference	Original	Absolute difference	Original	Absolute difference
	1	1	2	1	2	1
	2	0	4	1	3	0
	3	1	3	0	4	1
Sum	6		9		9	
N	3		3		3	
Mean	2		3		3	

level to take account of the fact that more than one comparison is being made. To calculate this, work out the total number of possible comparisons between any two groups, divide the chosen significance level (which is usually 0.05) by this number, and treat the result as the appropriate significance level for comparing more than three groups. In the case of three groups, the total number of possible comparisons is 3 which means the appropriate significance level is 0.017 (0.05/3).

To determine whether the variances of three or more related groups are different, Rosenthal and Rosnow (1991) recommend an extension of Levene's test. In this test a new score is created which is the absolute difference between the original score and the mean score for the group. The absolute deviation scores for pre-test, post-test and follow-up aggressiveness for boys in the reward condition are shown in Table 8.7.

We then perform a single factor repeated measures analysis of variance on these absolute deviation scores. The total and mean scores for the rows and columns are displayed in Table 8.8 together with the grand total and mean.

Although it is obvious in this case that the variances are the same, we will calculate the F ratio with the following steps to illustrate the test:

Table 8.8 Pre-test, post-test and follow-up individual, total and mean absolute deviation aggressiveness ratings in boys in the reward condition

	Pre-test	Post-test	Follow-up	Sum	Mean
	1	1	1	3	1.00
	0	1	0	1	0.33
	1	0	1	2	0.67
Sum	2	2	2	6	
N	3	3	3		
Mean	0.67	0.67	0.67		0.67

Step 1   The between-treatments sum of squares for our example is 0.00:

$[(0.67-0.67)^2 \times 3] + [(0.67-0.67)^2 \times 3] + [(0.67-0.67)^2 \times 3] =$
$(0.00^2 \times 3) + (0.00^2 \times 3) + (0.00^2 \times 3) =$
$(0.00 \times 3) + (0.00 \times 3) + (0.00 \times 3) = 0.00 + 0.00 + 0.00 =$
0.00

Step 2   The between-treatments degrees of freedom are 2 (3 − 1 = 2).

Step 3   The between-treatments mean is 0.00 (0.00/2 = 0.00).

Step 4   The between-subjects sum of squares is 0.69:

$[(1.00-0.67)^2 \times 3] + [(0.33-0.67)^2 \times 3] + [(0.67-0.67)^2 \times 3] =$
$(0.33^2 \times 3) + (-0.34^2 \times 3) + (0.00^2 \times 3) =$
$(0.11 \times 3) + (0.12 \times 3) + (0.00 \times 3) =$
$0.33 + 0.36 + 0.00 = 0.69$

Step 5   The within-treatments sum of squares is 2.01:

$(1-0.67)^2 + (0-0.67)^2 + (1-0.67)^2 + (1-0.67)^2 + (1-0.67)^2 +$
$(0-0.67)^2 + (1-0.67)^2 + (0-0.67)^2 + (1-0.67)^2 =$
$0.33^2 + -0.67^2 + 0.33^2 + 0.33^2 + 0.33^2 +$
$-0.67^2 + 0.33^2 + -0.67^2 + 0.33^2 =$
$0.11 + 0.45 + 0.11 + 0.11 + 0.11 + 0.45 + 0.11 + 0.45 + 0.11 =$
2.01

Step 6   The residual sum of squares is 1.32 (2.01 − 0.69 = 1.32).

Step 7   The residual degrees of freedom are 4 [(3 − 1) × (3 − 1) = 2 × 2 = 4].

Step 8   The residual mean square is 0.33 (1.32/4 = 0.33).

Step 9   The *F* ratio is 0.00 (0.00/0.33 = 0.00).

We look up the significance of this *F* ratio in the table in Appendix 3. We see that with 2 degrees of freedom in the numerator and 4 degrees of freedom in the denominator, *F* has to be 6.9443 or larger to be significant at the 0.05 level which it is not. Consequently, we would conclude that there is no significant difference in the variance of aggressiveness across the three tests.

The results of these steps are presented in Table 8.9 which shows the sums of squares, the degrees of freedom, the mean squares and the *F* ratio.

To conduct a single factor repeated measures analysis of variance with Minitab, we first have to create three new columns.

Table 8.9 Single factor repeated measures analysis of variance table comparing pre-test, post-test and follow-up absolute deviation aggressiveness in boys in the reward condition

Sources of variation	SS	df	MS	F	p
Between-treatments	0.00	2	0.00	0.00	ns
Within-treatments	2.01				
Between-subjects	0.69				
Residual	1.32	4	0.33		
Total	2.01				

The first column, called **agg** for **agg**ressiveness scores, contains the pre-test scores stacked on top of the post-test scores which in turn are stacked on top of the follow-up scores.

The second column, named **test** for time of **test**ing, consists of the code for specifying when aggressiveness was rated. The code is **1** for the pre-test, **2** for the post-test and **3** for the follow-up.

The third column, labelled **cases**, contains the identification number for each case.

The three new columns will contain the following values:

1 1 1
2 1 2
3 1 3
2 2 1
4 2 2
3 2 3
2 3 1
3 3 2
4 3 3

To carry out this single factor repeated-measures analysis of variance we would use the following **anova** command:

MTB > anova agg = test cases;
SUB C> means cases.

The dependent variable **agg** is listed first followed by an equals sign =, the factor **test** and the variable **cases** which orders participants. Note that the quotation marks around the variable names can be omitted in the **anova** command. If, as usual, we want to display the mean of the dependent variable across the levels of the categorising variable we add the **means** subcommand which lists the name of the categorising variable **test**.

The menu procedure for doing this is:

Table 8.10 **Anova** output for the single factor repeated measures analysis of variance comparing aggressiveness (**agg**) in boys in the reward condition across the three times of **test**ing

Analysis of Variance (Balanced Designs)

Factor	Type	Levels	Values		
test	fixed	3	1	2	3
cases	fixed	3	1	2	3

Analysis of Variance for agg

Source	DF	SS	MS	F	P
test	2	2.0000	1.0000	3.00	0.160
cases	2	4.6667	2.3333	7.00	0.049
Error	4	1.3333	0.3333		
Total	8	8.0000			

MEANS

test	N	agg
1	3	2.0000
2	3	3.0000
3	3	3.0000

→Stat →ANOVA →Balanced ANOVA... →agg →Select [this puts agg in the box beside Response:] →box under Model: →test →Select [this puts test in this box] →cases →Select →box under Display means for (list of terms): →test →Select →OK

The output from this procedure is shown in Table 8.10. The **F** ratio for **test** tells us whether aggressiveness differs significantly across the three occasions. It is calculated by dividing the mean square (**MS**) of **test** (**1.0000**) by the **Error** mean square (**0.3333**) which gives an **F** ratio of **3.00** (**1.0000/0.3333 = 3.00**). This **F** ratio is not significant since its p value is greater (**0.160**) than 0.05. Note that the factors in this model are described as being **fixed** as opposed to being **random**. This means that the levels of the factors have not been chosen at random so that the results cannot be generalised to the factors as a whole.

TWO-WAY ANALYSIS OF VARIANCE WITH REPEATED MEASURES ON ONE FACTOR

Two-way analysis of variance with repeated measures on one factor compares the means of groups consisting of two factors, one of which is

Table 8.11 Sources of variation and degrees of freedom in a two-way analysis of variance with repeated measures on one factor

Sources of variation	Degrees of freedom
Between-subjects factor (A)	No. of conditions in A − 1
Between-subjects error	No. of conditions in A × (no. of cases − 1)
Within-subjects factor (B)	No. of conditions in B − 1
Within-subjects error	No. of conditions in A × (no. of cases − 1) × (no. of conditions in B − 1)
A × B interaction	(No. of conditions in A − 1) × (no. of conditions in B − 1)
Total	(No. of cases × no. of conditions in A × no. of conditions in B) − 1

repeated. For example, we may employ this analysis if we wished to determine whether aggressiveness in boys is decreased in the punishment condition and increased in the reward condition. In this kind of analysis the total variation in the scores is broken down into five main sources of variation: (1) between-subjects factor (i.e. independent variable); (2) between-subjects error; (3) within-subjects factor (i.e. repeated measures); (4) within-subjects error; and (5) interaction of between- and within-subjects factor. These sources of variation are presented in Table 8.11 together with their associated degrees of freedom.

The *F* ratio for determining whether there is a significant effect for the between-subjects factor is the between-subjects mean square divided by the between-subjects error mean square. The *F* ratio for finding out whether the within-subjects factor is significant is the within-subjects factor mean square divided by the within-subjects error mean square. While the *F* ratio for seeing whether the interaction effect is significant is the interaction mean square divided by the within-subjects error mean square.

The procedure for calculating this analysis will be illustrated by comparing pre-test and post-test aggressiveness in the reward and punishment conditions for boys. Their individual scores are presented in Table 8.12. The total and mean score of the pre-test and post-test are shown in the last two columns of the table while the total and mean score for the two conditions are displayed at the bottom of each condition and in the last two rows. The overall total and mean score (grand mean) are in the bottom right-hand corner of the table. Means have been calculated to one decimal place.

Step 1 Compute the sum of squares for the between-subjects factor by subtracting the grand mean from the overall mean score for each condition (ignoring time of testing), squaring them, multiplying them by the number of scores in each condition and adding them together.

Table 8.12 Pre- and post-test aggressiveness ratings of boys in the reward and punishment conditions together with initial computations

Condition	Pre-test	Post-test	Sum	Mean
Reward	1	2	3	1.5
	2	4	6	3.0
	3	3	6	3.0
Sum	6	9	15	
N	3	3	6	
Mean	2	3	2.5	
Punishment	0	1	1	0.5
	1	2	3	1.5
	2	3	5	2.5
Sum	3	6	9	
N	3	3	6	
Mean	1	2	1.5	
Column sum	9	15	Grand sum	24
Column N	6	6	Grand N	12
Column mean	1.5	2.5	Grand mean	2.0

The sum of squares for the between-subjects factor for our example is 3.0:

$$[(2.5 - 2.0)^2 \times 6] + [(1.5 - 2.0)^2 \times 6] =$$
$$(0.5^2 \times 6) + (-0.5^2 \times 6) = (0.25 \times 6) + (0.25 \times 6) =$$
$$1.5 + 1.5 = 3.0$$

Step 2   Compute the between-subjects sum of squares by subtracting the grand mean from the mean score for each case, squaring them, multiplying them by the number of scores for each case and then summing them.

The between-subjects sum of squares for our example is 10.0:

$$[(1.5-2.0)^2 \times 2] + [(3.0-2.0)^2 \times 2] + [(3.0-2.0)^2 \times 2] +$$
$$[(0.5-2.0)^2 \times 2] + [(1.5-2.0)^2 \times 2] + [(2.5-2.0)^2 \times 2] =$$
$$(-0.5^2 \times 2) + (1.0^2 \times 2) + (1.0^2 \times 2) +$$
$$(-1.5^2 \times 2) + (-0.5^2 \times 2) + (0.5^2 \times 2) =$$
$$(0.25 \times 2) + (1.0 \times 2) + (1.0 \times 2) +$$
$$(2.25 \times 2) + (0.25 \times 2) + (0.25 \times 2) =$$
$$0.5 + 2.0 + 2.0 + 4.5 + 0.5 + 0.5 = 10.0$$

Step 3   Compute the sum of squares for the between-subjects error by subtracting the between-subjects factor sum of squares from the between-subjects sum of squares:

$$\text{between-subjects error sum of squares} = \text{between-subjects sum of squares} - \text{between-subjects factor sum of squares}$$

The between-subjects error sum of squares for our example is 7.0:

10.0 − 3.0 = 7.0

Step 4   Work out the sum of squares for the within-subjects factor by subtracting the grand mean from the overall mean score for each of the tests, squaring them, multiplying them by the number of cases and summing them.

The sum of squares for the within-subjects factor for our example is 3.0:

$$[(1.5 − 2.0)^2 \times 6] + [(2.5 − 2.0)^2 \times 6] =$$
$$(−0.5^2 \times 6) + (0.5^2 \times 6) = (0.25 \times 6) + (0.25 \times 6) =$$
$$1.5 + 1.5 = 3.0$$

Step 5   Calculate the sum of squares for the interaction term by subtracting the grand mean from the mean for each of the conditions formed by the two factors, squaring them, multiplying them by the number of cases in each condition, summing them and subtracting from the result the sum of squares for the between-subjects and within-subjects factors.

The sum of squares for the interaction term in our example is 0:

$$[(2 − 2.0)^2 \times 3] + [(3 − 2.0)^2 \times 3] +$$
$$[(1 − 2.0)^2 \times 3] + [(2 − 2.0)^2 \times 3] − 3.0 − 3.0$$
$$(−0.0^2 \times 3) + (1.0^2 \times 3) + (−1.0^2 \times 3) + (−0.0^2 \times 3) − 6.0 =$$
$$(0.0 \times 3) + (1.0 \times 3) + (1.0 \times 3) + (0.0 \times 3) − 6.93 =$$
$$0.0 + 3.0 + 3.0 + 0.0 − 6.0 = 6.0 − 6.0 = 0$$

Step 6   Calculate the total sum of squares by subtracting the grand mean from each score, squaring them and adding them together.

If we do this for our example, the total sum of squares is 14.0:

$$(1−2.0)^2 + (2−2.0)^2 + (3−2.0)^2 + (2−2.0)^2 +$$
$$(4−2.0)^2 + (3−2.0)^2 + (0−2.0)^2 + (1−2.0)^2 +$$
$$(2−2.0)^2 + (1−2.0)^2 + (2−2.0)^2 + (3−2.0)^2 =$$
$$−1.0^2 + 0.0^2 + 1.0^2 + 0.0^2 + 2.0^2 + 1.0^2 +$$
$$−2.0^2 + −1.0^2 + 0.0^2 + −1.0^2 + 0.0^2 + 1.0^2 =$$
$$1.0 + 0.0 + 1.0 + 0.0 + 4.0 + 1.0 +$$
$$4.0 + 1.0 + 0.0 + 1.0 + 0.0 + 1.0 = 14.0$$

Step 7   Calculate the sum of squares for the within-subjects error by subtracting from the total sum of squares the sum of squares for the between-subjects factor, the between-subjects error, the within-subjects factor, and the interaction.

The sum of squares for the within-subjects error for our example is 1.0:

14.0 − 3.0 − 7.0 − 3.0 − 0.0 = 1.0

Table 8.13 Two-way analysis of variance table with repeated measures on one factor comparing pre- and post-test aggressiveness in the reward and punishment condition in boys

Sources of variation	SS	df	MS	F	p
Between-subjects factor	3.0	1	3.00	1.71	ns
Between-subjects error	7.0	4	1.75		
Within-subjects factor	3.0	1	3.00	12.00	0.05
Within-subjects error	1.0	4	0.25		
Interaction	0.0	1	0.00	0.00	ns
Total	14.0	11			

The sums of squares for six of these sources of variation are presented in Table 8.13 together with the degrees of freedom, mean squares and *F* ratios.

Step 8   Compute the between-subjects factor mean square which is the between-subjects factor sum of squares divided by its degrees of freedom. The degrees of freedom are the number of conditions minus 1 which in this case is 1 (2 − 1 = 1). Consequently, the between-subjects factor mean square is 3.0 (3.0/1 = 3.0).

Step 9   Compute the between-subjects error mean square which is the between-subjects error sum of squares divided by its degrees of freedom. The degrees of freedom is the mean number of cases in each condition minus 1 multiplied by the number of conditions. As the mean number of cases in each condition is 3 and the number of conditions is 2 the degrees of freedom for the between-subjects error are 4 [2 × (3 − 1) = 2 × 2 = 4]. Thus the between-subjects error mean square for our example is 1.75 (7/4 = 1.75).

Step 10   The *F* ratio for the between-subjects factor is its mean square divided by the between-subjects error mean-square.

For our example the *F* ratio for the between-subjects factor is 1.71 (3.0/1.75 = 1.71). If we look up the significance of this value in the table in Appendix 3 with 1 and 4 degrees of freedom in the numerator and denominator respectively, the *F* ratio has to be 7.7086 or bigger to be significant at the 0.05 level, which it is not. Accordingly, we would conclude that the treatment effect is not significant. In this instance we would not be interested in this effect since it collapses the pre-test and post-test scores and so does not provide any evidence as to whether the post-test scores differ among the treatments.

Step 11 Work out the mean square for the within-subjects factor which is its sum of squares divided by its degrees of freedom. The degrees of freedom for the within-subjects factor are the number of conditions minus 1. Since the number of conditions in our example is 2 (pre- and post-test), the degree of freedom is 1 (2 − 1 = 1) and the within-subjects factor mean square is 3.0 (3.0/1 = 3.0).

Step 12 Compute the within-subjects error mean square which is the within-subjects error sum of squares divided by its degrees of freedom. The degrees of freedom for the within-subjects error are the average number of cases in each condition minus 1 multiplied by the number of within-subjects conditions minus 1 multiplied by the number of between-subjects conditions. The degrees of freedom for our example are 4 [(3 − 1) × (2 − 1) × 2 = 2 × 1 × 2 = 4]. The within-subjects error mean square, therefore, is 0.25 (1/4 = 0.25).

Step 13 The *F* ratio for the within-subjects factor is its mean square divided by the within-subjects error mean square.

The *F* ratio for the within-subjects factor of time of testing is 12.0 (3.0/0.25 = 12.0). From the table in Appendix 5, we can see that with 1 and 4 degrees of freedom in the numerator and denominator respectively the *F* ratio has to be 7.7086 or larger to be statistically significant at less than the 0.05 level which it is. Therefore, we would conclude that there was a significant time of testing effect across the two treatments. As the post-test scores would be expected to be different for the two conditions, we would not be interested in this effect either.

Step 14 The mean square for the interaction effect, which is of the main concern to us, is its sum of squares divided by its degrees of freedom. The degrees of freedom for the interaction effect are the number of between-subjects conditions minus 1 multiplied by the number of within-subjects conditions minus 1. The degree of freedom for our example is 1 [(2 − 1) × (2 − 1) = 1 × 1 = 1), giving a mean square of 0 (0/1 = 0).

Step 15 The *F* ratio for the interaction effect is its mean square divided by the mean square of the within-subjects error.

The *F* ratio for the interaction between the two conditions and time of testing is 0 (0/0.25 = 0.0). With 1 and 4 degrees of freedom in the numerator and denominator respectively, the *F* value has to be 7.7086 or greater to be statistically significant at less than the 0.05 level which it is not. So, we would conclude that the interaction effect was not statistically significant. If a significant interaction was predicted, *t* tests could be used to determine where the significant differences lay. If a significant interaction was not expected, then a *post hoc* test such as the Bonferroni test could be applied to related scores and the Scheffé test to unrelated scores.

To carry out with Minitab a two-way analysis of variance with repeated measures on one factor, it is necessary to have equal numbers of cases in the different conditions. The data for this analysis need to be organised into four new columns.

The first column, called **agg**, contains the pre-test aggressiveness scores stacked on top of the post-test aggressiveness scores.

The second column, named **test**, comprises the code which distinguishes the pre-test scores (coded as **1**) from the post-test scores (coded **2**).

The third column, labelled **cond**, holds the code for which of the scores come from the reward condition (coded **1**) and which from the punishment condition (coded **2**).

The fourth column, termed **cases**, identifies the cases.

These four columns would contain the following data:

```
1 1 1 1
2 1 1 2
3 1 1 3
0 1 2 1
1 1 2 2
2 1 2 3
2 2 1 1
4 2 1 2
3 2 1 3
1 2 2 1
2 2 2 2
3 2 2 3
```

To carry out an analysis of variance on these data we would use the following **anova** command:

MTB > anova agg=cond test cases cond*test cond*cases;
SUBC> means cond*test.

The dependent variable **agg** is listed after the **anova** keyword followed by an equals sign and the effects we want to test which include three main effects (**cond**, **test** and **cases**) and two interactions (**cond*test** and **cond*cases**). The quotes around the variable names can be omitted from the **anova** command. The **means** subcommand provides the means for the two tests in the two conditions.

The menu action for doing this is:

→**S̲tat** →**A̲NOVA** →**B̲alanced ANOVA...** →**agg** →**Select** [this puts **agg** in the box beside **Response:**] →box under **Model:** →**cond** →**Select** [this puts **cond** in this box] →**test** →**Select** →**cases** →**Select** →type **cond*test** →type **cond*cases** →**Options...** →in the box below **Display means for** [list of terms] type **cond*test** →**O̲K** →**O̲K**

Table 8.14 **Anova** output for the two-way analysis of variance with repeated measures on one factor comparing pre- and post-test aggressiveness in the reward and punishment condition in boys

Analysis of Variance (Balanced Designs)

Factor	Type	Levels	Values		
cond	fixed	2	1	2	
test	fixed	2	1	2	
cases	fixed	3	1	2	3

Analysis of Variance for agg

Source	DF	SS	MS	F	P
cond	1	3.0000	3.0000	12.00	0.026
test	1	3.0000	3.0000	12.00	0.026
cases	2	6.5000	3.2500	13.00	0.018
cond*test	1	0.0000	0.0000	0.00	1.000
cond*cases	2	0.5000	0.2500	1.00	0.444
Error	4	1.0000	0.2500		
Total	11	14.0000			

MEANS

cond	test	N	agg
1	1	3	2.0000
1	2	3	3.0000
2	1	3	1.0000
2	2	3	2.0000

The output from this procedure is shown in Table 8.14. The effect that we are interested in is the interaction between **cond** (i.e. the two conditions) and **test** (i.e. the two times of testing) which with an F ratio of **0.00** is not statistically significant with a p of **1.000**. This F ratio is formed by dividing the mean square of this interaction term (**0.0000**) by the mean square of the error term (**0.2500**). Note that the F ratio for **cond** in this analysis is its mean square divided by that of the within-subjects **Error** term (**3.0000/0.2500 = 12.00**) and not the between-subjects error term as it should be and which is not given. This is because this procedure has not been specifically designed to carry out this analysis but has been adapted to do so.

ONE-WAY ANALYSIS OF COVARIANCE

One-way analysis of covariance compares the means of two or more groups controlling for the effects of a second factor which is known to be

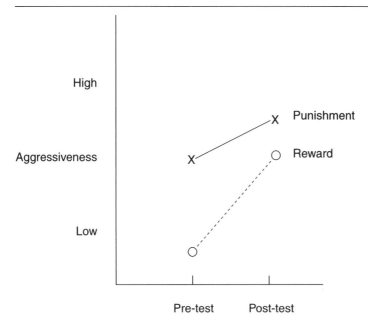

Figure 8.1 Example of pre-test and post-test differences

associated with the first factor. The variable which is controlled is called a *covariate*. Suppose, for example, that we found as shown in Figure 8.1 that the pre-test aggressiveness of the boys in the punishment condition was higher than that in the reward condition and that we knew that pre-test aggressiveness was positively correlated with post-test aggressiveness so that the more aggressive boys were at pre-test the more aggressive they were at post-test. If we observed that post-test aggressiveness was also higher in the punishment than in the reward condition, then this difference may be due not to the result of the punishment but to the fact that aggressiveness in these boys was initially higher. One way of taking into account these pre-test differences is to conduct a one-way analysis of covariance on the post-test scores covarying out the pre-test scores.

In an analysis of covariance the variation in the scores of the dependent variable is adjusted to take account of the relationship between the dependent variable and the covariate. In effect, variance in the dependent variable that is shared with the covariate is removed. In an analysis of variance the between-groups variance is compared with the within-group variance. If the between-groups variance is substantially bigger than the within-groups variance, then the means of the groups or treatments differ. Similarly, in an analysis of covariance the between-groups variance is compared with the within-groups variance except that the variances have been adjusted accordingly to their relationship with the covariate. In other words, the adjusted between-groups variance is compared with the adjusted within-groups variance.

The total variance in an analysis of covariance will generally be less than that in an analysis of variance since some of this variance will be shared with the covariate. The adjusted total variance will be the unadjusted total variance minus the total variance that is shared with the covariate:

adjusted total variance = unadjusted total variance − total variance shared with covariate

The extent to which the dependent variable is related to the covariate is expressed as the *unstandardised regression coefficient* (see Chapter 11), the square of which reflects the proportion of variance shared between the two variables. Consequently, the adjusted total variance is the unadjusted total variance minus the product of the squared unstandardised regression coefficient and the covariate total variance:

adjusted total variance = unadjusted total variance − (squared unstandardised regression coefficient × covariate total variance)

In other words, the adjusted total sum of squares of the dependent variable (TSS_{adj}) is the unadjusted total sum of squares for the dependent variable (TSS_{dep}) minus the product of the squared unstandardised regression coefficient (β^2) and the covariate total sum of squares (TSS_{cov}).

$$TSS_{adj} = TSS_{dep} - (\beta^2 \times TSS_{cov})$$

The formula for the unstandardised regression coefficient is the total sum of products divided by the covariate total sum of squares:

$$\beta = \frac{TSP}{TSS_{cov}}$$

The sum of products is simply the deviation of the dependent variable multiplied by the deviation of the covariate for each pair of scores summed across all scores. The formula for calculating the adjusted total sum of squares can be re-expressed as follows:

$$TSS_{adj} = TSS_{dep} - \left(\frac{TSP^2}{TSS_{cov^2}} \times TSS_{cov} \right)$$

which by cancelling the covariate total sum of squares in the denominator and numerator becomes:

$$TSS_{adj} = TSS_{dep} - \frac{TSP^2}{TSS_{cov}}$$

We follow a similar procedure for working out the adjusted within-groups sum of squares ($WGSS_{adj}$) where the unstandardised regression coefficient represents the relationship between the dependent variable and the covariate within the groups or treatments:

$$WGSS_{adj} = WGSS_{dep} - (\beta^2 \times WGSS_{cov})$$

$$= WGSS_{dep} - \left(\frac{WGSP^2}{WGSS_{cov^2}} \right) \times WGSS_{cov}$$

$$= WGSS_{dep} - \frac{WGSP^2}{WGSS_{cov}}$$

We cannot obtain the adjusted between-groups sum of squares ($BGSS_{adj}$) in the same way because the regression coefficient in this case is partly determined by the dependent variable which itself is partly determined by the treatments. Since the adjusted total sum of squares is the sum of the between- and within-groups sums of squares,

$$TSS_{adj} = BGSS_{adj} + WGSS_{adj}$$

the adjusted between-groups sum of squares is most easily derived by subtracting the adjusted within-groups sum of squares from the adjusted total sum of squares:

$$BGSS_{adj} = TSS_{adj} - WGSS_{adj}$$

The sources of variation in an analysis of covariance and their associated degrees of freedom are shown in Table 8.15. The between-groups mean square is simply the between-groups sum of squares divided by its degrees of freedom while the within-groups mean square is the within-groups sum of squares divided by its degrees of freedom. The F ratio is the between-groups mean square divided by the within-groups mean square.

In trying to understand and remember what an analysis of covariance is, it may be useful to think of it in terms of the *Venn diagram* shown in Figure 8.2 where the area enclosed by the circle represents the total variance of that variable. The total variance of the criterion or dependent variable has been divided into four sections labelled *a*, *b*, *c* and *d*. The extent of the relationship between the two variables is reflected in the overlap of the two circles. This area comprises the two sections *a* and *b* whereas the two remaining sections of *c* and *d* represent the adjusted total variance of the

Table 8.15 Sources of variation and degrees of freedom in a one-way analysis of covariance

Sources of variation	Degrees of freedom
Between-groups	No. of groups − 1
Within-groups	No. of cases − no. of groups −1
Total	No. of cases − 1

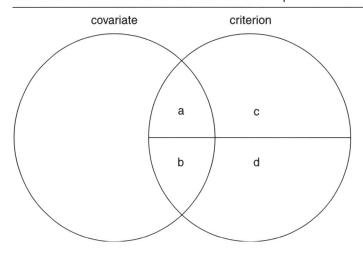

covariate   criterion

Figure 8.2 Venn diagram illustrating a one-way analysis of covariance

dependent variable. Sections *a* and *c* reflect the unadjusted between-groups variance while section *c* is the between-groups variance which has been adjusted for the covariate. Sections *b* and *d* represent the unadjusted within-groups variance whereas section *d* is the within-groups variance adjusted for the covariate. The *F* ratio is the adjusted between-groups mean square (represented by section *c*) divided by the within-groups mean square (signified by section *d*).

The procedure for carrying out a one-way analysis of covariance will be illustrated by comparing post-test aggressiveness in boys in the reward and punishment condition while covarying pre-test aggressiveness. The scores for these conditions are displayed in Table 8.16 together with the means for each condition and the grand means for the pre- and post-tests.

Step 1   Calculate the within-groups sum of squares for the dependent variable by subtracting the group mean from the individual score, squaring it and summing the squared difference for all scores:

within-groups sum of squares = sum of (individual score − group mean)^2 for all scores

The within-groups sum of squares for post-test aggressiveness is 4:

$$(2-3)^2 + (4-3)^2 + (3-3)^2 + (1-2)^2 + (2-2)^2 + (3-2)^2 =$$
$$-1^2 + 1^2 + 0^2 + -1^2 + 0^2 + 1^2 = 1 + 1 + 0 + 0 + 1 + 0 + 1 = 4$$

Step 2   Calculate the within-groups sum of products for the covariate and dependent variable by (1) subtracting the covariate group mean from each of the individual scores within that group; (2) subtracting the dependent variable group mean from each of the individual scores within that group;

Table 8.16 Pre- and post-test aggressiveness ratings of boys in the reward and punishment conditions together with initial computations

Condition	Pre-test	Post-test
Reward	1	2
	2	4
	3	3
Sum	6	9
N	3	3
Mean	2	3
Punishment	0	1
	1	2
	2	3
Sum	3	6
N	3	3
Mean	1	2
Grand sum	9	15
Grand N	6	6
Grand mean	1.5	2.5

(3) multiplying the deviation for each pair of scores of the covariate and dependent variable; and (4) summing the products for all the groups:

within-groups sum of products = sum of [(covariate individual score − covariate group mean) × (dependent variable individual score − dependent variable group mean)] for all groups

The within-groups sum of products for the covariate and the dependent variable is 3:

$$[(1-2) \times (2-3)] + [(2-2) \times (4-3)] + [(3-2) \times (3-3)] +$$
$$[(0-1) \times (1-2)] + [(1-1) \times (2-2)] + [(2-1) \times (3-2)] =$$
$$(-1 \times -1) + (0 \times 1) + (1 \times 0) + (-1 \times -1) + (0 \times 0) + (1 \times 1) =$$
$$1 + 0 + 0 + 1 + 0 + 1 = 3$$

Step 3   Calculate the within-groups sum of squares for the covariate by subtracting the group mean from the individual score, squaring it and summing the squared difference for all scores.

The within-groups sum of squares for pre-test aggressiveness is 4:

$$(1-2)^2 + (2-2)^2 + (3-2)^2 + (0-1)^2 + (1-1)^2 + (2-1)^2 =$$
$$-1^2 + 0^2 + 1^2 + -1^2 + 0^2 + 1^2 = 1 + 0 + 1 + + 1 + 0 + 1 = 4$$

Step 4   Calculate the adjusted within-groups sum of squares for the dependent variable by substituting the pertinent values in the following formula:

$$WGSS_{adj} = WGSS_{dep} - \frac{WGSP^2}{WGSS_{cov}}$$

The adjusted within-groups sum of squares for post-test aggressiveness is 1.75:

$$4 - \frac{3^2}{4} = 4 - \frac{9}{4} = 4 - 2.25 = 1.75$$

Step 5 Calculate the total sum of squares for the dependent variable by deriving the between-groups sum of squares and adding it to the within-groups sum of squares:

$$TSS_{dep} = = BGSS_{dep} + WGSS_{dep}$$

Work out the between-groups sum of squares for the dependent variable by subtracting its grand mean from its mean for each group, squaring these differences, multiplying them by the number of cases in each of the groups and summing the products for all the groups:

between-groups sum of squares = sum of [(group mean − grand mean)^2 ×
number of cases] for all groups

The between-groups sum of squares for post-test aggressiveness is 1.5:

$$[(3.0 - 2.5)^2 \times 3] + [(2.0 - 2.5)^2 \times 3] =$$
$$(0.5^2 \times 3) + (-0.5^2 \times 3) = (0.25 \times 3) + (0.25 \times 3) =$$
$$0.75 + 0.75 = 1.5$$

Consequently, the total sum of squares for post-test aggressiveness is 5.5:

$$1.5 + 4.0 = 5.5$$

Step 6 Calculate the total sum of products for the covariate and dependent variable by working out the between-groups sum of products and adding it to the within-groups sum of products

$$TSP = BGSP + WGSP$$

Calculate the between-groups sum of products for the covariate and dependent variable by (1) subtracting the covariate grand mean from each of its group means; (2) subtracting the dependent variable grand mean from each of its group means; (3) multiplying the deviation for each pair of group means of the covariate and dependent variable; (4) multiplying them by the number of pairs in each of the groups; and (5) summing the products for all the groups:

sum of [(covariate group mean − covariate grand mean) ×
between-groups sum of products = (dependent variable group mean − dependent variable
grand mean) × no. of cases] for all groups

The between-groups sum of products for pre-test and post-test aggressiveness is 1.5:

$[(2 - 1.5) \times (3 - 2.5) \times 3] + [(1 - 1.5) \times (2 - 2.5) \times 3] =$
$(0.5 \times 0.5 \times 3) + (-0.5 \times -0.5 \times 3) = 0.75 + 0.75 = 1.5$

Thus, the total sum of products for pre-test and post-test aggressiveness is 4.5:

$1.5 + 3.0 = 4.5$

Step 7   Calculate the total sum of squares for the covariate by obtaining the between-groups sum of squares and adding it to the within-groups sum of squares:

$$TSS_{cov} = BGSS_{cov} + WGSS_{cov}$$

Calculate the between-groups sum of squares for the covariate by subtracting its grand mean from its mean for each group, squaring these differences, multiplying them by the number of cases in each of the groups and summing the products for all the groups.

The between-groups sum of squares for pre-test aggressiveness is 1.5:

$[(2 - 1.5)^2 \times 3] + [(1 - 1.5)^2 \times 3] =$
$(0.5^2 \times 3) + (0.5^2 \times 3) = (0.25 \times 3) + (0.25 \times 3) =$
$0.75 + 0.75 = 1.5$

Accordingly, the total sum of squares for pre-test aggressiveness is 5.5:

$1.5 + 4.0 = 5.5$

Step 8   Calculate the adjusted total sum of squares for the dependent variable by substituting the appropriate values in the following formula:

$$TSS_{adj} = TSS_{dep} - \frac{TSP^2}{TSS_{cov}}$$

The adjusted total sum of squares for post-test aggressiveness is 1.82:

$$5.5 - \frac{4.5^2}{5.5} = 5.5 - \frac{20.25}{5.5} = 5.5 - 3.68 = 1.82$$

Step 9   Calculate the adjusted between-groups sum of squares for the dependent variable by subtracting its adjusted within-groups sum of squares from its adjusted total sum of squares:

$$BGSS_{adj} = TSS_{adj} - WGSS_{adj}$$

The adjusted between-groups sum of squares for post-test aggressiveness is 0.07:

$$1.82 - 1.75 = 0.07$$

Step 10   Calculate the adjusted between-groups mean square by dividing the adjusted between-groups sum of squares by its degrees of freedom which are the number of groups minus 1.

The adjusted between-groups mean square for post-test aggressiveness is 0.07 [0.07/(2 − 1) = 0.07/1= 0.07].

Step 11   Calculate the adjusted within-groups mean square by dividing the adjusted within-groups sum of squares by its degrees of freedom which are the total number of cases minus the number of groups minus 1.

The adjusted within-groups mean square for post-test aggressiveness is 0.58 [1.75/(6 − 2 − 1) = 1.75/3 = 0.58].

Step 12   Calculate the *F* ratio for the between-groups effect by dividing the adjusted between-groups mean square by the adjusted within-groups mean square.

The *F* ratio for the between-groups effect of treatment is 0.12 [0.07/0.58 = 0.12].

Step 13   Look up the *F* ratio in the table in Appendix 3.

With 1 and 3 degrees of freedom in the numerator and denominator respectively, *F* has to be 10.128 or larger to be significant at or less than the 0.05 level which it is not. Consequently, we would conclude that there is no significant difference in post-test aggressiveness between the reward and punishment conditions when pre-test aggressiveness is covaried.

The sums of squares, degrees of freedom, mean squares and *F* ratio for this analysis of covariance are shown in Table 8.17.

Since the means have been adjusted for the influence of the covariate, the adjusted means may differ from the unadjusted ones. Consequently, when interpreting the between-groups treatment effect, we should look at the

Table 8.17 One-way analysis of covariance table comparing post-test aggressiveness in the reward and punishment conditions in boys covarying out pre-test aggressiveness

Source of variation	SS	df	MS	F	p
Between-groups	0.07	1	0.07	0.12	ns
Within-groups	1.75	3	0.58		
Total	1.82	5			

adjusted means. The group means for the dependent variable can be adjusted according to the following formula:

adjusted group mean = unadjusted group mean −

$$\left[\frac{\text{WGSP}}{\text{WGSS}_{\text{cov}}} \times (\text{covariate group mean} - \text{covariate grand mean}) \right]$$

Substituting the pertinent values into this formula, the adjusted group mean for the reward condition is 2.625:

$$3 - \left[\frac{3}{4} \times (2 - 1.5) \right] = 3 - 0.375 = 2.625$$

For the punishment condition it is 2.375:

$$2 - \left[\frac{3}{4} \times (1 - 1.5) \right] = 2 - -0.375 = 2.375$$

Although the difference for the adjusted means for post-test aggressiveness is smaller than that for the unadjusted means, post-test aggressiveness in the reward condition is still higher than that in the punishment condition.

One condition that has to be met before a significant between-groups effect can be interpreted is that the statistical association known as the *regression coefficient* is the same within each of the treatment groups and is linear in the sense that higher levels of the dependent variable indicate higher levels of the covariate. This assumption is called *homogeneity of regression*. It is based on dividing or partitioning the adjusted within-groups sum of squares for the dependent variable into the *between-regressions* sum of squares and the remaining sum of squares (the remainder). These sums of squares and their associated degrees of freedom are shown in Table 8.18. The between-regressions mean square is its sum of squares divided by its degrees of freedom which are the number of groups minus 1. The remainder mean square is its sum of squares divided by its degrees of freedom which are the number of cases minus twice the number of groups. The *F* test for homogeneity of regression is the between-regressions mean square divided by the remainder mean square.

We have already described how to calculate the adjusted within-groups

Table 8.18 Between-regressions and remaining sums of squares and degrees of freedom

Source of variation	Degrees of freedom
Between-regressions	No. of groups − 1
Remainder	No. of cases − (2 × no. of groups)
Adjusted within-groups	No. of cases − no. of groups − 1

sum of squares for the dependent variable. The between-regressions sum of squares (BRSS) is the sum of the sum of products for each group (SP_1, SP_2 ...) squared and then divided by the covariate sum of squares for each group (SS_{1cov}, SS_{2cov} ...) from which is subtracted the within-groups sum of products (WGSP) squared and then divided by the within-groups sum of squares ($WGSS_{cov}$) for the covariate:

$$\text{BRSS} = \left(\frac{SP_1{}^2}{SS_{1cov}} + \frac{SP_2{}^2}{SS_{2cov}} + \cdots \right) - \frac{WGSP^2}{WGSS_{cov}}$$

The remainder sum of squares is simply obtained by subtracting the between-regressions sum of squares from the adjusted within-groups sum of squares:

$$\text{remainder SS} = WGSS_{adj} - BRSS$$

To compute the F test for homogeneity of regression we carry out the following steps which will be illustrated with the pre-test and post-test aggressiveness scores of the boys in the reward and punishment groups.

Step 1 Calculate the sum of products for each group by: (1) subtracting the covariate group mean from each of its individual scores in the group; (2) subtracting the dependent variable group mean from each of its individual scores in the group; (3) multiplying the deviation for each pair of covariate and dependent individual scores; and (4) summing the products within each group.

The sum of products for the reward condition is 1:

$$[(1 - 2) \times (2 - 3)] + [(2 - 2) \times (4 - 3)] + [(3 - 2) \times (3 - 3)] =$$
$$(-1 \times -1) + (0 \times 1) + (1 \times 0) = 1 + 0 + 0 = 1$$

The sum of products for the punishment condition is 2:

$$[(0 - 1) \times (1 - 2)] + [(1 - 1) \times (2 - 2)] + [(2 - 1) \times (3 - 2)] =$$
$$(-1 \times -1) + (0 \times 0) + (1 \times 1) = 1 + 0 + 1 = 2$$

Step 2 Calculate the covariate sum of squares for each group by (1) subtracting the covariate group mean from each of its individual scores in the group; (2) squaring them; and (3) summing the products within each group.

The sum of squares for pre-test aggressiveness in the reward condition is 2:

$$(1 - 2)^2 + (2 - 2)^2 + (3 - 2)^2 = -1^2 + 0^2 + 1^2 = 1 + 0 + 1 = 2$$

The sum of squares for pre-test aggressiveness in the punishment condition is 2:

$$(0 - 1)^2 + (1 - 1)^2 + (2 - 1)^2 = -1^2 + 0^2 + 1^2 = 1 + 0 + 1 = 2$$

Step 3 Calculate the between-regressions sum of squares by substituting the appropriate values into the following formula:

$$\text{BRSS} = \left(\frac{\text{SP}_1{}^2}{\text{SS}_{1\text{cov}}} + \frac{\text{SP}_2{}^2}{\text{SS}_{2\text{cov}}} + \cdots \right) - \frac{\text{WGSP}^2}{\text{WGSS}_{\text{cov}}}$$

The between-regressions sum of squares for post-test aggressiveness is 0.25:

$$\left(\frac{1^2}{2} + \frac{2^2}{2} \right) - \frac{3^2}{4} = \frac{1}{2} + \frac{4}{2} - \frac{9}{4} = 2.5 - 2.25 = 0.25$$

Step 4 Calculate the remainder sum of squares by subtracting the between-regressions sum of squares from the adjusted within-groups sum of squares.

The remainder sum of squares for post-test aggressiveness is 1.5 (1.75 − 0.25 = 1.5).

Step 5 Calculate the between-regressions mean square by dividing the between-regressions sum of squares by its degrees of freedom.

The between-regressions mean square for post-test aggressiveness is 0 [0/(2 − 1) = 0].

Step 6 Calculate the remainder mean square by dividing the remainder sum of squares by its degrees of freedom.

The remainder mean square for post-test aggressiveness is its sum of squares (1.5) divided by its degrees of freedom [6 − (2 × 2) = 2] which gives 0.75 (1.5/2).

Step 7 Calculate the *F* test for homogeneity of regression by dividing the between-regressions mean square by the remainder mean square.

The *F* test in this case is 0 (0/0.75).

Step 8 Look up the statistical significance of the *F* ratio in the table in Appendix 3.

With 1 and 2 degrees of freedom in the numerator and denominator respectively, *F* has to be 18.513 or bigger to be significant at or less than the 0.05 level which it is not. Therefore, the regression coefficient is the same in each of the groups.

The sum of squares, degrees of freedom, mean square and *F* ratio for these two sources of variation are presented in Table 8.19.

If we had more than two conditions, we would need to determine which of the adjusted means in the conditions differed significantly from one

Table 8.19 Analysis of covariance table for between-regressions and remaining sources of variation

Source of variation	SS	df	MS	F	p
Between-regressions	0.25	1	0.25	0.33	ns
Remainder	1.50	2	0.75		
Adjusted within-groups	1.75	3			

another. For planned or *a priori* comparisons we could run separate analyses of covariance on the pairs of groups being compared.

For unplanned or *post hoc* comparisons, we would use the Bryant-Paulson procedure (Stevens 1992). The following formula is used for a non-randomised study with one covariate where the subscripts 1 and 2 denote the two groups being compared and n is the sample size of the group.

$$\frac{\text{adjusted mean}_1 - \text{adjusted mean}_2}{\sqrt{\dfrac{\text{adjusted error}}{\text{mean square}} \times \left[\dfrac{2}{n} + \dfrac{(\text{covariate mean}_1 - \text{covariate mean}_2)^2}{\text{covariate error sum of squares}}\right]} }$$

The error term must be computed separately for each comparison.

For a randomised study with one covariate (such as the present example) we need to use the following formula:

$$\frac{\text{adjusted mean}_1 - \text{adjusted mean}_2}{\sqrt{\dfrac{\dfrac{\text{adjusted error}}{\text{mean square}} \times \left[1 + \dfrac{\text{covariate between-groups mean square}}{\text{covariate error sum of squares}}\right]}{\text{number of cases in each group}}}}$$

We will show the calculation of this procedure by comparing the adjusted post-test of the reward and punishment condition for boys. Inserting the pertinent values in this formula we find that the value for this procedure is 0.48:

$$\frac{2.625 - 2.375}{\sqrt{\dfrac{0.58 \times \left[1 + \dfrac{1.5}{4}\right]}{3}}} = \frac{0.25}{\sqrt{\dfrac{0.58 \times (1 + 0.375)}{3}}} =$$

$$\frac{0.25}{\sqrt{\dfrac{0.58 \times 1.375}{3}}} = \frac{0.25}{\sqrt{\dfrac{0.80}{3}}} = \frac{0.25}{\sqrt{0.27}} = \frac{0.25}{0.52} = 0.48$$

We look up the two-tailed 0.05 critical value of this procedure in the table in Appendix 18 where we see that with 3 degrees of freedom and two groups the value has to be 5.42 or bigger to be significant which it is not.

To carry out with Minitab an analysis of covariance on the the effect of reward and punishment on post-treatment aggressiveness in boys covarying pre-test aggressiveness, we need to arrange the data in three columns.

The first column, called **preb**, contains the **pre**-test aggressiveness ratings for **b**oys in the reward condition stacked on top of those in the punishment condition.

The second column, labelled **posb**, does the same for the **pos**t-test.

The third column, named **cond**, has the code for identifying the two conditions which is **1** for the reward condition and **2** for the punishment condition.

These three columns would contain the following values:

1 2 1
2 4 1
3 3 1
0 1 2
1 2 2
2 3 2

The following command is used to perform an analysis of covariance on these data:

MTB > glm posb = cond preb;
SUBC> covariates preb;
SUBC> means cond.

The dependent variable **posb** is listed first after the **glm** keyword, followed by an equals sign and the independent variable **cond** and the covariate **preb**. The **covariance** subcommand specifies that **preb** is to be the covariate in this analysis. The **means** subcommand provides the means of the three treatments adjusted for the effect of the covariate.

The menu procedure for doing this is:

→**Stat** →**ANOVA** →**General Linear Model...** →**posb** →**Select** [this puts **posb** in the box beside **Response:**] →box under **Model:** →**cond** [this puts **cond** in this box] →**preb** →**Select** →box under **Covariates [op-tional]:** →**preb** →**Select** →**Options...** →box under **Display means for (list of terms):** →**cond** →**Select** [this puts **cond** in this box] →**OK**

The output for this procedure is shown in Table 8.20. The coefficient for the covariate **preb** (**0.7500**) is not statistically significant ($p < 0.144$). This means that the first assumption that there is a significant linear relationship between the dependent variable and the covariate is not satisfied and that an analysis of covariance in this case is not warranted. The analysis of

Table 8.20 **Glm** output testing the effect of **cond**itions on **post**-test
aggressiveness in **boys** covarying **pre**-test aggressiveness

General Linear Model

Factor	Levels	Values	
cond	2	1	2

Analysis of Variance for posb

Source	DF	Seq SS	Adj SS	Adj MS	F	P
preb	1	3.6818	2.2500	2.2500	3.86	0.144
cond	1	0.0682	0.0682	0.0682	0.12	0.755
Error	3	1.7500	1.7500	0.5833		
Total	5	5.5000				

Term	Coeff	Stdev	t-value	P
Constant	1.3750	0.6522	2.11	0.126
preb	0.7500	0.3819	1.96	0.144

Means for Covariates

Covariate	Mean	Stdev
preb	1.500	1.049

Adjusted Means for posb

cond	Mean	Stdev
1	2.625	0.4805
2	2.375	0.4805

covariance table shows that the **cond**ition effect is not significant when pre-test aggressiveness is covaried out ($p<0.755$).

To determine if the second assumption, that the slope of the regression lines is the same in each cell, is met, we need to use the following commands:

MTB > glm posb = cond preb cond*preb;
SUBC> covariates preb;
SUBC> brief 1.

The dependent variable **posb** is listed first after the **glm** keyword, followed by an equals sign and the two variables and their interaction. It is the significance of this interaction that we are solely concerned with in this analysis. The **covariance** subcommand specifies that **preb** is to be the covariate in this analysis while **1** on the **brief** subcommand restricts the output to the analysis of covariance table.

The menu sequence for doing this is:

Table 8.21 **Glm brief 2** output showing the test of homogeneity of slope of regression line within cells

General Linear Model

Factor	Levels	Values	
cond	2	1	2

Analysis of Variance for posb

Source	DF	Seq SS	Adj SS	Adj MS	F	P
cond	1	1.5000	0.3158	0.3158	0.42	0.583
preb	1	2.2500	2.2500	2.2500	3.00	0.225
cond*preb	1	0.2500	0.2500	0.2500	0.33	0.622
Error	2	1.5000	1.5000	0.7500		
Total	5	5.5000				

Term	Coeff	Stdev	t-value	P
Consant	1.5000	0.7706	1.95	0.191
preb	0.7500	0.4330	1.73	0.225
preb*cond				
1	−0.2500	0.4330	−0.58	0.622

→**Stat** →**ANOVA** →**General Linear Model...** →**posb** →**Select** [this puts **posb** in the box beside **Response:**] →box under **Model:** →**cond** [this puts **cond** in this box] →**preb** →**Select** →type **cond*preb** →box under **Covariates [optional]:** →**preb** →**Select** →**OK**

The menu system does not have the **brief 1** output option, so the default output option (**brief 2**) is produced which includes the table of factor levels.

The **brief 2** output from this procedure is presented in Table 8.21. The interaction between the independent variable of **treat**ment and the covariate of **preb** is not significant since *p* is **0.662**. This means that the slope of the regression line in each of the cells is similar and the second assumption is met.

SUMMARY

The computation of parametric tests for assessing whether the means of interval or ratio data from two or more related samples differ significantly across the samples has been described. The related *t* test compares the difference between the means of the two related samples taking into account the extent to which the scores of the two samples are correlated by modifying the way the standard error of the difference in means is computed. Single factor repeated measures analysis of variance determines whether the means of three or more related samples differ. Differences between pairs of groups are examined with the related t test where differences were predicted and the Bonferroni test where differences were not predicted. Two-way analysis of variance with repeated measures on one factor compares the means of groups consisting of two factors, one of which is repeated. Where differences were predicted a related t test is used for related pairs of groups and an unrelated t test for unrelated pairs. Where differences were not predicted, the Bonferroni test could be applied to related scores and the Scheffé test to unrelated scores. One-way analysis of covariance compares the means of two or more groups controlling for the effects of a second factor known to be associated with the first factor and called a covariate. Interpretation of the analysis depends on the regression coefficient being the same within each of the groups. A two-group analysis of covariance tests for differences between pairs of groups which were predicted and the Bryan–Paulson procedure for differences which were not predicted.

EXERCISES

The data for these exercises are available in Table 6.23.

1 Use the related t test to compare educational interest at 12 and 15 for pupils from mixed-sex schools.
   (a) What is the value of the t test?
   (b) What are its degrees of freedom?
   (c) What is its two-tailed probability level?
   (d) Is educational interest significantly greater at 15 than at 12 for pupils from mixed-sex schools?
2 Use a single factor repeated measures analysis of variance to compare educational interest at 9, 12 and 15 for pupils from mixed-sex schools.
   (a) What is the value of the F test?
   (b) What are its degrees of freedom?
   (c) What is its probability level?
   (d) Does educational interest at 9, 12 and 15 differ significantly for pupils from mixed-sex schools?
3 Use a two-way analysis of variance with repeated measures on one factor to determine whether any change in educational interest between 12 and 15 differs for pupils from single- and mixed-sex schools.
   (a) What is the value of the F test?
   (b) What are its degrees of freedom?
   (c) What is its probability level?
   (d) Does any change in educational interest between 12 and 15 differ for pupils from single- and mixed-sex schools?
4 Use a one-way analysis of covariance to determine whether there is a

significant difference in educational interest at 12 between single- and mixed-sex schools when socio-economic status is covaried.

(a) What is the value of the F test for the adjusted between-groups effect?
(b) What are its degrees of freedom?
(c) What is its probability level?
(d) What is the value of the F test for homogeneity of regression?
(e) What are its degrees of freedom?
(f) What is its probability level?
(g) Is the regression coefficient the same in the two groups of single- and mixed-sex schools?
(h) What is the adjusted mean of educational interest at 12 for pupils from single-sex schools?
(i) What is the adjusted mean of educational interest at 12 for pupils from mixed-sex schools?
(j) Is educational interest at 12 significantly greater in single- than in mixed-sex schools when socio-economic status is covaried?

Chapter 9

Tests of association for categorical and ordinal data

So far we have looked at statistical tests which determine whether the distribution of two or more variables differs significantly. However, we are often interested in the extent to which two or more variables are associated, the direction of that association and the likelihood of that association occurring by chance. For example, we may wish to know whether women with children are less likely to watch violence on television than women without children and what the strength and statistical probability of any such association is. Or, as discussed in the previous chapter, we may want to find out whether higher pre-test aggressiveness is related to higher post-test aggressiveness and how strong and statistically significant such a relationship is. In addition, we may wish to discover whether an association between two variables, or the lack of one, is the result of their relationship with one or more other variables. For instance, if it was found that children who were least aggressive were also breastfed as babies, then this association may result from the fact that better educated mothers were more likely both to breastfeed their children and to encourage them to be less aggressive. To discover the answers to such questions, we would need to carry out the appropriate test of association, the selection of which partly depends on whether the data are categorical, ordinal or interval/ratio. In this chapter we will deal with tests which are suitable for categorical and ordinal data.

CATEGORICAL DATA

Tests of association for categorical data described in this chapter can be divided into those that are derived from chi-square (*phi coefficient, contingency coefficient* and *Cramer's V*) and those that are based on the *proportional reduction in error* (*Goodman and Kruskal's lambda* and *tau*). We will illustrate the computation of the first and last two of these tests with the data in Table 9.1 which show the number of women either with or without children who either watch violence on television or not.

Table 9.1 Number of women with and without children who watch violence on
television

| | | Children | | |
		No	Yes	Total
Watch violence	No	15	50	65
	Yes	55	20	75
Total		70	70	140

Phi coefficient

The phi coefficient is suitable as a measure of association where both
variables are dichotomous. One way of computing it is by dividing Pearson's chi-square by the total number of cases and taking the square root of
the result:

$$\text{phi} = \sqrt{\frac{\text{chi-square}}{\text{no. of cases}}}$$

With this formula phi can vary from zero to $+1.0$. Since the minimum
value of chi-square is 0, the minimum value of phi is also 0. If, however,
the formula involves subtracting the product of two of the cells from the
product of the other two cells, then the minimum value of phi can be -1.
This form of phi is the same as Pearson's product moment correlation
described in Chapter 10.

To calculate phi using the first formula, we first have to compute chi-
square. As described in Chapter 5, chi-square is the sum of the squared
difference between the observed and expected frequency for each cell
divided by the expected frequency for that cell. The expected frequency
for any cell is its row total multiplied by its column total divided by the
grand total. The expected frequencies for this example are shown in Table
9.2. In this example, chi-square is 35.18:

$$\frac{(15-32.5)^2}{32.5} + \frac{(50-32.5)^2}{32.5} + \frac{(55-37.5)^2}{37.5} + \frac{(20-37.5)^2}{37.5} =$$

$$\frac{306.25}{32.5} + \frac{306.25}{32.5} + \frac{306.25}{32.5} + \frac{306.25}{32.5} =$$

$$9.42 + 9.42 + 8.17 + 8.17 = 35.18$$

Consequently, phi is 0.50 ($\sqrt{35.18/140}$). Since chi-square equals phi
squared times the number of cases, the significance of phi can be tested
by looking up the statistical significance of the chi-square value (35.18),

Table 9.2 Expected frequency of married women with and without children who watch violence on television

		Children	
		No	Yes
Watch violence	No	32.5	32.5
	Yes	37.5	37.5

which has 1 degree of freedom, in the table in Appendix 5. With 1 degree of freedom, chi-square has to be larger than 3.84 to be significant at the two-tailed 0.05 level which it is. Therefore, we would conclude that there was a statistically significant association between having children and watching violence on television such that women with children were less likely to watch violence on television than women without children.

Contingency coefficient

When one or both variables have more than two categories, phi is not restricted to varying between zero and +1 because the chi-square value can be greater than the total number of cases in the sample. To obtain a measure that must lie between zero and +1, Pearson devised the contingency coefficient in which chi-square has been added to the denominator of the formula for phi:

$$\text{contingency coefficient } (C) = \sqrt{\frac{\text{chi-square}}{\text{chi-square} + \text{no. of cases}}}$$

The contingency coefficient does not have +1 as its upper limit as this limit depends on the number of categories. For a table made up of an equal number of rows and columns, $n \times n$, the upper limit is calculated by subtracting 1 from the number of n, dividing the result by n and then taking the square root of this division. So, for a 3 × 3 table the upper limit is 0.82 [$\sqrt{(3 - 1)/3} = 0.82$], while for a 4 × 4 table it would be 0.87 [$\sqrt{(4 - 1)/4} = 0.87$]. When the number of rows and columns differ, as in a 3 × 4 table, the upper limit is based on the smaller number. In this case the upper limit is 0.82.

We will demonstrate the calculation of the contingency coefficient with the example from Chapter 5 of the number of people in the past week who have either watched a violent film, watched a non-violent film or not watched any film in three different countries. These data are reproduced in Table 9.3. As calculated in Chapter 5, chi-square for these data is 12.64. Consequently, the contingency coefficent is 0.35 [$\sqrt{12.64/(12.64 + 90)} =$

Table 9.3 Film viewing in three countries

	Country			Row total
	US	UK	Canada	
Watched a violent film	14	3	5	22
Watched a non-violent film	6	5	15	26
Not watched a film	20	12	10	42
Column total	40	20	30	90

0.35]. To check the statistical significance of this coefficient, we look up the statistical significance of the chi-square value used to calculate it in the table in Appendix 5 with the appropriate degrees of freedom which is the number of rows minus 1 multiplied by the number of columns minus 1. With 4 degrees of freedom [(3 − 1) × (3 − 1)] the contingency coefficient has to be 9.49 or larger to be significant at the two-tailed 0.05 level which it is. Consequently, we would conclude that there was a statistically significant association between viewing films and the three countries.

Minitab does not compute the contingency coefficient directly but this can be worked out from the chi-square value which it provides.

Cramer's V

To make the upper limit of the association +1 for tables greater than 2 × 2, Cramer produced V which is computed by dividing chi-square by the total number of cases multiplied by the smaller number of rows or columns minus 1 and then taking the square root of the result:

$$\text{Cramer's } V = \sqrt{\frac{\text{chi-square}}{\text{no. of cases} \times (\text{smaller no. of rows/columns} - 1)}}$$

Where the smaller number of rows or columns is 2, the denominator effectively becomes the number of cases [N × (2 − 1) = N] and therefore Cramer's V is the same as phi.

For the data in Table 9.3, Cramer's V is 0.26 { √12.64/[(90 × (3 − 1)]} = 0.26]. As before, to check the statistical significance of this value, we look up the statistical significance of the chi-square value on which it is based in the table in Appendix 5 with the appropriate degrees of freedom which is the number of rows minus 1 multiplied by the number of columns minus 1. We would conclude that there was a statistically significant association between viewing films and the three countries.

Minitab does not calculate the contingency coefficient directly but it can be computed from the chi-square value which it provides.

Goodman and Kruskal's lambda

Lambda is the proportional increase in predicting the outcome of one categorical variable when knowing its combined outcome with a second categorical variable. The value of lambda can vary from zero to +1. Zero means that there is no increase in predictiveness whereas 1 indicates that prediction can be made without error. Suppose, for example, we wanted to predict from the data in Table 9.1 the larger number of cases with respect to women watching violence on television regardless of whether they had children. The larger category is women who watch violence (75). Consequently, if we had to predict whether a particular woman watched violence or not, our best guess would be to say she did. If we did this for all 140 women we would be wrong on 65 occasions (140 − 75 = 65).

How would our ability to predict whether a particular woman watched violence be enhanced by our knowledge as to whether they had children? Taking the women without children first, if we knew that 55 of these 70 women watched violence, our best guess for predicting which category a particular woman in this group was in is to say she watched violence. If we did this for all 70 women we would be wrong 15 times (70 − 55 = 15). Turning next to the women with children, if we knew that 50 of these 70 women did not watch violence, our best guess for predicting which category a particular women in this group was in is to say she did not watch violence. If we did this for all 70 women we would be wrong 20 times (70 − 50 = 20). Therefore, if we knew whether women had children or not, we would make 35 errors (15 + 20 = 35). Knowing this information reduces our errors by 30 (65 − 35 = 30) which as a proportion of the errors we made initially is 0.46 (30/65 = 0.46). In other words, knowledge of the second variable reduces the proportion of errors by 0.46. Predicting women who watched violence from having children results in a lambda of 0.46.

We could also work out lambda for predicting whether women have children based on knowing whether they watched violence. Lambda for this prediction is 0.5:

$$\frac{70 - (20 + 15)}{140 - 70} = \frac{35}{70} = 0.5$$

These two lambdas are called *asymmetric* since they are likely to vary depending on which variable is being predicted. The following formula is used for calculating asymmetric lambda:

$$\text{asymmetric lambda} = \frac{\text{sum of the largest cell frequencies in the columns} - \text{largest row total}}{\text{total number of cases} - \text{largest row total}}$$

Applying this formula to our data, we see that lambda for predicting watching violence is 0.46:

$$\frac{(50 + 55) - 75}{140 - 75} = \frac{30}{65} = 0.46$$

Lambda for predicting having children is 0.5:

$$\frac{(55 + 50) - 70}{140 - 70} = \frac{35}{70} = 0.5$$

The formula for computing symmetric lambda is:

$$\frac{\begin{array}{l}\text{sum of the largest cell} \\ \text{frequencies in the columns}\end{array} + \begin{array}{l}\text{sum of the largest cell} \\ \text{frequencies in the rows}\end{array} - \text{largest row total} - \text{largest column total}}{(2 \times \text{total number of cases}) - \text{largest row total} - \text{largest column total}}$$

Applying this formula to our data we find that symmetric lambda is 0.48:

$$\frac{(55 + 50) + (55 + 50) - 75 - 70}{(2 \times 140) - 75 - 70} = \frac{65}{135} = 0.48$$

Minitab does not compute Goodman and Kruskal's lambda.

Goodman and Kruskal's tau

Lambda assumes that the same prediction is made for all cases in a particular row or column. Goodman and Kruskal's tau, on the other hand, presumes that the predictions are randomly made on the basis of their proportions in row and column totals. For instance, if we predicted whether women watched violence on television ignoring whether they had children, then we would guess this correctly for 0.46 (65/140 = 0.46) of the 65 women who did not watch violence (i.e. 0.46 × 65 = about 30 women) and for 0.54 (75/140 = 0.54) of the 75 women who watched violence (i.e. 0.54 × 75 = about 40 women). In other words, we would guess correctly that about 70 of the women watched violence (140 − 30 − 40 = 70 women) and the probability of error would be 0.5 (70/140 = 0.5).

If we now took into account whether these women had children or not, then we would predict correctly whether women watched violence for 0.23 (15/65 = 0.23) of the 15 women without children and who did not watch violence (i.e. 0.23 × 15 = 3.5 women), 0.77 (50/65 = 0.77) of the 50 women with children and who did not watch violence (i.e. 0.77 × 50 = 38.5 women), 0.73 (55/75 = 0.73) of the 55 women without children and who watched violence (i.e. 0.73 × 55 = 40.3 women) and 0.27 (20/75 = 0.27) of the 20 women with children and who watched violence (i.e. 0.27 × 20 = 5.4 women). In other words, the probability of error for guessing whether women watched violence knowing whether they had children would be 0.37 [(140 − 3.5 − 38.5 − 40.3 − 5.4)/140 = 0.37]. Consequently, the proportional reduction of error in predicting women who watched violence knowing whether they have children is 0.26 [(0.5 − 0.37)/0.5 = 0.26]. In the same way, we could also work out Goodman and Kruskal's tau for predicting whether women have children knowing whether they watched violence.

Minitab does not provide Goodman and Kruskal's tau.

ORDINAL DATA

There are several tests of association for two ordinal variables. Apart from *Spearman's rank order correlation* and *Mantel–Haenszel's chi-square* measure of linear association, the tests discussed in this section (*Kendall's tau a*, *tau b* and *tau c*; *Goodman and Kruskal's gamma*; and *Somer's d*) are based on comparing all possible pairs of cases. To illustrate the general rationale behind these tests, imagine that two people or judges were asked to rank five women in terms of their aggressiveness where a rank of 1 indicated the most aggressive. The rankings given by these two judges are shown in Table 9.4 where the rankings for one judge (Judge A) have been listed in order and compared against the rankings of the other judge (Judge B). We can now compare the extent to which the rankings by Judge B are similar to Judge A by counting the number of pairs of cases for Judge B in which the first case is ranked higher than the second (called a *concordant* pair), lower (a *discordant* pair) or the same (a *tied* pair). For example, Judge B ranks Ann 2 and Mary 1, so this pair is discordant. On the other hand, both Ann and Jo are ranked 2, so this pair is tied, while both Sue and Jane are ranked higher than Ann, so that these two pairs are concordant.

If all pairs of cases for Judge B were concordant, then the rankings of Judge B would be the same as those of Judge A and there would be a perfect direct or *positive* association between the rankings of Judge A and B so that a higher ranking by Judge A would always correspond to a higher ranking by Judge B. Conversely, if all pairs of cases for Judge B were discordant, then there would be a perfect inverse or *negative* association between the rankings of Judge A and B so that a higher ranking by Judge A would always correspond to a lower ranking by Judge B. If there were an equal number of concordant and discordant pairs for Judge B, then there would be no association between the rankings of the two judges. If there are more concordant pairs than discordant pairs, then the association will

Table 9.4 Example of rankings by two judges

Women	Judge A	Judge B
Anne	1	2
Mary	2	1
Jo	3	2
Sue	4	4
Jane	5	5

be positive while if there are more discordant pairs than concordant pairs, then the association will be negative.

Kendall's rank correlation coefficient or tau *a*

Kendall's tau *a* is used when there are no tied pairs and can vary from -1 to $+1$. It is the number of concordant pairs minus the number of discordant pairs over the total number of pairs:

$$\text{tau } a = \frac{\text{no. of concordant pairs } - \text{ no. of discordant pairs}}{\text{total no. of pairs}}$$

Take the data in Table 9.5 which is the same as that in Table 9.4 except that the ranking by Judge B of Jo has been changed from 2 to 3 and where the number of concordant and discordant pairs has been counted. The number of concordant (or discordant) pairs is worked out by taking each case of Judge B in turn, starting with the first case, and counting the number of times that case is higher (or lower) than the cases below and adding the numbers for all cases. So the ranking by Judge B of Ann is higher than three of the other rankings (Jo, Sue and Jane), the ranking of Mary is also higher than three of the other rankings (Jo, Sue and Jane) and so on, giving a total of 9 concordant pairs. Tau *a* for this example is 0.8 [(9 $-$ 1)/10 = 0.8]. Note that the total number of pairs can be calculated by subtracting 1 from the number of pairs, multiplying the result by the number of pairs and then dividing by 2. If we do this, the total number of pairs is 10 [(5 $-$ 1) $\times$ 5/2 = 10].

Minitab does not offer Kendall's tau *a*.

Kendall's tau *b*

Kendall's tau *b* is used as a test of association for ordinal data when there are tied pairs. It is the number of concordant pairs (*C*) minus the number of

Table 9.5 Another example of rankings by two judges

Women	Judge A	Judge B	No. of concordant pairs	No. of discordant pairs
Ann	1	2	3	1
Mary	2	1	3	0
Jo	3	3	2	0
Sue	4	4	1	0
Jane	5	5	0	0
Total			9	1

discordant pairs (D) divided by the square root of the product of the total number of pairs (T) minus the number of tied pairs for one variable (T_1) and the total number of pairs (T) minus the tied pairs for the other variable (T_2):

$$\text{tau } b = \frac{C - D}{\sqrt{(T - T_1) \times (T - T_2)}}$$

Tau b can vary from -1 to $+1$ if the table is square and if none of the row and column totals is zero.

Take the data in Table 9.6 which are the same as those in Table 9.4. The number of ties for Judge B (the second variable) is 1, the number of concordant pairs is 8 and the number of discordant pairs is 1. There are no tied pairs for Judge A. Consequently, tau b is 0.74:

$$\frac{8 - 1}{\sqrt{(10 - 0) \times (10 - 1)}} = \frac{7}{9.49} = 0.74$$

If we arranged these data into the matrix displayed in Table 9.7 with the ranks of Judge A along the side and the ranks of Judge B along the bottom with the number of ranks in each cell, then we see that this table is not square since it consists of five rows and four columns.

An alternative method of counting the number of concordant, discordant and tied pairs is to use such a matrix. Concordant pairs for a joint ranking are represented by the sum of values which lie below and to the right of that position while discordant pairs are the sum of values which lie below and

Table 9.6 Number of concordant. discordant and tied pairs of rankings

Women	Judge A	Judge B	C	D	T_1	T_2
Ann	1	2	2	1	0	1
Mary	2	1	3	0	0	0
Jo	3	2	2	0	0	0
Sue	4	4	1	0	0	0
Jane	5	5	0	0	0	0
Total			8	1	0	1

Table 9.7 Matrix of ranks

	1	1		
	2	1		
Judge A	3	1		
	4		1	
	5			1
		1	2	4	5

Judge B

Table 9.8 Number of concordant, discordant and tied pairs of rankings for another example

Women	Judge A	Judge B	C	D	T_1	T_2
Ann	1	2	2	1	1	1
Mary	1	1	3	0	0	0
Jo	3	2	2	0	0	0
Sue	4	4	1	0	0	0
Jane	5	5	0	0	0	0
Total			8	1	1	1

Table 9.9 Another matrix of ranks

```
          1   1   1
          3       1
Judge A   4           1
          5               1
              1   2   4   5

              Judge B
```

to the left of that point. So, for the joint ranking located at rank 1 for Judge A and rank 2 for Judge B there are two values below and to the right of it (located at rank 4 of both judges and at rank 5 of both judges) and one value below and to the left of it (at rank 2 for Judge A and at rank 1 for Judge B). Proceeding in this way through the matrix, we can count 8 concordant pairs and one discordant pair. Ties are represented by values that lie along either the same rows (for Judge A) or the same columns (for Judge B). So, there is one tie for Judge B.

To illustrate that this second method of counting the number of concordant, discordant and tied pairs is easier to use than the first method, take the data in Table 9.8 which is the same as that in Table 9.6 except that the ranking of Mary by Judge A has been changed from 2 to 1. If we re-arrange the data in matrix form as shown in Table 9.9, we may work out more readily that there are now no discordant pairs since Judge A has given the same ranking to Ann and Mary.

An alternative formula for computing tau b is the difference between the number of concordant (C) and discordant (D) pairs multiplied by 2 and divided by the square root of the squared number of cases (N^2) minus the sum of squared row totals (RT^2) multiplied by the squared number of cases (N^2) minus the sum of squared column totals (CT^2):

$$\text{tau } b = \frac{2 \times (C - D)}{\sqrt{(N^2 - \text{sum of } RT^2) \times (N^2 - \text{sum of } CT^2)}}$$

If we substitute the appropriate values into this formula, then we see that tau b is 0.74:

$$\frac{2 \times (8 - 1)}{\sqrt{[5^2 - (1^2+1^2+1^2+1^2+1^2)] \times [5^2 - (1^2+2^2+1^2+1^2)]}} =$$

$$\frac{14}{\sqrt{(25 - 5) \times (25 - 7)}} = \frac{14}{\sqrt{360}} = \frac{14}{19} = 0.74$$

Minitab does not work out Kendall's tau b.

Kendall's tau c

For a rectangular table Kendall's tau c can come closer to -1 to $+1$. It is the number of concordant pairs (C) minus the number of discordant pairs (D) multiplied by twice the number of columns or rows whichever is the smaller (S), divided by the total number of cases (N) squared times 1 from the smaller number of columns or rows:

$$\text{tau } c = \frac{(C - D) \times 2 \times S}{N^2 \times (S - 1)}$$

Consequently, for the data in Table 9.8 where the number of columns (4) is smaller than the number of rows (5), tau c is 0.75:

$$\frac{(8 - 1) \times 2 \times 4}{5^2 \times (4 - 1)} = \frac{56}{75} = 0.75$$

Since tau is approximately normally distributed when the size of the sample (N) is larger than 10, we can calculate the significance level of tau by converting it into z according to the following formula:

$$z = \frac{\text{tau}}{\sqrt{\dfrac{2(2N + 5)}{9N(N - 1)}}}$$

Substituting the values in this formula for our example we find that z is 1.83.

$$\frac{0.75}{\sqrt{\dfrac{2 \times [(2 \times 5) + 5]}{9 \times 5 \times (5 - 1)}}} = \frac{0.75}{\sqrt{\dfrac{30}{180}}} = \frac{0.75}{0.41} = 1.83$$

We look up the significance of this z value in the table in Appendix 2. The area between the middle of the curve and a z value of 1.83 is 0.4664, indicating that the area beyond the z value on one side of the curve is 0.0336 (0.5000 − 0.4664 = 0.0336), which is the one-tailed probability. For the two-tailed probability we would double 0.0336 to give 0.0672 (0.0336 × 2 = 0.0672).

Minitab does not compute Kendall's tau c.

Goodman and Kruskal's gamma

Goodman and Kruskal's gamma can range from −1 to +1 and takes no account of ties or the size of the table. It is simply the number of concordant pairs (C) minus the number of discordant pairs (D) divided by the number of concordant and discordant pairs:

$$\text{gamma} = \frac{C - D}{C + D}$$

So, for the data in Table 9.6 gamma is 0.78:

$$\frac{8 - 1}{8 + 1} = \frac{7}{9} = 0.78$$

Minitab does not calculate Goodman and Kruskal's gamma.

Somer's d

Somer's d provides an asymmetric as well as a symmetric measure of association and takes account of tied pairs. The formula for computing asymmetric d for the first variable as the dependent variable is the difference between the number of concordant (C) and discordant (D) pairs divided by the number of concordant (C), discordant (D) and tied pairs for the first variable (T_1):

$$\text{asymmetric } d = \frac{C - D}{C + D + T_1}$$

For the data in Table 9.6, asymmetric d for Judge A as the dependent variable is 0.78:

$$\frac{8 - 1}{8 + 1 + 0} = \frac{7}{9} = 0.78$$

The formula for computing asymmetric d for the second variable as the dependent variable is the difference between the number of concordant (C) and discordant (D) pairs divided by the number of concordant (C), discordant (D) and tied pairs for the second variable (T_2):

$$\text{asymmetric } d = \frac{C - D}{C + D + T_2}$$

Asymmetric d for Judge B as the dependent variable is 0.7:

$$\frac{8 - 1}{8 + 1 + 1} = \frac{7}{10} = 0.7$$

The formula for computing symmetric d is the difference between the number of concordant (C) and discordant (D) pairs divided by the number of concordant (C), discordant (D) and tied pairs for the first variable (T_1) added to the number of concordant (C), discordant (D) and tied pairs for the second variable (T_2) divided by 2:

$$\text{symmetric } d = \frac{C - D}{(C + D + T_1 + C + D + T_2)/2}$$

Symmetric d for this example is 0.74:

$$\frac{8 - 1}{(8 + 1 + 1 + 8 + 1 + 0)/2} = \frac{7}{9.5} = 0.74$$

An alternative formula for computing asymmetric d, where the dependent variable is represented by the row totals of the matrix of ranks, is the difference between the number of concordant (C) and discordant (D) pairs multiplied by 2 and divided by the squared number of cases (N^2) minus the sum of squared column totals (CT^2):

$$\text{asymmetric } d = \frac{2 \times C - D}{N^2 - \text{sum of } CT^2}$$

For the data in Table 9.6, asymmetric d for Judge A as the dependent variable is 0.78:

$$\frac{2 \times (8 - 1)}{5^2 - (1^2 + 2^2 + 1^2 + 1^2)} = \frac{14}{25 - 7} = \frac{14}{18} = 0.78$$

The corresponding formula for computing asymmetric d, where the dependent variable is represented by the column totals of the matrix of ranks, is the difference between the number of concordant (C) and discordant (D) pairs multiplied by 2 and divided by the squared number of cases (N^2) minus the sum of squared row totals (RT^2):

$$\text{asymmetric } d = \frac{2 \times (C - D)}{N^2 - \text{sum of } RT^2}$$

Asymmetric d for Judge B as the dependent variable is 0.7:

$$\frac{2 \times (8 - 1)}{5^2 - (1^2 + 1^2 + 1^2 + 1^2 + 1^2)} = \frac{14}{25 - 5} = \frac{14}{20} = 0.7$$

The formula for computing symmetric d is the difference between the number of concordant (C) and discordant (D) pairs multiplied by 4 and divided by the squared number of cases (N^2) minus the sum of squared row totals (RT^2) added to the squared number of cases (N^2) minus the sum of squared column totals (CT^2):

$$\text{symmetric } d = \frac{4 \times (C - D)}{(N^2 - \text{sum of } RT^2) + (N^2 - \text{sum of } CT^2)}$$

Symmetric d is 0.74:

$$\frac{4 \times (8 - 1)}{[5^2 - (1^2 + 1^2 + 1^2 + 1^2 + 1^2)] + [5^2 - (1^2 + 2^2 + 1^2 + 1^2)]} =$$

$$\frac{28}{(25 - 5) + (25 - 7)} = \frac{28}{38} = 0.74$$

Minitab does not provide Somer's d.

Spearman's rank order correlation or rho

Spearman's rho ranges from -1 to $+1$ and is based on the amount of disagreement between the ranks for the two variables. More specifically, it involves squaring and then adding together the differences between paired ranks for the two variables for all cases. Rho can be described in terms of the following formula:

$$\text{rho} = 1 - \frac{2 \times \text{sum of differences squared}}{\text{maximum sum of differences squared}}$$

If there are no differences between the ranks, then there will be a perfect positive correlation of $+1$ ($1 - 0 = 1$) since the differences between the ranks will be zero and zero multiplied by 2 and divided by the maximum sum of differences squared will still be zero. If, on the other hand, the ranks of one variable are the exact reverse of the other, then there will be a perfect negative correlation of -1 ($1 - 2 = -1$) since the sum of differences squared will be the maximum sum which divided by itself will be 1.

When there are no tied ranks, the computational formula for rho is:

$$\text{rho} = 1 - \frac{6 \times \text{sum of differences squared}}{N^3 - N}$$

where N is the number of pairs or cases.

When there are tied ranks the computational formula for rho is:

Table 9.10 Initial computations for rho with no tied ranks

Women	Judge A	Judge B	Difference	Difference squared
Ann	1	2	−1	1
Mary	2	1	+1	1
Jo	3	3	0	0
Sue	4	4	0	0
Jane	5	5	0	0
Total				2

$$\text{rho} = \frac{T_1 + T_2 - \text{sum of differences squared}}{2 \times \sqrt{T_1 \times T_2}}$$

where T_1 or T_2 is:

$$\frac{[N \times (N^2 - 1)] - [\text{sum of } t \times (t^2 - 1)]}{12}$$

and t is the number of ties at a given rank for either the first or second variable.

We will illustrate the computation of rho with no tied ranks with the data in Table 9.10 which are the same as the data in Table 9.4 except that the ranking of Jo by Judge B has been changed from 2 to 3. Substituting the appropriate values in the formula for computing rho when there are no ties, we see that rho is 0.9:

$$1 - \frac{6 \times 2}{5^3 - 5} = 1 - \frac{12}{120} = 1 - 0.1 = 0.9$$

The significance level of rho can be computed by converting it into t using the following formula:

$$t = \text{rho} \times \sqrt{\frac{N - 2}{1 - \text{rho}^2}}$$

Substituting the values of our example into this formula we find that t is 3.57:

$$0.9 \times \sqrt{\frac{5 - 2}{1 - 0.9^2}} = 0.9 \times \sqrt{\frac{3}{0.19}} = 0.9 \times \sqrt{15.79} = 0.9 \times 3.97 = 3.57$$

We look up the statistical significance of t in the table in Appendix 15 against the appropriate degrees of freedom which is the number of cases (N) minus 2. We see that with three degrees of freedom t has to be 2.353 or bigger to be significant at the 0.05 one-tailed level. So if we had anticipated

Table 9.11 Initial computations for rho with some tied ranks

Women	Judge A	Judge B		Difference	Difference squared
Ann	1	2	2.5	−1.5	2.25
Mary	2	1	1.0	1.0	1.00
Jo	3	2	2.5	0.5	0.25
Sue	4	4	4.0	0.0	0.00
Jane	5	5	5.0	0.0	0.00
Total					3.50

that the two sets of rankings would be positively correlated, we could conclude that the correlation was significantly positive. Alternatively we could look up the statistical significance of rho in the table in Appendix 19 where we see that with three degrees of freedom rho has to be 0.9000 or bigger to be significant at the 0.05 one-tailed level.

Where some of the ranks are tied (as in Table 9.11) we first have to give these ranks the average rank they would have had if they had not been tied so that the average rank of Ann and Jo for Judge B is 2.5 [(2 + 3)/2 = 2.5]. For the first variable there are no ties, so T_1 is 10:

$$\frac{[5 \times (5^2 - 1)] - [0 \times (0 - 1)]}{12} = \frac{120 - 0}{12} = 10$$

For the second variable there are only two ties (2.5, 2.5) for one rank (2.5) so T_2 is 9.5:

$$\frac{[5 \times (5^2 - 1)] - [2 \times (2^2 - 1)]}{12} = \frac{120 - 6}{12} = 9.5$$

Substituting the appropriate values in the formula for computing rho when there are ties, we find that rho is 0.82:

$$\frac{10 + 9.5 - 3.5}{2 \times \sqrt{10 \times 9.5}} = \frac{16}{19.5} = 0.82$$

As we have already seen, with only five cases this correlation would have to be 0.9 or larger to be significant at the 0.05 one-tailed level.

To compute Spearman's rho with Minitab, we first have to rank the scores of our two variables and then carry out a Pearson's correlation on the ranked values. We will illustrate its use with the data in Table 9.11 although the data for the first variable have already been ranked. To calculate rho with the prompt system we rank scores with the **rank** command in which the variable to be ranked is listed first followed by the column number into which the ranked scores will be put as follows, for example:

MTB > rank 'judgeA' c3
MTB > rank 'JudgeB' c4

We then carry out a Pearson's correlation on these ranked values, for example:

MTB > correlation c3 c4

The output for this sequence is presented below:

Correlation of C3 and C4 = 0.821

The menu procedure for computing tau is:

→**Manip** →**Rank...** →**judgeA** →**Select** [this puts **judgeA** in the box beside **Rank data in:**]→in the box beside **Store ranks in:** type **c3** →**OK**
→**Manip** →**Rank...** →**JudgeB** →**Select** [this puts **JudgeB** in the box beside **Rank data in:**] →in the box beside **Store ranks in:** type **c4** →**OK**
→**Stat** →**Basic Statistics** →**Correlation...** →**c3** →**Select** [this puts **c3** in the box under **Variables:**] →**c4** →**Select** →**OK**

The significance level of rho has to be determined as described previously.

Mantel–Haenszel's chi-square

Mantel–Haenszel's chi-square is another linear measure of association for ordinal data. It is calculated by multiplying the squared Pearson's correlation coefficient by the number of cases minus 1 and it has 1 degree of freedom. The procedure for computing Pearson's correlation will be described in the next chapter. The critical values of Mantel–Haenszel's chi-square are those of chi-square with 1 degree of freedom.

A MEASURE OF PARTIAL ASSOCIATION

A significant association between two measures does not necessarily mean that the two variables are causally related. For instance, if people who watch more violence on television were found to be more aggressive, then this relationship does not necessarily imply that there is a causal link between these two variables such that violence on television leads to aggressiveness. It is possible that this association is *spurious* in the sense that it is the result of one or more other factors which are genuinely related to the two variables of watching violence on television and aggressiveness. For example, greater parental aggressiveness may be related to their children both watching more violence and being more aggressive. When parental aggressiveness is taken into account there may be no association between the viewing of violence and aggressiveness in their children.

Table 9.12 Data on parent's aggression, children's viewing of violence on television and children's aggression

Case no.	Parent's aggression	Children's viewing of TV violence	Children's aggression
01	1	1	2
02	1	1	2
03	1	1	1 *
04	1	1	1 *
05	1	1	1 *
06	1	1	1 *
07	1	1	1 *
08	1	1	1 *
09	1	2	1
10	1	2	2 *
11	2	1	2
12	2	1	2
13	2	2	2 *
14	2	2	2 *
15	2	2	2 *
16	2	2	2 *
17	2	2	2 *
18	2	2	1
19	2	2	1
20	2	2	1

The data in Table 9.12 have been made up to illustrate this point where a 1 indicates a lower level of these characteristics and a 2 a higher level. Comparing the overlap of values for the 20 cases, although we see that 12 (i.e. 60 per cent) of the cases (indicated with an asterisk at the end of the row) have the same values for their viewing of violence and their aggressiveness, 11 of these 12 cases (i.e. 92 per cent) also have the same status on parental aggressiveness. If we take out these 11 cases, then only one of the remaining 8 cases (i.e. about 12 per cent) has the same value on their viewing of violence and their aggressiveness. In other words, if we remove the influence of parental aggressiveness, then there does not appear to be any association between a person's own viewing of violence and their aggressiveness.

It may be easier to visualise the nature of this spurious relationship between children's viewing of violence on television and their aggressiveness if we first draw up a 2 × 2 contingency table for the sample as a whole as shown in Table 9.13 where we can see that the majority of children either watch less violence on television and are less aggressive (6) or watch more violence and are more aggressive (6).

Then we divide the sample according to parental aggressiveness and produce two 2 × 2 contingency tables between children's viewing of violence and their aggressiveness, one for children of less aggressive

Table 9.13 Contingency table of children's viewing of violence on television and children's aggression

			Children's viewing of TV violence	
			1 (less)	2 (more)
Children's aggression	1	(less)	6	4
	2	(more)	4	6

Table 9.14 Contingency table of parent's aggression, children's viewing of violence on television and children's aggression

				Children's viewing of TV violence	
				1 (less)	2 (more)
Parent's aggression	1 (less)	Children's aggression	1 (less)	6	1
			2 (more)	2	1
	2 (more)	Children's aggression	1 (less)	0	3
			2 (more)	2	5

parents and one for children of more aggressive parents, as shown in Table 9.14. If we compare the table for the whole sample with the subtable for children of less aggressive parents we see that all the children who watch less violence and are less aggressive (6) have less aggressive parents. If we do the same with the subtable for children with more aggressive parents we observe that five of the six children who watch more violence and are more aggressive have more aggressive parents. In other words, the relationship between children's viewing of violence and their aggressiveness may be explained in terms of their parent's aggressiveness.

A less extreme version of a spurious relationship is one in which part but not all of the association between two measures may be due to one or more other factors. For example, children who watch more violence may be more aggressive and may also have more aggressive parents. Part of the children's aggressiveness may be due to watching violence while another part may be due to their parent's aggression. If we removed the influence of their parent's aggression on the association between the children's viewing of violence and the children's aggression, then we can assume that the remaining association between these latter two variables is not the direct result of their parent's aggression. Similarly, we could remove the influence of the children's watching of violence from the relationship between their parent's aggression and their own aggression to determine how much of the association between these two variables was not due to the children's viewing of violence.

It is important to note that a significant reduction in the size of an association between two variables by partialling out the influence of a third variable does not necessarily mean that that reduction indicates the degree of spuriousness in the original relationship between the two variables. An alternative possibility that should be seriously considered is that one of the two variables is an *intervening* or *mediating* variable which is influenced by the third variable and which affects the other variable. For example, aggressive parents may make their children more aggressive (say, through modelling) which causes their children to be more interested in aggression as is reflected in their watching more violence on television. If this is the case, then the correlation between parent's and children's aggression and between children's aggression and watching violence should be more positive than that between parent's aggression and children's watching of violence. Whether parent's aggression is seen as a confounding variable or children's aggression as an intervening variable depends on theoretical argument and not statistical considerations and appears unclear in this situation.

The absence of a significant association between two measures, on the other hand, does not necessarily signify no causal connection between those two variables. It is possible that the relationship is suppressed or hidden by the influence of one or more other variables. For example, watching violence may appear not to be associated with aggression because greater physical weakness may result in watching more violence, on the one hand, and being less aggressive, on the other (due to the greater likelihood of being hurt). If we remove the effect of physical weakness, we may find that viewing violence is related to aggressiveness.

This kind of situation is exemplified by the data in Table 9.15 where 1 indicates a lower level and 2 a higher level of these factors. Comparing the extent to which the two scores are the same for all the cases, we see that 10 (i.e. 50 per cent) of the 20 cases (denoted with one asterisk at the end of their row) have the same values on the viewing of violence and aggression. However, for the remaining 10 cases (indicated by two asterisks at the end of their row) the physical weakness value is the same as the viewing of violence value but different from the aggression value. If in these cases the real relationship between the watching of violence and aggression was positive, then all 20 cases (i.e. 100 per cent) would have shown such a relationship.

Once again, it may be easier to picture the nature of this suppressed relationship between the viewing of violence on television and aggression if we first draw up a 2 × 2 contingency table for the whole sample as shown in Table 9.16 where we can see that there appears to be no relationship between these two variables as the number of cases in each of the four cells is the same (5).

Next, as before, we divide the sample according to physical weakness

Table 9.15 Data on physical weakness, viewing violence on television and
          aggression

Case	Physical weakness	Viewing TV violence	Aggression
01	1	2	2 *
02	1	2	2 *
03	1	2	2 *
04	1	1	2 **
05	1	1	2 **
06	1	1	2 **
07	1	1	2 **
08	1	1	2 **
09	1	1	1 *
10	1	1	1 *
11	2	1	1 *
12	2	1	1 *
13	2	1	1 *
14	2	2	1 **
15	2	2	1 **
16	2	2	1 **
17	2	2	1 **
18	2	2	1 **
19	2	2	2 *
20	2	2	2 *

Table 9.16 Contingency table of the viewing of violence on television and
          aggression

		Viewing of TV violence	
		1 (less)	2 (more)
Aggression	1 (less)	5	5
	2 (more)	5	5

Table 9.17 Contingency table of physical weakness, viewing of violence on
          television and aggression

			Viewing of TV violence	
			1 (less)	2 (more)
Physical weakness 1 (less)	Aggression	1 (less)	2	0
		2 (more)	5	3
2 (more)	Aggression	1 (less)	3	5
		2 (more)	0	2

and produce two 2×2 contingency tables between the viewing of violence and aggression, one for the physically stronger and one for the physically weaker, as displayed in Table 9.17. If we look at these two subtables there seems to be a relationship between viewing violence on television and aggression in both of them. In other words, in the sample as a whole the relationship between the viewing of violence and the aggression appears to be suppressed by their relationship with physical weakness.

An index of association between two variables where no other variables have been controlled or partialled out is known as a *zero-order* association. A *first-order* association is one where one other variable has been controlled, a *second-order* association is one in which two other variables have been controlled and so on. The two tests of partial association we shall discuss are *Kendall's partial rank correlation coefficient* and *partial gamma*.

Kendall's partial rank correlation coefficient

The formula for computing the partial rank correlation ($tau_{12.3}$) between two variables (1 and 2) partialling out a third (3) variable is the rank correlation between the first two variables (tau_{12}) minus the product of the rank correlation between one of the two variables (1) and the third variable (tau_{13}) and the rank correlation between the other variable (2) and the third variable (tau_{23}), divided by the square root of the product of 1 minus the squared rank correlation between one of the two variables (1) and the third variable (tau_{13}^2) times 1 minus the squared rank correlation between the other variable (2) and the third variable (tau_{23}^2):

$$tau_{12.3} = \frac{tau_{12} - (tau_{13} \times tau_{23})}{\sqrt{(1 - tau_{13}^2) \times (1 - tau_{23}^2)}}$$

The rank correlation is tau b.

To compute the rank correlation between children's viewing of violence and children's aggression controlling for parent's aggression using the data in Table 9.12 we would first calculate the Kendall's rank correlation for the three variables. The rank correlation between children's viewing of violence and children's aggression is 0.2, between children's viewing of violence and parent's aggression is 0.6 and between children's aggression and parent's aggression is 0.4. Substituting these values into the formula above, we see that the partial rank correlation is -0.05:

$$\frac{0.2 - (0.6 \times 0.4)}{\sqrt{(1 - 0.6^2) \times (1 - 0.4^2)}} = \frac{0.2 - 0.24}{\sqrt{0.64 \times 0.84}} = \frac{-0.04}{0.73} = -0.05$$

In other words, the rank correlation of 0.2 between children's viewing of violence and children's aggression is effectively reduced to zero (−0.05) when parent's aggression is controlled.

To determine the statistical significance of the partial rank correlation for samples of up to 90 we look at the appropriate value in the table in Appendix 20, which gives the 0.05 and 0.025 one-tailed values. The 0.05 two-tailed values correspond to the 0.025 one-tailed values. To be significant at the 0.05 one-tailed level with 20 cases the partial rank correlation needs to be 0.268 or bigger, which it is not.

Since partial tau is approximately normally distributed when the size of the sample (N) is large, we can calculate the significance level of partial tau by converting it into z according to the following formula:

$$z = \frac{3 \times tau \times \sqrt{N(N-1)}}{\sqrt{2(2N+5)}}$$

Substituting the values in this formula for our example we find that, ignoring the minus sign, z is 0.31

$$\frac{3 \times -0.05 \times \sqrt{20(20-1)}}{\sqrt{2[(2 \times 20)+5]}} = \frac{-0.15 \times \sqrt{380}}{\sqrt{2 \times 45}} =$$

$$\frac{-0.15 \times 19.49}{\sqrt{90}} = \frac{-2.92}{9.49} = -0.31$$

We look up the significance of this z value in the table in Appendix 2. The area between the middle of the curve and a z value of 0.31 is 0.1217, indicating that the area beyond the z value on one side of the curve is 0.3783 (0.5000 − 0.1217 = 0.3783), which is the one-tailed probability.

We will repeat this procedure for computing the rank correlation between the viewing of violence and aggression controlling for physical weakness using the data in Table 9.15. The rank correlation between the viewing of violence and aggression is 0.0, between the viewing of violence and physical weakness is 0.4 and between aggression and physical weakness is −0.6. Placing these values into the above formula, we find that the partial rank correlation is 0.33:

$$\frac{0.0 - (0.4 \times -0.6)}{\sqrt{(1-0.4^2) \times (1 - -0.6^2)}} = \frac{0.0 - -0.24}{\sqrt{0.84 \times 0.64}} = \frac{0.24}{0.73} = 0.33$$

The rank correlation of 0.0 between the viewing of violence and aggression is increased to 0.33 when the variable of physical weakness is held constant. Since the 0.05 one-tailed level of partial tau with 20 cases is 0.268, this coefficient is significant indicating that the viewing of violence on television is positively correlated with aggression when physical weakness is partialled out.

Minitab does not compute the partial rank correlation but as we have just seen this is fairly easy to do.

Partial gamma

The formula for partial gamma is the number of concordant pairs (C) minus the number of discordant pairs (D) for the two variables summed across the different levels of the third variable divided by the number of concordant and discordant pairs summed across the different levels of the third variable:

$$\text{partial gamma} = \frac{\text{sum of } C - D}{\text{sum of } C + D}$$

We will demonstrate the calculation of partial gamma with the data in Table 9.12. First we draw up a contingency table as we have done in Table 9.14 which contains two subtables, one for cases with less aggressive parents (1) and one for those with more aggressive parents (2). Taking each subtable in turn, we will use the matrix method of counting the number of concordant and discordant pairs for any cell in that subtable where the number of concordant pairs is the sum of cases which lie below and to the right of that cell multiplied by the number in that cell, whereas the number of discordant pairs is the sum of cases which lie below and to the left of that cell multiplied by the number of cases in that cell. Since each subtable only consists of a 2 × 2 table, there is only one cell below and to the right of the upper left-hand cell which can contain concordant pairs and there is only one cell below and to the left of the upper right-hand cell which can hold discordant pairs. Therefore, for cases with less aggressive parents, there are 6 concordant pairs (i.e. 1 in the bottom right-hand cell is multiplied by 6 in the top left-hand cell) and 2 discordant pairs (i.e. 2 in the bottom left-hand cell is multiplied by 1 in the top right-hand cell) whereas for those with more aggressive parents there are no concordant pairs (i.e. 5 in the bottom right-hand cell is multiplied by 0 in the top left-hand cell) and 6 discordant pairs (i.e. 2 in the bottom left-hand cell is multiplied by 3 in the top right-hand cell). Substituting these values into the formula for computing partial gamma, we see that partial gamma is -0.14:

$$\frac{(6 - 2) + (0 - 6)}{(6 + 2) + (0 + 6)} = \frac{4 + -6}{8 + 6} = \frac{-2}{14} = -0.14$$

We can work out what zero-order gamma is for the association between children's viewing of violence and children's aggression for the whole sample by looking at the contingency table as shown in Table 9.13. The number of concordant pairs is 36 (i.e. 6 in the bottom right-hand cell is multiplied by 6 in the top left-hand cell) while the number of discordant pairs is 16 (i.e. 4 in the bottom left-hand cell is multiplied by 4 in the top right-hand cell). Consequently, gamma is 0.38:

$$\frac{36 - 16}{36 + 16} = \frac{20}{52} = 0.38$$

In other words, the zero-order gamma of 0.38 between children's viewing of violence and children's aggression is reduced to -0.14 when parent's aggression is taken into account.

We will now work out partial gamma for the data in Table 9.15 which has been arranged into two contingency tables in Table 9.16. Partial gamma is 1:

$$\frac{(6 - 0) + (6 - 0)}{(6 + 0) + (6 + 0)} = \frac{6 + 6}{6 + 6} = \frac{12}{12} = 1$$

Gamma, computed from the contingency table for the whole sample in Table 9.17, is 0:

$$\frac{25 - 25}{25 + 25} = \frac{0}{50} = 0$$

Minitab does not give partial gamma.

SUMMARY

The computation of tests of association for categorical and ordinal data has been described in this chapter. Tests of association for categorical data can be divided into those derived from chi-square (phi coefficient, contingency coefficient and Cramer's V) and those based on the proportional reduction in error (Goodman and Kruskal's lambda and tau). The phi coefficient is appropriate for two dichotomous variables where it can vary from zero or -1 to $+1$ depending on the formula used. When one or both variables have more than two categories, the contingency coefficient may be preferable since it varies between zero and less than $+1$ whereas phi may be greater than $+1$. To make the upper limit $+1$ for tables greater than 2×2, Cramer's V should be used. Goodman and Kruskal's lambda, which varies from zero to $+1$, is the proportional increase in predicting one outcome of a categorical variable when knowing its combined outcome with a second categorical variable. Whereas lambda assumes the same prediction is made for all cases in a particular row or column, Goodman and Kruskal's tau presumes the predictions are randomly made based on their proportions in row and column totals.

Tests of association for two ordinal variables, which count the number of cases higher (concordant) and lower (discordant) than the others, include Somer's d, Goodman and Kruskal's gamma, Kendall's tau a, tau b and tau

Table 9.18 Opinion on increase in direct taxation of arts, social science and natural science students

	Yes	No	Undecided
Arts	45	15	9
Social science	77	13	11
Natural science	69	27	3

c. Kendall's tau a, which is the number of concordant pairs minus the number of discordant pairs over the total number of pairs, is used when there are no tied pairs and can vary from -1 to $+1$. Tau b is employed when there are tied pairs and can vary from -1 to $+1$ if the table is square and if none of the row and column totals is zero. For a rectangular table tau c can come closer to ± 1. Goodman and Kruskal's gamma, which is the number of concordant pairs minus the number of discordant pairs divided by the number of concordant and discordant pairs, can range from -1 to $+1$ and takes no account of ties or the size of the table. Somer's d provides an asymmetric as well as a symmetric measure of association and includes tied pairs. Spearman's rho ranges from -1 to $+1$ and is based on the squared difference between the ranks for the two variables. Mantel–Haenszel's chi-square is the squared Pearson's correlation coefficient multiplied by the number of cases minus 1. Partial gamma and Kendall's partial rank correlation coefficient are tests of partial association for ordinal data which partial out a third variable.

EXERCISES

1 Students reading an arts, social science or natural science subject were asked whether they supported an increase in direct taxation. The numbers in favour, against and undecided are shown in Table 9.18. Calculate the association between the students' area of study and their opinion on this issue using the following tests:
   (a) Phi coefficient
   (b) Contingency coefficient
   (c) Cramer's V
   (d) Goodman and Kruskal's asymmetric lambda with opinion as the dependent variable
   (e) Goodman and Kruskal's asymmetric tau with opinion as the dependent variable
2 Calculate the association between educational interest at 12 and at 15 for the data in Table 6.23 using the following tests:
   (a) Kendall's tau b

(b) Kendall's tau c

(c) Goodman and Kruskal's gamma

(d) Somer's asymmetric d with educational interest at 15 as the dependent variable

(e) Spearman's rho

(f) Kendall's partial rank correlation coefficent controlling for educational interest at 9

## Chapter 10

Tests of association for interval/ratio data

This chapter describes the Pearson's product moment correlation which assesses the strength, direction and probability of the linear association between two interval or ratio variables. Tests for determining whether Pearson's correlations differ for variables which come from the same or different samples are also discussed. We would use these tests to find out, for example, whether the correlation between aggressiveness at ages 9 and 12 is similar to that between aggressiveness at 12 and 15 for the same group of pupils, or whether the correlation between aggressiveness and watching violence on television is similar for girls and boys. In addition, Pearson's partial correlation which covaries out the effects of one or more variables which may be related to the two variables of interest is covered, as is eta which provides an index of the non-linear association between an interval/ratio variable and a categorical/ordinal one.

PEARSON'S PRODUCT MOMENT CORRELATION OR r

Pearson's product moment correlation or r is a measure of the linear association between two interval or ratio variables and varies between -1 and $+1$. Note also that it is the same as the point-biserial correlation which is a measure of the association between a dichotomous and an interval/ratio variable and the phi coefficient which is a measure of the association between two dichotomous variables. Note further that the statistical significance level of the point-biserial correlation is the same as that for the unrelated t test.

One way of conceptualising Pearson's correlation is to think of it as the ratio of the variance shared by two variables compared to the overall variance of the two variables. If the shared variance is high, then this variance will be similar to the overall variance and so the correlation will come close to -1 or $+1$. If there is no shared variance (i.e. zero shared variance), then the correlation will be zero. Variance is based on the extent to which scores differ from the mean. If high scores on one variable are associated with high scores on the other variable, then the differences will be in the same direction. A positive difference on one variable will tend to go together with a positive difference on the other variable. Similarly, a negative difference on one variable will tend to be associated with a negative difference on the other. If we multiply these differences, then the product of these differences will largely be positive in direction since a negative value multiplied by another negative value gives a positive value (e.g. $-2 \times -3 = 6$). On the other hand, if high scores on one variable are associated with low scores on the other variable, then a positive difference is likely to go together with a negative difference. If we multiply these differences, then the product of these differences will predominantly be negative since a positive value multiplied by a negative value forms a negative value (e.g. $2 \times -3 = -6$).

The formula for computing Pearson's r may be expressed in a number of ways. One formula is the covariance of the two variables divided by the product of the square root of the separate variances of those variables:

$$r = \frac{\text{covariance of variables } A \text{ and } B}{\sqrt{(\text{variance of variable } A) \times (\text{variance of variable } B)}}$$

$$= \frac{\text{covariance of variables } A \text{ and } B}{\sqrt{(\text{variance of variable } A)} \times \sqrt{(\text{variance of variable } B)}}$$

Since the square root of the variance is the standard deviation this formula may be written as:

$$r = \frac{\text{covariance of variables } A \text{ and } B}{(\text{standard deviation of variable } A) \times (\text{standard deviation of variable } B)}$$

The larger the covariance is, the stronger the relationship. The covariance can never be bigger than the product of the standard deviation of the two variables. If it is the same size as the product, then the correlation is either $+1$ or -1 depending on the sign of the covariance.

Covariance is the sum of products of the deviation of the score of one variable (A) from its mean multiplied by the deviation of the corresponding score of the other variable (B) for all pairs of scores, which is then divided by the number of cases or pairs minus 1:

$$\text{covariance} = \frac{\text{sum of } [(\text{mean } A - \text{each } A \text{ score}) \times (\text{mean } B - \text{each } B \text{ score})]}{\text{no. of cases} - 1}$$

Variance is the sum of squares of the deviation of each score from its mean, which is then divided by the total number of cases minus one:

$$\text{variance} = \frac{\text{sum of } (\text{mean} - \text{each score})^2}{\text{no. of cases} - 1}$$

If we replace the covariance and variance terms in the original formula with these expressions then the correlation formula becomes:

$$r = \frac{\text{sum of products of } A \text{ and } B/N - 1}{\sqrt{\text{sum of squares of } A/N - 1} \times \sqrt{\text{sum of squares of } B/N - 1}}$$

Since the product of $\sqrt{N-1}$ and $\sqrt{N-1}$ is $N-1$ (e.g $\sqrt{4} \times \sqrt{4} = 2 \times 2 = 4$), $N-1$ appears as a divisor on both the numerator and the denominator and so can be removed leaving this simpler formula:

$$r = \frac{\text{sum of products of } A \text{ and } B}{\sqrt{\text{sum of squares of } A \times \text{sum of squares of } B}}$$

Deviations are multiplied rather than added to indicate the direction of the relationship. If the deviations were added, then the sum of these deviations would be zero. This can be illustrated with the data in Table 9.5 which have been reproduced in Table 10.1. Table 10.1 shows the sum (15 and 15) and mean score (3 and 3) for the two variables (A and B), the difference of each score from their respective means (D_A and D_B), the squares (D_A^2 and D_B^2) and sum of squares of these differences (10 and 10), the cross product of these differences for the two variables (D_{AB}) together with their sum (9), and the cross sum of these differences for the two variables (D_{A+B}) together with their sum (0). Note that if we add together rather than multiply the deviations the sum of these additions would be 0. Pearson's correlation is 0.9 [$9/\sqrt{10 \times 10} = 0.9$]. The square root of the product of the sum of squares for the two variables needs to be taken to make the units of the denominator the same as those in the numerator.

The significance level of r can be computed by converting it into t using the following formula:

Table 10.1 Data and computations for Pearson's correlation showing a strong positive relationship

	A	B	D_A	D_A^2	D_B	D_B^2	D_{AB}	D_{A+B}
	1	2	2	4	1	1	2	3
	2	1	1	1	2	4	2	3
	3	3	0	0	0	0	0	0
	4	4	−1	1	−1	1	1	−2
	5	5	−2	4	−2	4	4	−4
Sum	15	15		10		10	9	0
N	5	5						
Mean	3	3						

Note: $r = \dfrac{9}{\sqrt{10 \times 10}} = \dfrac{9}{10} = 0.9$

$$t = r \times \sqrt{\frac{N - 2}{1 - r^2}}$$

The degrees of freedom are the number of cases (N) minus 2. Substituting the values of our example into this formula we find that t is 3.57:

$$0.9 \times \sqrt{\frac{5 - 2}{1 - 0.9^2}} = 0.9 \times \frac{3}{0.19} = 0.9 \times \sqrt{15.79} = 0.9 \times 3.97 = 3.57$$

We look up the statistical significance of t in the table in Appendix 15 where we see that with three degrees of freedom t has to be 2.353 or bigger to be significant at the 0.05 one-tailed level. So if we had anticipated that the two sets of values would be positively correlated, we could conclude that the correlation was significantly positive. Alternatively we could look up the statistical significance of r in the table in Appendix 21 where we see that with three degrees of freedom r has to be 0.8054 or larger to be significant at the 0.05 one-tailed level.

The percentage of variation that is shared between two variables can be calculated by squaring Pearson's r to give what is known as the *coefficient of determination*. So, the percentage of shared variation represented by a correlation of 0.9 is 81. It should be noted that the amount of shared variation is not a straight function of the size of a correlation since, for example, although a correlation of 0.4 is twice the size of a correlation of 0.2, the amount of shared variation denoted by a correlation of 0.4 (16 per cent) is four times that of a correlation of 0.2 (4 per cent). The size of a correlation is usually described verbally in terms of its amount of shared variation so that correlations in the range of 0.1 to 0.3 (reflecting 1 to 9 per cent of shared variation) are often described as small, weak or low; correlations in the range 0.4 to 0.6 (16 to 36 per cent) as moderate or modest; and correlations in the range 0.7 to 0.9 (49 to 81 per cent) as large, strong or high.

The Minitab command for conducting a Pearson's correlation is **correlation** followed by the variables to be correlated:

MTB > correlation 'a' 'b'

The output for this example is:

Correlation of a and b = 0.900

The menu procedure for computing r is:

→**S̲tat** →**B̲asic Statistics** →**C̲orrelation** . . . →**a** →**Select** [this puts **a** in the box under **V̲ariables:**] →**b** →**Select** →**O̲K**

The significance level of r has to be determined as described previously.

Pearson's r is a measure of linear association in that it assesses the extent

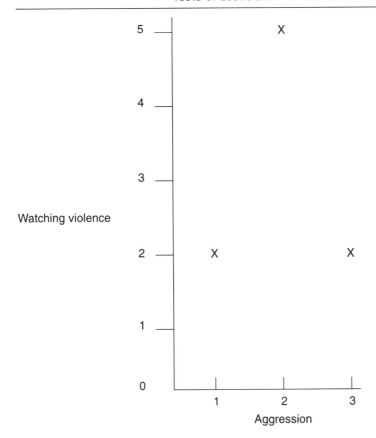

Figure 10.1 A scatterplot of watching violence on television and aggression

to which higher scores on one variable are related to higher scores on another variable. However, if there is a *curvilinear* relationship between the two variables such that up to a certain point the higher scores on one variable are associated with higher scores on the other variable but after that point the higher scores are associated with lower scores, then *r* may be zero. For example, people who watch little or much violence on television may be less aggressive than those watching an intermediate amount.

The most convenient way of determining whether there is a curvilinear relationship between two variables is to plot the position of the two variables on a graph as shown in Figure 10.1. Such a diagram is known as a *scatterplot* or *scattergram*.

The scatter of the points in this plot or diagram takes the shape of an inverted-U curve. The data for this graph are taken from Table 10.2 which presents the aggression and watching of violence scores for three cases. The watching violence scores are plotted along the vertical axis, *y*-axis or

Table 10.2 Data and computations for Pearson's correlation showing a curvilinear relationship between watching violence (*A*) and aggression (*B*)

	A	B	D_A	$D_A{}^2$	D_B	$D_B{}^2$	D_{AB}
	2	1	1	1	1	1	1
	5	2	-2	4	0	0	0
	2	3	1	1	-1	1	-1
Sum	9	6		6		2	0
N	3	3					
Mean	3	2					

Note: $r = \dfrac{0}{\sqrt{6 \times 2}} = \dfrac{0}{3.46} = 0.0$

ordinate while the aggression scores are arranged along the horizontal axis, *x*-axis or *abscissa*. The point on the graph of the aggression and watching violence scores for the first case is where the horizontal line drawn from 2 on the vertical axis intersects with the vertical line drawn from 1 on the horizontal axis. The two scores for each of the three cases are plotted in this way. When the relationship between two variables is curvilinear as in this case, a more appropriate measure of the relationship is *eta* which is described at the end of this chapter.

The Minitab command for producing a scatter diagram is **plot** followed by the variable on the *y*-axis, an asterisk and then the variable on the *x*-axis:

MTB > plot 'a' * 'b'

With the menu system, the sequence would be:

→**Graph** →**Plot** . . . →**a** →**Select** [a appears in **Y** column of →**Graph variables** box] →**b** →**Select** [b appears in **X** column of this box] →**OK**

The output for this procedure is displayed in Figure 10.2.

The size of Pearson's *r* is affected by the variance of one or both variables as well as the presence of extreme scores or *outliers* which will affect the variance. Take, for example, the data in Table 10.1 which represent a strong positive correlation. Now, we will introduce an extreme score in these data by replacing one of the 4's of the fourth case by a 9. When we do this, the Pearson's *r* is reduced from 0.9 to 0.7 as can be seen from the calculations in Table 10.3. Note that outliers may increase as well as decrease the size of a correlation.

If we reduced the variance in the original data by excluding the last two cases, Pearson's *r* decreases from 0.9 to 0.5 as shown in the calculations in Table 10.4.

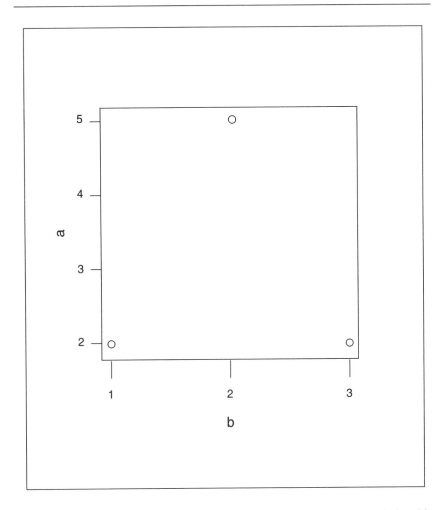

Figure 10.2 Basic **plot** output of a scatterplot showing a curvilinear relationship

TESTS OF DIFFERENCE FOR UNRELATED PEARSON'S CORRELATIONS

If we wanted to determine whether the size of a correlation differed between two unrelated samples we could carry out a z test where the difference between the two correlations converted into z correlations (z_1 and z_2) is divided by the the standard error of the difference between the transformed correlations of the two samples (N_1 and N_2):

$$z = \frac{z_1 - z_2}{\sqrt{[1/(N_1 - 3)] + [1/(N_2 - 3)]}}$$

Table 10.3 Data and computations for Pearson's correlation with one extreme score

	A	B	D_A	D_A^2	D_B	D_B^2	D_{AB}
	1	2	2	4	2	4	4
	2	1	1	1	3	9	3
	3	3	0	0	1	1	0
	4	9	−1	1	−5	25	5
	5	5	−2	4	−1	1	2
Sum	15	20		10		40	14
N	5	5					
Mean	3	4					

Note: $r = \dfrac{14}{\sqrt{10 \times 40}} = \dfrac{14}{20} = 0.7$

Table 10.4 Data and computations for Pearson's correlation with reduced variance

	A	B	D_A	D_A^2	D_B	D_B^2	D_{AB}
	1	2	1	1	0	0	0
	2	1	0	0	1	1	0
	3	3	−1	1	−1	1	1
Sum	6	6		2		2	1
N	3	3					
Mean	2	2					

Note: $r = \dfrac{1}{\sqrt{2 \times 2}} = \dfrac{1}{2} = 0.5$

Because the z and not the t distribution is being used, the sample size should be reasonable, say, at least above 20.

Suppose, for example, we wished to find out whether the correlation of 0.45 between aggression and watching violence for a sample of 30 women was different from that of 0.30 for a sample of 40 men. Using the table in Appendix 22 we first convert these two correlations into their respective z correlations which are 0.485 and 0.310. Inserting the appropriate values into the above formula, z is 0.69:

$$\frac{0.485 - 0.310}{\sqrt{[1/(30 - 3)] + [1/(40 - 3)]}} = \frac{0.175}{0.253} = 0.69$$

Looking up the significance of this value in the table in Appendix 2, we see that for z to be significant it would have to be 1.96 or more at the 0.05 two-tailed level and 1.65 or more at the 0.05 one-tailed level which it is not.

Consequently, we would conclude that there was no significant difference in the size of these two correlations. Note that it does not matter which way round into the formula we put the two z correlations or the two sample sizes.

If we had a large number of such correlations to compare it might be more convenient to write a macro to do this for us. To save us looking up the appropriate z correlations, we could compute these ourselves using the following formula:

$$z_r = 0.5 \times \log_e (1 + r) - 0.5 \times \log_e (1 - r)$$

The macro for carrying out this z test on these data could be as follows:

let 'zr1' = 0.5 * loge(1 + 'r1') − 0.5 * loge(1 − 'r1')
let 'zr2' = 0.5 * loge(1 + 'r2') − 0.5 * loge(1 − 'r2')
let 'def' = 'zr1' − 'zr2'
let 'se' = sqrt(1/('n1' − 3) + 1/('n2' − 3))
let 'z' = 'def'/'se'
print 'r1' 'zr1' 'n1' 'r2' 'zr2' 'n2' 'def' 'se' 'z'

We compute the two z correlations (**'zr1'** and **'zr2'**), the difference (**'dif'**) between them, the standard error of the difference (**'se'**) and the z value (**'z'**). The output of the listing of these variables is presented below:

Row	r1	zr1	n1	r2	zr2	n2	def	se
1	0.45	0.4847	30	0.3	0.309520	40	0.175181	0.253109

z
0.692116

If we are not interested in the values of the difference between the two z correlations and the standard error of the difference, we could compute the z value with this single command:

let 'z' = ('zr1' − 'zr2')/sqrt(1/('n1' − 3) + 1/('n2' − 3))

A TEST OF DIFFERENCE FOR RELATED PEARSON'S CORRELATIONS WITH A SHARED VARIABLE

The tests for comparing the size of two correlations from related data are more complicated and depend on whether the two correlations include the same variable (Steiger 1980). One test for comparing two related correlations (r_{12} and r_{13}) which have a variable in common is Williams' modification of Hotelling's T_1 which is called T_2. The formula for T_2 is:

$$(r_{12} - r_{13}) \times \sqrt{\frac{(N - 1) \times (1 + r_{23})}{[2 \times (N-1)/(N-3) \times A] + [B^2 \times (1 - r_{23})^3]}}$$

where

Table 10.5 Correlation matrix of children's aggression, parent's aggression and children's viewing of violence on television

	1	2
1 Children's aggression		
2 Parent's aggression	0.78	
3 Children's viewing of violence	0.49	0.85

$$A = (1 - r_{12}^2 - r_{13}^2 - r_{23}^2) + (2 \times r_{12} \times r_{13} \times r_{23})$$

and

$$B = 0.5 \times (r_{12} + r_{13})$$

Suppose that for a very small sample of seven cases we found that the correlation between children's aggression and their parent's aggression (r_{12}) was 0.78 while that between children's aggression and children's viewing of violence (r_{13}) was 0.49. We wished to find out whether the correlation between children's aggression and their parent's aggression was significantly bigger than that between children's aggression and children's viewing of violence. Since these two correlations were from the same sample of cases and had the variable of children's aggression in common we could use T_2 to determine whether the two correlations differed. To do this we also need to know the correlation between parent's aggression and children's viewing of violence (r_{23}) which was 0.85. These correlations are shown in Table 10.5.

Substituting the appropriate values in the above formula, we see that T_2 is 1.97:

$$A = (1 - 0.78^2 - 0.49^2 - 0.85^2) + (2 \times 0.78 \times 0.49 \times 0.85)$$
$$= (1 - 0.61 - 0.24 - 0.72) + 0.65 = 0.08$$

and

$$B = 0.5 \times (0.78 + 0.49) = 0.635$$

$$T_2 = (0.78 - 0.49) \times \sqrt{\frac{(7 - 1) \times (1 + 0.85)}{[2 \times (7-1)/(7-3) \times A] + [B^2 \times (1 - 0.85)^3]}}$$

$$= 0.29 \times \sqrt{\frac{11.10}{(3 \times 0.08) + (0.40 \times 0.003)}} = 0.29 \times \sqrt{\frac{11.10}{0.24 + 0.001}}$$

$$= 0.29 \times \sqrt{\frac{11.10}{0.24}} = 0.29 \times 6.80 = 1.97$$

We look up the value of T_2, whose degrees of freedom are the number of cases minus 3, in the table in Appendix 15. With 4 degrees of freedom, *t* has to be 2.132 or larger to be significant at the 0.05 one-tailed level which it is not. Thus, we would conclude that the correlation between children's aggression and parent's aggression was not significantly more positive than that between children's aggression and children's viewing of violence.

The following macro could be employed to compute T_2:

```
let 'a' = (1 − 'r12'**2 − 'r13'**2 − 'r23'**2) + (2*'r12'*'r13'*'r23')
let 'b' = 0.5*('r12' + 'r13')
let 'num' = ('n' − 1)*(1 + 'r23')
let 'den' = 2*('n' − 1)/('n' − 3)*'a' + 'b'**2*((1 − 'r23')**3)
let 't2' = ('r12' − 'r13')*sqrt('num'/'den')
print 'n' 'r12' 'r13' 'r23' 'a' 'b' 'num' 'den' 't2'
```

The relevant output for this macro is shown below:

Row	n	r12	r13	r23	a	b	num	den	t2
1	7	0.78	0.49	0.85	0.07874	0.635	11.1	0.237581	1.98223

A TEST OF DIFFERENCE FOR RELATED PEARSON'S CORRELATIONS WITH NO SHARED VARIABLE

A test for comparing two correlations from the same sample which have no variable in common is Z_2^*, which has the following formula:

$$\sqrt{(N − 3)} \times (z_{r12} − z_{r34}) \times 1/\sqrt{2 − (2 \times A/B)}$$

where

$$A = 0.5 \times \{\{[r_{13} − (r_{12} \times r_{23})] \times [r_{24} − (r_{23} \times r_{34})]\} +$$
$$\{[r_{14} − (r_{13} \times r_{34})] \times [r_{23} − (r_{12} \times r_{13})]\} +$$
$$\{[r_{13} − (r_{14} \times r_{34})] \times [r_{24} − (r_{12} \times r_{14})]\} +$$
$$\{[r_{14} − (r_{12} \times r_{24})] \times [r_{23} − (r_{24} \times r_{34})]\}\}$$

and

$$B = (1 − r_{12}^2) \times (1 − r_{34}^2)$$

Imagine that we wanted to find out whether the correlation between aggression and watching violence on television at 9 years of age differed from that at 15 for the same group of 10 individuals where the correlation at 9 and 15 was 0.30 (r_{12}) and 0.40 (r_{34}) respectively. In order to conduct a Z_2^* test we also need to know the four other correlations between the four variables. We shall say that the (test–retest) correlation between 9 and 15 for both these measures is 0.60 for aggression (r_{13}) and 0.80 for watching violence (r_{24}). The (cross-lagged) correlation between aggression at 9 and watching violence at 15 is 0.10 (r_{14}) and that between watching violence at 9 and aggression at 15 is 0.20 (r_{23}). All six correlations for this example are shown in Figure 10.3.

Placing the appropriate values in the formula we find that Z_2^* is −0.32:

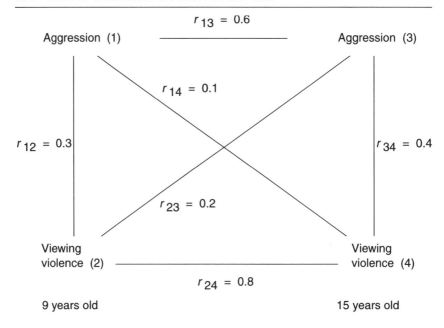

$r_{13} = 0.6$

Aggression (1)

Aggression (3)

$r_{14} = 0.1$

$r_{12} = 0.3$

$r_{34} = 0.4$

$r_{23} = 0.2$

Viewing
violence (2)

Viewing
violence (4)

$r_{24} = 0.8$

9 years old   15 years old

Figure 10.3 Correlations between aggression and viewing violence on television at ages 9 and 15

$$A = 0.5 \times \{\{[0.6 - (0.3 \times 0.2)] \times [0.8 - (0.2 \times 0.4)]\} +$$
$$\{[0.1 - (0.6 \times 0.4)] \times [0.2 - (0.3 \times 0.6)]\} +$$
$$\{[0.6 - (0.1 \times 0.4)] \times [0.8 - (0.3 \times 0.1)]\} +$$
$$\{[0.1 - (0.3 \times 0.8)] \times [0.2 - (0.8 \times 0.4)]\}\}$$

$$= 0.5 \times [(0.54 \times 0.72) + (-0.14 \times 0.02) +$$
$$(0.56 \times 0.77) + (-0.14 \times -0.12)]$$

$$= 0.5 \times (0.39 + -0.003 + 0.43 + 0.02) = 0.5 \times 0.84$$

$$= 0.42$$

and

$$B = (1 - 0.30^2) \times (1 - 0.40^2) = 0.91 \times 0.84 = 0.76$$
$$Z_2^* = \sqrt{(10 - 3)} \times (0.310 - 0.424) \times 1/\sqrt{2 - (2 \times 0.42/0.76)}$$
$$= 2.65 \times -0.114 \times 1/\sqrt{2 - 1.11} = -0.30 \times 1.06 = -0.318$$

We look up this value in the table in Appendix 2 where we see that to be significant a z value has to be ($\pm$) 1.96 or more at the 0.05 two-tailed level and ($\pm$) 1.65 or more at the 0.05 one-tailed level which it is not. Consequently, we would conclude that there was no significant difference in the size of these two correlations. Note that it does not matter which way round we put the two z correlations.

The following macro could be employed to compute Z_2^*:

```
let 'zr12' = 0.5*loge(1+'r12') − 0.5*loge(1 − 'r12')
let 'zr34' = 0.5*loge(1+'r34') − 0.5*loge(1 − 'r34')
let 'a1' = ('r13' − 'r12'*'r23')*('r24' − 'r23'*'r34')
let 'a2' = ('r14' − 'r13'*'r34')*('r23' − 'r12'*'r13')
let 'a3' = ('r13' − 'r14'*'r34')*('r24' − 'r12'*'r14')
let 'a4' = ('r14' − 'r12'*'r24')*('r23' − 'r24'*'r34')
let 'a' = 0.5*('a1' + 'a2' + 'a3' + 'a4')
let 'b' = (1 − 'r12'**2)*(1 − 'r34'**2)
let 'z2' = sqrt('n' − 3)*('zr12' − 'zr34')*(1/(sqrt(2 − 2*'a'/'b')))
print 'n' 'r12' 'r34' 'r13' 'r24' 'r14' 'r23' 'zr12' 'zr34' 'a' 'b' 'z2'
```

The relevant output for this example is shown below:

Row	n	r12	r34	r13	r24	r14	r23	zr12	zr34
1	10	0.3	0.4	0.6	0.8	0.1	0.2	0.309520	0.423649

Row	a	b	z2
1	0.417	0.7644	−0.316721

AVERAGING PEARSON'S CORRELATIONS

To find the average of a number of Pearson's correlations, we need to (1) convert them into z correlations; (2) weight each one of them by multiplying the z correlation by the number of cases in that sample minus 3; (3) sum the results and divide by the sum of, for each sample, the number of cases minus 3; and (4) convert this average z into an average r. We would use this procedure if we wanted to report, for instance, the average correlation between aggression and watching violence for a number of samples. An example of this procedure is shown in Table 10.6 where the average r for the three samples is 0.27. As you can see from the table in Appendix 22, r correlations are very similar in size to z_r correlations when they are small. For example, an r of 0.300 is equal to an z_r of 0.310. Consequently, when r correlations are small and when the number of cases

Table 10.6 Computations for averaging Pearson's correlations

Sample	N	N−3	r	z_r	$z_r \times (N-3)$
1	41	38	0.25	0.255	9.690
2	53	50	0.31	0.321	16.050
3	37	34	0.23	0.234	7.956
Sum		122			33.696

Notes: Average z_r = 33.696/122 = 0.276;
        Average r = 0.270

is similar in the different samples, simply summing the r correlations and dividing by the number of samples will provide a very close approximation to the more involved procedure. For instance, this simple procedure for our example will give an average r of 0.263 compared to an average r of 0.270 using the more complicated method.

PEARSON'S PARTIAL CORRELATION

To remove the influence of one or more variables from a Pearson's correlation (r_{12}) between the two main variables of interest, we calculate the Pearson's partial correlation. For a first-order partial correlation ($r_{12.3}$) the following formula is used:

$$r_{12.3} = \frac{r_{12} - (r_{13} \times r_{23})}{\sqrt{(1 - r_{13}^2) \times (1 - r_{23}^2)}}$$

To calculate a second-order partial correlation ($r_{12.34}$), which involves controlling two variables, the same general formula holds except that the zero-order correlations are replaced with first-order correlations:

$$r_{12.34} = \frac{r_{12.3} - (r_{14.3} \times r_{24.3})}{\sqrt{(1 - r_{14.3}^2) \times (1 - r_{24.3}^2)}}$$

Similarly, third-order partial correlations are based on second-order partial correlations and so on.

Suppose we wished to calculate the second-order partial correlation ($r_{12.34}$) between children's aggression (variable 1) and children's watching violence (variable 2) controlling for the two variables of parent's watching violence (variable 3) and parent's aggression (variable 4) which we knew to be positively related to these two variables. The correlations between these four variables are presented in Table 10.7 while the raw data on which they are based are shown in Table 10.8.

We would initially have to calculate the first-order partial correlations between children's aggression and children's watching violence partialling out each of these control variables. We will demonstrate the calculation of this first-order partial correlation controlling for parent's watching violence ($r_{12.3}$). Inserting the appropriate correlations into the formula, we see that this partial correlation is 0.78:

$$r_{12.3} = \frac{0.48 - (0.11 \times 0.87)}{\sqrt{(1 - 0.11^2) \times (1 - 0.87^2)}} = \frac{0.48 - 0.10}{\sqrt{0.99 \times 0.24}}$$

$$= \frac{0.38}{0.49} = 0.78$$

Table 10.7 Correlations between parent's aggression, parent's watching violence, children's watching violence and children's aggression

	4 Parent's aggression	3 Parent's watching violence	2 Children's watching violence
3 Parent's watching violence	0.15		
2 Children's watching violence	0.36	0.87	
1 Children's aggression	0.65	0.11	0.48

Table 10.8 Scores for parent's aggression, parent's watching violence, children's watching violence and children's aggression

Case no.	4 Parent's aggression	3 Parent's watching violence	2 Children's watching violence	1 Children's aggression
1	3	1	1	3
2	1	3	2	1
3	3	1	1	3
4	4	3	2	2
5	2	5	4	3
6	5	4	3	3
7	5	4	5	4

The correlation between children's aggression and children's watching violence is increased from 0.48 to 0.78 when we control for parent's watching violence. In other words, parent's watching violence acts as a suppressor variable.

To calculate the second-order partial correlation we also need to compute the first-order partial correlation of children's aggression and parent's aggression controlling for parent's watching violence ($r_{14.3}$) and that of children's watching violence and parent's aggression controlling for parent's watching violence ($r_{24.3}$). The partial correlation of children's aggression and parent's aggression controlling for parent's watching violence is 0.64:

$$r_{14.3} = \frac{0.65 - (0.11 \times 0.15)}{\sqrt{(1 - 0.11^2) \times (1 - 0.15^2)}} = \frac{0.65 - 0.02}{\sqrt{0.99 \times 0.98}}$$

$$= \frac{0.63}{0.98} = 0.64$$

In other words, controlling for parent's watching violence has little effect on the correlation between children's aggression and parent's aggression.

The partial correlation of children's watching violence and parent's aggression controlling for parent's watching violence is 0.48:

$$r_{24.3} = \frac{0.36 - (0.87 \times 0.15)}{\sqrt{(1 - 0.87^2) \times (1 - 0.15^2)}} = \frac{0.36 - 0.13}{\sqrt{0.24 \times 0.98}}$$

$$= \frac{0.23}{0.48} = 0.48$$

Parent's watching violence has a tendency to suppress the correlation between children's watching violence and parent's aggression.

The second-order partial correlation between children's aggression and children's watching violence covarying out parent's watching violence and parent's aggression is 0.70:

$$r_{12.34} = \frac{0.78 - (0.64 \times 0.48)}{\sqrt{(1 - 0.64^2) \times (1 - 0.48^2)}} = \frac{0.78 - 0.31}{\sqrt{0.59 \times 0.77}}$$

$$= \frac{0.47}{0.67} = 0.70$$

In other words, the correlation between children's aggression and children's watching violence increases from 0.48 to 0.70 when both parent's aggression and parent's watching violence are controlled.

The significance level of the partial correlation can be computed by converting it into t using the following formula

$$t = \text{partial } r \times \sqrt{\frac{\text{degrees of freedom}}{1 - \text{partial } r^2}}$$

The degrees of freedom are the number of cases (N) minus 2 minus the number of control variables. Substituting the values of our example into this formula we find that t is 1.69.

$$0.7 \times \sqrt{\frac{7 - 2 - 2}{1 - 0.7^2}} = 0.7 \times \sqrt{\frac{3}{0.51}} = 0.7 \times \sqrt{5.88} = 0.7 \times 2.42 = 1.69$$

We look up the statistical significance of t in the table in Appendix 15 where we see that with three degrees of freedom t has to be 2.353 or bigger to be significant at the 0.05 one-tailed level. Alternatively we could look up the statistical significance of r in the table in Appendix 21 where we see that with three degrees of freedom r has to be 0.8054 or larger to be significant at the 0.05 one-tailed level.

Partial correlations cannot be computed directly with Minitab but can be produced indirectly using the **regress** procedure. To explain the reasoning

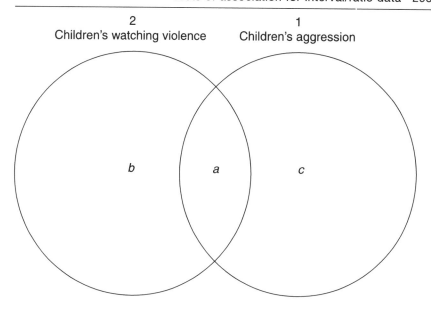

2
Children's watching violence

1
Children's aggression

b   *a*   *c*

Figure 10.4 Venn diagram showing a zero-order correlation between children's watching of violence and children's aggression

behind this procedure it is useful to think of correlations and partial correlations in terms of Venn diagrams as portrayed in Figures 10.4, 10.5 and 10.6. If you want information on regression turn to the next chapter where it is described. Figure 10.4 shows a correlation between two variables, say, the left circle representing the variance of children's watching violence and the right circle the variance of children's aggression. The overlap between the two circles (the section labelled *a*) indicates the size of the correlation: the bigger the overlap, the stronger the correlation. Section *b* represents the variance of the first variable that is not shared with, or explained, by the second variable while section *c* reflects the variance of the second variable that is not explained by the first variable. This unexplained variance is known as the residual variance or residual.

Figure 10.5 depicts a first-order partial correlation between two variables, say, the top left circle representing the variance of children's watching of violence and the top right circle the variance of children's aggression, controlling for a third variable, the bottom circle reflecting the variance of parent's watching of violence. Sections *a* and *b* together represent the zero-order correlation between the two variables while section *a* on its own reflects the first-order partial correlation between two variables controlling for a third variable.

Finally, Figure 10.6 portrays a second-order partial correlation between two variables, say, the top left circle representing the variance of children's

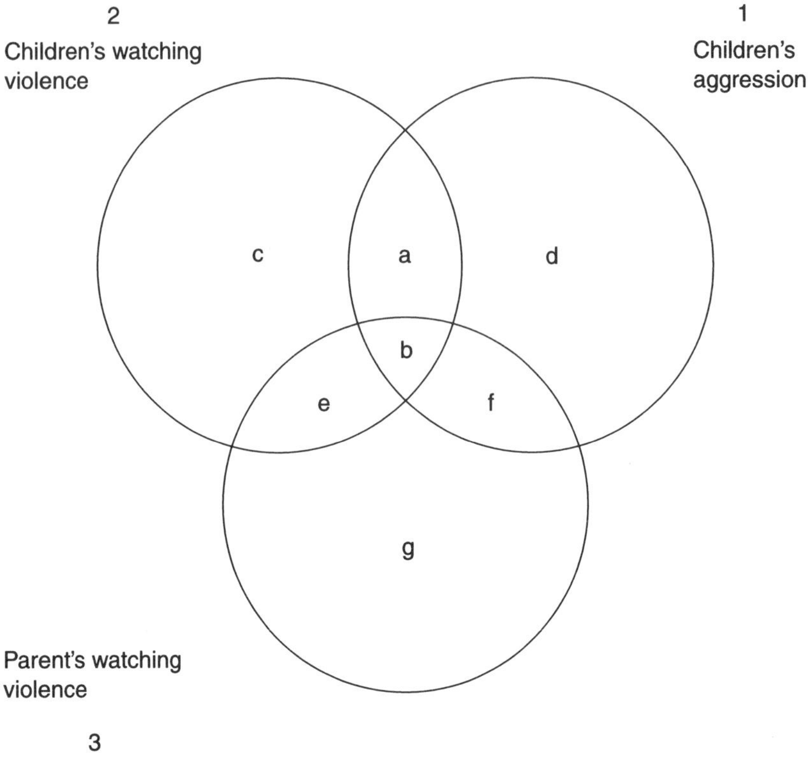

2
Children's watching
violence

1
Children's
aggression

c   a   d

b

e   f

g

Parent's watching
violence

3

Figure 10.5 Venn diagram showing a first-order partial correlation between children's watching of violence and children's aggression controlling for parent's watching of violence

watching of violence and the top right circle the variance of children's aggression, controlling for two variables, say the bottom left circle indicating the variance of parent's watching of violence and the bottom right circle parent's aggression. Sections *a*, *b*, *c* and *d* together denote the zero-order correlation between the two variables while section *a* on its own represents the second-order partial correlation controlling for the other two variables.

To conduct a first-order partial correlation with Minitab, we first regress one of the two variables (say, children's watching of violence) on the third variable (parent's watching of violence) and store the residual (sections *c* and *a* in Figure 10.5). We then regress the other variable (children's aggression) on the third variable (parent's watching of violence) and store the residual (sections *a* and *d* in Figure 10.5). Finally we correlate the two residuals to obtain the first-order partial correlation (section *a* in Figure 10.5).

To conduct a second-order partial correlation, regress one of the two

2
Children's watching
violence

1
Children's
aggression

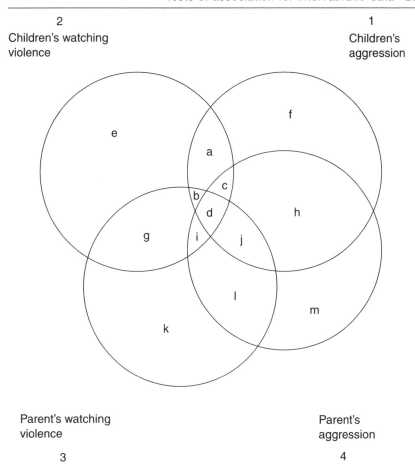

Parent's watching
violence

Parent's
aggression

3   4

Figure 10.6 Venn diagram showing a second-order partial correlation between children's watching of violence and children's aggression controlling for parent's watching of violence and parent's aggression

variables (say, children's watching of violence) on the third and fourth variables (parent's watching of violence and parent's aggression) and store the residual (sections *e* and *a* in Figure 10.6). Then regress the other variable (children's aggression) on the third and fourth variables and store the residual (sections *a* and *f* in Figure 10.6). Finally correlate the two residuals to obtain the second-order partial correlation (section *a* in Figure 10.6).

The prompt system for running a first-order partial correlation is as follows:

MTB > brief 0
MTB > regress 'ca1' 1 'pwv3';

SUBC> residuals c5.
MTB > regress 'cwv2' 1 'pwv3';
SUBC> residuals c6.
MTB > brief
MTB > correlation c5 c6

The first command (**brief 0**) suppresses all subsequent output. The regression command takes the following form. The dependent variable or criterion (e.g. **'ca1'** for children's **a**ggression variable **1**) is listed first after **regress** followed by the number of predictors to be entered into the regression equation (**1**) and the predictor (e.g. **'pwv3'** for **p**arent's **w**atching **v**iolence variable **3**). The subcommand specifies that the **residuals** be stored as a variable (e.g. **c5**). The second **brief** command cancels the first one and enables output to be displayed. The **correlation** command correlates the residuals in **c5** and **c6** and produces the following output:

Correlation of C5 and C6 = 0.767

This first-order partial correlation between children's aggression and children's viewing of violence controlling for parent's viewing of violence is similar to that of 0.78 previously calculated.

The prompt system for producing a second-order partial correlation is as follows:

MTB > brief 0
MTB > regress 'ca1' 2 'pwv3' 'pa4';
SUBC> residuals c5.
MTB > regress 'cwv2' 2 'pwv3' 'pa4';
SUBC> residuals c6.
MTB > brief
MTB > correlation c5 c6

The number of predictors in the regression equation is **2** rather than **1**. These commands produce the following output:

Correlation of C5 and C6 = 0.688

This second-order correlation between children's aggression and children's watching of violence controlling for parent's watching of violence and parent's aggression is similar to that of 0.70 previously worked out.

The menu system for computing a first-order partial correlation is as follows:

→**S**tat →**R**egression →**R**egression . . . →criterion [e.g. **ca1**] →**Select** [this puts the criterion in the box beside **Response:**] →predictor [e.g. **pwv3**] →**Select** [this puts this predictor in the box beside **Predictor:**] →**R**esiduals [stored in next available free column] →**O**K
→**S**tat →**B**asic Statistics →**C**orrelation . . . →residuals for first regres-

sion →**Select** [this puts these residuals in the box under →**V̲ariables:**] →residuals for second regression →**Select** →**O̲K**

The regression output is not suppressed in this procedure and can be ignored.

The menu system for calculating a second-order partial correlation is as follows:

→**S̲tat** →**Regression** →**Regression** . . . →criterion [e.g. **ca1**] →**Select** [this puts the criterion in the box beside **Response:**] →first predictor [e.g. **pwv3**] →**Select** [this puts this predictor in the box beside **Predic̲tor:**] →second predictor [e.g. **pa4**] →**Select** →**R̲esiduals** [stored in next available free column] →**O̲K**

→**S̲tat** →**Basic Statistics** →**C̲orrelation** . . . →residuals for first regression →**Select** [this puts these residuals in the box under **V̲ariables:**] →residuals for second regression →**Select** →**O̲K**

ETA

The eta coefficient provides a useful measure of the strength of the association between an interval/ratio variable (the dependent variable) and a categorical/ordinal variable (the independent variable) when this association is non-linear. Eta varies from zero to +1 and eta squared indicates the percentage of the total variation in the dependent variable that can be accounted for by the independent variable. As we have seen in Chapter 7, eta squared is the between-groups sum of squares divided by the total sum of squares. In this section we will demonstrate how eta can be calculated for the data in Table 10.2 which represent a curvilinear relationship between aggression and watching violence on television. As eta is an asymmetric measure we could compute eta with watching violence as the dependent variable and aggression as the independent variable, or vice versa. In drawing a graph it is customary to place the independent variable along the horizontal axis and the dependent variable along the vertical axis. Note that the shape of the relationship between aggression and watching violence would not be curvilinear if aggression was the dependent variable and watching violence the independent variable. Consequently, we will compute eta with watching violence as the dependent variable.

The data in Table 10.2 have been arranged in Table 10.9 so that the watching violence scores have been grouped in terms of the aggression scores.

Step 1   Calculate the between-groups sum of squares by subtracting the grand mean from the group means, squaring the differences, multiplying the squared differences by the number of cases in each group and summing the products for all the groups.

Table 10.9 Data and initial computations for eta

	Aggression				
	1	2	3		
	2	5	2		
Sum	2	5	2	Grand sum	9
N	1	1	1		
Mean	2	5	2	Grand mean	3

The between-groups sum of squares for these data is 6:

$$[(2 - 3)^2 \times 1] + [(5 - 3)^2 \times 1] + [(2 - 3)^2 \times 1] = 1 + 4 + 1 = 6$$

Step 2   Calculate the total sum of squares by subtracting each score from the grand mean, squaring them and summing them.

The total sum of squares for these data is 6:

$$(2 - 3)^2 + (5 - 2)^2 + (2 - 3)^2 = 1 + 4 + 1 = 6$$

Step 3   Divide the between-groups sum of squares by the total sum of squares and take the square root of the result to give eta.

For this example, eta is 1.0 ($\sqrt{1/1} = 1.0$).

Eta can be indirectly produced in Minitab by conducting a one-way analysis of variance and then dividing the between-groups sum of squares by the total sum of squares and taking the square root of the result. To do this the minimum number of cases in each group must be 2 which can be created by simply doubling the values in the original sample.

The prompt system for computing a one-way analysis of variance is:

MTB > oneway 'v' 'a'

The variable to be compared is listed first (**'v'**) followed by the grouping variable (**'a'**).

The menu sequence for doing this is:

→**Stat** →**ANOVA** →**Oneway** . . . →**v** →**Select** [this puts **v** in the box beside **Response:**] →**a** →**Select** [this puts **a** in the box beside **Factors:**] →**OK**

The output for this procedure is displayed in Table 10.10. Eta is the square root of the between-groups sum of squares (**a**) divided by the within-groups sum of squares (**ERROR**) which is 1.0 ($\sqrt{12.00000/12.00000} = 1.0$).

Table 10.10 One-way analysis of variance comparing number of violent films watched across three aggressiveness ratings

One-Way Analysis of Variance

Analysis of Variance on v

Source	DF	SS	MS	F	p
a	2	12.00000	6.00000	*	*
Error	3	0.00000	0.00000		
Total	5	12.00000			

Individual 95% CIs For Mean
Based on Pooled StDev

Level	N	Mean	StDev	———+———+———+———
1	2	2.00000	0.00000	*
2	2	5.00000	0.00000	*
3	2	2.00000	0.00000	*

———+———+———+———
Pooled StDev =   0.00000   3.0   4.0   5.0

SUMMARY

The computation of Pearson's product-moment correlation and first- and second-order partial correlations has been described together with the calculation of eta and tests for determining whether correlations from the same or different samples differ. Pearson's correlation assesses the strength, direction and probability of the linear association between two interval or ratio variables and varies from -1 to $+1$. It reflects the ratio of the variance shared by two variables compared to the overall variance of the two variables. This coefficient is the same as the point-biserial correlation (which measures the association between a dichotomous variable and an interval/ratio variable) and the phi coefficient (which assesses the association between two dichotomous variables). The percentage of variation shared by the two variables is the square of Pearson's correlation and is called the coefficient of determination. A correlation of close to zero may mean that the relationship between the two variables is curvilinear which can be checked with a scatterplot. The size of Pearson's correlation is affected by the variance of one or both variables as well as the presence of extreme scores which influence the variance. The z test determines whether the size of two correlations from two samples differs significantly. For correlations from the same sample, the T_2 test compares those having a variable in common while the Z_2* test compares those having no variable in common. Eta measures the strength of a non-linear association between an interval/ratio variable and a categorical/ordinal variable and varies from zero to $+1$. Eta squared indicates the percentage of the total variation in the dependent variable explained by the independent variable.

EXERCISES

Use the data in Table 6.23 for the following exercises.

1 Calculate Pearson's correlation between educational interest at 12 and at 15.
   (a) What is the size of the correlation?
   (b) What are its degrees of freedom?
   (c) Is educational interest at 12 and 15 significantly positively correlated at the 0.05 one-tailed level?
2 Compare the size of the correlation between educational interest at 12 and 15 for single- and mixed-sex schools.
   (a) Which test would you use?
   (b) What is the correlation for single-sex schools?
   (c) What is the correlation for mixed-sex schools?
   (d) What is the value of this test?
   (e) Do the two correlations differ significantly at the 0.05 two-tailed level?
3 Compare the size of the correlation of educational interest at 12 and 15 with that at 9 and 12.
   (a) Which test would you use?
   (b) What is the correlation between educational interest at 9 and 12?
   (c) What is the correlation between educational interest at 9 and 15?
   (d) What is the value of this test?
   (e) What are its degrees of freedom?
   (f) Do the two correlations differ significantly at the 0.05 two-tailed level?
4 Compare the size of the correlation between socio-economic status and educational interest at 9 with that of educational interest at 12 and 15.
   (a) Which test would you use?
   (b) What is the correlation between socio-economic status and educational interest at 9?
   (c) What is the correlation between socio-economic status and educational interest at 12?
   (d) What is the correlation between socio-economic status and educational interest at 15?
   (e) What is the value of this test?
   (f) Do the two correlations differ significantly at the 0.05 two-tailed level?
5 What is Pearson's correlation between educational interest at 12 and at 15 controlling for educational interest at 9?
6 What is the value of eta for socio-economic status and educational interest at 15 with socio-economic status as the independent variable?

## Chapter 11

Bivariate and multiple regression

Regression analysis estimates or predicts the scores of one variable (called the *criterion* or the dependent variable) from one or more other variables (called *predictors* or independent variables). In order to predict the criterion, the criterion is related to or regressed onto the predictor(s). *Simple* or *bivariate* regression involves one predictor whereas *multiple* regression uses two or more predictors. One of the main purposes of multiple regression in the social sciences is not so much to predict the score of one variable from others but to determine the minimum number of a set of variables which are most strongly related to the criterion and to estimate the percentage of variance in the criterion explained by those variables. For example, we may be interested in finding out which variables are most strongly related to aggressiveness and how much of the variance in aggressiveness those variables explain. Generally, the variable which is most highly related to aggression is entered first into the regression equation followed by variables which are the next most strongly related to aggressiveness once their relationship with the other variables is taken into account. If later variables are strongly associated with the variables already entered, then it is less likely that they will independently account for much more of the variance than those previously entered and so they are unlikely to be included as predictors. Although we will demonstrate the calculation of multiple regression with a few cases, this technique should only be used when a relatively large number of cases are available. Under these circumstances, multiple regression is a very valuable statistical procedure. We will begin by describing bivariate regression which just involves one predictor.

BIVARIATE REGRESSION

If we want to predict a score on a criterion from a score on another variable and we know that there is no association between the two variables, then our best guess is the mean of the criterion since this score is the closest to all other scores. If, on the other hand, the two variables are perfectly correlated, then we could predict the criterion perfectly. Indeed, the higher the correlation the more accurate our prediction could be. However, the correlation only tells us how much of the variance is shared by both variables. It does not by itself enable us to predict the actual score of the criterion from the score of the other variable. In order to do this we also need to know the way in which those scores are scaled. What linear regression does is to find the straight line that lies closest to the joint values of the two variables. Provided that there is variation on both variables, the closer the joint values are to the straight line the more accurately we can predict the scores of the criterion.

Linear regression may be best explained in terms of the scatterplot of two variables where it is possible to draw the straight line that comes closest to the points on the graph. Take our earlier example of the aggression rankings of the two judges A and B in Table 9.5 which have been represented in Table 11.1 and which we shall call scores. Previously we worked out (see Table 10.1) that the Pearson correlation between the scores of these two judges was 0.9. In other words, there is a near perfect association between these two sets of scores. Consequently, we should be able to predict the scores of one judge (say Judge A) from those of the other (Judge B) provided that we know the scales of the two sets of scores. The scatterplot of these two sets of scores is shown in Figure 11.1 where, as is usual, the vertical or y-axis represents the criterion (Judge A) and the horizontal or x-axis the predictor (Judge B).

Before we can draw a straight line in two-dimensional space (i.e. the space described by the horizontal and vertical axes) we need to know the slope of the line and its position. The position of the line can be described by the point where the line intercepts the vertical axis when the position on the horizontal axis corresponds to zero. This point is known as the *intercept*. The minimum number of points needed to draw a straight line is two. A point on a straight line can be defined by the following equation where y represents the position on the vertical or y-axis, a the intercept of the line on the y-axis, b the slope of the line and x the position on the horizontal or x-axis:

$$y = a + bx$$

While for any line the values of y and x vary, the values of a and b remain the same and are *constants*.

Table 11.1 Scores of two judges

Women	Judge A	Judge B
Ann	1	2
Mary	2	1
Jo	3	3
Sue	4	4
Jane	5	5

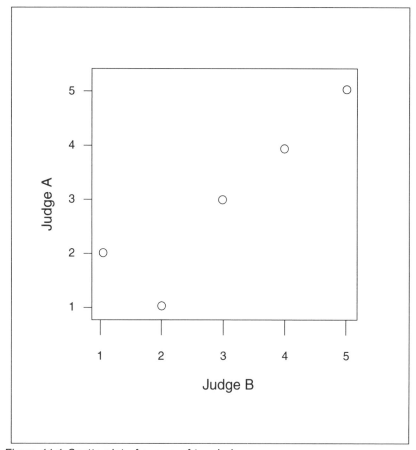

Figure 11.1 Scatterplot of scores of two judges

We will illustrate the formula for a straight line with the three following pairs of scores:

y   x
3   1
4   3
5   7

which represent a straight line and which are drawn are such in Figure 11.2. The slope of the line or *b* is the ratio of the vertical distance covered (called the *rise*) over a particular horizontal distance (called the *run*).

$$\text{slope or } b = \frac{\text{vertical distance (rise)}}{\text{horizontal distance (run)}}$$

We can see that the line rises by one unit for every two units along the

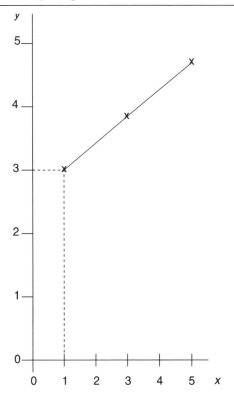

Figure 11.2 Three points representing a straight line

horizontal axis giving a slope of 0.5 (1/2 = 0.5). In effect, *b* is a measure of the change on the vertical axis which corresponds to a change of one unit on the horizontal axis:

$$b = \frac{b}{1}$$

In this case the line rises by 0.5 for every horizontal unit of 1. If we know any three of the four values in the equation for a straight line, we can work out the fourth. So, for example, we could work out *a* if we subtract *bx* from each side of the equation to give the following expression

$$y - bx = a$$

Substituting a pair of *y* and *x* values (3 and 1) in the equation we see that *a* is 2.5:

$$3 - (0.5 \times 1) = 2.5$$

Similarly, we can predict a particular y value from an x value if we know the other two values:

$a + bx = y$

For example, an x value of 1 corresponds to a y value of 3.0:

$2.5 + (0.5 \times 1) = 3.0$

If we know one pair of y and x values, we can define one point on the line which is simply the point where lines drawn from these two values intersect as shown in Figure 11.2. All we need now to draw the straight line is to determine the intersection of another pair of y and x values.

It is important to understand what the expression bx means. The value x indicates the distance from zero to the value x which is 1 unit where x is 1. Multiplying x by b gives the number of units on the vertical axis that y must change by over a horizontal distance of x units. So for one horizontal x unit y changes by 0.5 of a vertical unit ($0.5 \times 1 = 0.5$). To find out what value of y this represents we add a change of 0.5 vertical units to the vertical value of the intercept which in this example is 2.5 giving a y value of 3 ($0.5 + 2.5 = 3.0$).

In the social sciences, however, the relationship between two variables is rarely perfect and so determining the two points is more complicated. The formula for finding any point is the same as before except that we are interested in determining what the value of the criterion or y would be when a straight line is drawn that lies closest to the joint values of the criterion and the predictor. In this formula, the slope or b is known as the *regression* or *beta* coefficient:

criterion predicted score = intercept constant (or a) + [regression coefficient (or b) $\times$ predictor score]

To calculate the regression coefficient we use the following formula which is the sum of products of the deviation of the score of the criterion from its mean multiplied by the deviation of the corresponding score of the predictor for all pairs of scores, which is then divided by the sum of squares of the predictor:

$$b = \frac{\text{sum of products of the criterion and predictor}}{\text{predictor sum of squares}}$$

Note that the regression coefficient is similar to the correlation coefficient except that it describes the relationship between the predictor and the criterion in terms of the units of the predictor and not in terms of *standardised* units as does the correlation. The formula for the correlation coefficient expressed in the same terms as that for the regression coefficient is as follows:

$$r = \frac{\text{sum of products of the criterion and predictor}}{\sqrt{\text{criterion sum of squares} \times \text{predictor sum of squares}}}$$

Since the sum of products of the criterion and the predictor can equal but not exceed the square root of the product of the criterion and predictor sum of squares, the maximum value that the correlation coefficient can attain is ± 1.0. The value of the regression coefficient can be larger than ± 1.0 because the sum of products of the criterion and predictor can be bigger than the predictor sum of squares. We could draw a correlation line if we substitute the correlation for the regression coefficent.

We compute the intercept constant with the following formula which is the predictor mean score multiplied by the regression coefficient which is then subtracted from the criterion mean score:

$$a = \text{criterion mean} - (\text{regression coefficient} \times \text{predictor mean})$$

The regression line runs from the intercept constant on the vertical axis through the point where one of the predicted values of the criterion meets with the corresponding value for the predictor.

It is useful to understand the reason for this formula. The mean represents the centre of a distribution of values. In other words, the mean is the point in that set of values which lies closest to all the values. Multiplying the mean of the predictor by the regression coefficient gives the number of vertical units that the criterion must change by over the horizontal distance that the mean value of the predictor represents. If we subtract the number of vertical units from the mean value of the criterion, then that value of the predictor will correspond to a predictor value of zero.

So to determine the regression line we first have to compute the regression coefficient. The steps involved in calculating this coefficient for our example are presented in Table 11.2. The means of the criterion (A) and the

Table 11.2 Computations for a regression coefficient

	A	B	D_A	D_B	$D_B{}^2$	D_{AB}
	1	2	2	1	1	2
	2	1	1	2	4	2
	3	3	0	0	0	0
	4	4	−1	−1	1	1
	5	5	−2	−2	4	4
Sum	15	15			10	9
N	5	5				
Mean	3	3				

Note: $b = \dfrac{9}{10} = 0.9$

predictor (B) are first calculated, followed by the deviation of each score from its mean (D_A and D_B). Squaring ($D_B{}^2$) and summing the deviations of the predictor scores gives a sum of squares of 10, while multiplying the deviations of the criterion and predictor (D_{AB}) and summing them produces a sum of products of 9. Dividing the sum of products of the criterion and predictor by the sum of squares of the predictor produces a regression coefficient of 0.9 (9/10 = 0.9).

Once we have calculated the regression coefficient, we can work out from the predictor and criterion means the intercept constant which is 0.3 [3 − (0.9 × 3) = 0.3]. Using the intercept and one predictor value we work out the corresponding predicted value for the criterion. For example, the predictor value of 2 would give a predicted value for the criterion of 2.1 [0.3 + (0.9 × 2) = 2.1]. We can then draw a regression line which stretches from the point on the vertical axis of 0.3 through the point where the predictor value of 2 intersects with a predicted value for the criterion of 2.1 as shown in Figure 11.3.

Knowing the regression coefficient and the intercept constant, we can use the regression equation to predict the value of the criterion from any value of the predictor. For example, using this information we would predict that if Judge B gave a score of 1, Judge A would give a score of 1.2 [0.3 + (0.9 × 1) = 1.2]. Note that in the particular case where Judge B gave a score of 1, Judge A gave one of 2. In other words, there is a difference between the predicted score and the actual score of the criterion which in this case is 0.8 (2 − 1.2 = 0.8). This difference is called a *residual*. Although this residual is positive, others will be negative. For example, a score by Judge B of 2 would lead to a predicted score of 2.1 [0.3 + (0.9 × 2) = 2.1] by Judge A although the actual score of Judge A is 1. In other words, the difference between the actual and the predicted score is −1.1 (1 − 2.1 = −1.1). The actual criterion value is given by the following equation:

criterion value = a + (b × predictor value) + residual

Therefore, if Judge B gives a score of 1, the score of Judge A is 2.0:

0.3 + (0.9 × 1) + 0.8 = 2.0

The regression line is the straight line that is closest to the points on the scatterplot. To determine how close this line lies to these points we add together the squares of the residuals. If we simply added the residuals together, they would sum to zero since the sum of the negative differences equals the sum of the positive differences as shown in Table 11.3. Since the sum of squared residuals is the smallest it can be, the regression line is also called the *least-squares line* or *line of best fit*.

Since regression is sometimes used for prediction it is useful to know how accurate the prediction is. A measure of this is the *standard error of*

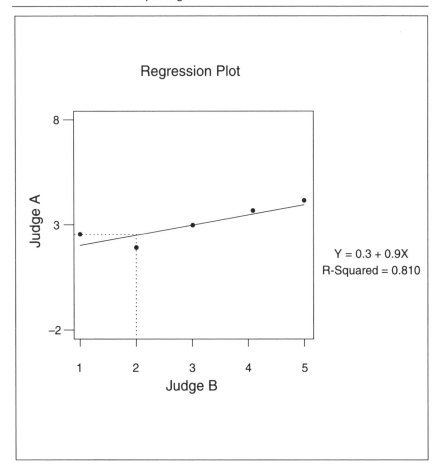

Figure 11.3 Regression line

Table 11.3 Sum of residuals and residuals squared

	Judge A scores		
Actual	*Predicted*	*Residuals*	*Residuals^2*
1	$0.3 + (0.9 \times 2) = 2.1$	$1 - 2.1 = -1.1$	1.21
2	$0.3 + (0.9 \times 1) = 1.2$	$2 - 1.2 = 0.8$	0.64
3	$0.3 + (0.9 \times 3) = 3.0$	$3 - 3.0 = 0.0$	0.00
4	$0.3 + (0.9 \times 4) = 3.9$	$4 - 3.9 = 0.1$	0.01
5	$0.3 + (0.9 \times 5) = 4.8$	$5 - 4.8 = 0.2$	0.04
Sum		0.0	1.90

estimate which is the square root of the sum of squared residuals divided by the number of cases minus 2:

$$\text{standard error of estimate} = \sqrt{\frac{\text{sum of squared residuals}}{N-2}}$$

It is the standard deviation of the errors of prediction. It provides an estimate of the probability of a particular criterion score occurring in that 68 per cent of scores will lie within one standard deviation of the predicted score, 95 per cent within two standard deviations and 99 per cent within three standard deviations. The standard error of estimate of the scores of Judge A is about 0.8 [$\sqrt{1.9/(5-2)} = 0.796$]. For example, when the score of Judge B is 2, the predicted score for Judge A is calculated to be 2.1 using the regression equation. As the standard error of estimate of the scores of Judge A is about 0.8 there is a 68 per cent probability that the actual score of Judge A will fall within the range of 2.1 ±0.8 (i.e. 1.3 to 2.9), a 95 per cent probability that it will fall within 2.1 ±1.6 (2 × 0.8 = 1.6) and a 99 per cent probability that it will fall within 2.1 ±2.4 (3 × 0.8 = 2.4).

A measure of the accuracy of the regression coefficient is the *standard error of the regression coefficient*. This is the square root of the sum of squared residuals divided by the number of cases minus 2 and then divided by the sum of squares of the predictor variable:

$$\text{standard error of } b = \sqrt{\frac{\text{sum of squared residuals}/(N-2)}{\text{sum of squares of predictor}}}$$

If the sample size is greater than 200, it gives an estimate of the probability of the regression coefficient occurring within one standard deviation of its value. For our example it is about 0.25:

$$\sqrt{\frac{1.90/(5-2)}{10}} = \sqrt{\frac{0.6333}{10}} = \sqrt{0.0633} = 0.25166$$

Consequently, the regression coefficient would have a 95 per cent probability of falling within the range 0.9 ±(0.25 × 1.96) if the sample was greater than 200. With smaller samples, the *b* estimates follow the *t* distribution with the degrees of freedom equal to the number of cases minus 2. According to the table in Appendix 15, the *t* value for 3 degrees of freedom is 3.182 at the 0.05 two-tailed level. Therefore, the regression coefficient has a 95 per cent probability of falling within the interval 0.9 ±(0.25 × 3.182).

We use a *t* test to determine the statistical significance of the regression coefficient. This *t* test is the unstandardised regression coefficient divided by its standard error which is 3.58 (0.9/0.25166 = 3.576). Its degrees of freedom are equal to those associated with the residual sum of squares which is the number of cases minus 2. Using the table in Appendix 15, we see that with 3 degrees of freedom t has to be 3.182 or bigger to be significant at the 0.05 level which it is.

An index of the accuracy of the intercept is the *standard error of the intercept* which is (1) the sum of squared residuals divided by the number of cases minus 2, which is then (2) multiplied by 1 divided by the number of cases plus the square of the predictor mean divided by the predictor sum of squares, and (3) the square root is then taken of this result:

standard error of a =

$$\sqrt{\frac{\text{sum of squared residuals}}{(n-2)} \times \left(\frac{1}{n} + \frac{\text{predictor mean squared}}{\text{predictor sum of squares}}\right)}$$

For our example it is about 0.83:

$$\sqrt{\frac{1.90}{(5-2)} \times \left(\frac{1}{5} + \frac{3^2}{10}\right)} = \sqrt{\frac{1.9}{3}} \times (0.2 + 0.9) = \sqrt{0.6966} = 0.834$$

With samples greater than 200, the intercept would have a 95 per cent probability of falling within the range $0.3 \pm (0.83 \times 1.96)$. With smaller samples, the a estimates follow the t distribution with the degrees of freedom equal to the number of cases minus 2. According to the table in Appendix 15, the t value for 3 degrees of freedom is 3.182 at the 0.05 two-tailed level. Therefore, the intercept has a 95 per cent probability of falling within the interval $0.3 \pm (0.83 \times 3.182)$.

We can use a t test to determine the statistical significance of the intercept constant. This t test is the intercept constant divided by its standard error which is 0.36 ($0.3/0.834 = 0.360$). Its degrees of freedom are equal to those associated with the residual sum of squares which is the number of cases minus 2. Using the table in Appendix 15, we see that with 3 degrees of freedom t has to be 3.182 or bigger to be significant at the 0.05 level which it is not. This means that the intercept constant does not differ significantly from zero.

In this example the regression coefficient is the same size as the correlation coefficient as the variance of the two variables is the same. If the variances differ, as is usually the case, the regression coefficient and correlation coefficient will differ. The formula for the correlation coefficient is essentially the sum of products of the criterion and predictor divided by the square root of the product of the sum of squares of the criterion and the predictor:

$$r = \frac{\text{sum of products of criterion and predictor}}{\sqrt{\text{criterion sum of squares} \times \text{predictor sum of squares}}}$$

Consequently, if the sum of squares for both the criterion and the predictor is the same, then the denominator of this formula is the sum of squares of the predictor.

When the variances of the two variables differ, the regression coefficient for predicting the scores of Judge B from those of Judge A will not be the same as that for predicting the scores of Judge A from those of Judge B since the sum of squares in the denominator will differ. However, when the criterion and the predictor are standardised so that they both have a standard deviation of 1, the regression coefficient is standardised so that the *standardised* regression coefficient or B is the same for predicting the scores of Judge A from those of Judge B and for predicting the scores of Judge B from those of Judge A. The standardised regression coefficient is the same as Pearson's correlation and can be calculated by multiplying the unstandardised regression coefficient by the standard deviation of the predictor and dividing by the standard deviation of the criterion:

$$\text{standardised regression coefficient} = \text{unstandardised regression coefficient} \times \frac{\text{predictor std dev}}{\text{criterion std dev}}$$

Since the standard deviations for our two variables are the same, the standardised and unstandardised regression coefficients are the same (i.e. 0.9).

This formula for the standardised regression coefficient is equivalent to the formula for the correlation coefficient given above. We can see this if we replace the terms in the formula for the standardised regression coefficient with their formulae as follows where SP stands for the sum of products for the criterion and predictor and SS their sum of squares:

$$B = \frac{SP}{\text{predictor SS}} \times \frac{\frac{\sqrt{\text{predictor SS}}}{\sqrt{N-1}}}{\frac{\sqrt{\text{criterion SS}}}{\sqrt{N-1}}}$$

To divide a numerator fraction by a denominator fraction, we inverse the denominator fraction and multiply it by the numerator fraction:

$$= \frac{SP}{\text{predictor SS}} \times \frac{\sqrt{\text{predictor SS}}}{\sqrt{N-1}} \times \frac{\sqrt{N-1}}{\sqrt{\text{criterion SS}}}$$

The $\sqrt{N-1}$ terms cancel out:

$$= \frac{SP}{\text{predictor SS}} \times \frac{\sqrt{\text{predictor SS}}}{\sqrt{\text{criterion SS}}}$$

The position of the denominators can be switched round:

$$= \frac{SP}{\sqrt{\text{criterion SS}}} \times \frac{\sqrt{\text{predictor SS}}}{\sqrt{\text{predictor SS}}}$$

The square root of a number ($\sqrt{\text{predictor SS}}$) divided by that number (predictor SS) gives the reciprocal square root of that number ($1/\sqrt{\text{predictor SS}}$):

$$= \frac{SP}{\sqrt{\text{criterion SS}}} \times \frac{1}{\sqrt{\text{predictor SS}}}$$

$$= \frac{SP}{\sqrt{\text{criterion SS}} \times \sqrt{\text{predictor SS}}}$$

$$= \frac{SP}{\sqrt{\text{criterion SS} \times \text{predictor SS}}}$$

The steps in this derivation can be checked using simple whole numbers.

Regression analysis can be thought of in terms of analysis of variance where the total sum of squares for the criterion can be divided or partitioned into a sum of squares due to regression and a residual sum of squares which is left over:

criterion total sum of squares = regression sum of squares + residual sum of squares

The total sum of squares for the criterion can be calculated by subtracting the criterion mean score from each of its individual scores, squaring and summing them. If we do this for the scores of Judge A, the total sum of squares for Judge A is 10:

$$(1 - 3)^2 + (2 - 3)^2 + (3 - 3)^2 + (4 - 3)^2 + (5 - 3)^2 =$$
$$-2^2 + -1^2 + 0^2 + 1^2 + 2^2 = 4 + 1 + 0 + 1 + 4 = 10$$

The regression sum of squares is the sum of squared differences between the predicted criterion score and the mean criterion score:

regression sum of squares = sum of (predicted criterion score − mean criterion score)^2

Alternatively, subtracting the residual sum of squares from the criterion total sum of squares gives the regression sum of squares:

regression sum of squares = criterion total sum of squares − residual sum of squares

The predicted criterion scores and squared residual scores are shown in Table 11.3. The residual sum of squares is 1.90. Therefore, the regression sum of squares for our example is 8.1 ($10 - 1.9 = 8.1$). The analysis of variance table for this regression is presented in Table 11.4.

The *squared multiple correlation* or R^2 is the proportion of the regression sum of squares over the criterion total sum of squares:

$$R^2 = \frac{\text{regression sum of squares}}{\text{criterion total sum of squares}}$$

It represents the proportion of variance in the criterion accounted for by the linear combination of the independent variables which in this case is only one variable. The squared multiple correlation for our example is 0.81 (8.1/ 10 = 0.81). In other words, 81 per cent of the variance in the scores of Judge A is explained by or shared with the scores of Judge B.

The adjusted squared multiple correlation is a more conservative estimate of explained variance than the squared multiple correlation since it takes into account the size of the sample and the number of predictors in the equation. Its formula is:

$$\text{adjusted } R^2 = R^2 - \frac{(1 - R^2) \times \text{no. of predictors}}{\text{no. of cases} - \text{no. of predictors} - 1}$$

Since there is only one predictor in this equation, the adjusted squared multiple correlation is about 0.75:

$$0.81 - \frac{(1 - 0.81) \times 1}{5 - 1 - 1} = 0.81 - \frac{0.19}{3} = 0.81 - 0.06333 = 0.747$$

The *multiple correlation* or R is the square root of the squared multiple correlation:

$$R = \sqrt{R^2}$$

The multiple correlation for our example is 0.9 ($\sqrt{0.81} = 0.9$).

The statistical significance of the squared multiple correlation can be tested by computing the F ratio of the regression mean square to the residual mean square:

$$F = \frac{\text{regression mean square}}{\text{residual mean square}}$$

Table 11.4 Analysis of variance table for regression

Sources of variation	SS	df	MS	F	p
Regression	8.10	1	8.1000	12.79	<.05
Residual	1.90	3	0.6333		
Total	10.00	4			

The regression mean square is the regression sum of squares divided by its degrees of freedom which is the number of predictors in the regression equation. The residual mean square is the residual sum of squares divided by its degrees of freedom which is the number of cases minus the number of predictors minus 1.

For our example the regression mean square is 8.1 (8.1/1 = 8.1) and the residual mean square is 0.6333 [1.9/(5 − 1 − 1) = 0.63333)]. Therefore, the F ratio is 12.79 (8.1/0.6333 = 12.79). With 1 and 3 degrees of freedom in the numerator and denominator respectively, the F ratio has to be 10.128 or larger to be significant at the 0.05 level which it is. Consequently we would conclude that the squared multiple correlation between the scores of Judge A and Judge B is significantly positive.

An alternative method of computing the F ratio for the squared multiple correlation is multiplying the squared multiple correlation by the degrees of freedom for the residual sum of squares and dividing the result by the squared multiple correlation subtracted from one and multiplied by the degrees of freedom for the regression sum of squares:

$$F = \frac{R^2 \times (\text{no. of cases} - \text{no. of predictors} - 1)}{(1 - R^2) \times \text{no. of predictors}}$$

This F ratio for our example is 12.79:

$$\frac{0.81 \times (5 - 1 - 1)}{(1 - 0.81) \times 1} = \frac{0.81 \times 3}{0.19 \times 1} = \frac{2.43}{0.19} = 12.789$$

The degrees of freedom for this F ratio are the same as the previous one.

With only one predictor, the statistical significance of the F ratio of the squared multiple correlation is the same as that of the t test of the unstandardised regression coefficient in that t^2 equals F ($3.576^2 = 12.787$).

The basic prompt procedure for running a regression analysis is as follows:

MTB > regress 'Judge A' 1 'Judge B'

The dependent variable or criterion (e.g. **'Judge A'**) is listed first after **regress** followed by the number of predictors to be entered into the regression equation (which is **1** in a simple or bivariate regression) and the predictor (e.g. **'Judge B'**).

The menu procedure for computing a regression analysis is:

→**Stat** →**Regression** →**Regression** . . . →criterion [e.g. **Judge A**] →**Select** [this puts the criterion in the box beside **Response:**] →predictor [e.g. **Judge B**] →**Select** [this puts this predictor in the box beside **Predictor:**] →**OK**

The output for this example is displayed in Table 11.5.

Table 11.5 Regression output of Judge A's scores regressed on Judge B's scores

Regression Analysis

The regression equation is
Judge A = 0.300 + 0.900 Judge B

Predictor	Coef	Stdev	t-ratio	p
Constant	0.3000	0.8347	0.36	0.743
Judge B	0.9000	0.2517	3.58	0.037

s = 0.7958   R-sq = 81.0%   R-sq(adj) = 74.7%

Analysis of Variance

SOURCE	DF	SS	MS	F	p
Regression	1	8.1000	8.1000	12.79	0.037
Error	3	1.9000	0.6333		
Total	4	10.0000			

The regression equation is displayed first with the values for the intercept (**0.300**) and the unstandardised regression coefficient (**0.900**). The statistical significance of the intercept (**Constant**) and the predictor (**Judge B**) is shown next together with the standard error of estimate (**s**), the squared multiple correlation (**R-sq**) and the adjusted squared multiple correlation [**R-sq(adj)**]. Finally, there is the analysis of variance table.

The original observations, the predicted values of the criterion (**Fit**), the standard deviations of the predicted values (**Stdev.Fit**), the residuals (**Residual**) and the standardised residuals (**St.Resid**) as presented in Table 11.6 are also displayed if the following command is entered prior to carrying out the regression:

MTB > brief 3

Residuals are standardised by dividing them by their standard deviation and have a variance of 1. Minitab prints an R next to standardised residuals over 2 which is usually considered large.

The following prompt command is used to produce a scatterplot with a

Table 11.6 Table of values including the predicted values and residuals

Obs.	Judge B	Judge A	Fit	Stdev.Fit	Residual	St.Resid
1	2.00	1.000	2.100	0.436	−1.100	−1.65
2	1.00	2.000	1.200	0.616	0.800	1.59
3	3.00	3.000	3.000	0.356	0.000	0.00
4	4.00	4.000	3.900	0.436	0.100	0.15
5	5.00	5.000	4.800	0.616	0.200	0.40

regression line where the variable listed first ('**Judge A**') forms the horizontal axis and the variable listed second ('**Judge B**') the vertical axis:

MTB > %fitline 'Judge A' 'Judge B'

The menu sequence for doing this is:

→**S̲tat** →**R̲egression** →**F̲itted Line Plot . . .** →criterion [e.g. **Judge A**] →**Select** [this puts the criterion in the box beside **Response** [**Y̲**]:] →predictor [e.g. **Judge B**] →**Select** [this puts the predictor in the box beside **Predictor** [**X̲**]:] →**O̲K**

The output for this procedure is displayed in Figure 11.3.

Correlation and regression provide a good index of the association between two variables when the assumptions of normality, linearity and *homoscedasticity* are met. Homoscedasticity refers to the variance of one variable being similar for all values of the other variable. A way of checking these three assumptions visually is to produce a scatterplot of the residuals with the predicted values. The assumption of normality is met if the residuals are normally distributed around each predicted score so that most of the residuals for that predicted score are concentrated at the centre of its distribution. The assumption of linearity holds if the overall shape of the distribution of points is rectangular. A curved shape implies that the relationship is not linear. The assumption of homoscedasticity is fulfilled if the spread of residuals does not change with an increase in the predicted values. An example of heteroscedasticity is when the distribution of residuals becomes wider at higher values.

To produce a scatterplot between the residuals and the predicted values we first have to store these. The prompt system for doing this is as follows:

MTB > regress 'Judge A' 1 'Judge B';
SUBC> residuals c3;
SUBC> fits c4.

The residuals are stored in **c3** and the predicted values (**fits**) in **c4**.
The menu sequence for doing this is:

→**S̲tat** →**R̲egression** →**R̲egression . . .** →criterion [e.g. **Judge A**] →**Se̲lect** [this puts the criterion in the box beside **R̲esponse:**] →predictor [e.g. **Judge B**] →**Select** [this puts this predictor in the box beside **Predi̲ctor:**] →**R̲esiduals** →**F̲its** →**O̲K**

The prompt command for producing the plot is

MTB > %resplots c3 c4

The corresponding menu action is:

→**Stat** →**Regression** →**Residual Plots . . .** →residuals [e.g. **c3**] →**Select** [this puts the residuals in the box beside **Residuals:**] →predicted values [e.g. **c4**] →**Select** [this puts the predicted values in the box beside **Fits:**] →**OK**

The output for this procedure is displayed in Figure 11.4. The bottom right figure is the scattergram of the residuals plotted against the predicted values of the criterion.

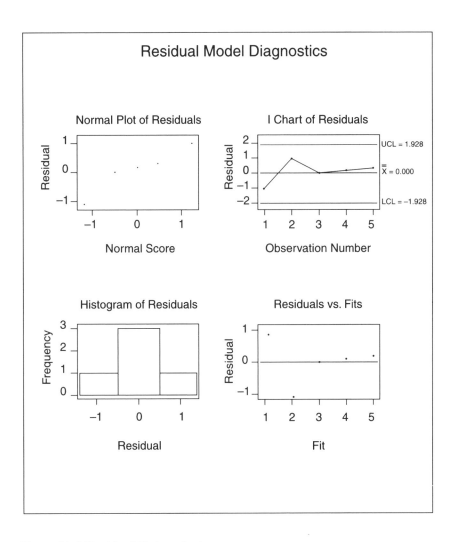

Figure 11.4 **Residual Plots** output

MULTIPLE REGRESSION

Multiple regression is the extension of bivariate regression to two or more predictors. We would use multiple regression if we wanted to find out, for example, how much of the variance in children's aggression was explained by the predictors of parent's aggression, children's watching violence and parent's watching violence. The regression equation for multiple regression is as follows:

criterion predicted score = $a + (b_1 \times$ predictor$_1$ score) + $(b_2 \times$ predictor$_2$ score)

where b_1 is the unstandardised partial regression coefficient of the criterion with the first predictor controlling for the other predictors in the equation, b_2 is the unstandardised partial regression coefficient of the criterion with the second predictor controlling for the other predictors in the equation and so on.

As the calculation of partial regression coefficients with more than two predictors is complicated and is more appropriately carried out with matrix algebra, we will only demonstrate the calculation of a multiple regression with two predictors. The formula for computing the standardised partial regression coefficient of the criterion (c) with the first predictor (1) controlling for the second predictor (2) is:

$$B_1 = \frac{r_{c1} - (r_{c2} \times r_{12})}{1 - r^2_{12}}$$

To convert the standardised partial regression coefficient into the unstandardised coefficient, we multiply the standardised coefficient by the standard deviation of the criterion divided by the standard deviation of the predictor:

$$b_1 = \frac{\text{criterion std dev}}{\text{predictor}_1 \text{ std dev}} \times B_1$$

Similarly, the formula for computing the standardised partial regression coefficient of the criterion (c) with the second predictor (2) controlling for the first predictor (1) is:

$$B_2 = \frac{r_{c2} - (r_{c1} \times r_{12})}{1 - r^2_{12}}$$

The formula for the unstandardised partial regression coefficient is:

$$b_2 = \frac{\text{criterion std dev}}{\text{predictor}_2 \text{ std dev}} \times B_2$$

As an illustration, we will compute the multiple regression between the criterion of children's aggression (c) and the two predictors of parent's aggression (1) and children's watching violence (2) for the data previously shown in Table 10.7. To be able to do this we need to know the means, standard deviations and intercorrelations of the three variables together with the number of cases in the sample which are presented in Table 11.7.

Using the above formulae we find that the standardised partial regression coefficient between children's aggression and parent's aggression is about 0.55 while the unstandardised partial regression coefficient is about 0.35:

$$B_1 = \frac{0.65 - (0.48 \times 0.36)}{1 - 0.36^2} = \frac{0.4772}{0.8704} = 0.548$$

$$b_1 = \frac{0.95}{1.50} \times 0.548 = 0.347$$

Similarly, the standardised partial regression coefficient between children's aggression and children's watching violence is about 0.28 while the unstandardised partial regression coefficient is about 0.18:

$$B_2 = \frac{0.48 - (0.65 \times 0.36)}{1 - 0.36^2} = \frac{0.2460}{0.8704} = 0.2826$$

$$b_2 = \frac{0.95}{1.51} \times 0.2826 = 0.1778$$

Note that both the standardised and the unstandardised partial regression coefficient for parent's aggression are bigger than those for children's watching violence which means that more of the variance in children's aggression is accounted for by parent's aggression than children's watching violence.

We can calculate the intercept constant from the following formula:

Table 11.7 Correlations, means and standard deviations for parent's aggression, children's watching violence and children's aggression

	1 Parent's aggression	2 Children's watching violence	c Children's aggression
1 Parent's aggression	0.15		
2 Children's watching violence	0.36	0.87	
c Children's aggression	0.65	0.11	0.48
Mean	3.29	2.57	2.71
Standard deviation	1.50	1.51	0.95

a = criterion mean − (b_1 × predictor$_1$ mean) + (b_2 × predictor$_2$ mean)

Substituting the appropriate values in the formula gives an intercept constant of about 1.10:

$$2.71 − (0.35 × 3.29) + (0.18 × 2.57) = 2.71 − 1.15 + 0.46 = 1.10$$

The formula for computing the squared multiple correlation is as follows:

$$R^2 = \frac{r^2_{c1} + r^2_{c2} − (2 × r_{c1} × r_{c2} × r_{12})}{1 − r^2_{12}}$$

Placing the appropriate correlations into this formula produces a squared multiple correlation of about 0.49:

$$\frac{0.65^2 + 0.48^2 − (2 × 0.65 × 0.48 × 0.36)}{1 − 0.36^2} =$$

$$\frac{0.4225 + 0.2304 − 0.2246}{0.8704} = \frac{0.4283}{0.8704} = 0.492$$

The formula for the adjusted squared multiple correlation is:

$$\text{adjusted } R^2 = R^2 − \frac{(1 − R^2) × \text{no. of predictors}}{\text{no. of cases } − \text{ no. of predictors } − 1}$$

Inserting the pertinent values into this formula we see that the adjusted squared multiple correlation for our example is about 0.24:

$$0.492 − \frac{(1 − 0.492) × 2}{7 − 2 − 1} = 0.492 − \frac{1.016}{4} = 0.492 − 0.254 = 0.238$$

The multiple correlation is the square root of the squared multiple correlation:

$$R = \sqrt{R^2}$$

Consequently, the multiple correlation for our example is about 0.70 ($\sqrt{0.492} = 0.70$).

The formula for computing the F ratio for testing the significance of the multiple correlation is:

$$F = \frac{R^2 × (\text{no. of cases } − \text{ no. of predictors } − 1)}{(1 − R^2) × \text{no. of predictors}}$$

The degrees of freedom are the number of predictors for the numerator and the number of cases minus the number of predictors minus 1 for the denominator.

The F ratio for our example is about 1.94:

$$\frac{0.492 \times (7 - 2 - 1)}{(1 - 0.492) \times 2} = \frac{0.492 \times 4}{0.508 \times 2} = 1.9370$$

Looking up this value in the table in Appendix 3, we see that with 2 and 4 degrees of freedom in the numerator and denominator respectively F has to be 6.9443 or bigger to be significant at the 0.05 level which it is not. Consequently, we would conclude that the multiple correlation between children's aggression and the two predictors of parent's aggression and children's watching violence is not significant.

Note that the size of the F test depends partly on the number of cases in the numerator. If the number of cases is increased then the size of the F ratio increases. For example, with 12 cases F is about 4.36:

$$\frac{0.492 \times (12 - 2 - 1)}{(1 - 0.492) \times 2} = \frac{0.492 \times 9}{0.508 \times 2} = 4.3582$$

With 2 and 9 degrees of freedom respectively F has to be 4.2565 or larger to be significant at the 0.05 level which it is.

The prompt procedure for running this multiple regression analysis is:

MTB > regress 'ca' 2 'cv' 'pa'

The criterion (e.g. **'ca'**) is listed first after **regress** followed by the number of predictors to be entered into the regression equation (which is **2** in this case) and the predictors (e.g. **'cv'** and **'pa'**).

The menu procedure for computing a regression analysis is:

→**Stat** →**Regression** →**Regression** . . . →criterion [e.g. **ca**] →**Select** [this puts the criterion in the box beside **Response:**] →first predictor [e.g. **cv**] →**Select** [this puts this predictor in the box beside **Predictor:**] →second predictor [e.g. **pa**] →**Select** →**OK**

The output for this example is displayed in Table 11.8. As we can see neither of the two predictors significantly predict the criterion in such a small sample.

Although the standardised and unstandardised partial regression coefficients provide an index of the contributions made by the predictors, they do not offer an estimate of the amount of variance in the criterion which is accounted for by each of the predictors. One coefficient which does this is the *part* (or *semipartial*) *correlation*. A first-order part correlation can be thought of as a simple correlation between the criterion and first predictor, from the latter of which the effect of the second predictor has been taken out. This is illustrated with the Venn diagram in Figure 11.5 in which

Table 11.8 Regression output for children's aggression (**ca**) regressed onto parent's aggression (**pa**) and children's watching violence (**cv**)

Regression Analysis

The regression equation is
ca = 1.10 + 0.351 pa + 0.178 cv

Predictor	Coef	Stdev	t-ratio	p
Constant	1.1050	0.8705	1.27	0.273
pa	0.3505	0.2418	1.45	0.221
cv	0.1779	0.2393	0.74	0.498

s = 0.8274   R-sq = 49.6%   R-sq(adj) = 24.3%

Analysis of Variance

SOURCE	DF	SS	MS	F	p
Regression	2	2.6901	1.3451	1.96	0.254
Error	4	2.7384	0.6846		
Total	6	5.4286			

SOURCE	DF	SEQ SS
pa	1	2.3116
cv	1	0.3786

sections *b* and *f* represent the variance that is common to both the first and second predictor and which is removed from the first predictor. A first-order part correlation should be distinguished from a first-order partial correlation in which the second predictor has been removed from both the criterion and the first predictor. This is shown in Figure 11.5 where sections *e*, *b* and *f* reflect the variance of the criterion and first predictor that is also shared with the second predictor. The squared part correlation indicates the proportion of variance in the criterion that is uniquely shared with the first predictor having taken into account the variance shared by the first and second predictor. This proportion can be thought of as the ratio of the variance represented by *a* to that represented by *a*, *b*, *c* and *e*. The squared partial correlation, in contrast, is the proportion of variance in the criterion that is shared with the first predictor taking into account the proportion of variance in the criterion that is also shared with the second predictor. This proportion can be conceptualised as the ratio of the variance represented by *a* to that represented by *a* and *c*. The squared first-order part correlation is the absolute increase in the amount of variance in the criterion which is explained by the first predictor taking the second predictor into account. Consequently, the squared part correlation is often used to determine whether adding a further variable to the regression

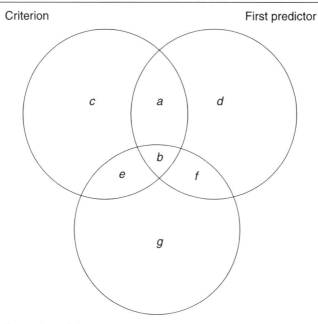

Criterion   First predictor

c   a   d

b

e   f

g

Second predictor

Squared semipartial correlation = $a/(a+b+c+e)$
Squared partial correlation = $a/(a+c)$

Figure 11.5 Areas representing a semipartial and a partial correlation between the criterion and the first predictor in standard multiple regression

equation provides a significant increase in the overall proportion of explained variance in the criterion.

The formula for the first-order part correlation between the criterion (c) and the first predictor (1) controlling for the second predictor (2) is:

$$r_{c1.2} = \frac{r_{c1} - (r_{c2} \times r_{12})}{\sqrt{(1 - r_{12}^2)}}$$

We will calculate the first-order part correlation between the criterion of children's aggression and the two predictors of parent's aggression and children's watching violence.

Using this formula, we find that the first-order part correlation between children's aggression (c) and parent's aggression (1) controlling for children's watching violence (2) is about 0.52:

$$\frac{0.65 - (0.48 \times 0.36)}{\sqrt{(1 - 0.36^2)}} = \frac{0.65 - 0.17}{\sqrt{1 - 0.13}} = \frac{0.48}{0.93} = 0.516$$

This first-order part correlation squared is about 0.27 (0.266) which means that adding the predictor of parent's aggression to that of children's watching violence increases the percentage of variance explained in children's aggression by about 27.

To determine whether the increase in variance explained by the additional variable of parent's aggression is significant we carry out the following F test:

$$F = \frac{\text{squared part correlation}/1}{(1 - R^2)/(\text{no. of cases} - \text{no. of predictors} - 1)}$$

The squared part correlation involves the additional variable in question while the squared multiple correlation (R^2) includes both the additional variable and the others in the regression equation. The degrees of freedom for the numerator is 1 and for the denominator is the number of cases minus the number of predictors minus 1.

The F ratio for adding parent's aggression to the regression equation is about 2.09:

$$\frac{0.266/1}{(1 - 0.492)/(7 - 2 - 1)} = \frac{0.266}{0.508/4} = \frac{0.266}{0.127} = 2.094$$

Turning to the table in Appendix 3, we see that with 1 and 4 degrees of freedom respectively, F has to be 7.7086 or bigger to be significant at the 0.05 level. Consequently, adding parent's aggression to the regression equation does not provide a significant increase to the proportion of variance already explained. Note, however, that if the number of cases had been increased to 13, including parent's aggression would have made a significant contribution to the percentage of variance explained. With 13 cases, F is about 5.24 [$0.266/(0.508/10) = 5.236$]. With 1 and 10 degrees of freedom respectively F has to be 4.9646 or larger to be significant at the 0.05 level which it is.

The first-order part correlation between children's aggression (c) and children's watching violence (2) controlling for parent's aggression (1) is about 0.27:

$$\frac{0.48 - (0.65 \times 0.36)}{\sqrt{(1 - 0.36^2)}} = \frac{0.48 - 0.23}{\sqrt{(1 - 0.13)}} = \frac{0.25}{0.93} = 0.2688$$

This first-order part correlation squared is about 0.07. In other words, adding children's watching violence to parent's aggression increases the percentage of variance explained in children's aggression by about 7.

The F ratio for adding children's watching violence to the regression equation is about 0.55:

$$\frac{0.07/1}{(1 - 0.492)/(7 - 2 - 1)} = \frac{0.07}{0.508/4} = \frac{0.07}{0.127} = 0.551$$

With 1 and 4 degrees of freedom respectively, F has to be 7.7086 or bigger to be significant at the 0.05 level which it is not. Therefore, we could conclude that adding children's watching violence to the regression equation does not result in a significant increase in the percentage of variance explained in children's aggression. Once again, however, note that if the number of cases were increased to 35 adding children's watching violence would have produced a significant increase in the proportion of variance explained. With 35 cases F is about 4.41 [0.07/(0.508/32) = 4.409]. With 1 and 32 degrees of freedom, F has to be 4.1709 or bigger to be significant at the 0.05 level which it is.

To find out with Minitab the proportion of variance explained by a particular predictor we run a regression analysis with all the other predictors (i.e. excluding that predictor) and subtract the resulting squared multiple correlation from the squared multiple correlation for the regression analysis with all the predictors (i.e. including that predictor). So, for example, to determine the percentage of variance explained by parent's aggression, we regress children's aggression onto children's watching violence and subtract the resulting squared multiple correlation (**23.1**) shown in Table 11.9 from the squared multiple correlation (**49.6**) presented in Table 11.8 for children's aggression regressed onto parent's aggression and children's watching violence. This difference (26.5) represents the percentage of variance in children's aggression explained by parent's aggression which is the same as that previously calculated.

Table 11.9 Regression output for children's aggression regressed onto children's violence

Regression Analysis

The regression equation is
ca = 1.94 + 0.302 cv

Predictor	Coef	Stdev	t-ratio	p
Constant	1.9375	0.7226	2.68	0.044
cv	0.3021	0.2468	1.22	0.275

s = 0.9140   R-sq = 23.1%   R-sq(adj) = 7.7%

Analysis of Variance

SOURCE	DF	SS	MS	F	p
Regression	1	1.2515	1.2515	1.50	0.275
Error	5	4.1771	0.8354		
Total	6	5.4286			

The prompt procedure for producing the output in Table 11.9 is:

MTB > regress 'ca' 1 'cv'

while the menu sequence is:

→$\underline{\text{S}}$tat →$\underline{\text{R}}$egression →$\underline{\text{R}}$egression . . . →ca →Select [this puts **ca** in the box beside $\underline{\text{R}}$esponse:] →cv →Select [this puts **cv** in the box beside Pred$\underline{\text{i}}$ctor:] →$\underline{\text{O}}$K

To work out the percentage of variance explained by children's watching violence, we regress children's aggression onto parent's aggression and subtract the resulting squared multiple correlation (**42.6**) displayed in Table 11.10 from the squared multiple correlation (**49.6**) shown in Table 11.8 for children's aggression regressed onto parent's aggression and children's watching violence. This difference (7.0) represents the percentage of variance in children's aggression explained by children's watching violence which is the same as that previously calculated.

The prompt procedure for producing the output in Table 11.10 is:

MTB > regress 'ca' 1 'pa'

while the menu sequence is:

→$\underline{\text{S}}$tat →$\underline{\text{R}}$egression →$\underline{\text{R}}$egression . . . →ca →Select [this puts **ca** in the box beside $\underline{\text{R}}$esponse:] →pa →Select [this puts **pa** in the box beside Pred$\underline{\text{i}}$ctor:] →$\underline{\text{O}}$K

Table 11.10 Regression output for children's aggression regressed onto parent's aggression

Regression Analysis

The regression equation is
ca = 1.35 + 0.415 pa

Predictor	Coef	Stdev	t-ratio	p
Constant	1.3511	0.7683	1.76	0.139
pa	0.4149	0.2155	1.93	0.112

s = 0.7896   R-sq = 42.6%   R-sq(adj) = 31.1%

Analysis of Variance

SOURCE	DF	SS	MS	F	p
Regression	1	2.3116	2.3116	3.71	0.112
Error	5	3.1170	0.6234		
Total	6	5.4286			

PROCEDURES FOR SELECTING PREDICTORS

The number of potential regression equations increases with the number of predictors and is a function of 2 to the power of the number of predictors minus 1. With only two predictors the maximum number of regression equations or models that can be tested is three ($2^2 - 1 = 3$): the two predictors on their own and combined. With three predictors seven different equations can be examined ($2^3 - 1 = 7$): three with only one predictor, three with two predictors and one with all three. With four predictors there are fifteen different equations ($2^4 - 1 = 15$). As the number of predictors increases it takes more and more time to investigate and compare the different equations. In order not to have to examine every possible equation, a number of different approaches for selecting and testing predictors have been suggested, including *hierarchical* (or *blockwise*) *selection*, *forward selection*, *backward elimination* and *stepwise selection*. The first of these selects predictors on practical or theoretical grounds while the last three involve statistical criteria and are used to choose the smallest set of predictors that might explain most of the variance in the criterion. In contrast to these methods, entering all predictors into the equation is known as *standard* multiple regression while comparing all possible sets of predictors is called *setwise* regression. The method(s) used should mirror the purpose of the analysis. Standard multiple regression is carried out in Minitab with the **regress** command or **Regression** menu. Hierarchical, forward, backward and stepwise regression are executed with the **stepwise** command or **Stepwise** menu.

In hierarchical selection predictors are entered singly or in blocks according to some rationale. For example, potentially confounding variables such as socio-demographic factors may be entered first in order to control for their effects. Or similar variables may be grouped together (such as attitudes) and entered as a block. With the data in Table 10.8, for instance, if we wanted to enter parent's watching violence (**pv**) first we would use the following prompt and menu procedures respectively:

MTB > stepwise 'ca' 'pa' 'cv' 'pv';
SUBC> enter 'pv';
SUBC> force 'pv'.

→**Stat** →**Regression** →**Stepwise** . . . →**ca** →**Select** [this puts **ca** in the box beside **Response:**] →**pa** →**Select** [this puts **pa** in the box beside **Predictor:**; repeat with **cv** and **pv**] →**pv** →box beside **Enter:** →**Select** [this puts **pv** in the box beside **Enter:**] →**pv** →box beside **Force:** →**Select** [this puts **pv** in the box beside **Force:**] →**OK**

If we wanted to enter both parent's watching violence (**pv**) and children's watching violence (**cv**) first we would use the following prompt and menu procedures respectively:

MTB > stepwise 'ca' 'pa' 'cv' 'pv';
SUBC> enter 'pv' 'cv';
SUBC> force 'pv' 'cv'.

→**S̲tat** →**R̲egression** →**S̲tepwise** . . . →**ca** →**Select** [this puts **ca** in the box beside **R̲esponse:**] →**pa** →**Select** [this puts **pa** in the box beside **Predi̲ctor:**; repeat with **cv** and **pv**] →**pv** →box beside **E̲nter:** →**Select** [this puts **pv** in the box beside **E̲nter:**] →**cv** →**Select** →**pv** →box beside **F̲orce:** →**Select** [this puts **pv** in the box beside **F̲orce:**] →**cv** →**Select** →**O̲K**

In forward selection the predictor with the largest F ratio is considered first for entry into the regression equation. This predictor is entered into the equation if the previously specified F ratio is exceeded. In Minitab this F ratio is set at 4.0 by default but can be changed. If the previously specified F ratio is not exceeded, this variable is not entered and the analysis ends. If this value is exceeded, then this predictor is entered and the analysis continues. The next predictor considered for entry is that with the next largest F. If it meets the statistical criterion, it will be entered into the regression equation and the predictor with the next largest F will be evaluated. The selection stops when no other predictor satisfies the entry criterion. Once a predictor has been entered into the equation it remains there even though it may no longer make a significant contribution to the amount of variance explained. The following prompt and menu procedures respectively are used to run a forward analysis:

MTB > stepwise 'ca' 'pa' 'cv' 'pv';
SUBC> fremove 0.

→**S̲tat** →**R̲egression** →**S̲tepwise** . . . →**ca** →**Select** [this puts **ca** in the box beside **R̲esponse:**] →**pa** →**Select** [this puts **pa** in the box beside **Predi̲ctor:**; repeat with **cv** and **pv**] →**O̲ptions** . . . →box beside **F to r̲emove:**, delete **4.0** and type **0** →**O̲K** →**O̲K**

Setting the F ratio for removal at zero means that no predictor is removed.

In backward elimination all the predictors are initially entered into the regression equation. The predictor with the smallest F ratio is examined first. If it meets the previously specified F ratio for removing predictors (which is set by default at 4.0 in Minitab), it is excluded from the regression equation and the predictor with the next smallest F ratio is considered. No predictor can ever reenter the model. The analysis stops when no further predictors satisfy this criterion. The following prompt and menu procedures respectively are used to run a forward analysis:

MTB > stepwise 'ca' 'pa' 'cv' 'pv';
SUBC> fenter 100000.

→**Stat** →**Regression** →**Stepwise** . . . →**ca** →**Select** [this puts **ca** in the box beside **Response:**] →**pa** →**Select** [this puts **pa** in the box beside **Predictor:**; repeat with **cv** and **pv**] →**Options** . . . →box beside **F to enter:**, delete **4.0** and type **100000** →**OK** →**OK**

Setting the F ratio for entry at 100000 means that no predictor is ever reentered into the model.

Stepwise selection is a combination of forward selection and backward elimination. The predictor which has the lowest F ratio is removed first if the previously specified F ratio for removing predictors is met. The second predictor to be considered is that which has the next lowest F ratio. If this meets the statistical criterion it is removed from the regression equation. If no predictor can be removed, the predictor with the highest F ratio for entry is considered. If it exceeds the criterion for entry it is entered and the predictor with the next highest F ratio is considered. If the predictor does not meet the criterion for entry, the analysis stops. Note that these three different selection methods may give different results with the same data so it may be worthwhile comparing the results of the three methods.

We will illustrate stepwise regression with the data in Table 10.8. As we have seen in the previous section the size of the sample is too small for either predictor (children's watching violence or parent's aggression) to explain a significant proportion of the variance in the criterion (children's aggression). Consequently, we will increase the size of the sample seven-fold to 49. We can do this in the prompt system with the **set** command in which the numbers to be repeated are enclosed in brackets and the number of times the sequence is to be repeated precedes the brackets. We would use the following procedure, for example, to repeat the values for parent's aggression seven times:

MTB > set c1
DATA> 7(3,1,3,4,2,5,5)
DATA> end

We would replicate these data seven times with the menu system as follows:

→data in **Data** window by moving cursor to cell in column 1 row 1, hold down left button, move cursor to cell in column 4 row 7 and release left button →**Edit** →**Copy Cells** →cursor to cell in column 1 row 1 →**Edit** →**Paste/Insert Cells** (six times)

The following prompt and menu procedures respectively would be used to run a stepwise regression:

MTB > stepwise 'ca' 'pa' 'cv' 'pv'

→**Stat** →**Regression** →**Stepwise** . . . →**ca** →**Select** [this puts **ca** in the box beside **Response:**] →**pa** →**Select** [this puts **pa** in the box beside **Predictor:**; repeat with **cv** and **pv**] →**OK**

The output for this procedure is presented in Table 11.11. Parent's aggression (**pa**) is the predictor that explains the highest percentage of the variance in children's aggression (**42.58**) followed by children's watching violence (**cv**) which accounts for a further 6.98 per cent (**49.56** − **42.58** = 6.98) and parent's watching violence (**pv**) a further 20.24 per cent (**69.80** − **49.56** = 20.24). Altogether these three predictors account for **69.80** (42.58 + 6.98 + 20.24 = 69.80) per cent of the variance in children's aggression.

In this example, parent's watching violence acts as a suppressor variable. Suppressor variables have a low correlation with the criterion and a strong correlation with one or more of the predictors. As shown in Table 10.7 parent's watching violence has a low positive correlation of 0.11 with children's aggression and a high positive correlation of 0.87 with children's watching violence. Including this suppressor variable in the regression equation increases the proportion of variance explained in the criterion because it suppresses variance shared with a predictor but not with the criterion. This may be more readily understood if we look at the formula for the first-order partial correlation shown in Chapter 10. The second

Table 11.11 Stepwise multiple regression output showing children's aggression (**ca**) regressed onto parent's aggression (**pa**), children's watching violence (**cv**) and parent's watching violence (**pv**)

Stepwise Regression

F-to-Enter: 4.00 F-to-Remove: 4.00

Response is ca on 3 predictors, with N = 49

Step	1	2	3
Constant	1.351	1.105	1.827
pa	0.415	0.351	0.235
T-Ratio	5.90	4.92	3.95
cv		0.178	0.742
T-Ratio		2.52	6.36
pv			−0.60
T-Ratio			−5.49
S	0.681	0.646	0.505
R-Sq	42.58	49.56	69.80

More? (Yes, No, Subcommand, or Help)
SUBC>

expression in the denominator $[(1 - r_{23}{}^2)]$ indicates the proportion of variance remaining when the variance shared by the predictor (2) and the suppressor (3) is removed. The greater the correlation between the predictor and the suppressor variable, the greater the variance is that is shared by the two variables and the smaller the remaining variance is. The smaller the remaining variance is, the smaller the denominator is and so the bigger the partial correlation is. In the example the correlation between the predictor (children's watching violence) and the suppressor variable (parent's watching violence) is 0.87 giving a partial correlation of 0.78:

$$r_{12.3} = \frac{0.48 - (0.11 \times 0.87)}{\sqrt{(1 - 0.11^2) \times (1 - 0.87^2)}} = \frac{0.48 - 0.10}{\sqrt{0.99 \times 0.24}} = \frac{0.38}{0.49} = 0.78$$

If the correlation between the predictor and the suppressor had been smaller, say 0.30, then the partial correlation would have been smaller at 0.47:

$$r_{12.3} = \frac{0.48 - (0.11 \times 0.30)}{\sqrt{(1 - 0.11^2) \times (1 - 0.30^2)}} = \frac{0.48 - 0.03}{\sqrt{0.99 \times 0.91}} = \frac{0.45}{0.95} = 0.47$$

SUMMARY

The computation of bivariate regression and multiple regression with two predictors has been described. One use of regression analysis is to estimate the likely score of a criterion from one or more predictors. Another use is to determine the minimum number of predictors needed to explain the maximum variance in the criterion. The regression coefficient (b) is the straight line lying closest to the points on the scatterplot. It provides a good index of the association between two variables when the assumptions of normality, linearity and homoscedasticity are met, which can be visually checked through a scatterplot of the residuals with the predicted values. The accuracy of prediction is given by the standard error of estimate. The proportion of variance in the criterion accounted for by the linear combination of predictors is assessed by the squared multiple correlation (R^2), the statistical significance of which is tested by the F ratio. A more conservative estimate of explained variance which takes account of the size of the sample and the number of predictors is the adjusted squared multiple correlation. Multiple regression uses partial regression coefficients. The squared part correlation is the absolute increase in the amount of variance in the criterion explained by the predictors and is often used to determine whether adding a further variable to the regression equation significantly increases the overall proportion of variance explained. With a large number of potential predictors, various procedures may be used to select those predictors which maximise the explained variation.

EXERCISES

Use the data in Table 6.23 for the following exercises.

1 Conduct a bivariate regression with educational interest at 15 as the criterion and educational interest at 12 as the predictor.
  (a) What is the unstandardised regression coefficient?
  (b) What is the standardised regression coefficient?
  (c) What is the intercept constant?
  (d) What is the predicted value of educational interest at 15 if the value of educational interest at 12 is 2?
  (e) What is the standard error of estimate?
  (f) What is the standard error of the regression coefficient?
  (g) What is the standard error of the intercept?
  (h) What is the squared multiple correlation?
  (i) What is the adjusted squared multiple correlation?
  (j) What is the F ratio of the squared multiple correlation?
  (k) What are its degrees of freedom?
  (l) What is its probability value?
2 Carry out a multivariate regression with educational interest at 15 as the criterion and educational interest at 12 and at 9 as the predictors.
  (a) What is the standardised partial regression coefficient between educational interest at 15 and at 12?
  (b) What is the unstandardised partial regression coefficient between educational interest at 15 and at 12?
  (c) What is the standardised partial regression coefficient between educational interest at 15 and at 9?
  (d) What is the unstandardised partial regression coefficient between educational interest at 15 and at 9?
  (e) What is the squared multiple correlation?
  (f) What is the adjusted squared multiple correlation?
  (g) What is the F ratio of the squared multiple correlation?
  (h) What are its degrees of freedom?
  (i) What is its probability value?
  (j) What is the part correlation between educational interest at 15 and educational interest at 12 controlling for educational interest at 9?
  (k) What is the F ratio for adding educational interest at 12 to the regression equation?
  (l) What are its degrees of freedom?
  (m) What is its probability value?
  (n) What is the part correlation between educational interest at 15 and educational interest at 9 controlling for educational interest at 12?
  (o) What is the F ratio for adding educational interest at 9 to the regression equation?
  (p) What are its degrees of freedom?
  (q) What is its probability value?

## Chapter 12

Measurement reliability and agreement

This chapter describes statistical tests which provide an index of how reliable a particular measure is or how much agreement exists between two or more judges. For instance, we may wish to find out to what extent two or more judges categorise or rate subjects in the same way, or to what extent the answers to questions devised to measure the same quality are consistent. The type of test to use depends on whether the data are categorical or not. The most widely recommended index of agreement between two or more judges is Cohen's *kappa coefficient* for categorical data. The most common measure of the reliability of non-categorical data from three or more judges is Ebel's *intraclass correlation* while the most frequently used index of the internal reliability of a set of questions is Cronbach's *alpha*.

CATEGORICAL DATA

Kappa coefficient

Kappa indicates the extent of agreement for categorical data between two judges or raters and can be extended to apply to more than two judges (Fleiss 1971). It measures the proportion of agreements between two judges taking into account the proportion of agreements that may occur simply by chance. It has the following formula:

$$k = \frac{\text{observed proportion of agreement} - \text{chance-expected proportion of agreement}}{1 - \text{chance-expected proportion of agreement}}$$

which can be expressed in frequencies:

$$k = \frac{\text{observed frequency of agreement} - \text{chance-expected frequency of agreement}}{\text{no. of subjects} - \text{chance-expected frequency of agreement}}$$

Kappas can range from -1 to $+1$. A kappa of 0 means that the observed agreement is exactly equal to the agreement that would be expected by chance, a negative kappa a less than chance agreement, a positive kappa a greater than chance agreement and a kappa of 1 perfect agreement. A kappa of 0.7 or more is usually considered to be an acceptable level of agreement. As shall be demonstrated below, kappa is an index of agreement whereas tests such as the contingency coefficient and phi are measures of association. Both the contingency coefficient and phi vary between 0 and 1. If there is substantial disagreement between two judges on a dichotomous judgement task, then both the contingency coefficient and phi will be positive whereas kappa will be negative.

To illustrate the computation of kappa we will take the case where two judges are asked to indicate whether they consider each of 100 events to be aggressive or not. The results of these two judges are shown in Table 12.1. Judge A thinks that 90 out of 100 or 90 per cent of the events are aggressive while Judge B believes that only 40 per cent of them are. The decisions of the two judges agree on only 30 per cent of the events.

To calculate kappa we first find the chance-expected frequency of agreement for the two cells. This is done for each cell by multiplying its row total by its column total and dividing by the overall total. So the chance-expected frequency for the non-aggressive category is 6 (10 $\times$ 60/100 = 6) and for the aggressive category 36 (90 $\times$ 40/100 = 36) giving a total of 42.

Applying the above formula we find that kappa is about -0.21:

$$\frac{30 - 42}{100 - 42} = \frac{-12}{58} = -0.2069$$

This indicates that the agreement between the two judges is less than would be expected by chance which implies that they are using different criteria to make their judgements.

Let us now compare this kappa with the contingency coefficient and phi. To calculate these two coefficients we first have to find chi-square which is about 16.67:

$$\frac{(0 - 6)^2}{6} + \frac{(10 - 4)^2}{4} + \frac{(60 - 54)^2}{54} + \frac{(30 - 36)^2}{36} =$$

$$6 + 9 + 0.67 + 1 = 16.67$$

Table 12.1 Categorisation of events by two judges

		Judge B		
		Non-aggressive	Aggressive	
Judge A	Non-aggressive	0	10	10
	Aggressive	60	30	90
Total		60	40	100

Consequently, the contingency coefficient is about 0.38 [$\sqrt{16.67/(16.67 + 100)} = 0.378$] and phi is 0.41($\sqrt{16.67/100} = 0.408$). Note that both the contingency coefficient and phi are positive and larger than kappa even though the amount of disagreement is greater than the amount of agreement. What these two coefficients indicate is that there is a tendency for certain decisions of Judge A to be associated with certain decisions of Judge B but they provide no information as to whether the actual decisions are the same.

Minitab does not calculate kappa.

NON-CATEGORICAL DATA

When measuring a hypothetical construct such as aggression or educational interest, it is useful to obtain a number of separate indices of that variable in order to determine how reliably that construct is being assessed. These indices might consist of either the independent ratings of a number of judges asked to assess that variable or the answers to a number of items designed to measure that variable. These ratings or answers represent the score on that variable for the person being assessed. These scores can be thought of as reflecting two components consisting of a true score plus some error:

actual score = true score + error

For example, a person may understand the question correctly and may answer appropriately, in which case the actual score will mainly reflect the true score with very little error. Alternatively, the person may misunderstand the question and therefore respond inappropriately, in which situation the actual score will largely consist of error.

The reliability of that score can be thought of as the proportion of the true score over the true score plus the error:

$$\text{reliability of a score} = \frac{\text{true score}}{\text{true score} + \text{error}}$$

Alternative ways of expressing this measure of reliability are as follows:

$$\text{reliability of a score} = \frac{\text{actual score} - \text{error}}{\text{actual score}} = \frac{\text{true score}}{\text{actual score}}$$

With only one measure of a variable it is not possible to estimate the error in that measure. In order to do this, it is necessary to have a number of indices (i.e. judges or items), where the error of those indices can be estimated with analysis of variance. Reliability is the proportion of the true variance in the scores of subjects as a function of the true variance together with the error variance:

$$\text{reliability} = \frac{\text{true variance}}{\text{true variance} + \text{error variance}}$$

Two measures of reliability are Ebel's intraclass correlation and Cronbach's alpha coefficient. The intraclass correlation is used to estimate the individual or average reliability of the ratings of judges whereas alpha is employed to assess the internal consistency of a set of items making up a scale. The difference between these two measures of reliability lies in the kind of analysis of variance conducted. Intraclass correlation is calculated with a one- or two-way analysis of variance where the ratings of the judges are treated as an unrelated factor in which the ratings are made by different people. Alpha, on the other hand, is computed with a single factor repeated measures analysis of variance in which the different items are treated as a repeated measure in that the answers to the different items are given by the same individual.

INTRACLASS CORRELATION

The reliability of the non-categorical ratings of two judges is estimated with Pearson's correlation coefficient and of three or more judges with the intraclass correlation. There are four different forms of the intraclass correlation. The intraclass correlation can be generally thought of as the proportion of the true or between-subjects variance in the ratings of the subjects in relation to the between-subjects variance together with the error variance:

$$\text{intraclass correlation} = \frac{\text{between-subjects variance}}{\text{between-subjects variance} + \text{error variance}}$$

This formula gives the reliability of the average rating for all the judges and would be used as the appropriate measure of reliability if the ratings of the judges were averaged to form a score for each case. For example, if three judges rated the aggressiveness of 80 individuals and these three ratings were averaged for each individual to give them an aggressiveness rating, then it would be suitable to use this index as the measure of reliability.

If, on the other hand, only one of every four of these 80 individuals was rated by all three judges while the other three were rated by only one of the three judges, then it would be more suitable to provide the reliability of the average rating for an individual judge. The reliability of the average rating for an individual judge will be lower than that for all three judges since in this formula the error variance is multiplied by the number of judges minus 1:

$$\frac{\text{between-subjects variance}}{\text{between-subjects variance} + [\text{error variance} \times (\text{no. of judges} - 1)]}$$

Using the error variance on its own provides an index of the extent to which the judges rank the subjects in a similar order, ignoring the extent to which a similar rating (rather than ranking) is given to each case. Take, for example, the ratings shown in Table 12.2 of four subjects made by three judges. Note that while there is perfect agreement between the three judges in the rank order of the four subjects, there is total disagreement over the particular ratings given. For example, all three judges agree in giving the first case the highest rating (low numbers reflecting higher ratings) but give that case a different rating of 1, 2 and 3. An intraclass correlation which uses error variance on its own is sometimes referred to as interjudge reliability.

To determine the extent to which the mean ratings are also similar, the error variance is combined with the between-judges variance:

$$\frac{\text{between-subjects variance}}{\text{between-subjects variance} + \text{error variance} + \text{between-judges variance}}$$

An intraclass correlation which includes the between-judges variance is sometimes known as a measure of interjudge agreement since it assesses the extent to which the judges also give a similar rating.

So the following four forms of intraclass correlation may be distinguished:

$$\text{interjudge reliability of all judges} = \frac{\text{between-subjects variance}}{\text{between-subjects variance} + \text{error variance}}$$

$$\text{interjudge reliability of individual judges} = \frac{\text{between-subjects variance}}{\text{between-subjects variance} + [\text{error variance} \times (\text{no of judges} - 1)]}$$

$$\text{interjudge agreement of all judges} = \frac{\text{between-subjects variance}}{\text{between-subjects variance} + \text{error variance} + \text{between-judges variance}}$$

$$\text{interjudge agreement of individual judge} = \frac{\text{between-subjects variance}}{\text{between-subjects variance} + [(\text{error variance} + \text{between-judges variance}) \times (\text{no. of judges} - 1)]}$$

When the between-judges variance is to be included in the error var-

Table 12.2 Ratings by three judges

Subjects	Judges		
	A	B	C
1	1	2	3
2	2	3	4
3	3	4	5
4	4	5	6

iance, a one-way analysis only need be worked out as the error term will incorporate the between-judges variance:

one-way anova − between-subjects variance + error variance

When the between-judges variance is to be excluded from the error variance, then a two-way analysis of variance is necessary as the between-judges variance will be given separately from the error variance:

two-way anova − between-subjects variance + between-judges variance + error variance

Note that if a two-way analysis of variance is performed, the between-judges variance can be combined with the error variance to give the appropriate error variance for inter-rater reliability.

So, to demonstrate the calculation of these four kinds of intraclass correlation for the data in Table 12.2, we will carry out a two-way analysis of variance. The means for the three judges and four subjects are shown in Table 12.3 together with the grand mean.

The between-subjects sum of squares is calculated by subtracting the grand mean from each of the subject means, squaring this difference, multiplying this squared difference by the number of judges and summing the products for all the subjects. This makes it 15:

$$[(2 - 3.5)^2 \times 3] + [(3 - 3.5)^2 \times 3] + [(4 - 3.5)^2 \times 3] +$$
$$[(5 - 3.5)^2 \times 3] =$$
$$[2.25 \times 3] + [0.25 \times 3] + [0.25 \times 3] + [2.25 \times 3] =$$
$$6.75 + 0.75 + 0.75 + 6.75 = 15$$

The between-subjects mean square is its sum of squares divided by its degrees of freedom (the number of subjects minus 1) which gives 5.0 (15/3 = 5).

The between-judges sum of squares is calculated by subtracting the grand mean from the mean of each judge, squaring this difference, multi-

Table 12.3 Sums and means of ratings of subjects and judges

Subjects	Judges			Sum	Mean
	A	B	C		
1	1	2	3	6	2
2	2	3	4	9	3
3	3	4	5	12	4
4	4	5	6	15	5
Sum	10	14	18	42	
N	4	4	4		
Mean	2.5	3.5	4.5		3.5

plying this squared difference by the number of subjects and summing the products for all the judges. This makes it 8:

$$[(2.5 - 3.5)^2 \times 4] + [(3.5 - 3.5)^2 \times 4] +$$
$$[(4.5 - 3.5)^2 \times 4] = 4 + 0 + 4 = 8$$

The between-judges mean square is its sum of squares divided by its degrees of freedom (the number of judges minus 1) which gives 4.0 (8/2 = 4).

The residual or error sum of squares can be calculated by subtracting the between-subjects and between-judges sum of squares from the total sum of squares. The total sum of squares is the grand mean subtracted from each rating, squared and added together which makes it 23.0:

$$(1 - 3.5)^2 + (2 - 3.5)^2 + (3 - 3.5)^2 + (4 - 3.5)^2 +$$
$$(2 - 3.5)^2 + (3 - 3.5)^2 + (4 - 3.5)^2 + (5 - 3.5)^2 +$$
$$(3 - 3.5)^2 + (4 - 3.5)^2 + (5 - 3.5)^2 + (6 - 3.5)^2 =$$
$$6.25 + 2.25 + 0.25 + 0.25 + 2.25 + 0.25 + 0.25 +$$
$$2.25 + 0.25 + 0.25 + 2.25 + 6.25 = 23.0$$

The error sum of squares is 0 (23.0 − 15.0 − 8.0 = 0.0). The degrees of freedom for the error sum of squares are the number of subjects minus 1 multiplied by the number of judges minus 1. Since the error sum of squares is 0 its mean square is also 0 [0/(4 − 1) × (3 − 1) = 0]. The sums of squares, degrees of freedom and mean squares for these data are presented in Table 12.4.

Using the between-subjects and error mean square we find that the reliability of the average rating for an individual judge is 1.0:

$$\frac{5 - 0}{5 + [0 \times (3 - 1)]} = \frac{5}{5} = 1.0$$

If no account is taken of the differences in the average ratings of the judges, then the intraclass correlation indicates that there is perfect agreement between the judges even though no judge gave the same case the same rating. In other words, when the average ratings of the judges are ignored the intraclass correlation is similar to an average intercorrelation.

However, if the between-judges variance is included in the error term,

Table 12.4 Analysis of variance table for the intraclass correlation

Sources of variation	SS	df	MS
Between-subjects	15.0	3	5.0
Between-judges	8.0	2	4.0
Error	0.0	6	0.0
Total	23.0		

the intraclass correlation is substantially smaller. To calculate the error sum of squares which includes the between-judges variance either subtract the between-subjects sum of squares from the total sum of squares which gives 8.0 (23.0 − 15.0 = 8.0) or add the between-judges sum of squares to the residual sum of squares (8.0 + 0.0 = 8.0). The degrees of freedom for this residual sum of squares are 1 subtracted from the number of judges for each case summed together. Therefore the residual mean square is 1.0 [8/(3 − 1 + 3 − 1 + 3 − 1) = 1]. Using this value, we find that the intraclass correlation is 0.57:

$$\frac{5 - 1}{5 + [1 \times (3 - 1)]} = \frac{4}{7} = 0.57$$

Note that the intraclass correlation is still positive even though none of the ratings is the same.

To produce the necessary statistics with Minitab to derive the intraclass correlation the data for this analysis need to be organised into three columns.

One column, called **'ratings'**, contains rating values of the judges.

Another column, named **'judges'**, comprises the code for the judges with the first judge coded **1**, the second **2** and the third **3**.

A third column, termed **'subjects'**, identifies the subjects.

These three columns would contain the following data

1 1 1
2 1 2
3 1 3
4 1 4
2 2 1
3 2 2
4 2 3
5 2 4
3 3 1
4 3 2
5 3 3
6 3 4

The **twoway** command is then used to perform a two-way analysis of variance on the effect of the **'judges'** and **'subjects'** on the **'ratings'**:

MTB > twoway 'ratings' 'judges' 'subjects'

The menu procedure for doing this is

→**Stat** →**ANOVA** →**Twoway...** →**ratings** →**Select** [this puts **ratings** in the box beside **Response:**] →**judges** →**Select** [this puts **judges** in the box beside **Row factor:**] →**subjects** →**Select** [this puts **subjects** in the box beside **Column factor:**] →**OK**

The output for these procedures is displayed in Table 12.5.

ALPHA

The alpha coefficient determines the internal reliability or consistency of a set of items designed to measure a particular characteristic. It can be thought of as the proportion of variation in the subjects which is explained by the items:

$$\text{alpha} = \frac{\text{between-subjects variance} - \text{error variance}}{\text{between-subjects variance}} \quad \text{or}$$

$$1 - \frac{\text{error variance}}{\text{between-subjects variance}}$$

The difference between this formula and that for the intraclass correlation lies in the different way in which the error variance is derived. We can calculate alpha as a single factor repeated measures analysis of variance in which the error mean square is divided by the between-subjects mean square and the result subtracted from 1.

We will illustrate the computation of alpha with the data shown in Table 12.6 which represent the dichotomous answers of four subjects to three items measuring, say aggression. A '1' might indicate a 'No' or 'Disagree' response and a '2' a 'Yes' or 'Agree' answer. Each of the three items is worded so that a 'Yes' reply indicates greater aggression than a 'No' response. Apart from the fourth case the scores for each person are the same for all three items so that if a person answers 'Yes' to one question they answer 'Yes' to the other two. This pattern of responding implies that the items are measuring the same characteristic. If some of the items had been worded so that a 'Yes' signified lower aggression than a 'No', then

Table 12.5 **Twoway ANOVA** output for calculating the intraclass correlation

Two-way Analysis of Variance

Analysis of Variance for ratings

Source	DF	SS	MS
judges	2	8.00000	4.00000
subjects	3	15.00000	5.00000
Error	6	0.00000	0.00000
Total	11	23.00000	

Table 12.6 Dichotomous answers to three items

Subjects	Items		
	1	2	3
1	1	1	1
2	2	2	2
3	1	1	1
4	1	2	2

the scoring of these items would have to be reversed (i.e. a 'Yes' coded as a '1' and a 'No' as '2') so that the direction of the scoring was consistent.

The total and mean scores for the subjects and items are presented in Table 12.7 together with the grand mean. To calculate the between-subjects and error mean squares carry out the following steps:

Step 1 Calculate the total sum of squares by subtracting the grand mean from each score, squaring them and adding them together.

The total sum of squares for our example is 2.92:

$$(1 - 1.42)^2 + (2 - 1.42)^2 + (1 - 1.42)^2 + (1 - 1.42)^2 +$$
$$(1 - 1.42)^2 + (2 - 1.42)^2 + (1 - 1.42)^2 + (2 - 1.42)^2 +$$
$$(1 - 1.42)^2 + (2 - 1.42)^2 + (1 - 1.42)^2 + (2 - 1.42)^2 = 2.917$$

Step 2 Compute the between-subjects sum of squares by subtracting the grand mean from the mean score for each case, squaring them, multiplying them by the number of items and adding them together.

The between-subjects sum of squares for our example is 2.25:

$$[(1.00 - 1.42)^2 \times 3] + [(2.00 - 1.42)^2 \times 3] +$$
$$[(1.00 - 1.42)^2 \times 3] + [(1.67 - 1.42)^2 \times 3] =$$
$$0.529 + 1.009 + 0.529 + 0.188 = 2.25$$

Table 12.7 Sum and means of items and subjects

Subjects	Items			Sum	Mean
	1	2	3		
1	1	1	1	3	1
2	2	2	2	6	2
3	1	1	1	3	1
4	1	2	2	5	1.67
Sum	5	6	6	17	
N	4	4	4		
Mean	1.25	1.5	1.5		1.42

Step 3 Work out the within-factor (i.e. items) sum of squares by subtracting the grand mean from the mean score for each of the items, squaring them, multiplying them by the number of subjects and summing them.

The within-factor sum of squares for our example is 0.17:

$$[(1.25 - 1.42)^2 \times 4] + [(1.5 - 1.42)^2 \times 4] +$$
$$[(1.5 - 1.42)^2 \times 4] = 0.116 + 0.026 + 0.026 = 0.168$$

Step 4 Calculate the residual sum of squares by adding together the between-subjects and within-subjects sum of squares and subtracting them from the total sum of squares.

For our example the residual sum of squares is 0.50 [2.92 − (2.25 + 0.17) = 0.50].

Step 5 Calculate the error mean square by dividing its sum of squares by its degrees of freedom which are the number of subjects minus 1 multiplied by the number of items minus 1.

For our example the degrees of freedom are 6 [(4 − 1) × (3 − 1) = 6] so the error mean square is 0.08 (0.50/6 = 0.08).

Step 6 Calculate the between-subjects mean square by dividing its sum of squares by its degrees of freedom which are the number of subjects minus 1.

The between-subjects mean square for our example is 0.75 (2.25/3 = 0.75).

The results of these steps are presented in Table 12.8.

To calculate alpha divide the error mean square by the between-subjects mean square and subtract the result from 1. For our example alpha for the three items is 0.89:

$$1 - \frac{0.08}{0.75} = 1 - 0.1067 = 0.8933$$

Since an alpha of 0.80 or higher is generally thought to indicate an acceptable level of internal reliability, this set of three items would be considered as constituting a reliable scale.

Table 12.8 Analysis of variance table for alpha

Sources of variation	SS	df	MS
Between-subjects	2.25	3	0.75
Within-subjects			
Within-factor	0.17		
Residual	0.50	6	0.08
Total	2.92		

To produce the necessary statistics with Minitab to derive alpha, the data for this analysis need to be organised into three columns.

One column, called **ratings**, contains answer codes for the items. Another column, named **items**, comprises the code for the items with the first item coded **1**, the second **2** and the third **3**. A third column, termed **subjects**, identifies the subjects.

These three columns would contain the following data

```
1 1 1
2 1 2
1 1 3
1 1 4
1 2 1
2 2 2
1 2 3
2 2 4
1 3 1
2 3 2
1 3 3
2 3 4
```

To carry out a two-way analysis of variance with repeated measures on one factor we would use the following **anova** command:

MTB > anova ratings = items subjects

The menu action for doing this is:

→**S̲tat** →**A̲NOVA** →**B̲alanced ANOVA** ... →**ratings** →**Select** [this puts **ratings** in the box beside **R̲esponse:**] →**box under M̲odel:** →**items** →**Select** [this puts **items** in this box] →**subjects** →**Select** →**O̲K**

The output for these procedures is displayed in Table 12.9.

If the wording of one or more of a series of items was reversed, then the **code** procedure could be used to reverse the scores of these items. Imagine, for example, that of a scale of 10 dichotomously-scored items the wording of the odd-numbered ones was reversed. We could reconvert the scores for these items so that a 1 becomes a 2 and a 2 a 1 using the **code** procedure described in Chapter 3.

SPEARMAN–BROWN PROPHECY FORMULA

One way of estimating the number of judges or items necessary for providing a measure of acceptable reliability is to use the following Spearman–Brown prophecy formula:

Table 12.9 **Anova** output for calculating alpha

Analysis of Variance (Balanced Designs)

Factor	Type	Levels	Values			
items	fixed	3	1	2	3	
subjects	fixed	4	1	2	3	4

Analysis of Variance for ratings

Source	DF	SS	MS	F	P
items	2	0.16667	0.08333	1.00	0.422
subjects	3	2.25000	0.75000	9.00	0.012
Error	6	0.50000	0.08333		
Total	11	2.91667			

$$\text{estimated reliability} = \frac{n \times \text{known reliability}}{1 + [(n - 1) \times \text{known reliability}]}$$

where n is the ratio by which the number of judges or items is to be increased or decreased. For example, we could use this formula to estimate the reliability of having six rather than three items to assess aggression where the alpha reliability of the three items was 0.89. The estimated reliability of the six item scale is 0.94:

$$\frac{2 \times 0.89}{1 + [(2 - 1) \times 0.89]} = \frac{1.78}{1.89} = 0.94$$

We can check the accuracy of this estimate by adding to our data an identical set of three scores as shown in Table 12.10.

The following formula is used for estimating the ratio by which the number of judges or items has to be changed in order to achieve a measure of a specified reliability:

$$\text{ratio} = \frac{\text{specified reliability} \times (1 - \text{known reliability})}{\text{known reliability} \times (1 - \text{specified reliability})}$$

Suppose, for instance, we had a scale of three items with an alpha of 0.5

Table 12.10 Dichotomous answers to six items

Subjects	Items					
	1	2	3	4	5	6
1	1	1	1	1	1	1
2	2	2	2	2	2	2
3	1	1	1	1	1	1
4	1	2	2	1	2	2

and we wished to increase it to about 0.9. According to this formula, the number of items we would need to do this is 9 times 3 (i.e. 27):

$$\frac{0.9 \times (1 - 0.5)}{0.5 \times (1 - 0.9)} = \frac{0.45}{0.05} = 9$$

CORRECTION FOR ATTENUATION

Many variables are measured with a certain degree of unreliability. Consequently, the correlation between unreliably measured variables will always be less strong than that between reliably measured variables. This reduced correlation is known as *attenuation*. If we wanted to find out the 'true' or theoretical correlation between two measures which had been assessed without error then we need to make a correction for their unreliability.

The following formula has been proposed for calculating the correlation between two variables where the unreliability of both measures has been taken into account:

$$r_c = \frac{\text{correlation between measure}_1 \text{ and measure}_2}{\sqrt{\text{measure}_1 \text{ reliability} \times \text{measure}_2 \text{ reliability}}}$$

When the reliability of only one of the measures is being adjusted, then the formula is:

$$r_c = \frac{\text{correlation between measure}_1 \text{ and measure}_2}{\sqrt{\text{measure}_1 \text{ or measure}_2 \text{ reliability}}}$$

For instance, if the observed correlation between aggression and watching violence was 0.30 and the reliability of the aggression and watching violence measure was 0.80 and 0.70 respectively, then the theoretical correlation between aggression and watching violence is 0.40:

$$\frac{0.30}{\sqrt{0.80 \times 0.70}} = \frac{0.30}{0.75} = 0.40$$

If the attenuated correlation between two measures is close to 1.0, then the two measures would be interpreted as two forms of the same measure.

SUMMARY

The computation of various tests for assessing the agreement and reliability between judges and the internal reliability of a scale of items has been described. Kappa indicates the amount of agreement for categorical data between two judges taking into account the agreement expected by chance. While it can range from -1 to $+1$, a kappa of 0.7 or higher indicates an

Table 12.11 Categorisation of patients' problems by two clinicians

Clinician A	Clinician B		
	Anxiety	Depression	Other
Anxiety	7	2	1
Depression	6	35	4
Other	2	13	30

acceptable level of agreement. For non-categorical data Pearson's correlation assesses the reliability of the ratings made by two judges and the intraclass correlation the reliability of three or more judges. Alpha assesses the internal reliability of a set of items for measuring a particular characteristic. Spearman–Brown's prophecy formula estimates the number of judges or items needed to provide a specified level of reliability. The correlation between two variables can be corrected for the known unreliability of both or either measure.

EXERCISES

1 Two clinicians categorise the problems of 100 patients into the three classes of anxiety, depression and other as shown in Table 12.11. What is the kappa coefficient of agreement for the diagnoses of the two clinicians?

2 Three judges rate the physical attractiveness of four people on a 4-point scale as presented in Table 12.12.
   (a) What is the reliability of the average rating for an individual judge not taking into account the mean levels of the judges' ratings?
   (b) What is the reliability of the average rating for an individual judge taking into account the mean levels of the judges' ratings?
   (c) What is the reliability of the average rating for all three judges not taking into account the mean levels of the judges' ratings?

Table 12.12 Physical attractiveness ratings by three judges

Subjects	Judges		
	A	B	C
1	1	2	2
2	2	2	1
3	3	1	2
4	4	3	2

(d) What is the reliability of the average rating for all three judges taking into account the mean levels of the judges' ratings?

(e) What is the alpha reliability of the judges' ratings?

(f) By what factor would we have to increase the number of judges to achieve an alpha of 0.80?

(g) How many judges would be needed to attain this alpha?

Appendices

APPENDIX 1: MINITAB COMMANDS

This appendix provides a convenient summary of Minitab commands described in this book, listed in alphabetical order. Only Minitab terms are printed in bold. Variables are denoted as **c** which stands for column number and constants as **k**.

---

anova dependent variable **c** = first independent variable **c** second independent variable **c** interaction **c*c;**
  means first independent variable **c** second independent variable **c** interaction **c*c.**

anova dependent variable **c** = first independent variable **c** blocking variable **c;**
  means blocking variable **c.**

aovoneway first group variable **c** second group variable **c** . . .

brief 0
brief

cdf number of successes;
  binomial number of trials   probability of a success.

center first variable **c** second variable **c** . . . (into) standardised first variable **c** standardised second variable **c** . . .

chisquare first column **c** second column **c** . . .

code (old values) new value (old values) old variable **c** new variable **c**

copy old variable **c** new variable **c;**
  use selecting variable **c** = code.

correlation first variable **c** second variable **c** . . .

delete row number(s)   first variable **c** second variable **c** . . .

describe first variable **c** second variable **c** . . .

end (data entry)

erase first variable **c** second variable **c** . . .

execute 'macro name ending in **.mtb**'

friedman dependent variable **c** independent variable **c** blocking variable **c**

ghistogram [Release 8] first variable **c** second variable **c** . . .

glm dependent variable **c** = first independent variable **c** second independent variable **c** interaction **c*c**;
   means first independent variable **c** second independent variable **c** interaction **c*c**;
   brief 1.

glm dependent variable **c** = independent variable(s) **c**. . . covariate(s) **c**. . .;
   covariates c. . .;
   means independent variable(s) **c**. . . interaction(s) **c*c**;
   brief 1.

help (commands)

histogram first variable **c** second variable **c** . . .

insert first variable **c** second variable **c** . . .(into data file)

invcdf .95; (for 0.05 probability level)
   f numerator df   denominator df.
   chisquare df.

kruskal-wallis dependent variable **c** independent variable **c**

let variable **c** (or constant **k**)= expression
   +   addition
   –   subtraction
   /   division
   *   multiplication
   **   raise to a power
   absolute(c. . .)   absolute values
   sqrt(c. . .)   square root
   loge(c. . .)   base e or natural logarithm
   logten(c. . .)   base 10 logarithm

let variable **c** (row number)=new value

mann–whitney first variable **c** second variable **c**;
   alternative 1 or **−1.**

mean variable **c** as a constant **k**

mood dependent variable **c** independent variable **c**

n variable **c** as a constant **k**

name c 'variable name' **c** 'variable name'

nooutfile (ends saving outfile)

oneway dependent variable **c** independent variable **c**

outfile='listing file name'
ow=width of outfile

plot vertical axis variable **c** * horizontal axis variable **c**

print first variable **c** second variable **c** . . .(or constant **k**)

rank old variable **c** new variable **c**

read first variable **c** second variable **c** . . .(enter data)

regress criterion variable **c**   number of predictors   predictor variable(s)
c. . .

regress criterion variable **c** **1** predictor variable **c;**
  residuals store in **c;**
  fits store in **c.**

retrieve 'file name'

save 'file name'

set variable **c** (enter data)

stack one variable **c** on another variable **c** and store as another variable **c**

stdev variable **c** as a constant **k**

stepwise criterion variable **c** predictor variable(s) **c. . .;**
  enter first predictor variable **c;**
  force first predictor variable **c.**
  fremove 0.
  fenter 100000.

stest difference **c;**
  alternative 1 or $-1.$

stop (session)

sum variable **c** as a constant **k**

tinterval confidence level **95** variable **c**

ttest difference **c;**
  alternative 1 or **−1.**

ttest population mean   variable **c;**
  alternative 1 or **−1.**

twosample first variable **c** second variable **c;**
  alternative 1 or **−1;**
  pooled.

twot dependent variable **c** independent variable **c**

twoway dependent variable **c** first independent variable **c** second independent variable **c**

wtest difference **c;**
  alternative 1 or **−1.**

%fitline vertical axis variable **c** horizontal axis variable **c**

%resplots vertical axis variable **c** horizontal axis variable **c**

%vartest dependent variable **c** independent variable **c**

Macros (Release 9 onwards)

gmacro
name.**mac**
endmacro

if logical expression

and or **&**	and
or or **|**	or
not or **~**	not
eq or **=**	equal to
ne or **~=**	not equal to
le or **<=**	less than or equal to
lt or **<**	less than
ge or **>=**	greater than or equal to
gt or **>**	greater than

else logical expression
endif

comment
% macro name ending in **.mac**

APPENDIX 2: STANDARD NORMAL DISTRIBUTION

z	0.00	0.01	0.02	0.03	0.04	0.05	0.06	0.07	0.08	0.09
0.0	0.0000	0.0040	0.0080	0.0120	0.0160	0.0199	0.0239	0.0279	0.0319	0.0359
0.1	0.0398	0.0438	0.0478	0.0517	0.0557	0.0596	0.0636	0.0675	0.0714	0.0754
0.2	0.0793	0.0832	0.0871	0.0910	0.0948	0.0987	0.1026	0.1064	0.1103	0.1141
0.3	0.1179	0.1217	0.1255	0.1293	0.1331	0.1368	0.1406	0.1443	0.1480	0.1517
0.4	0.1554	0.1591	0.1628	0.1664	0.1736	0.1700	0.1772	0.1808	0.1844	0.1879
0.5	0.1915	0.1950	0.1985	0.2019	0.2054	0.2088	0.2123	0.2157	0.2190	0.2224
0.6	0.2258	0.2291	0.2324	0.2357	0.2389	0.2422	0.2454	0.2486	0.2518	0.2549
0.7	0.2580	0.2612	0.2642	0.2673	0.2704	0.2734	0.2764	0.2794	0.2823	0.2852
0.8	0.2881	0.2910	0.2939	0.2967	0.2996	0.3023	0.3051	0.3078	0.3106	0.3133
0.9	0.3159	0.3186	0.3212	0.3238	0.3264	0.3289	0.3315	0.3340	0.3365	0.3389
1.0	0.3413	0.3438	0.3461	0.3485	0.3508	0.3531	0.3554	0.3577	0.3599	0.3621
1.1	0.3643	0.3665	0.3686	0.3708	0.3729	0.3749	0.3770	0.3790	0.3810	0.3830
1.2	0.3849	0.3869	0.3888	0.3907	0.3925	0.3944	0.3962	0.3980	0.3997	0.4015
1.3	0.4032	0.4049	0.4066	0.4082	0.4099	0.4115	0.4131	0.4147	0.4162	0.4177
1.4	0.4192	0.4207	0.4222	0.4236	0.4251	0.4265	0.4279	0.4292	0.4306	0.4319
1.5	0.4332	0.4345	0.4357	0.4370	0.4382	0.4394	0.4406	0.4418	0.4429	0.4441
1.6	0.4452	0.4463	0.4474	0.4484	0.4495	0.4505	0.4515	0.4525	0.4535	0.4545
1.7	0.4554	0.4564	0.4573	0.4582	0.4591	0.4599	0.4608	0.4616	0.4625	0.4633
1.8	0.4641	0.4649	0.4656	0.4664	0.4671	0.4678	0.4686	0.4693	0.4699	0.4706
1.9	0.4713	0.4719	0.4726	0.4732	0.4738	0.4744	0.4750	0.4756	0.4761	0.4767
2.0	0.4772	0.4778	0.4783	0.4788	0.4793	0.4798	0.4803	0.4808	0.4812	0.4817
2.1	0.4821	0.4826	0.4830	0.4834	0.4838	0.4842	0.4846	0.4850	0.4854	0.4857
2.2	0.4861	0.4864	0.4868	0.4871	0.4875	0.4878	0.4881	0.4884	0.4887	0.4890
2.3	0.4893	0.4896	0.4898	0.4901	0.4904	0.4906	0.4909	0.4911	0.4913	0.4916
2.4	0.4918	0.4920	0.4922	0.4925	0.4927	0.4929	0.4931	0.4932	0.4934	0.4936
2.5	0.4938	0.4940	0.4941	0.4943	0.4945	0.4946	0.4948	0.4949	0.4951	0.4952
2.6	0.4953	0.4955	0.4956	0.4957	0.4959	0.4960	0.4961	0.4962	0.4963	0.4964
2.7	0.4965	0.4966	0.4967	0.4968	0.4969	0.4970	0.4971	0.4972	0.4973	0.4974
2.8	0.4974	0.4975	0.4976	0.4977	0.4977	0.4978	0.4979	0.4979	0.4980	0.4981
2.9	0.4981	0.4982	0.4982	0.4983	0.4984	0.4984	0.4985	0.4985	0.4986	0.4986
3.0	0.4987	0.4987	0.4987	0.4988	0.4988	0.4989	0.4989	0.4989	0.4990	0.4990
3.1	0.4990	0.4991	0.4991	0.4991	0.4992	0.4992	0.4992	0.4992	0.4992	0.4993
3.2	0.4993	0.4993	0.4994	0.4994	0.4994	0.4994	0.4994	0.4995	0.4995	0.4995
3.3	0.4995	0.4995	0.4995	0.4996	0.4996	0.4996	0.4996	0.4996	0.4996	0.4997
3.4	0.4997	0.4997	0.4997	0.4997	0.4997	0.4997	0.4997	0.4997	0.4997	0.4998
3.5	0.4998	0.4998	0.4998	0.4998	0.4998	0.4998	0.4998	0.4998	0.4998	0.4998
3.6	0.4998	0.4998	0.4999	0.4999	0.4999	0.4999	0.4999	0.4999	0.4999	0.4999
3.7	0.4999	0.4999	0.4999	0.4999	0.4999	0.4999	0.4999	0.4999	0.4999	0.4999
3.8	0.4999	0.4999	0.4999	0.4999	0.4999	0.4999	0.4999	0.4999	0.4999	0.4999
3.9	0.5000	0.5000	0.5000	0.5000	0.5000	0.5000	0.5000	0.5000	0.5000	0.5000

Note: Proportion of area from the mean (0) to z

APPENDIX 3: TWO-TAILED 0.05 VALUES OF F

df_2	df_1								
	1	2	3	4	5	6	7	8	9
1	161.45	199.50	215.71	224.58	230.16	233.99	236.77	238.88	240.54
2	18.513	19.000	19.164	19.247	19.296	19.330	19.353	19.371	19.385
3	10.128	9.5521	9.2766	9.1172	9.0135	8.9406	8.8867	8.8452	8.8323
4	7.7086	6.9443	6.5914	6.3882	6.2561	6.1631	6.0942	6.0410	5.9938
5	6.6079	5.7861	5.4095	5.1922	5.0503	4.9503	4.8759	4.8183	4.7725
6	5.9874	5.1433	4.7571	4.5337	4.3874	4.2839	4.2067	4.1468	4.0990
7	5.5914	4.7374	4.3468	4.1203	3.9715	3.8660	3.7870	3.7257	3.6767
8	5.3177	4.4590	4.0662	3.8379	3.6875	3.5806	3.5005	3.4381	3.3881
9	5.1174	4.2565	3.8625	3.6331	3.4817	3.3738	3.2927	3.2296	3.1789
10	4.9646	4.1028	3.7083	3.4780	3.3258	3.2172	3.1355	3.0717	3.0204
11	4.8443	3.9823	3.5874	3.3567	3.2039	3.0946	3.0123	2.9480	2.8962
12	4.7472	3.8853	3.4903	3.2592	3.1059	2.9961	2.9134	2.8486	2.7964
13	4.6672	3.8056	3.4105	3.1791	3.0254	2.9153	2.8321	2.7669	2.7444
14	4.6001	3.7389	3.3439	3.1122	2.9582	2.8477	2.7642	2.6987	2.6458
15	4.5431	3.6823	3.2874	3.0556	2.9013	2.7905	2.7066	2.6408	2.5876
16	4.4940	3.6337	3.2389	3.0069	2.8524	2.7413	2.6572	2.5911	2.5377
17	4.4513	3.5915	3.1968	2.9647	2.8100	2.6987	2.6143	2.5480	2.4943
18	4.4139	3.5546	3.1599	2.9277	2.7729	2.6613	2.5767	2.5102	2.4563
19	4.3807	3.5219	3.1274	2.8951	2.7401	2.6283	2.5435	2.4768	2.4227
20	4.3512	3.4928	3.0984	2.8661	2.7109	2.5990	2.5140	2.4471	2.3928
21	4.3248	3.4668	3.0725	2.8401	2.6848	2.5727	2.4876	2.4205	2.3660
22	4.3009	3.4434	3.0491	2.8167	2.6613	2.5491	2.4638	2.3965	2.3219
23	4.2793	3.4221	3.0280	2.7955	2.6400	2.5277	2.4422	2.3748	2.3201
24	4.2597	3.4028	3.0088	2.7763	2.6207	2.5082	2.4226	2.3551	2.3002
25	4.2417	3.3852	2.9912	2.7587	2.6030	2.4904	2.4047	2.3371	2.2821
26	4.2252	3.3690	2.9752	2.7426	2.5868	2.4741	2.3883	2.3205	2.2655
27	4.2100	3.3541	2.9604	2.7278	2.5719	2.4591	2.3732	2.3053	2.2501
28	4.1960	3.3404	2.9467	2.7141	2.5581	2.4453	2.3593	2.2913	2.2360
29	4.1830	3.3277	2.9340	2.7014	2.5454	2.4324	2.3463	2.2783	2.2329
30	4.1709	3.3158	2.9223	2.6896	2.5336	2.4205	2.3343	2.2662	2.2507
40	4.0847	3.2317	2.8387	2.6060	2.4495	2.3359	2.2490	2.1802	2.1240
60	4.0012	3.1504	2.7581	2.5252	2.3683	2.2541	2.1665	2.0970	2.0401
120	3.9201	3.0718	2.6802	2.4472	2.2899	2.1750	2.0868	2.0164	1.9688
∞	3.8415	2.9957	2.6049	2.3719	2.2141	2.0986	2.0096	1.9384	1.8799

APPENDIX 3: *continued*

					df_1					
10	**12**	**15**	**20**	**24**	**30**	**40**	**60**	**120**	**∞**
241.88	243.91	245.95	248.01	249.05	250.10	251.14	252.20	253.25	254.31
19.396	19.413	19.429	19.446	19.454	19.462	19.471	19.479	19.487	19.496
8.7855	8.7446	8.7029	8.6602	8.6385	8.6166	8.5944	8.5720	8.5594	8.5264
5.9644	5.9117	5.8578	5.8025	5.7744	5.7459	5.7170	5.6877	5.6381	5.6281
4.7351	4.6777	4.6188	4.5581	4.5272	4.4957	4.4638	4.4314	4.3085	4.3650
4.0600	3.9999	3.9381	3.8742	3.8415	3.8082	3.7743	3.7398	3.7047	3.6689
3.6365	3.5747	3.5107	3.4445	3.4105	3.3758	3.3404	3.3043	3.2674	3.2298
3.3472	3.2839	3.2184	3.1503	3.1152	3.0794	3.0428	3.0053	2.9669	2.9276
3.1373	3.0729	3.0061	2.9365	2.9005	2.8637	2.8259	2.7872	2.7475	2.7067
2.9782	2.9130	2.8450	2.7740	2.7372	2.6996	2.6609	2.6211	2.5801	2.5379
2.8536	2.7876	2.7186	2.6464	2.6090	2.5705	2.5309	2.4901	2.4480	2.4045
2.7534	2.6866	2.6169	2.5436	2.5055	2.4663	2.4259	2.3842	2.3410	2.2962
2.6710	2.6037	2.5331	2.4589	2.4202	2.3803	2.3392	2.2966	2.2524	2.2064
2.6022	2.5342	2.4630	2.3879	2.3487	2.3082	2.2664	2.2229	2.1778	2.1307
2.5437	2.4753	2.4034	2.3275	2.2878	2.2468	2.2043	2.1601	2.1141	2.0658
2.4935	2.4247	2.3522	2.2756	2.2354	2.1938	2.1507	2.1058	2.0589	2.0096
2.4499	2.3807	2.3077	2.2304	2.1898	2.1477	2.1040	2.0584	2.0107	1.9604
2.4117	2.3421	2.2686	2.1906	2.1497	2.1071	2.0629	2.0166	1.9681	1.9168
2.3779	2.3080	2.2341	2.1555	2.1141	2.0712	2.0264	1.9795	1.9302	1.8780
2.3479	2.2776	2.2033	2.1242	2.0825	2.0391	1.9938	1.9464	1.8963	1.8432
2.3210	2.2504	2.1757	2.0960	2.0540	2.0102	1.9645	1.9165	1.8657	1.8117
2.2967	2.2258	2.1508	2.0707	2.0283	1.9842	1.9380	1.8894	1.8380	1.7831
2.2747	2.2036	2.1282	2.0476	2.0050	1.9605	1.9139	1.8648	1.8128	1.7570
2.2547	2.1834	2.1077	2.0267	1.9838	1.9390	1.8920	1.8424	1.7896	1.7330
2.2365	2.1649	2.0889	2.0075	1.9643	1.9192	1.8718	1.8217	1.7684	1.7110
2.2197	2.1479	2.0716	1.9898	1.9464	1.9010	1.8533	1.8027	1.7488	1.6906
2.2043	2.1323	2.0558	1.9736	1.9299	1.8842	1.8361	1.7851	1.7306	1.6717
2.1900	2.1179	2.0411	1.9586	1.9147	1.8687	1.8203	1.7689	1.7138	1.6541
2.1768	2.1045	2.0275	1.9446	1.9005	1.8543	1.8055	1.7537	1.6981	1.6376
2.1646	2.0921	2.0148	1.9317	1.8874	1.8409	1.7918	1.7396	1.6835	1.6223
2.0772	2.0035	1.9245	1.8389	1.7929	1.7444	1.6928	1.6373	1.5766	1.5089
1.9926	1.9174	1.8364	1.7480	1.7001	1.6491	1.5943	1.5343	1.4673	1.3893
1.9105	1.8337	1.7505	1.6587	1.6084	1.5543	1.4952	1.4290	1.3519	1.2539
1.8307	1.7522	1.6664	1.5705	1.5173	1.4591	1.3940	1.3180	1.0214	1.0000

Source: Adapted from Merrington, M. and Thompson, C.M. (1943) 'Table of percentage points of the inverted beta (F) distribution', *Biometrika* 33: 73–88
Notes: df_1 are the degrees of freedom for the numerator; df_2 are the degrees of freedom for the denominator

APPENDIX 4: ONE-TAILED PROBABILITIES OF SMALL OBSERVED VALUES IN THE BINOMIAL TEST

N								n								
	0	1	2	3	4	5	6	7	8	9	10	11	12	13	14	15
1	0.500															
2	0.250	0.750														
3	0.125	0.500	0.875													
4	0.062	0.312	0.687	0.937												
5	0.031	0.188	0.500	0.812	0.969	*										
6	0.016	0.109	0.344	0.656	0.891	0.984	*									
7	0.008	0.062	0.227	0.500	0.773	0.938	0.992	*								
8	0.004	0.035	0.145	0.363	0.637	0.855	0.965	0.996	*							
9	0.002	0.020	0.090	0.254	0.500	0.746	0.910	0.980	0.998	*						
10	0.001	0.011	0.055	0.172	0.377	0.623	0.828	0.945	0.989	0.999	*					
11		0.006	0.033	0.113	0.274	0.500	0.726	0.887	0.967	0.994	*	*				
12		0.003	0.019	0.073	0.194	0.387	0.613	0.806	0.927	0.981	0.997	*	*			
13		0.002	0.011	0.046	0.133	0.291	0.500	0.709	0.867	0.954	0.989	0.998	*	*		
14		0.001	0.006	0.029	0.090	0.212	0.395	0.605	0.788	0.910	0.971	0.994	0.999	*	*	
15			0.004	0.018	0.059	0.151	0.304	0.500	0.696	0.849	0.941	0.982	0.996	*	*	*
16			0.002	0.011	0.038	0.105	0.227	0.402	0.598	0.773	0.895	0.962	0.989	0.998	*	*
17			0.001	0.006	0.025	0.072	0.166	0.315	0.500	0.685	0.834	0.928	0.975	0.994	0.999	*
18			0.001	0.004	0.015	0.048	0.119	0.240	0.407	0.593	0.760	0.881	0.952	0.985	0.996	0.999
19				0.002	0.010	0.032	0.084	0.180	0.324	0.500	0.676	0.820	0.916	0.968	0.990	0.998
20				0.001	0.006	0.021	0.058	0.132	0.252	0.412	0.588	0.748	0.868	0.942	0.979	0.994
21				0.001	0.004	0.013	0.039	0.095	0.192	0.332	0.500	0.668	0.808	0.905	0.961	0.987
22					0.002	0.008	0.026	0.067	0.143	0.262	0.416	0.584	0.738	0.857	0.933	0.974
23					0.001	0.005	0.017	0.047	0.105	0.202	0.339	0.500	0.661	0.798	0.895	0.953
24					0.001	0.003	0.011	0.032	0.076	0.154	0.271	0.419	0.581	0.729	0.846	0.924
25						0.002	0.007	0.022	0.054	0.115	0.212	0.345	0.500	0.655	0.788	0.885

Source: Adapted from Table IV, B of Walker, H. and Lev, J. (1953) *Statistical Inference*, New York: Holt, Rinehart & Winston, by permission of the publishers

APPENDIX 5: TWO-TAILED CRITICAL VALUES OF CHI-SQUARE

df	Level of significance		
	0.10	*0.05*	*0.01*
1	2.71	3.84	6.64
2	4.60	5.99	9.21
3	6.25	7.82	11.34
4	7.78	9.49	13.28
5	9.24	11.07	15.09
6	10.64	12.59	16.81
7	12.02	14.07	18.48
8	13.36	15.51	20.09
9	14.68	16.92	21.67
10	15.99	18.31	23.21
11	17.28	19.68	24.72
12	18.55	21.03	26.22
13	19.81	22.36	27.69
14	21.06	23.68	29.14
15	22.31	25.00	30.58
16	23.54	26.30	32.00
17	24.77	27.59	33.41
18	25.99	28.87	34.80
19	27.20	30.14	36.19
20	28.41	31.41	37.57
21	29.62	32.67	38.93
22	30.81	33.92	40.29
23	32.01	35.17	41.64
24	33.20	36.42	42.98
25	34.38	37.65	44.31
26	35.56	38.88	45.64
27	36.74	40.11	46.96
28	37.92	41.34	48.28
29	39.09	42.69	49.59
30	40.26	43.77	50.89

Source: Adapted from Table IV of Fisher, R.A. and Yates, F. (1974) *Statistical Tables for Biological, Agricultural and Medical Research*, 6th edn, London: Longman, by permission of the publishers

APPENDIX 6: 0.05 CRITICAL VALUES OF THE DUNN MULTIPLE COMPARISON TEST

No. of comparisons	df											
	5	7	10	12	15	20	24	30	40	60	120	∞
2	3.17	2.84	2.64	2.56	2.49	2.42	2.39	2.36	2.33	2.30	2.27	2.24
3	3.54	3.13	2.87	2.78	2.69	2.61	2.58	2.54	2.50	2.47	2.43	2.39
4	3.81	3.34	3.04	2.94	2.84	2.75	2.70	2.66	2.62	2.58	2.54	2.50
5	4.04	3.50	3.17	3.06	2.95	2.85	2.80	2.75	2.71	2.66	2.62	2.58
6	4.22	3.64	3.28	3.15	3.04	2.93	2.88	2.83	2.78	2.73	2.68	2.64
7	4.38	3.76	3.37	3.24	3.11	3.00	2.94	2.89	2.84	2.79	2.74	2.69
8	4.53	3.86	3.45	3.31	3.18	3.06	3.00	2.94	2.89	2.84	2.79	2.74
9	4.66	3.95	3.52	3.37	3.24	3.11	3.05	2.99	2.93	2.88	2.83	2.77
10	4.78	4.03	3.58	3.43	3.29	3.16	3.09	3.03	2.97	2.92	2.86	2.81
15	5.25	4.36	3.83	3.65	3.48	3.33	3.26	3.19	3.12	3.06	2.99	2.94
20	5.60	4.59	4.01	3.80	3.62	3.46	3.38	3.30	3.23	3.16	3.09	3.02
25	5.89	4.78	4.15	3.93	3.74	3.55	3.47	3.39	3.31	3.24	3.16	3.09
30	6.15	4.95	4.27	4.04	3.82	3.63	3.54	3.46	3.38	3.30	3.22	3.15
35	6.36	5.09	4.37	4.13	3.90	3.70	3.61	3.52	3.43	3.34	3.27	3.19
40	6.56	5.21	4.45	4.20	3.97	3.76	3.66	3.57	3.48	3.39	3.31	3.23
45	6.70	5.31	4.53	4.26	4.02	3.80	3.70	3.61	3.51	3.42	3.34	3.26
50	6.86	5.40	4.59	4.32	4.07	3.85	3.74	3.65	3.55	3.46	3.37	3.29
100	8.00	6.08	5.06	4.73	4.42	4.15	4.04	3.90	3.79	3.69	3.58	3.48
250	9.68	7.06	5.70	5.27	4.90	4.56	4.4*	4.2*	4.1*	3.97	3.83	3.72

* Obtained by graphical interpolation

Source: Adapted from Table 1 of Dunn, O. J. (1961) 'Multiple comparisons among means', *American Statistical Association Journal* 56: 52–64

APPENDIX 7: ONE-TAILED 0.05 CRITICAL VALUES OF *d* (OR *c*) IN FISHER'S TEST WHEN FREQUENCIES OF *b* (OR *a*) ARE ENTERED

Row totals		Cells	
a + b	*c + d*	*b* (or *a*)	*d* (or *c*)
3	3	3	0
4	4	4	0
	3	4	0
5	5	5	1
		4	0
	4	5	1
		4	0
	3	5	0
	2	5	0
6	6	6	2
		5	1
		4	0
	5	6	1
		5	0
		4	0
	4	6	1
		5	0
	3	6	0
		5	0
	2	6	0
7	7	7	3
		6	1
		5	0
		4	0
	6	7	2
		6	1
		5	0
		4	0
	5	7	2
		6	1
		5	0
	4	7	1
		6	0
		5	0
	3	7	0
		6	0
	2	7	0

Row totals		Cells	
a + b	*c + d*	*b* (or *a*)	*d* (or *c*)
8	8	8	4
		7	2
		6	1
		5	0
		4	0
	7	8	3
		7	2
		6	1
		5	0
	6	8	2
		7	1
		6	0
		5	0
	5	8	2
		7	1
		6	0
		5	0
	4	8	1
		7	0
		6	0
	3	8	0
		7	0
	2	8	0
9	9	9	5
		8	3
		7	2
		6	1
		5	0
		4	0
	8	9	4
		8	3
		7	2
		6	1
		5	0
	7	9	3
		8	2
		7	1
		6	0
		5	0

Row totals		Cells	
a + b	c + d	b (or a)	d (or c)
9	6	9	3
		8	2
		7	1
		6	0
		5	0
	5	9	2
		8	1
		7	0
		6	0
	4	9	1
		8	0
		7	0
		6	0
	3	9	1
		8	0
		7	0
	2	9	0
10	10	10	6
		9	4
		8	3
		7	2
		6	1
		5	0
		4	0
	9	10	5
		9	4
		8	2
		7	1
		6	1
		5	0
	8	10	4
		9	3
		8	2
		7	1
		6	0
		5	0
	7	10	3
		9	2
		8	1
		7	1
		6	0
		5	0

Row totals		Cells	
a + b	c + d	b (or a)	d (or c)
10	6	10	3
		9	2
		8	1
		7	0
		6	0
	5	10	2
		9	1
		8	1
		7	0
	4	6	0
		10	1
		9	1
		8	0
	3	7	0
		10	1
		9	0
	2	8	0
		10	0
		9	0
11	11	11	7
		10	5
		9	4
		8	3
		7	2
		6	1
		5	0
		4	0
	10	11	6
		10	4
		9	3
		8	2
		7	1
		6	1
		5	0
	9	11	5
		10	4
		9	3
		8	2
		7	1
		6	0
		5	0

Row totals		Cells		Row totals		Cells	
$a + b$	$c + d$	b (or a)	d (or c)	$a + b$	$c + d$	b (or a)	d (or c)
11	8	11	4	12	11	12	7
		10	3			11	5
		9	2			10	4
		8	1			9	3
		7	1			8	2
		6	0			7	1
		5	0			6	1
	7	11	4			5	0
		10	3		10	12	6
		9	2			11	5
		8	1			10	4
		7	0			9	3
		6	0			8	2
	6	11	3			7	1
		10	2			6	0
		9	1			5	0
		8	1		9	12	5
		7	0			11	4
		6	0			10	3
	5	11	2			9	2
		10	1			8	1
		9	1			7	1
		8	0			6	0
		7	0			5	0
	4	11	1		8	12	5
		10	1			11	3
		9	0			10	2
		8	0			9	2
	3	11	1			8	1
		10	0			7	0
		9	0			6	0
	2	11	0		7	12	4
		10	0			11	3
12	12	12	8			10	2
		11	6			9	1
		10	5			8	1
		9	4			7	0
		8	3			6	0
		7	2				
		6	1				
		5	0				
		4	0				

Row totals		Cells		Row totals		Cells	
		b	d			b	d
a + b	c + d	(or a)	(or c)	a + b	c + d	(or a)	(or c)
12	6	12	3	13	11	13	7
		11	2			12	6
		10	1			11	4
		9	1			10	3
		8	0			9	3
		7	0			8	2
		6	0			7	1
	5	12	2			6	0
		11	1			5	0
		10	1		10	13	6
		9	0			12	5
		8	0			11	4
		7	0			10	3
	4	12	2			9	2
		11	1			8	1
		10	0			7	1
		9	0			6	0
		8	0			5	0
	3	12	1		9	13	5
		11	0			12	4
		10	0			11	3
		9	0			10	2
	2	12	0			9	2
		11	0			8	1
						7	0
13	13	13	9			6	0
		12	7			5	0
		11	6		8	13	5
		10	4			12	4
		9	3			11	3
		8	2			10	2
		7	2			9	1
		6	1			8	1
		5	0			7	0
		4	0			6	0
	12	13	8		7	13	4
		12	6			12	3
		11	5			11	2
		10	4			10	1
		9	3			9	1
		8	2			8	0
		7	1			7	0
		6	1			6	0
		5	0				

Row totals		Cells		Row totals		Cells	
		b	d			b	d
a + b	c + d	(or a)	(or c)	a + b	c + d	(or a)	(or c)
13	6	13	3	14	13	14	9
		12	2			13	7
		11	2			12	6
		10	1			11	5
		9	1			10	4
		8	0			9	3
		7	0			8	2
	5	13	2			7	1
		12	2			6	1
		11	1			5	0
		10	1		12	14	8
		9	0			13	6
		8	0			12	5
	4	13	2			11	4
		12	1			10	3
		11	0			9	2
		10	0			8	2
		9	0			7	1
	3	13	1			6	0
		12	0			5	0
		11	0		11	14	7
		10	0			13	6
	2	13	0			12	5
		12	0			11	4
						10	3
14	14	14	10			9	2
		13	8			8	1
		12	6			7	1
		11	5			6	0
		10	4			5	0
		9	3		10	14	6
		8	2			13	5
		7	1			12	4
		6	1			11	3
		5	0			10	2
		4	0			9	2
						8	1
						7	0
						6	0
						5	0

Row totals		Cells		Row totals		Cells	
		b	d			b	d
a + b	c + d	(or a)	(or c)	a + b	c + d	(or a)	(or c)
14	9	14	6	14	4	14	2
		13	4			13	1
		12	3			12	1
		11	3			11	0
		10	2			10	0
		9	1			9	0
		8	1		3	14	1
		7	0			13	0
		6	0			12	0
	8	14	5			11	0
		13	4		2	14	0
		12	3			13	0
		11	2			12	0
		10	2				
		9	1	15	15	15	11
		8	0			14	9
		7	0			13	7
		6	0			12	6
	7	14	4			11	5
		13	3			10	4
		12	2			9	3
		11	2			8	2
		10	1			7	1
		9	1			6	1
		8	0			5	0
		7	0			4	0
	6	14	3		14	15	10
		13	2			14	8
		12	2			13	7
		11	1			12	6
		10	1			11	5
		9	0			10	4
		8	0			9	3
		7	0			8	2
	5	14	2			7	1
		13	2			6	1
		12	1			5	0
		11	1				
		10	0				
		9	0				
		8	0				

Row totals		Cells		Row totals		Cells	
		b	d			b	d
a + b	c + d	(or a)	(or c)	a + b	c + d	(or a)	(or c)
15	13	15	9	15	9	15	6
		14	7			14	5
		13	6			13	4
		12	5			12	3
		11	4			11	2
		10	3			10	2
		9	2			9	1
		8	2			8	1
		7	1			7	0
		6	0			6	0
		5	0		8	15	5
	12	15	8			14	4
		14	7			13	3
		13	6			12	2
		12	5			11	2
		11	4			10	1
		10	3			9	1
		9	2			8	0
		8	1			7	0
		7	1			6	0
		6	0		7	15	4
		5	0			14	3
	11	15	7			13	2
		14	6			12	2
		13	5			11	1
		12	4			10	1
		11	3			9	0
		10	2			8	0
		9	2			7	0
		8	1		6	15	3
		7	1			14	2
		6	0			13	2
		5	0			12	1
	10	15	6			11	1
		14	5			10	0
		13	4			9	0
		12	3			8	0
		11	3		5	15	2
		10	2			14	2
		9	1			13	1
		8	1			12	1
		7	0			11	0
		6	0			10	0
						9	0

Row totals		Cells	
		b	d
a + b	c + d	(or a)	(or c)
15	4	15	2
		14	1
		13	1
		12	0
		11	0
		10	0
	3	15	1
		14	0
		13	0
		12	0
		11	0
	2	15	0
		14	0
		13	0

Source: Adapted from Finney, D.J. (1948) 'The Fisher–Yates test of significance in 2 × 2 contingency tables', *Biometrika* 35, pp. 149–54

APPENDIX 8: TWO-TAILED CRITICAL VALUES OF THE LARGEST DIFFERENCE IN THE KOLMOGOROV-SMIRNOV ONE-SAMPLE TEST

N	0.10	0.05
1	0.950	0.975
2	0.776	0.842
3	0.642	0.708
4	0.564	0.624
5	0.510	0.565
6	0.470	0.521
7	0.438	0.486
8	0.411	0.457
9	0.388	0.432
10	0.368	0.410
11	0.352	0.391
12	0.338	0.375
13	0.325	0.361
14	0.314	0.349
15	0.304	0.338
16	0.295	0.328
17	0.286	0.318
18	0.278	0.309
19	0.272	0.301
20	0.264	0.294
25	0.24	0.27
30	0.22	0.24
35	0.21	0.23
36+	$\dfrac{1.22}{\sqrt{N}}$	$\dfrac{1.36}{\sqrt{N}}$

Source: Adapted from F. J. Massey, Jr. (1951) 'The Kolmogorov-Smirnov test for goodness of fit', Journal of the American Statistical Association 46: 70

APPENDIX 9: ONE-TAILED 0.05 CRITICAL VALUES OF THE KOLMOGOROV-SMIRNOV TEST FOR SMALL SAMPLES

	n_1																						
n_2	3	4	5	6	7	8	9	10	11	12	13	14	15	16	17	18	19	20	21	22	23	24	25
3	9	10	13	15	16	19	21	22	25	27	28	31	33	34	35	39	40	41	45	46	47	51	52
4	10	16	16	18	21	24	25	28	29	36	33	38	38	44	44	46	49	52	52	56	57	60	61
5	13	16	20	21	24	26	28	35	35	36	40	42	50	46	49	51	56	60	60	62	65	67	75
6	15	18	21	30	25	30	33	36	38	48	43	48	51	54	56	61	56	66	69	70	73	78	78
7	16	21	24	25	35	34	36	40	43	45	50	56	56	58	61	64	68	72	77	77	79	83	85
8	19	24	26	30	34	40	40	44	48	52	53	58	60	72	65	72	73	80	81	84	89	96	95
9	21	25	28	33	36	40	54	46	51	57	57	63	69	68	74	81	80	83	90	91	94	99	101
10	22	28	35	36	40	44	46	60	57	60	62	68	75	76	77	82	85	100	91	98	101	106	110
11	25	29	35	38	43	48	51	57	66	64	67	72	76	80	83	87	92	95	101	110	108	111	116
12	27	36	36	48	45	52	57	60	64	72	71	78	84	88	89	96	98	104	108	110	112	124	120
13	28	33	40	43	50	53	57	62	67	71	78	78	91	90	94	98	102	108	112	117	120	124	131
14	31	38	42	48	56	58	63	68	72	78	78	92	105	101	109	104	108	114	126	130	126	132	136
15	33	38	50	51	56	60	69	75	76	84	91	105	101	112	109	113	125	125	126	130	134	141	145
16	34	44	46	54	58	72	68	76	80	88	90	101	112	109	116	120	128	128	130	136	140	152	148
17	35	44	49	56	61	65	74	77	83	89	94	109	109	116	118	125	130	130	135	141	146	150	156
18	39	46	51	61	64	72	81	82	87	96	98	104	113	120	125	127	144	136	144	148	151	162	161
19	40	49	56	56	68	73	80	85	92	98	102	108	125	128	130	144	152	144	147	151	159	162	168
20	41	52	60	66	72	80	83	100	95	104	108	114	125	128	130	136	144	152	154	160	163	162	180
21	45	52	60	69	77	81	90	91	101	108	112	126	126	130	135	144	147	154	168	160	163	172	182
22	46	56	62	70	77	84	91	98	110	110	117	130	130	136	141	148	151	160	160	163	173	182	188
23	47	57	65	73	79	89	94	101	108	112	120	126	134	140	146	151	159	163	163	173	207	183	194
24	51	60	67	78	83	96	99	106	111	124	124	132	141	152	150	162	162	162	172	182	183	216	204
25	52	61	75	78	85	95	101	110	116	120	131	136	145	148	156	161	168	180	182	188	194	204	225

Source: Adapted from Gail, M. H. and Green, S. B. (1976) 'Critical values for the one-sided two-sample Kolmogorov-Smirnov statistic', *Journal of the American Statistical Association* 71: 757–60

APPENDIX 10: TWO-TAILED 0.05 CRITICAL VALUES OF THE KOLMOGOROV-SMIRNOV TEST FOR SMALL SAMPLES

n_1

n_2	2	3	4	5	6	7	8	9	10	11	12	13	14	15	16	17	18	19	20	21	22	23	24	25
2							16	18	20	22	24	26	26	28	30	32	34	36	38	38	40	42	44	46
3				15	18	21	21	24	27	30	30	33	36	36	39	42	45	45	48	51	51	54	57	60
4			16	20	24	28	28	28	30	33	36	39	42	44	48	48	50	53	60	59	62	64	68	68
5		15	20	25	30	28	30	35	40	39	43	45	46	55	54	55	60	61	65	69	70	72	76	80
6		18	20	24	30	30	34	39	40	43	48	52	54	57	60	62	72	70	72	75	78	80	90	88
7		21	24	28	34	42	40	42	46	48	53	56	63	62	64	68	72	76	79	91	84	89	92	97
8	16	21	28	30	39	40	48	46	48	53	60	62	64	67	80	77	80	82	88	89	94	98	104	104
9	18	24	28	35	40	42	46	54	53	59	63	65	70	75	78	82	90	89	93	99	101	106	111	114
10	20	27	30	40	43	46	48	53	70	60	66	70	74	80	84	89	92	94	110	105	108	114	118	125
11	22	30	33	39	48	48	53	59	60	77	72	75	82	84	89	93	97	102	107	112	121	119	124	129
12	24	30	36	43	52	53	60	63	66	72	84	81	86	93	96	100	108	116	116	124	125	144	144	138
13	26	33	39	45	54	56	62	65	70	75	81	91	89	96	101	105	110	114	120	126	130	135	140	145
14	26	36	42	46	57	63	64	70	74	82	86	89	112	98	106	111	116	121	126	140	138	142	146	150
15	28	36	44	55	60	62	67	75	80	84	93	96	98	120	114	116	123	127	135	138	144	149	156	160
16	30	39	48	54	62	64	80	78	84	89	100	101	106	114	128	124	128	133	140	145	150	157	168	167
17	32	42	48	55	64	68	77	82	89	93	108	105	111	116	124	136	133	141	146	151	157	163	168	173
18	34	45	50	60	70	72	80	90	92	97	108	110	116	123	128	133	162	142	152	159	164	170	180	180
19	36	45	53	61	72	76	82	89	94	102	116	114	121	127	133	141	142	171	160	163	169	177	183	187
20	38	48	60	65	75	79	88	93	110	107	120	120	126	135	140	146	152	160	180	173	176	184	192	200
21	38	51	59	69	78	91	89	99	105	112	124	126	140	138	145	151	159	163	173	189	183	189	198	202
22	40	51	62	70	80	84	94	101	108	121	125	130	138	144	150	157	164	169	176	183	198	194	204	209
23	42	54	64	72	88	89	98	106	114	119	144	135	142	149	157	163	170	177	184	189	194	230	205	216
24	44	57	68	76	90	92	104	111	118	124	144	140	146	156	168	168	180	183	192	198	204	205	240	225
25	46	60	68	80	88	97	104	114	125	129	138	145	150	160	167	173	180	187	200	202	209	216	225	250

Source: Adapted from Table 51 of Pearson, E. S. and Hartley, H. O. (1972) *Biometrika Tables for Statisticians*, vol. 2, Cambridge University Press, New York, by permission of the publishers

APPENDIX 11: TWO-TAILED CRITICAL VALUES OF THE KOLMOGOROV-SMIRNOV TEST FOR LARGE SAMPLES

Significance level	D
0.10	$1.22 \sqrt{\dfrac{n_1 + n_2}{n_1 \times n_2}}$
0.05	$1.36 \sqrt{\dfrac{n_1 + n_2}{n_1 \times n_2}}$
0.025	$1.48 \sqrt{\dfrac{n_1 + n_2}{n_1 \times n_2}}$
0.01	$1.63 \sqrt{\dfrac{n_1 + n_2}{n_1 \times n_2}}$
0.005	$1.73 \sqrt{\dfrac{n_1 + n_2}{n_1 \times n_2}}$
0.001	$1.95 \sqrt{\dfrac{n_1 + n_2}{n_1 \times n_2}}$

Source: Adapted from Smirnov, N. (1948) 'Tables for estimating the goodness of fit of empirical distributions', *Annals of Mathematical Statistics* 19: 280–1

APPENDIX 12: CRITICAL VALUES OF U AT 0.05 ONE-TAILED LEVEL AND 0.10 TWO-TAILED LEVEL

n_1

n_2	1	2	3	4	5	6	7	8	9	10	11	12	13	14	15	16	17	18	19	20
1	–	–	–	–	–	–	–	–	–	–	–	–	–	–	–	–	–	–	0	0
2	–	–	–	–	0	0	0	1	1	1	1	2	2	2	3	3	3	4	4	4
3	–	–	0	0	1	2	2	3	3	4	5	5	6	7	7	8	9	9	10	11
4	–	–	0	1	2	3	4	5	6	7	8	9	10	11	12	14	15	16	17	18
5	–	0	1	2	4	5	6	8	9	11	12	13	15	16	18	19	20	22	23	25
6	–	0	2	3	5	7	8	10	12	14	16	17	19	21	23	25	26	28	30	32
7	–	0	2	4	6	8	11	13	15	17	19	21	24	26	28	30	33	35	37	39
8	–	1	3	5	8	10	13	15	18	20	23	26	28	31	33	36	39	41	44	47
9	–	1	3	6	9	12	15	18	21	24	27	30	33	36	39	42	45	48	51	54
10	–	1	4	7	11	14	17	20	24	27	31	34	37	41	44	48	51	55	58	62
11	–	1	5	8	12	16	19	23	27	31	34	38	42	46	50	54	57	61	65	69
12	–	2	5	9	13	17	21	26	30	34	38	42	47	51	55	60	64	68	72	77
13	–	2	6	10	15	19	24	28	33	37	42	47	51	56	61	65	70	75	80	84
14	–	2	7	11	16	21	26	31	36	41	46	51	56	61	66	71	77	82	87	92
15	–	3	7	12	18	23	28	33	39	44	50	55	61	66	72	77	83	88	94	100
16	–	3	8	14	19	25	30	36	42	48	54	60	65	71	77	83	89	95	101	107
17	–	3	9	15	20	26	33	39	45	51	57	64	70	77	83	89	96	102	109	115
18	–	4	9	16	22	28	35	41	48	55	61	68	75	82	88	95	102	109	116	123
19	0	4	10	17	23	30	37	44	51	58	65	72	80	87	94	101	109	116	123	130
20	0	4	11	18	25	32	39	47	54	62	69	77	84	92	100	107	115	123	130	138

Source: Adapted from Table I of Runyon, R.P. and Haber, A. (1991) Fundamentals of Behavioral Statistics (7th edn), McGraw–Hill, New York, by permission of the publishers

APPENDIX 13: CRITICAL VALUES OF U AT 0.025 ONE-TAILED LEVEL AND 0.05 TWO-TAILED LEVEL

n_1

n_2	1	2	3	4	5	6	7	8	9	10	11	12	13	14	15	16	17	18	19	20
1	—	—	—	—	—	—	—	—	—	—	—	—	—	—	—	—	—	—	—	—
2	—	—	—	—	—	—	—	0	0	0	0	1	1	1	1	1	2	2	2	2
3	—	—	—	—	0	1	1	2	2	3	3	4	4	5	5	6	6	7	7	8
4	—	—	—	0	1	2	3	4	4	5	6	7	8	9	10	11	11	12	13	13
5	—	—	0	1	2	3	5	6	7	8	9	11	12	13	14	15	17	18	19	20
6	—	—	1	2	3	5	6	8	10	11	13	14	16	17	19	21	22	24	25	27
7	—	—	1	3	5	6	8	10	12	14	16	18	20	22	24	26	28	30	32	34
8	—	0	2	4	6	8	10	13	15	17	19	22	24	26	29	31	34	36	38	41
9	—	0	2	4	7	10	12	15	17	20	23	26	28	31	34	37	39	42	45	48
10	—	0	3	5	8	11	14	17	20	23	26	29	33	36	39	42	45	48	52	55
11	—	0	3	6	9	13	16	19	23	26	30	33	37	40	44	47	51	55	58	62
12	—	1	4	7	11	14	18	22	26	29	33	37	41	45	49	53	57	61	65	69
13	—	1	4	8	12	16	20	24	28	33	37	41	45	50	54	59	63	67	72	76
14	—	1	5	9	13	17	22	26	31	36	40	45	50	55	59	64	67	74	78	83
15	—	1	5	10	14	19	24	29	34	39	44	49	54	59	64	70	75	80	85	90
16	—	1	6	11	15	21	26	31	37	42	47	53	59	64	70	75	81	86	92	98
17	—	2	6	11	17	22	28	34	39	45	51	57	63	67	75	81	87	93	99	105
18	—	2	7	12	18	24	30	36	42	48	55	61	67	74	80	86	93	99	106	112
19	—	2	7	13	19	25	32	38	45	52	58	65	72	78	85	92	99	106	113	119
20	—	2	8	13	20	27	34	41	48	55	62	69	76	83	90	98	105	112	119	127

Source: Adapted from Table I of Runyon, R.P. and Haber, A. (1991) *Fundamentals of Behavioral Statistics* (7th edn), McGraw-Hill, New York, by permission of the publishers

APPENDIX 14: TWO-TAILED CRITICAL VALUES OF *T* FOR THE WILCOXON TEST

N	Significance level			N	Significance level		
	0.10	0.05	0.02		0.10	0.05	0.02
5	0	—	—	28	130	116	101
6	2	0	—	29	140	126	110
7	3	2	0	30	151	137	120
8	5	3	1	31	163	147	130
9	8	5	3	32	175	159	140
10	10	8	5	33	187	170	151
11	13	10	7	34	200	182	162
12	17	13	9	35	213	195	173
13	21	17	12	36	227	208	185
14	25	21	15	37	241	221	198
15	30	25	19	38	256	235	211
16	35	29	23	39	271	249	224
17	41	34	27	40	286	264	238
18	47	40	32	41	302	279	252
19	53	46	37	42	319	294	266
20	60	52	43	43	336	310	281
21	67	58	49	44	353	327	296
22	75	65	55	45	371	343	312
23	83	73	62	46	389	361	328
24	91	81	69	47	407	378	345
25	100	89	76	48	426	396	362
26	110	98	84	49	446	415	379
27	119	107	92	50	466	434	397

Source: Adapted from Table I of Wilcoxon, F. (1949) *Some Rapid Approximate Statistical Procedures*, American Cyanamid Company, New York, by permission of the publishers

APPENDIX 15: TWO-TAILED CRITICAL VALUES OF *t*

df	Significance level		
	0.10	*0.05*	*0.02*
1	6.314	12.706	31.821
2	2.920	4.303	6.965
3	2.353	3.182	4.541
4	2.132	2.776	3.747
5	2.015	2.571	3.365
6	1.943	2.447	3.143
7	1.895	2.365	2.998
8	1.860	2.306	2.896
9	1.833	2.262	2.821
10	1.812	2.228	2.764
11	1.796	2.201	2.718
12	1.782	2.179	2.681
13	1.771	2.160	2.650
14	1.761	2.145	2.624
15	1.753	2.131	2.602
16	1.746	2.120	2.583
17	1.740	2.110	2.567
18	1.734	2.101	2.552
19	1.729	2.093	2.539
20	1.725	2.086	2.528
21	1.721	2.080	2.518
22	1.717	2.074	2.508
23	1.714	2.069	2.500
24	1.711	2.064	2.492
25	1.708	2.060	2.485
26	1.706	2.056	2.479
27	1.703	2.052	2.473
28	1.701	2.048	2.467
29	1.699	2.045	2.462
30	1.697	2.042	2.457
40	1.684	2.021	2.423
60	1.671	2.000	2.390
120	1.658	1.980	2.358
∞	1.645	1.960	2.326

Source: Adapted from Table III of Fisher, R. A. and Yates, F. (1974) *Statistical Tables for Biological, Agricultural and Medical Research* (6th edn), Longman, London, by permission of the publishers

APPENDIX 16: TWO-TAILED 0.5 CRITICAL VALUES OF F_{max}

$n-1$	Number of groups								
	2	3	4	5	6	7	8	9	10
4	9.60	15.5	20.6	25.2	29.5	33.6	37.5	41.4	44.6
5	7.15	10.8	13.7	16.3	18.7	20.8	22.9	24.7	26.5
6	5.82	8.38	10.4	12.1	13.7	15.0	16.3	17.5	18.6
7	4.99	6.94	8.44	9.70	10.8	11.8	12.7	13.5	14.3
8	4.43	6.00	7.18	8.12	9.03	9.78	10.5	11.1	11.7
9	4.03	5.34	6.31	7.11	7.80	8.41	8.95	9.45	9.91
10	3.72	4.85	5.67	6.34	6.92	7.42	7.87	8.28	8.66
12	3.28	4.16	4.79	5.30	5.72	6.09	6.42	6.72	7.00
15	2.86	3.54	4.01	4.37	4.68	4.95	5.19	5.40	5.59
20	2.46	2.95	3.29	3.54	3.76	3.94	4.10	4.24	4.37
30	2.07	2.40	2.61	2.78	2.91	3.02	3.12	3.21	3.29
60	1.67	1.85	1.96	2.04	2.11	2.17	2.22	2.26	2.30
∞	1.00	1.00	1.00	1.00	1.00	1.00	1.00	1.00	1.00

Source: Adapted from Table 31 of Pearson, E.S. and Hartley, H.O. (1958) *Biometrika Tables for Statisticians*, vol. 1, 2nd edn, New York: Cambridge University Press, by permission of the publishers

APPENDIX 17: TWO-TAILED 0.05 CRITICAL VALUES OF COCHRAN'S C

$n-1$	Number of groups										
	2	3	4	5	6	7	8	9	10	15	20
1	0.9985	0.9669	0.9065	0.8412	0.7808	0.7271	0.6798	0.6385	0.6020	0.4709	0.3894
2	0.9750	0.8709	0.7679	0.6838	0.6161	0.5612	0.5157	0.4775	0.4450	0.3346	0.2705
3	0.9392	0.7977	0.6841	0.5981	0.5321	0.4800	0.4377	0.4027	0.3733	0.2758	0.2205
4	0.9057	0.7457	0.6287	0.5441	0.4803	0.4307	0.3910	0.3584	0.3311	0.2419	0.1921
5	0.8772	0.7071	0.5895	0.5065	0.4447	0.3974	0.3595	0.3286	0.3029	0.2195	0.1735
6	0.8534	0.6771	0.5598	0.4783	0.4184	0.3726	0.3362	0.3067	0.2823	0.2034	0.1602
7	0.8332	0.6530	0.5365	0.4564	0.3980	0.3535	0.3185	0.2901	0.2666	0.1911	0.1501
8	0.8159	0.6333	0.5175	0.4387	0.3817	0.3384	0.3043	0.2768	0.2541	0.1815	0.1422
9	0.8010	0.6167	0.5017	0.4241	0.3682	0.3259	0.2926	0.2659	0.2439	0.1736	0.1357
16	0.7341	0.5466	0.4366	0.3645	0.3135	0.2756	0.2462	0.2226	0.2032	0.1429	0.1108
36	0.6602	0.4748	0.3720	0.3066	0.2612	0.2278	0.2022	0.1820	0.1655	0.1144	0.0879
144	0.5813	0.4031	0.3093	0.2513	0.2119	0.1833	0.1616	0.1446	0.1308	0.0889	0.0675

Source: Adapted from Eisenhart, C., Hastay, M. W. and Wallis, A. (1947) *Techniques of Statistical Analysis*, McGraw-Hill, New York, by permission of the publishers

APPENDIX 18: TWO-TAILED 0.05 CRITICAL VALUES OF THE BRYANT-PAULSON PROCEDURE

Error df	Number of covariates	Number of groups										
		2	3	4	5	6	7	8	10	12	16	20
3	1	5.42	7.18	8.32	9.17	9.84	10.39	10.86	11.62	12.22	13.14	13.83
	2	6.21	8.27	9.60	10.59	11.37	12.01	12.56	13.44	14.15	15.22	16.02
	3	6.92	9.23	10.73	11.84	12.72	13.44	14.06	15.05	15.84	17.05	17.95
4	1	4.51	5.84	6.69	7.32	7.82	8.23	8.58	9.15	9.61	10.30	10.82
	2	5.04	6.54	7.51	8.23	8.80	9.26	9.66	10.31	10.83	11.61	12.21
	3	5.51	7.18	8.25	9.05	9.67	10.19	10.63	11.35	11.92	12.79	13.45
5	1	4.06	5.17	5.88	6.40	6.82	7.16	7.45	7.93	8.30	8.88	9.32
	2	4.45	5.68	6.48	7.06	7.52	7.90	8.23	8.76	9.18	9.83	10.31
	3	4.81	6.16	7.02	7.66	8.17	8.58	8.94	9.52	9.98	10.69	11.22
6	1	3.79	4.78	5.40	5.86	6.23	6.53	6.78	7.20	7.53	8.04	8.43
	2	4.10	5.18	5.87	6.37	6.77	7.10	7.38	7.84	8.21	8.77	9.20
	3	4.38	5.55	6.30	6.84	7.28	7.64	7.94	8.44	8.83	9.44	9.90
7	1	3.62	4.52	5.09	5.51	5.84	6.11	6.34	6.72	7.03	7.49	7.84
	2	3.87	4.85	5.47	5.92	6.28	6.58	6.83	7.24	7.57	8.08	8.46
	3	4.11	5.16	5.82	6.31	6.70	7.01	7.29	7.73	8.08	8.63	9.03
8	1	3.49	4.34	4.87	5.26	5.57	5.82	6.03	6.39	6.67	7.10	7.43
	2	3.70	4.61	5.19	5.61	5.94	6.21	6.44	6.82	7.12	7.59	7.94
	3	3.91	4.88	5.49	5.93	6.29	6.58	6.83	7.23	7.55	8.05	8.42
10	1	3.32	4.10	4.58	4.93	5.21	5.43	5.63	5.94	6.19	6.58	6.87
	2	3.49	4.31	4.82	5.19	5.49	5.73	5.93	6.27	6.54	6.95	7.26
	3	3.65	4.51	5.05	5.44	5.75	6.01	6.22	6.58	6.86	7.29	7.62
12	1	3.22	3.95	4.40	4.73	4.98	5.19	5.37	5.67	5.90	6.26	6.53
	2	3.35	4.12	4.59	4.93	5.20	5.43	5.62	5.92	6.17	6.55	6.83
	3	3.48	4.28	4.78	5.14	5.42	5.65	5.85	6.17	6.43	6.82	7.12
14	1	3.15	3.85	4.28	4.59	4.83	5.03	5.20	5.48	5.70	6.03	6.29
	2	3.26	3.99	4.44	4.76	5.01	5.22	5.40	5.69	5.92	6.27	6.54

Source: Adapted from Bryant, J. L. and Paulson, A. S. (1976) 'An extension of Tukey's method of multiple comparisons to experimental designs with random concomitant variables', *Biometrika* 63, 631–638

Error df	Number of covariates	Number of groups										
		2	3	4	5	6	7	8	10	12	16	20
16	3	3.37	4.13	4.59	4.93	5.19	5.41	5.59	5.89	6.13	6.50	6.78
	1	3.10	3.77	4.19	4.49	4.72	4.91	5.07	5.34	5.55	5.87	6.12
	2	3.19	3.90	4.32	4.63	4.88	5.07	5.24	5.52	5.74	6.07	6.33
	3	3.29	4.01	4.46	4.78	5.03	5.23	5.41	5.69	5.92	6.27	6.53
18	1	3.06	3.72	4.12	4.41	4.63	4.82	4.98	5.23	5.44	5.75	5.98
	2	3.14	3.82	4.24	4.54	4.77	4.96	5.13	5.39	5.60	5.92	6.17
	3	3.23	3.93	4.35	4.66	4.90	5.10	5.27	5.54	5.76	6.09	6.34
20	1	3.03	3.67	4.07	4.35	4.57	4.75	4.90	5.15	5.35	5.65	5.88
	2	3.10	3.77	4.17	4.46	4.69	4.88	5.03	5.29	5.49	5.81	6.04
	3	3.18	3.86	4.28	4.57	4.81	5.00	5.16	5.42	5.63	5.96	6.20
24	1	2.98	3.61	3.99	4.26	4.47	4.65	4.79	5.03	5.22	5.51	5.73
	2	3.04	3.69	4.08	4.35	4.57	4.75	4.90	5.14	5.34	5.63	5.86
	3	3.11	3.76	4.16	4.44	4.67	4.85	5.00	5.25	5.45	5.75	5.98
30	1	2.94	3.55	3.91	4.18	4.38	4.54	4.69	4.91	5.09	5.37	5.58
	2	2.99	3.61	3.98	4.25	4.46	4.62	4.77	5.00	5.18	5.46	5.68
	3	3.04	3.67	4.05	4.32	4.53	4.70	4.85	5.08	5.27	5.56	5.78
40	1	2.89	3.49	3.84	4.09	4.29	4.45	4.58	4.80	4.97	5.23	5.43
	2	2.93	3.53	3.89	4.15	4.34	4.50	4.64	4.86	5.04	5.30	5.50
	3	2.97	3.57	3.94	4.20	4.40	4.56	4.70	4.92	5.10	5.37	5.57
60	1	2.85	3.43	3.77	4.01	4.20	4.35	4.48	4.69	4.85	5.10	5.29
	2	2.88	3.46	3.80	4.05	4.24	4.39	4.52	4.73	4.89	5.14	5.33
	3	2.90	3.49	3.83	4.08	4.27	4.43	4.56	4.77	4.93	5.19	5.38
120	1	2.81	3.37	3.70	3.93	4.11	4.26	4.38	4.58	4.73	4.97	5.15
	2	2.82	3.38	3.72	3.95	4.13	4.28	4.40	4.60	4.75	4.99	5.17
	3	2.84	3.40	3.73	3.97	4.15	4.30	4.42	4.62	4.77	5.01	5.19

APPENDIX 19: TWO-TAILED CRITICAL VALUES OF SPEARMAN'S rho

N	Significance level	
	0.10	0.05
5	0.900	1.000
6	0.829	0.886
7	0.715	0.786
8	0.620	0.715
9	0.600	0.700
10	0.564	0.649
11	0.537	0.619
12	0.504	0.588
13	0.484	0.561
14	0.464	0.539
15	0.447	0.522
16	0.430	0.503
17	0.415	0.488
18	0.402	0.474
19	0.392	0.460
20	0.381	0.447
21	0.371	0.437
22	0.361	0.426
23	0.353	0.417
24	0.345	0.407
25	0.337	0.399
26	0.331	0.391
27	0.325	0.383
28	0.319	0.376
29	0.312	0.369
30	0.307	0.363

Source: Adapted from Glasser, G. J. and Winter, R. F. (1961) 'Critical values of the coefficient of rank correlation for testing the hypothesis of independence', Biometrika 48, 444–8

APPENDIX 20: ONE-TAILED CRITICAL VALUES OF KENDALL'S PARTIAL RANK-ORDER CORRELATION

N	0.05	0.025
4	0.707	1.000
5	0.667	0.802
6	0.600	0.667
7	0.527	0.617
8	0.484	0.565
9	0.443	0.515
10	0.413	0.480
11	0.387	0.453
12	0.465	0.430
13	0.347	0.410
14	0.331	0.391
15	0.319	0.377
16	0.305	0.361
17	0.294	0.348
18	0.284	0.336
19	0.275	0.326
20	0.268	0.318
25	0.236	0.279
30	0.213	0.253
35	0.196	0.232
40	0.182	0.216
45	0.171	0.203
50	0.161	0.192
60	0.147	0.174
70	0.135	0.160
80	0.126	0.150
90	0.119	0.141

Source: Adapted from Maghsoodloo, S. (1975) 'Estimates of the quantiles of Kendall's partial rank correlation coefficient', *Journal of Statistical Computing and Simulation*, 4, 155–64; Maghsoodloo, S. and Pallos, L.L. (1981) 'Asymptotic behavior of Kendall's partial rank correlation coefficient and additional quantile estimates', *Journal of Statistical Computing and Simulation*, 13, 41–8

APPENDIX 21: TWO-TAILED CRITICAL VALUES OF PEARSON'S r

$N-2$	Significance level	
	0.10	0.05
1	0.9877	0.9969
2	0.9000	0.9500
3	0.8054	0.8783
4	0.7293	0.8114
5	0.6694	0.7545
6	0.6215	0.7067
7	0.5822	0.6664
8	0.5494	0.6319
9	0.5214	0.6021
10	0.4973	0.5760
11	0.4762	0.5529
12	0.4575	0.5324
13	0.4409	0.5139
14	0.4259	0.4973
15	0.4124	0.4821
16	0.4000	0.4683
17	0.3887	0.4555
18	0.3783	0.4438
19	0.3687	0.4329
20	0.3598	0.4227
25	0.3233	0.3809
30	0.2960	0.3494
35	0.2746	0.3246
40	0.2573	0.3044
45	0.2428	0.2875
50	0.2306	0.2732
60	0.2108	0.2500
70	0.1954	0.2319
80	0.1829	0.2172
90	0.1726	0.2050
100	0.1638	0.1946

Source: Adapted from Table VII of Fisher, R. A. and Yates, F. (1974) *Statistical Tables for Biological, Agricultural and Medical Research* (6th edn), Longman, London, by permission of the publishers

APPENDIX 22: TRANSFORMATION OF PEARSON'S r TO Z_r

r	Z_r	r	Z_r	r	Z_r	r	Z_r	r	Z_r
0.000	0.000	0.200	0.203	0.400	0.424	0.600	0.693	0.800	1.099
0.005	0.005	0.205	0.208	0.405	0.430	0.605	0.701	0.805	1.113
0.010	0.010	0.210	0.213	0.410	0.436	0.610	0.709	0.810	1.127
0.015	0.015	0.215	0.218	0.415	0.442	0.615	0.717	0.815	1.142
0.020	0.020	0.220	0.224	0.420	0.448	0.620	0.725	0.820	1.157
0.025	0.025	0.225	0.229	0.425	0.454	0.625	0.733	0.825	1.172
0.030	0.030	0.230	0.234	0.430	0.460	0.630	0.741	0.830	1.188
0.035	0.035	0.235	0.239	0.435	0.466	0.635	0.750	0.835	1.204
0.040	0.040	0.240	0.245	0.440	0.472	0.640	0.758	0.840	1.221
0.045	0.045	0.245	0.250	0.445	0.478	0.645	0.767	0.845	1.238
0.050	0.050	0.250	0.255	0.450	0.485	0.650	0.775	0.850	1.256
0.055	0.055	0.255	0.261	0.455	0.491	0.655	0.784	0.855	1.274
0.060	0.060	0.260	0.266	0.460	0.497	0.660	0.793	0.860	1.293
0.065	0.065	0.265	0.271	0.465	0.504	0.665	0.802	0.865	1.313
0.070	0.070	0.270	0.277	0.470	0.510	0.670	0.811	0.870	1.333
0.075	0.075	0.275	0.282	0.475	0.517	0.675	0.820	0.875	1.354
0.080	0.080	0.280	0.288	0.480	0.523	0.680	0.829	0.880	1.376
0.085	0.085	0.285	0.293	0.485	0.530	0.685	0.838	0.885	1.398
0.090	0.090	0.290	0.299	0.490	0.536	0.690	0.848	0.890	1.422
0.095	0.095	0.295	0.304	0.495	0.543	0.695	0.858	0.895	1.447
0.100	0.100	0.300	0.310	0.500	0.549	0.700	0.867	0.900	1.472
0.105	0.105	0.305	0.315	0.505	0.556	0.705	0.877	0.905	1.499
0.110	0.110	0.310	0.321	0.510	0.563	0.710	0.887	0.910	1.528
0.115	0.116	0.315	0.326	0.515	0.570	0.715	0.897	0.915	1.557
0.120	0.121	0.320	0.332	0.520	0.576	0.720	0.908	0.920	1.589
0.125	0.126	0.325	0.337	0.525	0.583	0.725	0.918	0.925	1.623
0.130	0.131	0.330	0.343	0.530	0.590	0.730	0.929	0.930	1.658
0.135	0.136	0.335	0.348	0.535	0.597	0.735	0.940	0.935	1.697
0.140	0.141	0.340	0.354	0.540	0.604	0.740	0.950	0.940	1.738
0.145	0.146	0.345	0.360	0.545	0.611	0.745	0.962	0.945	1.783
0.150	0.151	0.350	0.365	0.550	0.618	0.750	0.973	0.950	1.832
0.155	0.156	0.355	0.371	0.555	0.626	0.755	0.984	0.955	1.886
0.160	0.161	0.360	0.377	0.560	0.633	0.760	0.996	0.960	1.946
0.165	0.167	0.365	0.383	0.565	0.640	0.765	1.008	0.965	2.014
0.170	0.172	0.370	0.388	0.570	0.648	0.770	1.020	0.970	2.092
0.175	0.177	0.375	0.394	0.575	0.655	0.775	1.033	0.975	2.185
0.180	0.182	0.380	0.400	0.580	0.662	0.780	1.045	0.980	2.298
0.185	0.187	0.385	0.406	0.585	0.670	0.785	1.058	0.985	2.443
0.190	0.192	0.390	0.412	0.590	0.678	0.790	1.071	0.990	2.647
0.195	0.198	0.395	0.418	0.595	0.685	0.795	1.085	0.995	2.994

Source: Adapted from Edwards, A. L. (1967) *Statistical Methods* (2nd edn), Holt, Rinehart & Winston, New York, by permission of the publishers

APPENDIX 23: WRITING UP THE RESULTS OF A STATISTICAL TEST IN A RESEARCH PAPER

As space is at a premium in research papers, the results of statistical analyses are written as succinctly as possible. To find out how this is done, it is useful to look at the way such analyses have been presented in journal articles and only a few general guidelines will be offered here. Different journals may have slightly different 'house styles' but these differences are unlikely to be important.

Descriptive statistics such as the mean, standard deviation and correlation should be reported. If there are relatively few such statistics they may be reported in sentences such as in the following examples:

The mean age in years for women was 21.35 (SD = 1.72) and for men 20.42 (SD = 0.96).

Mean aggressiveness was significantly higher (t = 1.95, df = 19, one-tailed $p<.05$) in the reward condition (M = 3.13, SD = 1.07) than in the punishment condition (M = 2.21, SD = 1.01).

Self-reported aggressiveness was significantly positively correlated (r = 0.33, df = 49, one-tailed $p<.01$) with the number of violent television programmes seen over the previous week.

If there are a relatively large number of such statistics then it may be more convenient to present them in a table. Tables are generally preferable to figures such as histograms since the exact values can be more readily presented. The table should have a number and a brief title describing its contents and may have notes at the bottom where this is appropriate. Means and standard deviations should be presented for variables which are correlated. It is not usual to report the distribution of values of variables, although this may be useful.

It is usually necessary to describe the nature of the inferential statistic used for a particular analysis as in the following examples:

A two-way analysis of variance was carried out with gender and treatment as the two factors.

Pre-test-post-test changes on the two measures were evaluated with related t tests.

A stepwise multiple regression was conducted for women and men separately with self-reported aggression as the criterion.

When describing a statistically significant finding, the test statistics which should be presented in the sentence are:

1 The test statistic symbol (e.g. t, r or F) and its value;
2 Its degrees of freedom particularly where these may differ for different analyses;
3 Its probability level and whether this was one-tailed where this is appropriate.

These statistics are placed either within brackets as in the two of the examples above or within commas as in the example below. The degrees of freedom are sometimes alternatively presented as a subscript of the test statistic or in brackets as shown respectively in the two examples below:

The interaction between gender and treatment was significant, $F_{1,20} = 10.95$, $p<.01$.

Test statistics are also sometimes presented for findings which are not significant in which case the significance level is usually reported as *ns*:

The interaction between gender and treatment was not significant, F (1, 20) = 3.27, *ns*.

Answers to exercises

2 MEASUREMENT AND UNIVARIATE ANALYSIS

1 Ordinal
2 Ratio
3 (a) 3 and 4
  (b) 7
  (c) 4.0
  (d) 3.5
  (e) 4.3
  (f) 44.1
  (g) 4.9
  (h) 2.21

3 INTRODUCING MINITAB

1 You could assign a single number to each category such as 1 for single and never married, 2 for married, 3 for separated, 4 for divorced and 5 for widowed.
2 With no other information, you could code marital status for this person as missing.
3 With the prompt system:

MTB > let 'age'=2000-year-of-birth

With the menu system:

→**Calc** →**Mathematical Expressions** ... →variable column or name [e.g. **age**] →**Select** [this puts **age** in the box beside **Variable [new or modified]:**] →box under **Expression:** and in it type the desired expression [e.g. **2000-**year-of-birth] →**OK**

4 With the prompt system use the following kinds of commands:
  (a) **read c1-c13**
    1 . . . .

2

.

. (data)

.

10 . . . .
end

(b) **code (1) 2 (2) 1 c5 c7 c9 c11 c13 c14-c18**

(c) **let c19=c4+c6+c8+c10+c12+c14+c15+c16+c17+c18**

(d) **let c20=c19/10**

or

let c20=(c4+c6+c8+c10+c12+c14+c15+c16+c17+c18)/10

(e) **describe c20**

With the menu system use the following kinds of steps:

(a) Input the information into the **Data** window

(b) →**Manip** →**Code Data Values . . . →c5 c7 c9 c11 c13 →Select** [this puts these variables in the box beneath **Code data from columns:**] →box under **Into columns** and in it type **c14-c18** →first box under **Original values [eg, 1:4 12]:** and **1** →first corresponding box under **New:** and in it type **2** →second box under **Original values [eg, 1:4 12]:** and in it type **2** →second corresponding box under **New:** and in it type **1** →**OK**

(c) →**Calc** →**Mathematical Expressions . . . →c19** →**Select** →box under **Expression:** and in it type **c4+c6+c8+c10+c12+c14+c15+c16+c17+c18** →**OK**

(d) →**Calc** →**Mathematical Expressions . . . →c20** →**Select** →box under **Expression:** and in it type **c19/10** →**OK**

(e) →**Stat** →**Basic Statistics** →**Descriptive Statistics . . . →c20 →Select →OK**

5 If one or more scores were coded as missing (*), the total score will be set as missing.

4   STATISTICAL SIGNIFICANCE AND CHOICE OF TEST

1 1 out of 64 ($2 \times 2 \times 2 \times 2 \times 2 \times 2 = 64$) or 0.015625 (1/64 or $0.5 \times 0.5 \times 0.5 \times 0.5 \times 0.5 \times 0.5 = 0.015625$)

2 1 out of 8 ($2 \times 2 \times 2 = 8$) or 0.125 (1/8 or $0.5 \times 0.5 \times 0.5 = 0.125$)

3 0.421875 ($0.75 \times 0.75 \times 0.75 = 0.421875$)

4 25

5 No

6 Two-tailed

7 (a) 0.661

   (b) 0.717

   (c) 0.92

(d) 0.4641

(e) 0.9282

(f) Symmetrical with a nonsignificant tendency of a positive skew

(g) −0.153

(h) 1.400

(i) 0.11

(j) 0.4562

(k) 0.9124

(l) Mesokurtic with a nonsignificant tendency towards platykurtosis

8 (a) 55.56

(b) 3

(c) 4

(d) Less than 0.05

(e) Yes

(f) 135.38

(g) Less than 0.05

(h) Yes

5   TESTS OF DIFFERENCE FOR CATEGORICAL DATA

1 (a) Chi-square. Observed frequencies need to be converted into percentages.

(b) 10.32

(c) 3

(d) Two-tailed

(e) Less than 0.05

(f) Yes

2 (a) Chi-square

(b) 6.95

(c) 1

(d) Two-tailed

(e) Less than 0.05

(f) Yes

3 (a) McNemar test

(b) 4.05

(c) 1

(d) Two-tailed

(e) Less than 0.05

(f) Yes

6   TESTS OF DIFFERENCE FOR ORDINAL DATA

1 (a) $U = 6.0$

(b) 0.0649

(c) No

2 (a) 3.09
  (b) 1
  (c) 0.079
  (d) No

3 (a) 2.51
  (b) 2
  (c) 0.286 (adjusted for ties)
  (d) No

4 (a) 0.1875
  (b) No

5 (a) 0.225
  (b) No

6 (a) 6.52 (adjusted for ties)
  (b) 2
  (c) 0.039 (adjusted for ties)
  (d) Yes

7   TESTS OF DIFFERENCE FOR INTERVAL/RATIO DATA IN UNRELATED SAMPLES

1 (a) 1.41
  (b) 5 in the numerator and 5 in the denominator
  (c) Greater than 0.05
  (d) No
  (e) Yes
  (f) 2.44
  (g) 10
  (h) Less than 0.05
  (i) Yes

2 (a) 5.98
  (b) 1 in the numerator and 10 in the denominator
  (c) Less than 0.05
  (d) Yes
  (e) 0.37

3 (a) 1.1
  (b) 2 in the numerator and 9 in the denominator
  (c) Greater than 0.05
  (d) No
  (e) 4.13
  (f) None

4 (a) 1.86
  (b) 2 in the numerator and 6 in the denominator
  (c) Greater than 0.05

(d) No

(e) 7.00

(f) 1 in the numerator and 6 in the denominator

(g) Less than 0.05

(h) Yes

(i) 1.00

(j) 1 in the numerator and 6 in the denominator

(k) Greater than 0.05

(l) No

8 TESTS OF DIFFERENCE FOR INTERVAL/RATIO DATA IN RELATED AND MIXED SAMPLES

1 (a) −1.58

  (b) 5

  (c) Greater than 0.05

  (d) No

2 (a) 1.86

  (b) 2 in the numerator and 10 in the denominator

  (c) Greater than 0.05

  (d) No

3 (a) 1.00

  (b) 1 in the numerator and 10 in the denominator

  (c) Greater than 0.05

  (d) No

4 (a) 7.60

  (b) 1 in the numerator and 9 in the denominator

  (c) Less than 0.05

  (d) 0.92

  (e) 1 in the numerator and 8 in the denominator

  (f) Greater than 0.05

  (g) Yes

  (h) 3.00

  (i) 1.83

  (j) Yes

9 TESTS OF ASSOCIATION FOR CATEGORICAL AND ORDINAL DATA

1 (a) 0.21

  (b) 0.20

  (c) 0.15

  (d) 0.00

  (e) 0.02

2 (a) 0.35
  (b) 0.33
  (c) 0.43
  (d) 0.35
  (e) 0.41
  (f) 0.32

10   TESTS OF ASSOCIATION FOR INTERVAL/RATIO DATA

1 (a) 0.37
  (b) 10
  (c) No
2 (a) z test
  (b) 0.0
  (c) 0.54
  (d) -0.74
  (e) No
3 (a) T_2 test
  (b) 0.35
  (c) 0.16
  (d) 0.05
  (e) 9
  (f) No
4 (a) Z_2^* test
  (b) -0.64
  (c) -0.43
  (d) -0.40
  (e) -2.34
  (f) Yes
5 0.34
6 0.40

11   BIVARIATE AND MULTIPLE REGRESSION

1 (a) 0.39
  (b) 0.37
  (c) 1.81
  (d) 2.59
  (e) 1.03
  (f) 0.31
  (g) 0.81
  (h) 0.14
  (i) 0.05
  (j) 1.56

(k) 1 in the numerator and 10 in the denominator
(l) Greater than 0.05
2 (a) 0.36
(b) 0.38
(c) 0.04
(d) 0.06
(e) 0.14
(f) 0
(g) 0.71
(h) 2 in the numerator and 9 in the denominator
(i) Greater than 0.05
(j) 0.33
(k) 1.15
(l) 1 in the numerator and 9 in the denominator
(m) Greater than 0.05
(n) 0.03
(o) 0.01
(p) 1 in the numerator and 9 in the denominator
(q) Greater than 0.05

12 MEASUREMENT RELIABILITY AND AGREEMENT

1 0.54
2 (a) −0.18
(b) −0.17
(c) −0.46
(d) −0.78
(e) 0.42
(f) 5.5
(g) 17

Bibliography

Berenson, M. L. and Levine, D. M. (1992) *Basic Business Statistics: Concepts and Applications*, 5th edn, Englewood Cliffs, NJ: Prentice-Hall.

Bliss, C. I. (1967) *Statistics in Biology, Statistical Methods for Research in the Natural Sciences*, vol. 1, New York: McGraw-Hill.

Boneau, C. A. (1960) 'The effects of violations of assumptions underlying the *t* test', *Psychological Bulletin* 57: 49–64.

Box, G. E. P. (1953) 'Non-normality and tests on variances', *Biometrika* 40: 318–35.

Bradley, D. R., Bradley, T. D., McGrath, S. G. and Cutcomb, S. D. (1979) 'Type I error rate of the chi-square test of independence in $R \times C$ tables that have small expected frequencies', *Psychological Bulletin* 86: 1290–7.

Bryman, A. and Cramer, D. (1996) *Quantitative Data Analysis with Minitab: A Guide for Social Scientists*, London & New York: Routledge.

Camilli, G. and Hopkins, K. D. (1978) 'Applicability of chi-square to 2×2 contingency tables with small expected cell frequencies', *Psychological Bulletin* 85: 163–7.

Camilli, G. and Hopkins, K. D. (1979) 'Testing for association in 2×2 contingency tables with very small sample sizes', *Psychological Bulletin* 86: 1011–14.

Campbell, D. T. and Stanley, J. C. (1966) *Experimental and Quasi-Experimental Designs for Research*, Chicago: Rand McNally.

Cochran, W. G. (1954) 'Some methods for strengthening the common X^2 tests', *Biometrics* 10: 417–51.

Fleiss, J. L. (1971) 'Measuring nominal scale agreement among many raters', *Psychological Bulletin* 76: 378–82.

Hays, W. L. (1994) *Statistics*, 5th edn, New York: Harcourt Brace.

Hollander, M. and Wolfe, D. A. (1973) *Nonparametric Statistical Methods*, New York: Wiley.

Keppel, G. (1991) *Design and Analysis: A Researcher's Handbook*, 3rd edn, Englewood Cliffs, NJ: Prentice-Hall.

Levene, H. (1960) 'Robust tests for equality of variances', in I. Olkin (ed.) *Contributions to Probability and Statistics*, Stanford, CA: Stanford University Press.

Lord, F. M. (1953) 'On the statistical treatment of football numbers', *American Psychologist* 8: 750–1.

Marascuilo, L. A., and McSweeney, M. M. (1977) *Nonparametric and Distribution-Free Methods for the Social Sciences*, Monterey, CA: Brooks/Cole.

Maxwell, S. E. (1980), 'Pairwise multiple comparisons in repeated measures designs', *Journal of Educational Statistics* 5: 269–87.

McNemar, Q. (1969) *Psychological Statistics*, 4th edn, New York: Wiley.

Minitab Inc. (1989) *MINITAB Reference Manual Release 7*, State College, PA: Minitab Inc.

Minitab Inc. (1991) *MINITAB Reference Manual PC Version Release 8*, State College, PA: Minitab Inc.

Minitab Inc. (1992) *MINITAB Reference Manual Release 9*, State College, PA: Minitab Inc.

Minitab Inc. (1995) *MINITAB Reference Manual Release 10Xtra for Windows and Macintosh*, State College, PA: Minitab Inc.

Mosteller, F. and Tukey, J. W. (1977) *Data Analysis and Regression*, Reading, MA: Addison-Wesley.

Overall, J. E. (1980) 'Power of chi-square tests for 2×2 contingency tables with small expected frequencies', *Psychological Bulletin* 87: 132–5.

Rosenthal, R. and Rosnow, R. L. (1991) *Essentials of Behavioral Research: Methods and Data Analysis*, 2nd edn, New York: McGraw-Hill.

Siegel, S. (1956) *Nonparametric Statistics for the Behavioral Sciences*, 1st edn, New York: McGraw-Hill.

Siegel, S. and Castellan, Jr., N. J. (1988) *Nonparametric Statistics for the Behavioral Sciences*, 2nd edn, New York: McGraw-Hill.

Steiger, J. H. (1980) 'Tests for comparing elements of a correlation matrix', *Psychological Bulletin* 87: 245–51.

Stevens, J. (1992) *Applied Multivariate Statistics for the Social Sciences*, 2nd edn, Hillsdale, NJ: Lawrence Erlbaum.

Stevens, S. S. (1946) 'On the theory of scales of measurement', *Science* 103: 677–80.

Yates, F. (1934) 'Contingency tables involving small numbers and the X^2 test', *Journal of the Royal Statistical Society* Supplement 1: 217–35.

Walker, H. M. (1940) 'Degrees of freedom', *Journal of Educational Psychology* 31: 253–69.

Wilcox, R. R. (1987) 'New designs in analysis of variance', *Annual Review of Psychology*, 38: 29–60.

Index

(Entries in **bold** are Minitab keywords.)